# MURDER IN THE CITY
## Parts I-II
## By
## Bobby Legend

# MURDER IN THE CITY
## Parts I & II

Published through Legend Publishing Company

This is a work of fiction. Names, characters, places, and incidents are the product of the author's imagination or are used fictitiously. Any resemblance to actual persons, living or dead, events, or locales is entirely coincidental.

All rights reserved
Copyright © 2014 Bobby Legend
Interior Book Design and Layout by Mickey Strange
ISBN 978-0-9821687-1-4

No part of this publication may be reproduced, stored in a retrieval system, or transmitted in any form or by any means electronic, mechanical, photocopying, recording, or otherwise, without the written permission of the author or publisher.

# Introduction

This is a story about a man that loves women for their money. He uses them, spends all their savings, and then moves on to another. He loves 'em and leaves 'em—that is, until he winds up dead. There is no shortage of suspects, all with the motive for murder.

Detective Hero finally arrests a suspect. But is this person really the killer, or is there an innocent person now sitting on death row? He answers that question months later when he becomes involved in another gruesome murder investigation concerning four victims found dead in the city park. The investigation leads to many other murders that are intertwined and connected until he finally gets his man. Or does he? Find out when you read:
Murder in the City—Parts I-II.

# Chapter 1

I was awakened at three o'clock in the morning by a telephone call from the precinct.

"Detective Hero," stated desk Sergeant Keller, "your expertise is needed on the far side of town."

"What's up?" I asked.

"Another murder. I don't want to say any more until you've seen it. It's not pretty."

Oh heck, I thought to myself, still half a sleep. I'd been a homicide Detective for over twenty-five years, called to hundreds of gruesome murders, but that never made them easy to stomach. I surmised that this one would be no different.

As I stumbled out of bed, sleepy and hung over, I reached for my cigarettes on the nightstand. I took one out of the half-empty pack and sucked it into my mouth. I lit it and inhaled deeply, coughing up the phlegm that had settled in my throat during my short sleep. Two cigarettes later, I was dressed and in my kitchen drinking a hot cup of black Colombian coffee. But as I looked at my watch, I noticed thirty minutes had passed since I'd answered the phone.

I poured the half-empty pot of Colombian nectar into my thermos and walked out the door, my head still spinning. I jumped into my car and headed to the address the dispatcher had given me over the phone. By the time I reached the victim's apartment building, my thermos was empty and I was wide-awake.

I pulled alongside the flashing red and blue lights and noticed that the coroner and three other police units were already there. I quickly stepped out of my vehicle and headed for the crime scene.

As I entered the Admore apartment building, I was escorted by a patrol officer to the tenth floor, where thirty or more city employees were scurrying about investigating and doing their jobs. Before I entered the victim's apartment, I put on the usual scrubs—rubber gloves and cotton slippers—so I wouldn't contaminate the crime scene. Now I was ready to start my investigation.

When I noticed the victim, I became weak in the knees and nauseated. As I said before...I never get used to crime scenes—and this one was no different.

The male victim was lying face down on the white, linoleum floor—although the floor was no longer white but red with blood. It was his blood—all thirteen pints of it. It appeared as though he had been tied up to the bedposts and stabbed in the bedroom. Then dragged to the kitchen floor, where he died. The reason being was that his penis had been completely severed and placed into his left hand, as if he were the Statue of Liberty holding the torch. Plus, his neck had been cut from ear to ear...and the head nearly decapitated—with only the spinal cord holding it to the body.

We knew he had been tied up to the bedposts because of the ropes, which were still tied to the bed, and the rope burns and bruises on his wrists and ankles, as though he had fought to get away. Obviously, he hadn't made it—or at least, he made it only as far as the kitchen.

The bedspread, pillowcases, and rug leading to the kitchen were covered in blood. There was blood everywhere. But most of it was lying on the kitchen floor.

The victim had over fifty deep stab wounds to the heart and chest area. Each wound was nearly two inches long and a quarter of an inch in width—and all of the wounds came from the front to the back.

We didn't see any obvious bloody footprints or fingerprints and would need special laser equipment to pick up anything the forensic crew might have overlooked.

While the investigative team was busy looking for clues, the photographer was busy taking photos of everything in the victim's apartment. Once all the evidence was bagged and tagged, the forensic team and photographer were allowed to leave.

While investigating the murder scene, many questions had been answered...except the most important one: Who did it? We weren't sure if the murderer was a male or female. This could have been a sex crime, or a robbery gone awry. But we'd know more once we had determined whether there were any valuables missing...and once we had questioned the neighbors to see if they had any pertinent information concerning this hideous murder. We would also have to canvas the neighborhood—someone may have heard screams or a loud argument. Perhaps by chance someone had seen a strange car in the area, or even the perpetrator or perpetrators.

We had been on the scene for about four hours. The sun was out and saying "good morning." I had just stepped into the hallway of the apartment complex to have a smoke when I noticed a black-haired woman walking nervously towards the victim's apartment. Before she could get within ten feet of the door, one of the police officers stopped her and asked her where she was going.

"Why are you people here?" she whined, trying to push her way into the apartment. "Please, tell me why all of you are here."

"I'm sorry, but you can't go in there right now," said one of the patrol officers.

They didn't want her to contaminate the murder scene. I interrupted their conversation and introduced myself.

"Hello, ma'am," I said. "I'm Detective Hero. I'm investigating the crime scene. I need to have a few words with you." I held onto her left arm, directing her away from the apartment. "Let's get a cup of coffee."

As we walked to a coffee machine next to a snack machine in the hallway approximately twenty-five feet from the victim's apartment, she kept hounding me to explain what had happened and began to cry uncontrollably. When she tried to speak, I could hardly understand her. I asked for her name but it was as if she was in a trance.

"Why won't you tell me?" she sobbed.

"Get hold of yourself and settle down," I said, putting a pocket full of change into the machine and handed her a cup of black coffee.

She drank two or three big gulps before she finally began to settle down, but she still couldn't stop shaking. I didn't know if she was acting guilty or just very nervous.

"Now would you please tell me what's going on?" she pleaded.

"Do you know the person that lives in this apartment? Is he a relative of yours?"

But again she didn't seem to care about answering my question. She wanted answers.

"No. He's not a relative ... he's my boyfriend. Why ... is something wrong with him?"

She became upset again, flailing her arms and spilling her cup of coffee onto the floor, some landing on my wrinkled white shirt.

"Please tell me. What has happened? Is he all right?"

"Please, Miss. Calm down," I told her, wiping off spots of coffee from my shirt.

"What's happened to him?"

"I'll answer your questions in a minute. But first, you must answer mine. What is your name and when did you leave your boyfriend's apartment?"

"I've been away for the weekend trying to think over my problems."

"Oh. You two were having problems then?"

"Yes. But I had hoped we could work them out. That's why I came back this morning," she said, biting her fingernail as we were walking towards the apartment.

I was just about to ask for her name and a few more pertinent questions when I was called into the apartment by one of the officers.

"Excuse me, will you?" I told her. "And *don't* go anywhere. Wait here, until I return."

She nodded, and then I told an officer standing at the front door of the apartment, not to let her go anywhere.

I then returned to the apartment. As I entered, the coroner stopped me.

"Is it all right to remove the body, Detective Hero?" Doc Grady asked.

"Sure. I have all the information I need for now. But I think I'm about to get more."

"What do you mean, Detective?" asked Grady.

"I'm about to question the victim's girlfriend again and this time, get her name... she's waiting for me in the hallway. And I think she will give me the answers I need. She's just as good a suspect as anyone," I said, winking at him.

Once I had answered the coroner's questions, I returned to the hallway to talk with the dark-haired woman again. I looked all over for her, but she had disappeared. She wasn't anywhere around. I couldn't find the officer who I had explicitly asked not to allow the woman to leave but couldn't find him so I asked a few of the uniformed policemen standing in the hallway if they'd seen her leave, but they hadn't. How they hadn't noticed that hysterical woman moaning and crying was beyond me. During all the confusion, and all the drinking I had done the night before, I had forgotten to get the young woman's name.

If I was to blame anyone for not getting and writing down her name, it was me. As I stood in the hallway venting my anger, another detective walked up to me and handed me a handful of Polaroid photos. I quickly looked them over. They were all pictures of women. Some were nude and others were dressed in formal attire. There were pictures of more than ten different women. Most of them were in their early twenties—but some looked to be in their early forties. One photo in particular stood out from all the others. It was a picture of a sweet and innocent teenager. She must have been his daughter, I thought.

Well, it was time for breakfast and more coffee, so I decided to drive to my favorite café—a little out of the way restaurant that had the best home-cooked meals in the city called Gabrielles Hoagies. I had been going there since I was a rookie in the police force. The couple that ran it was like my adopted parents. I would do anything for them if they ever needed my help.

As I sat eating my bacon and eggs, I looked over the photos that had been given to me at the murder scene. I noticed names on the backs of some of the photos. This would be a big help in locating these women. Now the real investigating would begin.

Once we finished canvassing the neighborhood and questioning neighbors and close business associates, if he had any, the pieces of the jigsaw puzzle should begin falling into place.

It sure seemed like this guy was a real woman's man. The woman that I had met at the apartment was also in two of the pictures—one looked to be taken some years before, when she was a young teenager, assuming it was the same woman and on the back was the name Sammy. It might have been her sister or some other relative. And the other looked similar to the teenager, but much older. But the picture was out of focus and the name on the back of the picture was smeared and unreadable, so I wasn't sure about her. I was sure to find out in time.

    I finished my breakfast, paid the bill, and headed out the door. My hangover was finally subsiding. I jumped into my car, started the engine, and headed to the station. Within ten minutes, I was back in my old stomping grounds. I quickly signed in at the front desk and headed to my department. Once at my desk, I pulled the pictures from my jacket pocket and dumped them on top of it. I grabbed a notebook and pencil and began making a list of the different names of the females in the photos. Now I had to run background checks on each of them to see if they had any criminal records or any violent actions against anyone. This would help me form a little better psychological profile on each person. This would also help me decide which ones were the most viable suspects. Right now, they were all suspects. Within a few days, I would have it narrowed down a bit.

    The other investigators and uniformed officers would be dropping off their reports of the investigation after they'd questioned the witnesses and neighbors of the victim. Hopefully someone had seen or heard something that terrible night.

    The apartments on either side of the victim's were vacant. The apartment complex supervisor had told me that the two elderly couples that had lived in those apartments had just moved out within the last few weeks because they were fed up with all the partying and noise at all hours of the day and night. But I would have to talk with them if I needed any more information. That's exactly what I intended to do later that afternoon.

I had copied the elderly couples' new addresses into my notebook from the supervisor's address book...and even did the supervisor a favor and saved him a few cents in stamps when I agreed to deliver the couple's mail, which had been sent to the vacant apartments. Heck, I was a civil servant. I figured doing something nice for these senior citizens might get them to open up more during our interview. They might have had a grudge against the guy and not care if his murderer was caught. This, to me, was a revenge killing. It had to be someone he knew and was close to.

We still had lab tests to do on the bloody sheets, pillowcases, and other pieces of evidence. The tests would tell us if he'd had sex before he was killed. But, if the tests did come back positive for semen and fluid stains, it might only prove that he'd had sex hours before he was killed. He could have been with one of his girlfriends and then was killed later by her ex-boyfriend.

I still wondered who would cut off the guy's penis and stick it in his fist. That's why I thought it might be a male killer. He might have cut off the guy's penis to get back at him for balling his girlfriend. The coroner would be able to tell me if he had been alive or not while his penis was being sliced off. For the victim's sake, I hoped that he was already dead before that occurred. There were still many, many questions to be answered. This had become a complex murder investigation.

I still needed to question the woman that I had met at the victim's apartment that morning. But I didn't have an address, full name, or telephone number to locate her other than a photo, which looked very similar to the woman at the apartment; it had the name Sammy written on the back.

In the photo she looked much younger than when I met her this morning. The victim's girlfriend was much older than many of the women in the photos.

Before I had made any background checks on anyone, I needed to do one on the victim. That might reveal something. I needed to pin down a motive for this horrendous killing.

I walked down to the computer operator's office and asked if I could get the printouts of the criminal records of the people that I wanted checked out. They agreed to help me out.

The first criminal record I wanted to look at was the victim's. With all his female lovers, he had to have done something illegal. I thought that if he had a criminal record, this might give me some insight into his murder. It was a start, anyway. The suspects might also have had something in their criminal past, which would put a light on this murder.

The female computer operator explained that it would take an hour or so to finish the order. She would bring them to my desk when she was finished. I thanked her and walked back to my desk. Within a few seconds, I was deep in contemplation. I put myself in the victim's place and could feel the pain, as he did—as he was being butchered and killed.

Suddenly, I was awakened from my trance by one of the uniformed officers dropping off his report on the questioning of the victim's immediate neighborhood. Soon, more and more investigators, in half-hour intervals, were dropping off their reports. By mid-afternoon, nearly all the reports were in. Now it was up to me to question the rest of the people. Most of the ones left to question were either suspects or elderly witnesses.

I began looking over the mound of reports and interviews. The first interview I looked at was from two old ladies that lived in the same apartment complex on the same floor as the victim. Both were senior citizens, nearly ninety years old that had lived there since the late thirties and were sisters. They seemed like a great old ladies. I had no last names, just first names: Anna and Mira. I decided they would be the first witnesses I would question.

I took the elevator to the tenth floor, the location of the victim's apartment. I was surprised and amazed to see that there wasn't anyone guarding the murder scene. However, the crime tape that was stretched across the doorway kept people from entering the apartment. I continued down the hall to Annie and Mira's apartment and knocked on the door. A small, hunchbacked, toothless woman answered.

"Yes. May I help you?" she asked.

"I'm Detective Hero. I'm investigating the murder in the apartment a few doors down the hall from you. I would like to ask you a few questions, if you don't mind. I'm hoping you can help me with my investigation."

"I'm Annie. You want to talk with my sister. She is the one with the big ears," she said, motioning to the bedroom. "Mira, come out into the living room. This nice, young detective wants to ask you some questions."

Within a few minutes, another frail and tiny, hunchbacked old woman came out. She moved slowly, with the help of a walker. I quickly apologized for getting her out of bed, but she didn't seem to mind. In fact, she was rather eager to find out what had happened at the apartment. For the first few minutes, we exchanged small talk. She said she had lived at this apartment complex since the late thirties when Bugsy Siegel had rented the penthouse and stayed there when he was in town. She said he was a very nice man. He had been very nice to her and always flirted with her. But she was just a teenager at the time.

But she knew more about the murder victim. She was in her apartment nearly ninety-nine percent of the time, unless she had to go to the hospital.

"He lived in that apartment for thirteen years," Mira said.

Jim Palter was quite a partier from her perspective. She noticed more than a dozen different women that spent time at his apartment. She said they would stay in for days at a time.

"Mira, were you friends with any of his girlfriends?" I asked.

She shook her head. "Not really. We did meet one or two of them. But he brought home a different woman almost every night. He upset everyone around here...especially the people on this floor."

"Why is that?"

"He didn't have any respect for anyone. He was a selfish pig. He only cared about himself. I even heard that he lived off of the women. He was nothing more than a gigolo. My sister called him a male prostitute." She whispered this last part, as if the word "prostitute" was a dirty word. I hid a smile by covering my mouth briefly. She was adorable.

"I think he only used the apartment for his dates," she added.

"Why do you say that, Mira?"

"Because he would be gone for weeks at a time. Then, when he returned to the apartment, he had a habit of making excessive noise and waking up his neighbors. Two couples that had the apartments next to his have already moved out."

"Do you know the reason for their moving?" I asked.

"They finally got fed up with all the partying and noise," she said, fanning her face as though she was having a hot flash. "So they left the building. I couldn't blame them. Sometimes he had two or three females there at the same time. They made such a racket with their loud music and laughter that the noise became unbearable at times. I had to put pieces of cotton into my ear canals so I wouldn't have to listen to all of that loud music. And they didn't leave the apartment until the following morning."

That old lady sure knew a lot about the guy. She had learned all that information from within her apartment. Imagine what she could have learned if she had nosed around a little?

"Mira, did you or your sister see anything suspicious or out of the ordinary the night of the murder?"

"What night was that?" she asked.

"That would be two nights ago—Sunday night. Did you see anyone—man or woman—go in or out of the victim's apartment that night?"

"Well, I'm sorry. Unfortunately, my sister and I have been very ill for the past week. We have been sick in bed for the past six to seven days."

"I'm very sorry to hear that, Mira. I hope you're feeling better. If I had known that you both were ill, I would have waited to question you. I truly am sorry for disturbing you."

She smiled. "That's all right. We each came down with a little cold and it turned into pneumonia. We're feeling better today. At least I am. My sister wasn't able to keep her eye at the peephole...or her ear to the door. The only time one of us got out of bed was to let our doctor into the apartment. He was the only person that we saw on Sunday. In fact, he stopped by twice that day."

"Why did he stop by twice?"

"He treated us for the pneumonia," interjected Annie. She was standing in the doorway. "We each received a penicillin and vitamin B-12 shot. Remember, Mira? I wasn't able to watch my favorite television program."

"And what program was that, ma'am?" I asked.

"Oh, it's called *Deep Space, Nine*... I think? It's one of those flying saucer movies."

"Oh. So you're a Trekie?" I joked.

"A what?" asked Mira.

"That's one of those Star Trek people that dress and act like one of the characters on the *Star Trek* show."

They acted as if they didn't know what I was talking about, so I changed the subject. "Well, if you can remember anything else, please contact me any time at this number." I handed Mira my business card.

I thanked them for their time and let myself out of their apartment.

Within twenty minutes, I was back at my desk with coffee in hand. As I sipped the warm brew, I continued to pore over the investigative reports. I wanted to find out for sure about the victim's nightlife. The next-door neighbors should know, I hoped. I was betting that the apartment walls at the victim's complex were very thin. The adjoining neighbors might have heard everything that was said in his apartment.

I also tried to get in contact with the victim's mother, but I was unable to reach any relatives except one older brother, who lived out of state on the other side of the country. He made it clear that he wanted nothing to do with his brother. At first, he even denied having a brother. He didn't give me a reason, but he refused to acknowledge him. He was absolutely of no help in my investigation.

Over the next few hours, I continued to read through the stack of reports. Most of them were of no help whatsoever. Eventually, the computer operator brought me the criminal records I had asked for, but by then my eyes were becoming blurry. All the reading had given me a headache. I put my reports to the side and decided to take a ride out to visit one of the two couples that had moved out of the next-door apartments. I hoped they could tell me something of importance.

Within thirty minutes, I was knocking at their front door. I introduced myself as the elderly couple invited me into their abode.

"Mr. Carmen, you lived at the Admore apartments, didn't you?" I asked, once I was seated in the living room.

"Yes," he said, as his wife stood nearby. "We lived there for many, many years—until a few weeks ago."

"Was there any particular reason you moved out?"

"Why? What is this all about?" asked Mrs. Carmen.

"I'm sorry to say that Jim Palter, your next door neighbor at the Admore Apartments, was found murdered in his apartment on Sunday night. Did you hear or see anything suspicious coming from his apartment when you still lived there?"

"The only thing we saw or heard were women going in and out at all hours of the day and night," said Mr. Carmen. "We would see two or three different women stay overnight during the week. Then he wouldn't be around for a few days—or even weeks sometimes."

"Did you ever hear any fighting or yelling come from Palter's apartment?"

He nodded. "There were a few times that we heard loud arguing and yelling. More than once, there were loud thuds followed by glass breaking. We figured they were having love spats."

"Did you ever hear him argue with any men?"

"No, I don't think so. Well, wait. Yeah…just a few weeks ago, there was an old gentleman that was pounding on Palter's door…and when I heard the pounding and yelling, I went outside to see what all the fuss was about. Just as I opened my door, Palter's door opened… I saw this big, old man raise his right hand in a fist. He let Palter have it right across the jaw."

"Was Palter hurt?"

"He was sent flying backward into his apartment. I heard a loud bang, and then I heard him cry out. The old man yelled a few obscene words about leaving his daughter alone or the next time would be his last. Then the man stormed off down the hall."

"Do you remember what this old man looked like?"

"No. I didn't get a good look at his face."

"So what happened next…after the guy stormed off?"

"When the old man had gone, I ran over to Palter's apartment and looked in just as he was standing up. Two small tables and a lamp were knocked about. I asked him if he wanted me to call the police, but he rejected the idea."

"Why is that?"

"He just wanted to forget about everything that had just happened. He quickly showed me the door. I walked away thinking…the heck with him."

"Did you ever speak with him again after that day?"

"I asked him one day, 'Why don't you settle down with one woman and have a family?'"

"What did Palter say to that?"

"He said, 'Are you kidding? These women take care of me. They're my paycheck.' He told me that every girl he went out with gave him her paycheck each and every week. He was arrogant," said Mr. Carmen. "Then I asked him 'What if they don't give you their money?'"

"What did he say to that?"

"He said he wouldn't go out with them...and that they weren't worthy of his time. He said it in a cocky voice, too. Then he just laughed and went into his apartment."

"So, what did you do?"

"We just got fed up with his shenanigans and all night parties. We finally made up our minds and moved into this complex."

"And I'm glad we did," interjected Mrs. Carmen.

"Well, if you can remember anything else, call me at this number," I said, as I handed Mr. Carmen my business card. "Thank you for your time and help."

I said goodbye, then drove back to the city. It was getting late so I decided to head home to get a good night's sleep. I would look over the rest of the investigative reports in the morning.

Although I was exhausted, I couldn't sleep that night. I tossed and turned thinking about Jim Palter's murder. I kept thinking about the brutal way he had been killed. In my dream, I was the victim, and it was my severed penis in my hand. I woke up in a cold sweat.

The next morning, I drove to my favorite cafe to eat breakfast. As I sat waiting for my order, I noticed a beautiful, young, blonde-haired woman sway past and sit in a cubicle a few feet away. As I stared at her beautiful face and full lips, I could have sworn I had seen her before...but I couldn't put a finger on it. I pulled out the pile of photos from my jacket pocket thinking she might have been in one of them, but before I could look through them, the waitress approached with my food. I placed the photos back into my pocket.

The only thing I was interested in at this particular moment was my bacon, eggs, hash browns, toast, coffee, and orange juice. That would give me enough energy to keep me going full steam until lunch. When I finished my excellent breakfast, I sat back and relaxed. As I drank my coffee and smoked a cigarette, I again thought about the investigation. I suddenly remembered that I hadn't questioned the other elderly couple about the victim. So I decided that before I returned to the station, I would take a ride to the couple's address. I believed it to be another retiree's apartment complex, one of those places for senior citizens only.

I paid the bill for my meal, left a nice tip for the waitress, and headed to the elderly couple's address. They had lived on the left side of the victim's apartment.

I finally reached my intended address an hour after leaving the restaurant. And I was right—it was an apartment complex for retired people only. It looked like a beautiful place to live out the golden years.

I found their apartment with no problem. An elderly man answered the door after my second knock.

"Hello, I'm Detective Hero. Are you Mr. Smith?" I asked, showing him my badge and police identification, then handing him my business card.

"Yes, can I help you?" he asked. His wife came to the door and stood next to him.

"I need to ask you and your wife a few questions concerning your next door neighbor from the Admore Apartments, Mr. Jim Palter."

"Why do you want to question us?" asked Mr. Smith. "Heck, we moved away from there over two weeks ago. What is this all about?"

"Mr. Palter was murdered a few nights ago," I said, looking into the old man's eyes for his reaction.

"Murdered?" he said, as his wife turned and walked away into another room.

"Yes, that's right. Did you hear or see anything while you lived next door to him that might help me in my investigation?"

When he answered, he pitched his voice into a whisper so his wife couldn't hear him talking about her.

"My wife is the one that has a knack for listening in on conversations," he said. "She has a fine-tuned ear."

"I do not," yelled his wife from the kitchen, two rooms away.

"See what I mean," he said. We both laughed.

"Mr. Smith, did you ever have any friendly conversations with Jim Palter?"

He nodded. "Yes, a few times. He was always trying to sell my wife and me time shares for vacations in far off places."

"What exactly are time shares?" I asked, not knowing much about the subject.

"For a few thousand dollars, we could buy into these time shares that would allow us to vacation in a land of paradise for seven days and seven nights of luxurious living."

"That's what he was selling?"

"Yes. He handed out brochures full of beautiful pictures of luxurious hotel rooms and condos that we could rent once a year for a set price. Plus, we could trade with any other time share members."

"Like what?"

"For instance, another member might want to spend a week in our vacation spot. We could either trade with them for their vacation spot and he for ours...or we could trade with any number of other members. It all sounded like a good deal, until I talked with friends who had been sucked into his swindle," said Mr. Smith.

"What did they say about it?"

"They told us to 'forget about it because it wasn't worth the money that he charged.'"

"Why?" I asked.

"He sold time-shares in beautiful parts of the world, but the hotels or condos that the members were to use were in the slums of the city...usually across from the garbage dump."

"That doesn't sound very nice."

"One member's room was only one hundred feet from the city dump...and it was a cramped, small, one-room cabana that had a dirt floor. They said the garbage dump looked better to live at than their hotel room...and it had no air conditioning or fans."

"That's terrible."

"Not only that, but they weren't allowed to leave early."

"Why not?" I asked.

"They had to wait out their seven nights. That's the way their airline ticket was made out."

"Why didn't they ask to have their money refunded?"

"I guess when they arrived back home they tried to get a refund from him. But he refused. They took him to small claims court. Mr. Palter told my friends that even though they didn't get what they paid for, it wasn't his fault that they were given a crummy hotel room."

"How did the judge rule?"

"He ruled in favor of Mr. Palter. Everything else on my friend's trip was in order...so they lost their case. After listening to their story, we didn't want to take the chance. So we declined Palter's offer."

"Mr. Smith, did you say anything to Mr. Palter about that situation?"

"Yes. When I asked him about our friend's trip, he explained to me that the only thing they'd complained about was the lack of air-conditioning, and he had no control over that. That's what he told me. So I never bought any of his time-shares."

"It seems you were lucky but your friends weren't."

"But I do know that our friends were very angry with him after that episode. They said that they'd trusted him as a friend and that he took advantage of them. They never talked to him or had anything to do with him after that incident."

"Mr. Smith, did your friend say anything other than that he was angry with Palter?"

"My friend did mention that he would like to kill him...but he was just kidding. A few weeks later, we moved out of the building complex."

"Mr. Smith could you give me your friend's name who wanted to kill Mr. Palter? I'm sure your friend isn't involved in Palter's murder. People, when in an angry mood usually say things they don't mean. But being a detective I may want to ask your friend a few questions." I then pulled out my notebook to write down the information.

"Well detective, I don't think my friend, John Smithers will be able to help you much."

"And why is that?"

"Because him and his wife were coming back from a movie a few nights ago and were hit head on by a drunk driver."

I'm sorry to hear that," I said, saddened by the news. "I just have a few more questions and I'll get out of your hair."

"Go ahead. You have a job to do."

"Did you ever talk to or meet any of Palter's girlfriends?"

"As a matter of fact I did. I thought the young woman was a relative, like his niece. But she said she was a good friend."

"How long ago was that?"

"That was almost a year ago. I also met his newest girlfriend just before we moved out of the apartment. She was quite older than many of his other girlfriends."

"Do you know this woman's name?"

He shook his head. "I remember him telling me that they had been high school sweethearts more than twenty-five years ago. My wife thought that was very romantic. You know how women are."

"Did Palter ever mention who his business partner was...or did he have a business office that you know of?"

"No. I didn't know any of his business partners. But I know he was in business before, some years back. I think he sold out...or it went bankrupt? I'm not real sure."

"Do you know the name of the company?" I asked, hoping he had the answer.

"No. But I think I have his old business card somewhere. Let me check." He took out his wallet from his back pocket and began looking through it. "Here it is," he said, pulling it out of his wallet and handing it to me.

I quickly grabbed it from his hand and glanced over the name and address, then gave it back to him.

"Thank you, Mr. Smith. This should help me in my investigation. Hopefully he is still in business. I'll check the telephone number when I return to the police station. You have helped me immensely."

"I'm glad I could be of some help."

"It has been a pleasure talking with you. If you can think of anything else that might be pertinent to my investigation, you can reach me using the telephone number on the card I gave you." With that said, Mr. Smith walked me through the apartment complex and to my car.

We shook hands and said goodbye. Then I hopped into my car and headed for my precinct.

## Chapter 2

By the time I reached the station, it was lunchtime, so I turned around and drove directly to my favorite cafe. Ten minutes later, I was there, sitting at my favorite table in the smoking section. I had an hour to kill before I had to return to the station.

After I ordered my food, I sat back to relax and enjoy a cigarette. While thinking about the investigation, I remembered the girl this morning at breakfast. She reminded me of one of the women in the pictures.

Once again, I pulled the photos out of my jacket pocket. But just at that moment, I remembered that I hadn't shown them to the elderly couples I had talked with. I'd forgotten all about them. My mind just wasn't what it used to be. I was angry with myself over my forgetfulness. But my anger quickly subsided as I looked through the photos.

Just as I got to the one that reminded me of the girl I had seen, my food arrived. Again, I put the photos back into my jacket pocket and began eating my lunch.

About an hour later, I was back at my desk at the precinct sifting through the mound of investigative reports on Jim Palter's murder. I had more than sixty reports still to read and a number of statements. The victim seemed to be well known around the neighborhood. For someone who didn't stay or live at his apartment much, the neighbors sure knew a lot about him.

I didn't read one report where the person being interviewed liked the guy. And many were his neighbors from the Admore Apartments. Many of them, over a period of time, had loaned him different items, which had never been returned. When they asked for their items back, Mr. Palter told them that he'd never borrowed it, or he told them that they must have loaned it to someone else.

One report told a story of how he went around to different neighbors and borrowed one or two items of food from each one of them. He borrowed enough food to make himself breakfast. One neighbor loaned him three eggs and a pint of milk. Another gave him five strips of bacon and two slices of bread. He even borrowed a toaster from one of them so he could make his toast. The only thing he didn't borrow was a frying pan. The neighbors gave him everything that he had asked for. But it became a habit.

*Boy*, I thought, *this guy is one of a kind.* Finally, many of the neighbors refused to let him borrow anything. Some even gave him verbal reprimands. But that didn't work. He just borrowed from other neighbors in the apartment complex that didn't know about his reputation. He had even borrowed large sums of money from a few of the elderly residents, promising to pay it back within a week or so...but that never happened. Most of these elderly tenants lived on limited budgets and needed that money....

This guy used everyone he met. It didn't seem like it would be difficult to find two or three of his neighbors that hated him enough to kill him. Here I was trying to narrow down the suspects, and I kept finding more and more people that might have had a motive to kill him. The guy was pond scum. The more I read and learned about him and his antics, the more I hated him, too. Hell, if I had known him, I would probably have been another name on the suspect list.

I wondered if this guy had any good friends. Were there any people that he *hadn't* used? The ones that loved him were vulnerable women. But that was no concern of mine. My concern was finding his killer. My next step in my investigation was to make a new list of suspects, find them, and bring them in for questioning.

At the top of my list was the woman I had met at the apartment earlier. Somehow, she had slipped through my fingers. But I would find her again, soon.

Just then, I remembered seeing a telephone number on the back of her photo. I reached into my jacket pocket, pulled out the photos, and quickly looked through the stack of lovely women. "Here it is," I said to myself. I flipped it over and saw a number with the word "mother" written over it. I figured it must be her mother's telephone number. But it was an out-of-state number...and a New York area code.

Just as I picked up the phone to make the telephone call, an investigator walked over to my desk and handed me a small, brown paper sack. I hung up the phone, deciding that if I didn't hear from the girl within the next twenty-four hours, I would make the phone call to New York. Now I was more interested in this paper bag.

When I opened the bag, I noticed it was full of items that belonged to the murder victim. At first, I was elated. But then I became angry at the investigator.

"Why wasn't I given these things two days ago?" I asked. "Why am I just now receiving them?"

He shrugged. "I'm sorry. But I was ordered to investigate another crime scene, so I shoved them into a lower drawer in my desk and forgot about them until today. I brought it as soon as I remembered."

I listened intently to his excuse while dumping the contents onto my desk. I was very surprised by what I saw. Among the items were almost a dozen different identification cards. Each one had a different name but one picture—his picture. What was this guy into, I wondered?

I thanked the investigator for bringing me the items as he turned to walk back to his department. Now I wondered...what, if anything, did these phony identifications have to do with Jim Palter's killing?

I placed the items back into the bag, set it to one side of my desk, and began reading the investigative reports once again. One stated that the murder victim had had a dozen girlfriends over the last five years—and that included the girl I had met at the apartment, plus many of the girls in the photos. It seems I had a number of people to question, not only his girlfriends but also his business partner and his ex-business partner. It seemed the victim had screwed everybody one way or another. He had many enemies. Any one of them could have committed the dastardly deed. But I still needed a motive...and right now, I had a few different theories.

Had he been killed by a lover during or after the lovemaking? Or had he made love with another man's woman and been killed by a jealous husband or boyfriend? These were my two main theories. There could have been others. It was simply too early in the investigation to know for sure. Maybe the killer saw the woman leave, and then came in and killed him over a business deal. The more reports I read about the victim, the more the suspect list grew. I hadn't even gotten to the criminal reports yet.

From the investigative reports, I learned that many people were angry with the victim. Most of them were the vulnerable women that he had used and abused. But there were also others. One was his ex-business partner. Another was his present business partner...and a few were clients who were angry with him for screwing them over a business deal, in which they had lost thousands of dollars. But who was angered to the point of murder?

Then, while looking over Palter's criminal report, I noticed some disgusting crimes of which he had been accused. One was a one-count indictment of statutory rape. He had been accused of molesting a fifteen-year-old girl. But the jury acquitted him. The girl's father didn't like the verdict and didn't take the outcome very well. He was... very upset. In the courtroom, he stood up for all to hear and threatened to kill Palter. He said he would do what the jury had failed to do...and no matter how long it took, he would get his revenge. I wondered if this guy might be angry enough to cut off Palter's penis, stab him more than fifty times in the chest, and leave him lying face down in his own blood?

The female Palter had allegedly raped was in one of the photos. It was the one torn in half. Maybe the half that wasn't there was a picture of the girl's father...or possibly another boyfriend? Evidently, the victim didn't want to look at it.

Palter had quite a criminal file with our department. He had been arrested on fraud charges. It seemed two different women had pressed charges against him for taking their money under false pretense. But the district attorney had refused to prosecute, so the charges were dropped. He had also been arrested and tried more than once for assault. Again, no convictions.

Upon leaving the courtroom, after being acquitted on assault charges of two different women, Palter said—to anyone that would listen—that the women had gotten what they deserved. They knew he was having affairs on the side, but they put up with it anyway...and when he tried to leave them, they became angry and attacked him.

Palter rambled on that these women had had him arrested so he couldn't leave town. They knew that he would need their help and money to post bail...and they'd bailed him out of jail each time he was arrested.

The women were asked why they would bail him out and take him back after pressing charges against him. They always gave the same idiotic answer: "Because I love him!" Evidently, they didn't know the definition of "love."

Well, this guy, Palter, sure had a lot of enemies. My list had at least six probable suspects on it already. The more investigating I did, the more suspects I came up with—and many of them were women. Many of the people I had checked out had fairly decent records—nothing that really stood out, anyway...and the crime I was concerned with at the moment was "murder"...but that didn't mean they weren't capable. Plus, there were still a few that were lacking identities. I hoped to be able to narrow the field with a few more rounds of questioning. Then, within a month or so, I would have the DNA test results...and that would, hopefully, narrow my list to one. That is, if there weren't any problems at the lab.

Another case might have top priority over mine, and my evidence would get put on the back burner until their testing was completed. My evidence didn't have the highest priority. The task force investigating a serial killer had that.

I was beginning to grow tired, so I took a short restroom break. Then I walked to the snack room and poured myself a cup of hot, black coffee. I needed to wake up.

With coffee in hand, I returned to my desk. I wanted to make a few phone calls to the suspects, to have them to come to the station so I could question them on my turf and away from their comfortable surroundings.

Once I had the suspects at the station, I would question them in the interrogating room and look into their very souls. I knew what questions to ask and how to ask them. I would look directly into their eyes so I could judge their reactions. I could tell a lot from a person's body language.

But first, I wanted to call the number that was on the back of the woman's photo. Also written on the back of the photo was the word, "mother." I had also found the same telephone number and the word, "mother," written beneath it in the victim's wallet on a small, folded-up piece of paper.

Before I dialed the number, I called the long distance operator to get the name of the person that lived at this particular number. The operator not only told me the occupant's name but also the city in which she lived. Her name was Myra Manner, and she lived in New York City.

As I dialed the number and waited for someone to answer, I prayed that this phone call would help in my quest to find Jim Palter's murderer. After three or four rings, a woman finally answered the phone.

"Hello?" she said.

"Hello. Is this Mrs. Manner?" I asked.

"Yes. Who is this, please?"

"I'm Detective Hero from the St. Louis police department. I'm a homicide detective, and I'm calling concerning your daughter."

"Why? What happened to my daughter, Sammy?" she asked. "I told her that the son of a bitch would not only take all of her money, like he did over twenty-five years ago, but he would end up killing her this time."

"Mrs. Manner, please get a hold of yourself," I said. "Is your daughter in her mid-forties and about five feet five, one hundred and thirty pounds...with long, black hair and a small, black mole on her left cheek, next to her nose?"

"Yes. That sounds like the description of my daughter. Now what has happened to her? Is she dead?" she whined. "Please. I have to know."

"Mrs. Manner, your daughter is fine. Her boyfriend, Mr. Palter, is the one that was murdered. That is her boyfriend, correct?"

"Yes, unfortunately. I tried to talk her out of it...but she was adamant. He walked out on her before, more than twenty-five years ago, when they were high school sweethearts. He left her high and dry."

"High and dry. What do you mean?"

"He talked her into withdrawing her college funds to start him in business so they could settle down, get married, and start a family. She ate it up, hook, line and sinker. But within a year the money was gone...and so was he."

"Excuse me, Mrs. Manner. If I can just interrupt you for one minute, I need to ask you a few questions about your daughter."

"Oh, I'm sorry. What do you want to ask me?"

"I met her a few days ago while investigating her boyfriend's homicide. But I was unable to get her name or address. Mrs. Manner, I just need you to give me your daughter's address and a phone number where she can be reached."

"Why?"

"I need to ask her some very pertinent questions concerning my murder investigation."

"I'm sorry. She calls me, but I never asked her for her address."

"Why is that?"

"Because I can't write due to my arthritis...and my memory is bad. I can't remember a telephone number or address if my life depended on it. But I'm sure glad it's Jim that's dead and not her."

"When did you last talk with your daughter?"

"I just talked to her a little over a week ago. She was leaving him for a few days to get away so she could think."

"Leaving who? Mr. Palter?"

"Yes. She told me he was having affairs while they had been living together."

"How did she find that out?"

"She found the apartment that he kept on the side. He used it to seduce women. She was fed up with it. She had spent all her savings—what she'd been saving for retirement. I told her not to do it. I knew he hadn't changed. But she refused to heed my warning."

"So, what happened?"

"She packed up...lock, stock, and barrel. She quit her job, withdrew all her savings, and traveled to Missouri to start a new life with him—just like they'd done over twenty-five years before. She hadn't gotten over him."

"What is her last name?"

"She never married. Her last name is the same as mine, Manner."

"Wasn't she happy where she was at?"

"She had a great life here. But when Jim began calling her and told her what she wanted to hear...she fell for it."

"When did he phone her?"

"She hadn't heard from him in all these years, but out of the blue he phoned her here about a year ago. I told her not to talk with him, but she wouldn't listen to me."

"Why not?"

"She was always deaf to me when he was in the picture. But now she is in the same predicament as before."

"How did she sound when she last talked with you?"

"She seemed very upset when she called me last."

"But you don't know where she is living now?"

"She'd been house-sitting for a friend she met while living out there. That's where she was the last time she phoned me."

"Mrs. Manner, how was your daughter's demeanor when you spoke with her?"

"She was in quite a state of confusion. That man uses everyone. He is a pig. And I'm glad he's dead. He deserved what he got."

"Excuse me, Mrs. Manner. I'm sorry I have to ask you this...but do you think your daughter was angry enough with him that she wanted him dead...or angry enough to kill him herself?" I tried to ask the question without upsetting her or making her angry.

"Well, she was very angry at him...and I would be lying if I told you she never said that she wished him dead...or that he should hurt like he made her hurt. But to actually kill him. No! She is not that kind of person. She couldn't harm a flea."

"Well, if you hear from her, would you give me a call...or better yet...tell her to contact me at the St. Louis police department. Just tell her to contact Detective Hero in the homicide department. I just need to ask her a few more questions to clear up any misconceptions I have of her...in this horrible situation."

"Yes. When and if she calls, I will relay your message. I just hope I can remember. I would write it down, but I can't hold a pencil in my hand. I'm sorry."

"That's all right. Just remind her to contact the homicide department...and in the meantime, I'll try to hunt down her address now that I have her last name. I thank you for your time. You have been a big help to my investigation."

I hung up the phone feeling dejected. She hadn't given me the information I'd wanted. Now I had more digging to do. More than ever, I wanted to question her daughter, Sammy. After talking with her mother, I thought Sammy was an excellent suspect. She was angry about the adultery which was an excellent motive to kill ones spouse or to have him killed, I thought to myself.

## MURDER IN THE CITY PARTS I-II

It was near quitting time, but I wasn't finished for the evening. I decided to take some of the reports with me and go through them at home...just in case there was something I had missed earlier. I also picked up all the phony identification cards and other personal items, then placed them back into their paper bag and stuck them in the top center drawer of my desk. But before I left for home, I decided to call the victim's most recent business partner. I wanted him to come down to the station for an interview.

I found the guy's telephone number and business address, which had been given to me by the elderly couple, the Smiths. I just hoped that he was still in business.

The phone rang four times before the answering machine came on. The company wouldn't open until the morning. I hung up the phone, grabbed my stack of reports, and left the station for the day.

I drove directly home. I wanted to relax and try to get some rest. The last few nights I had been tossing and turning, waking up from nightmares trying to piece this crazy puzzle together. During a case like this, the nightmares always came. It had happened before; it would happen again. Murders like this ate me up inside.

At home, I grabbed my bottle of scotch and poured myself a stiff drink. It would be one in a line of many. Sometimes, it kept the nightmares at bay. Soon, I passed out on the couch; this time, there were no dreams.

The next morning, I was nursing my hangover headache with a cup of strong black coffee at Gabrielles, my favorite café when I saw her. She was the same innocent, beautiful young woman that I had seen at the cafe at dinnertime a few days before. I recognized her face, but I couldn't put a finger on it. I had left my six-inch stack of reports in the car, but I had the photos in my jacket pocket. This time, without being interrupted, I found the photo that reminded me of her.

But the woman in the photo was much older. In fact, it was the same woman I had met in the hallway of the murder victim's apartment building—Samantha Manner, or Sammy to her mother. The woman in the photo could have been her sister or a close relative. Or maybe it was just a coincidence. The photo wasn't that clear, anyway. I put the thought out of my mind.

I finished my coffee and donuts and went on my way. My first stop was to the victim's business in the warehouse district. I found the address easily. The building was a big warehouse with a couple of small offices up front. A few minutes later, I was standing inside, at the receptionist desk. I asked the receptionist for Mr. Palter's associate, Mr. Tom Walters. After waiting more than ten minutes, he finally came out and introduced himself.

"Hello," he said, holding out his hand, "I'm Mr. Walters. Can I help you?"

I shook his hand and nodded. "I hope so. I'm homicide Detective Hero. I need to ask you to come down to the station with me."

"May I ask, why?" he said, chewing on a fingernail.

"I need to ask you a few questions concerning the death of your business partner, Jim Palter."

"Can't you ask them here?" Beads of sweat began to pour out of his forehead.

I shook my head. "No. I'm sorry. We need to get your statements recorded and filed. It's better that you come down to the station."

"Can't I come to the station later this afternoon...after I finish work?"

"I'm sorry. You'll have to come down to the station with me."

"But I'll lose plenty of money if I close up shop now."

"Please sir," I said. "It's better that you come with me now and get it over with. The sooner we can get your statements on record, the quicker you can get back to your business affairs."

He sighed. "Well then. Let's get this over with. I have lots of work to do, and this isn't helping matters any."

"You can follow me to the station in your car if you'd like, or you can ride with me and an officer will return you to your place of business when our interview is finished. It's up to you."

"Okay, I'll follow you in my car."

I waited for him to get his coat and then we walked out the front door to the parking lot.

I wanted him to drive his car to the station just in case we needed to search it. He may have hidden evidence in the car. You never know.

When he reached the station, I placed him in the interrogation room. Before I went in, I asked Mr. Brenner, another detective, to help me question the witness. Two heads are better than one, I thought.

"I can't," he said. "I'm too busy with the task force."

When I pressed him...he relented.

"Ok, I'll do it, but I won't participate in the questioning." Instead, he would watch and listen from the adjacent room with the one-way mirror. So I reluctantly agreed.

As Brenner walked into the adjacent room, I walked into the interrogation room and sat across the table from Palter's business partner. I questioned him not as a witness but as a suspect.

"Mr. Walters, how long did you know Jim Palter...your business partner?" I asked, switching on the recorder sitting on the table in front of me.

"I'd known him for little more than two years," he said, biting his fingernails.

"Mr. Walters, where did you meet him?"

"I met him one night at a local bar. We began our friendship by talking and drinking while playing a game of darts. The more we talked, the more our friendship grew."

"How did he become your business partner?"

"During our conversation, I mentioned that I had just lost my business partner a few weeks before and was thinking about filling his position."

"What did Palter say to that?"

"He said that he had also lost his business partner...and their business."

"Did he say how?"

"He never explained to me what had happened...but I never prodded any further. He said he was interested in my business proposition. So I invited him to my place of business the following day."

"I take it he came to your office the next day?"

"Yes. I showed him around the warehouse and explained to him the type of business I was involved in, and I offered him a piece of it."

"Why would you do that when you just met the man the night before?" I asked.

"He was the type of salesman I needed," he replied. "He had wit, charm, charisma...and a great personality. He was perfect for taking clients out on the town to get them in a favorable mood to buy our time shares."

"Just like that ... with no strings attached?"

He shook his head. "No. There was a price to be paid."

"How much did he pay you?"

"The agreed upon amount was ten thousand dollars."

"To be paid all at once?"

"Yes."

"He had that kind of money just lying around...just after losing his other business?"

"Yes. But I never asked him how he got the money."

"Did he give you cash or a check?"

He cleared his throat. "He gave me a cashier's check in the amount of ten thousand dollars a few days later."

"What did he get for that money?" I watched as he squirmed nervously in the chair.

"I gave him twenty percent of my business. I didn't learn until later how he *really* got his money."

"What did you find out?"

"He told me he collected his girlfriend's paychecks each week and put them in his savings account. He said that women had been living off of men for centuries, so he lived off of rich and well-off women."

"So he lived off of women? ... Mr. Walters, how many women did he have at one time?"

"I remember one time he had at least three that he was dating...and living with."

"How did he get away with that?"

"He would stay with each girl for two or three days at a time and then tell them he was leaving on a business trip...but really he was leaving them to stay at another girlfriend's house."

"Mr. Walters, did any of these girls know about the other?"

"A few times he had some problems with the females coming to the office and confronting him about other women in his life. But he would always deny it and tell them that the women were just business clients. He usually squirmed out of it somehow." Walters shook his head in admiration. "He was one smooth talker."

"Do you remember any of his girlfriends? Tell me if you remember seeing any of these women with him, recently."

I handed him a handful of Polaroid photos that I had been carrying in my jacket pocket.

"What are these?" he asked, grabbing the pile of photos and shuffling through them.

"Mr. Walters, do you recognize any of these women?"

"Yes." He nodded his head, still flipping through the stack. "I think I have seen them all at one time or another." He removed two photos from the pile and placed them on the desk in front of me. "These two women are the ones I had seen him with recently," he said.

The first picture was the girl I had met at the victim's apartment building. The other was the young girl in the photo that had been torn in half.

"Mr. Walters, did you notice whether any of the women might have been angry enough to kill him?"

"Well, I didn't try to get too nosey. I tried to mind my own business. But when the women came to our business to scream and yell at him...I couldn't help but get involved. After a year being in business with him, I was sorry I had ever gotten involved with him."

"Why do you say that?"

"Not only did I witness ugly confrontations with angry girlfriends but there were also constant run-ins with angry clients. Just last week he had a confrontation with his most recent girlfriend."

"Which female? Is she in these photos?" I asked, pointing to the pile of photos I had given him.

"Yes, this one," he said, pointing to Samantha Manner. "Jim called her Sam."

"How long had she been his girlfriend?"

"She had been his girlfriend for about seven or eight months when she barged into our office and began screaming at him for having affairs while they were living together."

"What else did she have to say?"

"She ranted and raved about how she'd left her family back east to make a life with him. She was angry that he was just using her for her money like he had done over twenty-five years before. I felt sorry for her. She was quite older than many of his past girlfriends. I figured she must have had a big pocketbook."

"Mr. Walters, do you think she was angry enough to kill him?" I asked, looking directly into his eyes, trying to get his reaction.

"Well, she could have been…but then many of the other women were just as angry," he said, shrugging. "Some men, also."

"Like who, for instance?"

"There were many of his clients that were even angrier. I remember one guy telling him the reason he didn't own any guns was so he wouldn't shoot scum like him."

"Anything else?"

"One couple came in and reamed him from one end of our building to the other. He couldn't get away from their outrage fast enough. I also remember him telling me about his ex-partner." Walters dug through his shirt pocket and came out with a cigarette.

"About what?"

"They were angry at each other for their business going belly up," he said, lighting the cigarette.

"Whose fault was it?"

"They each blamed each other for the downfall. I never really got the whole story. Of course, it was all one-sided. I never heard his ex-business partner's story about the bankruptcy of their business. … Excuse me, could I have something to drink? I'm getting a little parched. I could sure use a cold soda."

"Sure. Is a Coke all right?"

"That'll be fine."

We stopped the interview while I went out into the hallway to the pop machine and bought our witness his soda. Next to the pop machine was the coffeepot, so I poured myself a cup of coffee. With soda and coffee in hand, I stepped back inside the interrogating room.

"Here you go, Mr. Walters," I said, handing him his ice-cold soda.

"Thank you." He opened the can and quickly took a big gulp.

"Now. Let's get back to the questioning," I said. "Did you know Mr. Palter's ex-partner?"

He shook his head and tapped his cigarette against the ashtray on the table. "I don't know him, personally. But I do know of him. I think his name is Don Cadwell. He blamed Palter for their business failing...and for having to file bankruptcy. Not only that...but he blamed Palter for getting him arrested for grand larceny."

"How did he do that?"

"It seems that their salvage business needed a quick shot in the arm. I didn't listen to the whole story, but I guess Palter wasn't winning any bids for salvaged goods, and the warehouse was sitting pretty empty. So he began ordering four thousand dollars or less of new merchandise from the manufacturers. Then he sold the stuff at salvage prices."

"Why? ... He couldn't make any money that way. How was he going to pay for the merchandise?"

"He never intended to pay back the manufacturers. When they complained, he would make excuses and say the check was in the mail...or that there'd been a fire."

"How long did he get away with that?"

"I guess he did this for more than a year before it all came tumbling down. Because the business was in his partner's name, Palter's partner was responsible and liable."

"Was Cadwell angry with Palter over this?"

"I believe he was. But I just learned about this two months ago."

"Was Cadwell arrested for fraud?"

"I'm not sure. You might want to question him and get the whole story."

"Yes, I plan on it," I said. "Mr. Walters, you also mentioned that some of your clients were angry and had confronted Palter about the time-shares that he sold them. Is that right?"

"Yes. But it wasn't one angry couple that came into our place to complain that day—it was two different couples. I guess they were close friends and bought their time shares together."

"How much money did they pay for them?"

"They paid a total of seven thousand dollars for the one week time share that they each acquired."

"When did they come in to complain?"

"They came in about three weeks ago in a vile mood," he said, taking another sip of his soda. "They were really steamed. They nearly broke the glass out of the front door from slamming it against the wall. Then they stormed into Palter's office...but when they couldn't find him there, they began yelling and screaming for him."

"Then what happened?"

"Jim came running out of the restroom, half-dressed, wondering what all the fuss was about. He thought the place was on fire. When the clients finally saw him, they were so angry they couldn't get the words out of their mouths."

"What did they do?"

"One of the men stammered and stuttered, but he made his anger visible. Palter told them to 'quiet down' and then asked them why they were so 'angry and upset' at him."

"What did the clients say?"

"They wanted their money back."

"What did Palter say to that?"

"He told them that he hoped they could come to some kind of understanding. Palter was very good at apologizing. He knew all the right words. He must have practiced saying the words over and over because he had them memorized." Walters took a long drag on his cigarette.

"What happened then?" I asked.

"He finally got the two couples to calm down long enough to take them into his office and out of ear shot of the other workers. But within ten minutes, both couples stormed out of his office and started yelling about how they were going to the cops to press fraud charges. As they stomped out of the building, they nearly broke the front door."

"What did Palter have to say about them?"

"When he came out of his office, I asked him if he had refunded any of their money."

"Did he?"

Walters laughed. "Hell no! He said they vacationed in the cities they'd asked for...and just because their vacation hadn't gone according to their plans didn't mean they could blame it all on him. That's all he would say about it."

"Did that client ever press fraud charges?"

"I don't know. Two days after that incident, some police officers stopped by and asked him some questions about it...but they said it was out of their hands."

"Your clients could have bypassed the police and gone directly to the district attorney."

"They did. But the district attorney refused to press charges...saying that the people that had bought the time-shares got what they paid for. He said that...just because they didn't get the hotel room that they wanted they wanted their money refunded. He said that it wasn't Palter's fault about the room...or that the air conditioner didn't work. He believed they got exactly what they paid for. I know the clients were really pissed off about it."

"Did Mr. Palter have any good friends that you know of? ... Was there anyone that wasn't angry at him? ... Were you angry at him, Mr. Walters?" I asked. I waited for a reaction, but I got none.

"I'll ask you once again, Mr. Walters. ... Were you angry at Mr. Palter for any reason?"

Walters ground the last of his cigarette out in the ashtray and sighed. "Well . . . I might as well tell you. You'll probably learn about it sooner or later, anyway. That is, if you don't know about it already."

"Well. Let's hear it."

"My company was a profitable and soluble company. We had over one hundred thousand dollars in the company's account. But when I checked the account more than a month ago...we were broke."

"Why is that?"

"Palter had been embezzling the funds right under my nose. I guess it was my fault." He slouched down in his chair. "I trusted the guy!"

"Were you mad enough to kill him?"

"No, of course not," he said, pounding the top of the table with his fist. "I'm not a murderer."

"You could have paid to have him killed, though. Isn't that right, Mr. Walters?"

"No. I didn't have anything to do with his murder!" Walters finished his soda and then set the can to the side.

"Okay, calm down, Mr. Walters," I said. "Tell me ... when did you find out Palter was embezzling funds from your company? ... When did you become aware of his criminal activity?" I was sure he was hiding something.

Walters refused to answer. He just sat at the table, staring blankly ahead, as if he were in a trance.

I wiped off my sweating palms with a napkin I'd brought in with the soda, then reached over and, using the napkin as a glove, grabbed the empty can of soda. I stepped out of the room for just a short minute, found an evidence bag, and placed the soda can into it. I wanted to have the fingerprints on the can checked out...to make sure I was talking to the person Walters said he was. After finding all those phony identification cards, I didn't want to take a chance.

I had one of the uniformed officers take the can down to the forensics lab for fingerprint analysis and identification before returning to the interrogation room. By tomorrow afternoon, I would know whether he'd been truthful concerning his identity.

"Okay. Now tell me, Mr. Walters...when was the first time you found out about Palter embezzling funds?" I asked.

"Before I tell you anything else, I just want to say for the record...I did not, I repeat...I did not kill Palter or have him killed!"

"Then what are you afraid of? Tell us what we want to know."

"Well, the first time I noticed money missing out of our account was when some bills went unpaid. Usually Palter took care of the bills. But he didn't come into work on that day and I found the unpaid notices."

"What bills are you talking about?"

"I don't know. Lots of bills. The lease on our building hadn't been paid. The electric bill hadn't been paid in months...and some other utility bills."

"Let me ask you this, Mr. Walters. Did you or Mr. Palter have any life insurance policies through the company?"

"Yes. We both had policies just in case the company went belly up."

"Let me see if I've got this straight," I said, leaning on the table to look him directly in the eyes. "First you find out your partner has embezzled funds from the company's account. And he didn't just steal a few thousand dollars out of the till but damn near busted your company. Is that right?"

"Yes. But it wasn't like that."

"Well, tell me how it was," I said, getting right up into his face. "I want to know! I want to know how you felt when you found out that he damn near put your company in bankruptcy court!"

Walters remained silent. I pressed the point. "And now you tell me that you have a quarter of a million dollar life insurance policy on him. That's a good motive for murder. ... Hell, not one good motive...but two."

This seemed to wake him up. "But I'm innocent!"

"This should put you on top of my suspect list," I said, looking coldly into Walters's eyes. "But I'm sure you have a perfect alibi for the night of the murder. Don't you?"

"And what day was that?" asked Walters.

"That would be on Sunday night between seven and eleven in the evening. Does that bring back any memories?"

"Well, first of all, I didn't know I would need an alibi. Second, I didn't kill him...and third, I was at my home all night long on Sunday. I didn't go anywhere that night."

"Mr. Walters, do you have any witnesses that can verify that you were at home at that time?"

"No. I was home alone Sunday night. I'm alone most every night. But I didn't kill anyone!"

"All right, Mr. Walters, settle down.... That quarter of a million dollars from the insurance policy should get your company back on its feet. Shouldn't it? It seems that your partner died at just the right time. That's what I call perfect timing."

"Well, I think I want a lawyer," he said, wiping his brow with his shirt sleeve.

"Why do you need a lawyer if you aren't guilty?" I looked directly into his eyes.

He squirmed in his chair and said, "Because...you are going to arrest me. You think I killed my own business partner."

"I can't remember saying that I was going to arrest you," I replied. "Why would you think I was going to arrest you?"

He again wiped the perspiration from his brow. "You guys arrest innocent people all the time. You don't do your job thoroughly, and the public and your boss want someone arrested for a crime...so you are pressured into arresting anyone...even someone that is innocent. It happens all the time!"

"Mr. Walters, I hate to bust your bubble, but we don't work that way," I told him. "Believe me. If and when we arrest you, we will arrest you based on the evidence against you...and nothing else. So if I were you, I wouldn't be leaving town anytime soon."

"May I go now?"

I nodded. "Yes, for now. But I'm sure I'll be questioning you about this, again," I said. He stood up, slowly, and I watched him leave the room. I then went to speak with Detective Brenner to see what he thought of my possible suspect. He had been an experienced homicide detective for over twenty years and one of the best in the business.

"That interrogation went well," said Brenner.

"Come on, Detective Brenner, let's get a cup of coffee."

"That sounds like a good idea."

I followed him out of the room.

"What do you think? Is Walters my man?" I asked, lighting a cigarette.

"Well, I think he's a good start. He does have two very good motives for wanting his partner dead."

"Yeah. But do I have enough on him to get a search warrant from a judge to search his home?"

Brenner shrugged. "Maybe. You should ask the district attorney about it first."

"I think I'm going to wait until I question a few more witnesses," I said. "I don't want to jump the gun too fast. Right now I'm going to give him the benefit of doubt."

"Well, it's past lunchtime already," Brenner said, looking down at his watch. "I think I'm going to take a rain check on that coffee. I need to get back to my own investigation. If you need me for anything, I'll be at my desk."

"Thank you, Detective Brenner."

I returned to my desk and spent the rest of the day poring over the reports. I still hadn't gotten the complete coroner's report or the report from the forensic lab. I also tried to get the telephone number of Samantha Manner...but was unable to acquire it. I did find an address, however.

Soon, my mind wandered as I sat back in my chair, thinking about what I would do tomorrow—hoping to question the ex-business partner and Samantha Manner... that is, if I could find her. I also wanted to question the two couples that had been unhappy clients—and the young girl that Palter had allegedly raped. Her father was still a good bet, too. In addition to that, I still had to find out the names of the other women that were in the Polaroid photos and stop by the coroner's office and forensic lab. I wanted to check on the date my evidence would be tested and examined. I had so many things to do...and only myself to do them. Everyone else in my department was on the serial killer task force looking for a serial killer. The force wouldn't rest until he was found. I knew *I* wouldn't rest until I caught Palter's killer.

# Chapter 3

Just as I was waking up from yet another horrendous nightmare, the phone rang. Déjà vu. It was the desk sergeant telling me to go over to the Admore apartment building.

"You might want to get over to the Admore building," he said.

"Why?" I asked, shrugging back the covers. The residuals of yet another nightmare sat on my shoulders like lead weights.

"Investigators found what they think might be the murder weapon."

"Great." I hung up the phone and quickly dressed. I took a cup of hot coffee with me.

When I arrived at the apartment complex parking lot it was nearing 8 a.m. and saw that two police cars were already there. I quickly finished my cup of coffee, set the empty cup on my front seat, then hopped out of my car and walked over to the officers standing next to a large trash container.

I pulled a pair of rubber gloves out of my jacket pocket.

"What's up, guys?" I asked, as I put the gloves on.

"Not a whole lot, Detective Hero." One of the uniformed officers flipped up the lid on the four-foot square garbage container. "Let me show you where we found what we think is the murder weapon. As soon as the blood is tested for DNA evidence and blood type, we'll know more about the weapon. ... Whether it belongs to this murder investigation or another."

The container was completely full of garbage. The murder weapon was sitting directly on top of the garbage heap, as if it had just been tossed into the container. Picking up the weapon, I noticed someone had wrapped it in two large, clear plastic bags. The weapon was covered in blood. Without opening the plastic bags, I gently placed the weapon into a large evidence bag. But something was unclear to me. We had searched this dumpster the day we found the victim. Why had it suddenly appeared there now, I wondered? I believed this to be the knife that had been used in the stabbing of the murder victim, Jim Palter, but now I wasn't so sure. I was keeping my fingers crossed that there might also be fingerprints on the handle. Finding the weapon really brightened up my morning. I believed I was that much closer to solving this homicide.

After bagging the knife I handed it to an officer so he could take it to the lab for testing, and as I pulled the gloves off and placed them back into my jacket pocket, I looked up and noticed an old but elegant gentleman carrying a doctor's bag. He was walking out of the apartment complex, heading in my direction. As I watched him approach, I wondered if he was the doctor that had treated those two old ladies on the tenth floor. As the doctor passed by me, presumably heading towards his automobile, I called out to him.

"Excuse me, doctor...can I have a minute of your time?" He was bending down to unlock his car door and didn't respond. I talked a little louder. "Excuse me, doctor...can I have your attention, please?"

He finally turned and answered me.

"Yes ... what can I help you with, son?" asked the old man, peering over his wire- rimmed eyeglasses.

I approached him. "Hello, I'm Detective Hero...and I'm investigating a homicide that happened a few days ago on the tenth floor of the Admore apartments.... You are a doctor, aren't you?"

"Yes, I'm a medical doctor," he said, shifting his bag in his hands. "What can I help you with?"

"You're not, by chance, the doctor that treats those two dear, old ladies up on the tenth floor—apartment 1002?" I asked, hoping I had guessed right.

"You mean the Weinburg sisters?" He frowned. "Yes, I am their attending and treating physician. I have been...for nearly fifty years."

"Well, when I questioned the ladies a few days ago, they told me you had treated them at their apartment, twice, on the day of the murder. Do you remember why you were at their apartment?... I mean...what were you treating them for?"

"What day was that murder on?... Who was murdered?"

"That would have been last Sunday," I said. "What time did you stop by their apartment on that day? Do you remember?"

"As near as I can remember...the first time I stopped by to see how the Weinburg sisters were doing was approximately at this time...about eight or nine in the morning. I was treating them for a lingering illness. They were each diagnosed and treated for pneumonia." He frowned again, then looked at his watch. "I'm sorry, but is this going to take much longer? I have more patients to see this morning."

"I only have a couple more questions for you. But if you would, when you get some free time, please come into the station and give a formal statement. You may help us in our investigation."

"Okay, I can do that," he said, as he opened his car door and stepped into the vehicle. "But right now...I must be on my way. If I don't leave now, I'll never catch up...and won't be able to see all of my patients that need my attention."

"Well, I would like to ask you a few more questions, but I know you are busy. Did you see or hear anything suspicious on that day, while you were visiting the sisters' apartment?"

The doctor climbed into his car and shut the door, but he rolled down the window, started the engine, put his car into gear, and then turned to me. "I can't remember anything, off hand," he said. "But if I do, I'll contact your office."

"Here's my business card," I said, handing him the card through the window. "Call before you come into the station...to make sure I'm there."

He grabbed the card out of my hand and quickly sped off in his old 1954 Nash Rambler.

I turned to the forensic investigators, who were busy taking fingerprints off of the garbage container, and told them to leave their reports on my desk as soon as they were written. I needed to return to the station. I had much to do.

Palter's business partner, Walters, who I had already questioned...was my number one suspect. He had been angry with the victim for screwing his clients and embezzling funds that nearly bankrupted his company. The kicker was the life insurance policy he had on Palter for the sum of a quarter of a million dollars. He had the motive, opportunity, and means to kill his business partner.

But I still needed the lab tests to narrow the suspect field. That was the one thing I wanted to get across to the people at the forensics lab—that the forensic evidence was very important to my investigation. Unless the killer was going to break down and "spill his guts," it was the forensic and DNA evidence that would verify my choice in suspects—especially if there were fingerprints on the murder weapon. First, they had to determine if that particular butcher knife was the actual murder weapon. I was fairly certain that it was. Now we had to figure out when it had been thrown into that garbage container...and who put it there? Hopefully, someone that lived at the apartment complex had seen the killer throw away the knife.

When I returned to the station, I found two new reports on my desk concerning my investigation. On top of the neat stack was a large photo of a woman with the name "Rita" written on the back of it. I sat down and began flipping through the papers. One was on the victim...about his childhood through to adulthood. The other report...and photo...was on a woman who had been Palter's girlfriend at one time. When I got a good look at her picture, I noticed that I had seen her face before. Then it finally dawned on me. I pulled the pile of photos out of my jacket pocket and quickly glanced through them. The last picture I looked at revealed the same woman. Now I had a name to go along with the picture. Two down, eight to go.

I decided to read the victim's report first. I figured I might find something that might put me closer to the murderer.

Palter spent most of his childhood with his father, John—a man who had been married seven different times...and never seemed able to hold on to a job. His wives worked to support him. He would beat his son when he didn't obey him and he also beat his wives.

Palter's father was very possessive of his women. He wanted to know where they were at all hours of the day. He demanded that his women dress to his specifications and were there only to serve him.

While the wife and his mistresses worked, Palter had to stay at home and do all the chores, such as the housework. He had to take out the garbage, wash the clothes, and wash and dry the dishes. He did all the vacuuming, scrubbed the floors, and cleaned the bathroom. He was basically a slave to his father, just as his father's wives were slaves to their husband.

Palter was never allowed to attend school because he had to do the housework. When the school board found out, John simply moved his family out of the area. When his wife lost her job—or all of the money was depleted from her savings account—John would leave that woman and move in with one of his mistresses. When he felt comfortable living with his new woman—and if she had a fat savings account—John and son would move in, permanently. He would then marry the woman, even though he hadn't been divorced yet from his former wife. Once they married, he controlled her and her money. He played the part of the happy husband—once again, until his wife's funds were depleted.

While the wife worked and paid all of the bills, Palter's father would be out partying and spending her money. He used her money to buy sex, drugs, and anything else that struck his fancy. Plus, he had one or two other financially-sound and vulnerable women on the side—to use when he tired of his present wife. But they were all disposable. The women he left behind were stuck paying off his bills.

John often convinced the women to buy a new and very expensive car or truck—and then register the vehicle in his name. Now they would be liable for the vehicle's payments, but he got to keep the car. Then he would sell the car for cash before the bank could repossess it...sticking the unlucky woman with the bills.

Palter stayed with his father until he was eighteen. Then he left. Actually, his father kicked him out...because he was lazy and refused to work. So Palter went out and began dating rich and lonely women. His father had taught him well. The difference was, Palter never married them as his father had. He learned the dangers of that when his father was arrested for polygamy. Shortly thereafter, while out on bail, the police found his father lying dead in the street.

The autopsy report stated that Palter's father had died from food poisoning, and the coroner signed the death certificate as an accidental death. But many in the police department thought a murder had been committed. When they investigated his background and found all the heartache he had caused these lonely, vulnerable women, they didn't challenge the coroner's report. They let it stand as an accidental death. They figured the guy finally got what he deserved—especially if the murderer was one of the women that he had abused.

So it was easy to see how Palter had learned his trade. They always say, "Like father like son." And also, much like his father, it seemed that his way of living had finally caught up with him. Jim Palter had caused a lot of pain to many vulnerable women. Now it was possible that one of those women had decided to return the favor. You could say it was "payback time." This guy was a real slime ball...just like his old man.

At lunchtime, I headed to the cafe but shunned my usual table in the back. I planned to get the order to go and head back to the station. After I placed my order—two grilled steak and cheese hoagies—I looked around. That's when I noticed a young, beautiful woman seated near the back. She looked like one of the women in the Polaroid photos, similar to Samantha Manner, the girl I had talked to at Jim Palter's apartment.

A few minutes later, Bonnie brought me my order. I paid the bill, then walked out of the café to my car. Ten minutes later, I was at the station, sitting at my desk, eating and enjoying my meal. When that task was completed, I finished reading the victim's report, and then began reading an investigative report on one of the victim's ex-girlfriends. Her name was Rita Margaw. She'd been with him until about a year ago. She was a nude dancer and danced for some rough and tough customers. It appeared that she made decent money—about three thousand dollars per week—but worked in a "hellhole."

When Palter and Rita met, she had just inherited a large sum of money from her dead father's estate. Palter found a gold mine when he met her. But they broke up shortly after her inheritance was depleted. The story didn't end there. Evidently, Rita couldn't get over him...because she was arrested for trespass at the Admore apartment building the day Palter's body was discovered and was now being held in our jail.

I decided to walk down to the women's cellblock, two floors below, and bring her up to the interrogation room. I wanted to see if she had an alibi for the night of the murder. If she did, I could cross her off my suspect list...once I had checked out her story. If not, she would be added to the list for further investigation.

An hour and twenty minutes later, she was sitting at a table across from me in the interrogation room.

"Miss Margaw, can I get you anything? ... A cup of coffee? ... A soda?" I asked.

"No. Nothing to drink," she said. "But I could use a cigarette."

"Here, have one of mine." I handed her a cigarette from the pack I carried in my shirt pocket, then lit it for her.

"Do you know of a Mr. Jim Palter?" I asked.

Before answering, she took a long drag on her cigarette, then exhaled and blew a big cloud of smoke in my face. "Yes ... I know him. Why do you think I'm in jail?"

"I don't know. Why are you in jail, Rita?" I asked, testing her.

"I guess they arrested me for stalking him. I'm not sure...but I think that's the charge."

"Why were you stalking him?"

"I wanted to see if he was living with anyone. I thought I could get him to come back to me. ... I loved him."

"Did you know him by any other name?"

"What do you mean?" She took another deep drag on her cigarette and exhaled the smoke, once again, into my face.

"Well, did he ever use any aliases? Did you ever see these?" I asked, as I fanned the smoke away and pulled a small paper bag out of my jacket pocket. I spilled its contents on the table in front of her, then placed the ten pieces of phony identification in a neat row so she could look at the different names...different names but Jim Palter's photo on them.

"Rita, did he ever mention any of these names?"

"No. I don't know anything about these," she said after a moment. She shoved the pieces of plastic across the table. "As far as I knew...he was Jim Palter. That's what I've always known him as. That is his real name ... isn't it?" She looked confused as she crushed out her cigarette on the edge of the table and threw it to the floor.

"As far as I know." I picked up the phony identification and placed them back into the paper sack and then back into my jacket pocket. "When were you arrested, Rita?"

"Can I have a cigarette, first?"

"Sure."

I pulled another one from the pack in my shirt pocket and handed it to her.

"Thank you," she said, and placed it between her lips. I lit it for her and watched as she took a long drag. Then I began my questioning again.

"Now, when were you arrested?"

"Let's see. I was arrested Sunday night...standing out in front of the Admore apartment complex...about ten that evening."

"Who called the police on you?"

"I guess the security guard from the apartment complex must have called the police."

"Why? ... What did you do that would warrant a call to the police?"

"I had been banned from that complex for disturbing the peace...so the security guard must have called them when he saw me standing near the front doors of the building. ... Why is that so important?"

"Rita, let me ask you this. Did you see or hear anything suspicious that night? Did you see anyone that might have visited Mr. Palter's apartment that night?"

"Well, I'm aware of possibly three different people that visited him while I was standing outside, watching the apartment complex for his departure from the building. Within three or four hours that afternoon, I saw two women and one or two men go into the complex."

"But who did they visit?"

"I was certain they visited Jim's apartment."

"Did you recognize anyone else that might have visited Palter that night?"

"I thought I saw his ex-business partner visit that night. I think his name is Cadwell. But, I'm not real sure about him."

"Why is that?"

"I saw him just as I was being hassled by the police. The cops blocked my view...that's why I didn't get a good look at him. But I'm pretty sure it was him."

"Rita, do you know anyone...by name...that you think might have visited Palter on that Sunday night?"

"Yes. Some of them. ... Oh! ... I forgot to tell you that I was also chased away two different times from the building by the security guard."

"Where did you go during that time?"

"I ran to a small cafe, a block away."

"How long did you stay there?"

"I sat in the cafe for about thirty minutes each time I was chased away from the apartment building. So anyone could have visited Jim during those two times I was away from the building."

"All right, Rita. So tell me the names of the people you saw go into the building."

"One man was his business partner...but I forget what his name is. The young woman that I saw first, around six that evening, I had only seen once before."

"Where?"

"That was when I saw them together, going out to dinner. I followed them to the restaurant."

"Do you know the woman's name?"

"I believe her name was either Ellen, Helen...or Helena? But I'm not one hundred percent sure."

"What about the other girl? Did you see her before? Do you know her name?"

"Yes, I have seen her before. She was one of his sluts," she replied angrily, raising her voice and flipping her cigarette against the wall. "Jim kept her around because she gave him lots of money and anything else he wanted. I believe her name was Elaine."

"How long have you known about her?"

"I had never seen her before two weeks ago. She was someone he had just met not too long ago."

"Rita, I have some photos I want you to look at." I pulled the photos out of my jacket pocket and placed them on the table in front of her. "Can you put a name to their pictures?

See if any of these women are named Helen or Ellen or Elaine?"

"Well, I'll do my best." She glanced through the stack of women's photos. After looking over all the photos of the different women, she picked out only one of them. "This one is Helen or Helena." The photo was of a pretty, blonde-haired woman. "But you don't have a picture of Elaine...unless it's this one...I can't really tell." She pointed to the photo of a young woman that looked similar to Samantha Manner.

"You don't happen to know any of the names of any of the women in the other photos, do you?" I hoped she could fill in some of the blanks...to make my investigation a bit easier.

"Oh, I might be able to help you...if you give me another cigarette," she said. Rita picked up the stack of photos and began glancing through them once again.

"You've got a deal." I handed her another cigarette...and lit it for her. "But you better cut down on those cancer sticks. It's gonna end up killing you."

She shrugged. "Everybody dies some time."

"But then you won't be able to stalk, I mean...chase your old boyfriend anymore."

It was another test. I wanted to see if she knew he was dead. But she ignored my statement and continued to look over the photos.

"Out of these ten photos, I know the names of seven of them," she said, confidently.

"Who are they?"

"A few of them were his mistresses or girlfriends before I became his girlfriend. The others' came after me...or while I was dating him."

"He sure had a lot of girlfriends."

"He was having affairs all throughout our relationship. I was a fool...but I loved him. I'm still in love with him...even though he uses me...and abuses me. I just can't help myself." She dropped her head, as if ashamed.

"Rita, why don't you put a name to each one of the women in the photos...if you can?" I asked.

"This one's me," she said, pointing to a photo with her picture on it. She placed it away from the others. Then she picked up another. "This woman's name is Mary Ann. I think her last name is Milford." She showed me a picture of a petite brunette before setting it on top of hers. Then she pointed to another photo...this time of a dark-haired beauty. "This one's name is Carmen Sanders. She owned a small kiln and pottery shop. She had a long affair with Jim while he was living with another woman." She took a long drag on her cigarette and blew the smoke in my face.

"Is that other woman amongst these photos?" I asked, pointing to the rest of the photos.

"Yeah...this one," she said, pointing at the photo of a beautiful, blonde-haired goddess. She picked it up a moment later and tossed it onto the floor.

"Rita, why did you do that?" I asked, picking up the photo and returning it to the pile.

"Because I knew her."

"Who is she?"

"She had been a close friend of mine. In fact, she had been one of my roommates."

"How did she meet Jim Palter?"

"I introduced her to him...but I didn't know they would have an affair together."

"Rita, what's your roommate's name?"

"Ex-roommate," she exclaimed, slapping her hand on the tabletop.

"Okay, Rita...ex-roommate. What's her name?" I asked again, writing their names on the backs of their cards.

"Janet Gray," she said, flicking her cigarette butt to the floor. "And this lady's name is Judy Brown." She pointed to the photo of a pretty redhead. "She was also seeing Jim during the same time I was living with him...or should I say when he was living with me."

I handed her another cigarette and then lit it for her. I watched as she took a long drag and blew the smoke into my face...and then asked her my next question.

"Rita, what about the other women in the photos?"

"These other women came after me," she said. Then she picked up one of the pictures and tossed it in front of me. "But I think this is the woman he's living with now...well, for the last nine or ten months anyway." It was the photo of Samantha Manner.

"Rita, when you say Jim lived with you...was that at the Admore apartments?"

"Hell no! He lived with me...at my apartment. He always lived with his women at their place."

"Why is that?"

"The women supported him."

"What about his apartment at the Admore building?"

"I just found out a few months ago that he had his own apartment."

"How did you find out where his secret apartment was?"

"When Jim would leave me for days at a time...I thought he was going out of town on business."

"Was he?"

"No. He was actually having affairs with other women," she snarled.

"What did you do when you found out about it?"

"We broke up," she snapped.

"But how did you find out where his apartment was?"

"When I found about his affairs...I wondered where he was taking those other women, so I followed him—which led me to that apartment building...the Admore Apartments."

"There are many apartment units in that complex. How did you find Jim's apartment? Did you follow him?"

"Yeah...right to his apartment on the tenth floor. Then I went back down to the lobby and found the apartment manager and asked him when Jim had rented the apartment. I was shocked to learn that it had been leased to Jim nearly thirteen years ago. I couldn't believe it."

"Rita, how long did he live with you before you broke up with him?"

"He lived off of me for over a year."

"Didn't Jim work?"

"Sometimes. He was always telling me he was broke...or all of his money was invested in his salvage business. He always had one excuse or another for not having any money."

"How did he make his money?"

"I usually gave him my weekly paycheck."

"How would you pay your bills if Jim took all of your money?"

"He would give me just enough money from my check to pay the bills and buy groceries. Then he would pocket the rest of the money."

"You liked those arrangements?"

She shook her head. "Not really. But I never complained...because I was deeply in love with him. Like an idiot, I thought he was also in love with me."

"What about the other women?"

"I didn't know at that time that he was seeing other women. When he told me he was going out of town on business, I believed him."

"Rita, what about the other women in the photos?"

"I believe these other women were having affairs with him while he was living with Samantha Manner," she said, pointing to the last few photos.

"Why do you say that? Did you know Miss Manner?"

"Jim told me about her just before he left me. I guess he'd known her since they were young teenagers. She was his first love...or so he told me. She came all the way from back east somewhere."

"Rita, what about these other women?" I pointed to the few remaining photos. "Do you know their names?"

"I'm not positive about their names," she said, shrugging her shoulders. "I think this one is Jeanie." She pointed to the photo of a pretty brunette. "And this one is Carol." This time, she pointed to another beautiful blonde. "But Samantha Manner could probably tell you better than me."

"Why her? ... How did you know her? I thought you said that Jim told you about her?"

"Well, he did...but that was just before we broke up. And then I met her...right after he moved out of my apartment."

"When?"

"She came up to my apartment with Jim one day...when he came over to get some of his clothes he had left behind. But then I ran into her again a few days ago."

"What did you say to her?"

"We talked for a little while. In fact, we ran into each other at Jim's apartment building. She had just found out he was cheating on her. ... I'm sorry, may I bum another cigarette from you?"

"Sure." I handed her another cigarette, then lit it for her. "Rita, how do you know all of these women's names?" I asked. "Did you spy on them, too?"

She nodded. "Sure. Most of them were with Jim at one time or another. When I followed them they would end up at their apartment or some restaurant. A few of the women I met at Small Claims court."

"When was that?"

"We were all put on the same docket when the court noticed we all had claims against Jim within the same time frame," she said, as she blew cigarette smoke in my face, as she moved uncomfortably in her chair. "So, all of us got together over lunch and began discussing our love lives. That's when I learned that Jim was having affairs behind my back, while we were living together."

I still hadn't told Rita about her ex-boyfriend's mishap. When I did tell her, I wanted to catch her off guard. I wanted to see her reaction to his death.

"So tell me, what were you women suing Palter for?"

"We were all suing him for monetary reasons. Two of the girls were suing to get their jewelry from him, and one was suing him to get her car returned."

"Why would you sue someone you supposedly love?"

"I will admit, I was angry with him. Even angrier when I found out about all those other women."

"Rita, is that why you sued him...for having affairs?"

"That's one reason. Also, I wanted him to pay the bills he ran up on my credit card, and I wanted him to return the card to me so I could cut it up to get rid of it. He had caused me enough trouble. But that didn't mean I didn't have feelings for him. That didn't mean I didn't love him. You know, we all make mistakes."

I just sat in my chair too stunned to move. I couldn't believe what I was hearing. I had no sympathy for her whatsoever. She moaned and groaned about the guy using her and having multiple affairs...but she still loved him...and wanted to get back with him.

"You know, I don't feel sorry for you at all," I said. "You let the guy walk all over you. You let him use you. You let him take all your hard-earned money. He spent all your savings... and to top it all off, he told you he was leaving you for another woman because he didn't love you anymore. After all that, you still want to take him back."

"Yeah! So!"

"Rita, I just don't understand you," I exclaimed, shaking my head. "Hell, I would have been angry as hell. I would have wanted to break his neck if he had spent all my life savings."

"I wanted to, believe me."

"Not only that...but he had affairs while he was living off of your money. That sure would have pissed me off. I hope you don't get AIDS from him."

"Oh, believe me, I am *very* angry with him," she retorted. "In fact, all of the girls that sued him were also angry with him."

"How angry?"

"One day, after leaving the courtroom, all of us girls went over to Carol's apartment and spewed out our frustrations. We each said what we wanted to do with him."

"Like what?" I asked her quizzically.

"I mean, we all wanted to skin him alive. One even wanted to cut off his penis and shove it up his ass."

"Why would you want to do that?"

"To let him feel what it's like to get screwed. We talked for hours about the different ways we'd do Jim in."

"Give me a for instance."

"One girl wanted to run over him with the car that she had bought for him. We all had kind of crazy ideas. We were all pretty angry that day."

"What happened to your court case? Did you girl's win?"

"No, we lost the case," she said. "That was the day we all drove over to Carol's house and got drunk. That's the day we ranted and raved about Jim using us like we were his personal toys." She flicked her cigarette butt to the floor and asked for another.

"Rita, you must be what they call a chain smoker," I said, as I handed her another cigarette, then lit it for her. "Would you like a soda or coffee…or maybe a glass of water?"

"No, I'm not thirsty. But thanks anyway."

"Rita, you said that you knew all the women in the photos I showed you. Right?"

"Well, I've seen them…but I don't really know them. The only one you didn't have a picture of was his recent slut. I think her name is Elaine. I believe she was his newest find.

"Can you give me a description of her?"

"I never really got that close to her so I didn't see her face that clearly."

"So you saw Helen first…and then a few hours later you saw her leave the building. Is that right?"

"Yes. Her name is either Ellen, Helen, or Helena…I'm not real sure."

"Let's just call her Helen for now. When did you see her?"

"She came to the apartment building about two in the afternoon. Then about four-thirty, I saw her leave the building and drive away."

"Rita, when did you see the other woman visit the apartment?"

"She came about an hour later…after Helen left."

"How long did she visit Jim?"
"She was in his apartment for almost four hours."
"How do you know?"
"I watched as she left the building."
"How did she look?"
"She was upset about something."
"Why do you say that?"
"The front of the apartment building is all lit up at night...and I could see that she was crying because her eyes were all red and puffy and she rubbed them with a handkerchief. Then I watched as she ran from the building to the parking lot. She jumped into her vehicle, gunned the engine, and tore out of there like a bat out of hell. She was definitely upset. I figured Jim had probably told her he was leaving her for another woman. That's what I was thinking, anyway...at the time."

"Rita, what time did you get arrested that Sunday evening?"

"I told you before. I think it was around ten o'clock that evening. It was about fifteen or twenty minutes after that young girl left the apartment building."

"How do you know?"

"I remember...because there was an old man coming out of the building just as I was being arrested. I heard him tell the security guard that he had to be somewhere by ten o'clock. I couldn't hear exactly where he said he was going because I was struggling with the police officer as he was handcuffing me."

"What were you doing as the police officer was arresting you?"

"I was crying for the old man to help me, but he acted like I wasn't there. He acted like he didn't even notice me. He must have been going to the airport because he was carrying a little black suitcase. That's when I saw...or thought I saw...his ex-business partner going into the building. I thought he was going to visit Jim, too. Then the police handcuffed me and hauled me to this dungeon. I've been in jail ever since," she said, flicking her lit cigarette butt against the wall, five feet away.

"Rita, you never explained to me why you lost the court case?"

"Well, the judge's ruling was unfair. He said that we gave Jim the money. That Carol had bought the car for him as a gift...and that Carmen had given Jim the credit card to use."

"How did the judge rule on your case?"

"The judge told me that I let Jim spend my life savings. He also told Mary Ann the same thing...that she allowed him to withdraw the funds out of her savings account. Mary Ann explained to the judge that the money Jim had spent was her inheritance. But the judge didn't care. So he dismissed her case...and mine. "

"Rita, who was the angriest at Jim that day? Was it Carmen? Was it Mary Ann? Or were you the angriest?"

"On that particular day, I was probably the angriest. I was the drunkest, that's for sure. So I probably hated him the most that day."

"Rita, did you visit Jim that Sunday night? ... Were you so angry that you went to his apartment to see whom he was with? Were you angry enough to kill him? Were you angry enough to stab him thirty or forty times in the chest, then cut his throat? You said you wanted to cut off his penis and shove it up his ass. Didn't you?" I looked deep into her eyes as she sat in silence, dazed, stunned, and confused.

"What are you saying?"

"Did you kill your boyfriend, Jim Palter, that Sunday evening?"

"Is he dead?" she cried. "Please, tell me. Is he dead?"

"Rita, you know he is. You killed him."

"No... no," she said, shaking her head. Tears streamed down her face. "I loved Jim. I wouldn't kill him. When we talked about it at Carol's house, we didn't mean it. We were just joking around."

"You know, Rita, it's funny. But you told me that you wanted to cut off his penis and stick it up his ass. Guess what? His penis was cut off!" I made that statement hoping to get a reaction out of her, but she stayed as cool as a cucumber.

"If Jim is dead, I had nothing to do with his murder," she said, angrily beating her fists on the tabletop. "Why don't you ask some of the other women these questions? We all wanted to cut off his penis and shove it up his ass."

"Rita, I think you were angry at Jim for dumping you...so you went up there and killed him."

"You're crazy," she said, crying harder.

"You might as well tell me now. If you tell me now, I'll be able to help you later on. If you don't...you're on your own. When the jury finds you guilty, you'll get the death penalty. But you like doing drugs, don't you? In this state, you'll get that last rush from a needle."

"I don't have to listen to this! I want a lawyer! Either charge me with a crime...or take me back to my cell!"

"Rita, if you don't help yourself now, I won't be able to help you later on."

"Just take me back to my cell! Now!" she yelled.

I had the guard return Rita to her cell. That was all she was going to tell me. I couldn't arrest her—yet. I hadn't gotten the lab work back yet. My evidence was still being held up due to the serial killer task force. Right now, I could only go on my gut instinct.

The forensics lab was my next stop. Then I'd stop by the coroner's office. I wanted to find out how much longer I would have to wait before I would receive the forensics report on the fingerprints, weapon, and other microscopic evidence. I wasn't even certain yet of the exact time of death. All I had was a very wide, approximate time. The coroner had given me about a five-hour window for the death.

I still needed to track down the ex-business partner and the other women I wanted to interview and interrogate. But with only one person working the case, it was taking longer to crack. But I figured it was job security, so I couldn't complain. Hell, it wouldn't have done me any good anyway.

At the very least, I had added a few more names to my suspect list—thanks to my jailbird, Rita. She had made my investigation that much harder. I wanted to call it a day. I wanted to leave my investigation at the station. Tonight, I wanted to clear my mind, a la "tabula rasa." This case was beginning to drive me crazy. I wanted to test my willpower to see if I was strong enough not to bring the case home with me anymore. It was eating me alive. Every murder case that crossed my desk always drove me buggy. That is until it was solved.

I signed myself out and drove home singing along with the songs on the radio. "So good, so far," I said to myself, as I drove up into my driveway. I jumped out of my car, then swaggered into the house in a jovial mood. I ate a light dinner, then sat down on the couch to relax by listening to some beautiful, soothing classical music on the radio. My mind was finally at ease and completely blank. Definitely "tabula rasa."

I felt so relaxed that I decided to have a drink to celebrate. I decided that from now on, I wouldn't bring my work home with me. If I continued, the stress would get so bad I'd get ulcers.

I walked to the kitchen cabinet and grabbed my favorite bottle of twenty-year-old scotch. Once back in the living room, I returned to the couch and opened the bottle, pouring myself a shot. Within a few minutes, I had chugged three more shots. I began feeling giddy. I hadn't felt this good in a very long time.

I flicked off the radio and turned on the TV. I flipped through the channels until I settled on a police movie.

I stared, blankly, into the screen. I might have even faded out, but the local news cut into the movie, and then I was awake—wide awake. The wheels began to grind in my head. My mind was no longer "tabula rasa." My willpower crumbled. My mind began to roar like the engine of a Mack truck.

The investigation slammed, full force, back into my mind. An explosion of thoughts ripped through my brain. Who wanted Jim Palter killed, I thought to myself? Maybe the better question would have been, who *didn't* want him killed. There were too many suspects, and not enough answers.

None of the people I had questioned had a good alibi, and all of my evidence was purely circumstantial until I received the reports from the forensic lab. Instead of subtracting from the list of suspects, I just kept adding more. And almost everyone had motive.

I decided to contact Palter's ex-business partner in the morning and bring him into the station. If I were lucky, I'd have him there by lunchtime. That was the last thing I remembered before I passed out on the couch. When I awoke, the television was blaring the "Star Spangled Banner" and my head was pounding out a "Gene Krupa" drum solo. What "willpower," I thought to myself, as I shook my head in disgust.

# Chapter 4

I awoke, once again, with a hangover. But that was nothing new. It was a daily habit and had been for the last twenty years. After smoking a cigarette, I put my feet to the floor and stood up, then stumbled to the bathroom for a quick shave and shower. When those tasks were complete, I tugged on the same wrinkled suit I had worn the day before.

After a quick breakfast of two three-minute, soft-boiled eggs, toast, and coffee, I headed for work. There was a lab report waiting for me when I got to my desk. It was an exciting moment—until I noticed that it was only the fingerprint information from the soda can, which I had taken from Tom Walters, the victim's business partner. Evidently, the man was who he said he was. He hadn't lied. He had given us his real name. His fingerprints were on file in the main computer database. It seems he had been picked up, more than once, for driving under the influence.

Hell, I wanted more information than that. The forensics lab had been sitting on my evidence for almost a week. Now, I was angry. I wanted to find out what the heck was happening over there.

The coroner's office was in the same building, adjacent to the forensic lab. I hadn't received any reports from them, either. I hadn't heard whether that knife we had found in the garbage bin, at the apartment complex, was the murder weapon or not. I decided it was time to put my foot down. I needed something to go on. I wasn't a psychic. I didn't have a magic wand to wave. I put cases together with solid and hard evidence.

I left my desk and walked out of the precinct to my car. Ten minutes later, I was at the medical examiner's building. As I entered the building, I couldn't believe what I was seeing. The forensics lab was a madhouse. People were everywhere. Lab assistants and secretaries were running like chickens with their heads cut off. Uniformed officers, undercover detectives, inspectors, captains, and even the police commissioner seemed to be roaming the halls.

I immediately sought out the supervisor of the lab, Dr. Charlie Stork. I was hoping he could tell me what the heck was going on. I noticed a number of officers and detectives from the serial killer task force. Putting two and two together, I figured it had something to do with that investigation. It really wasn't the right time to ask about my case, but I was adamant. I had been waiting long enough. It was only fair that I get the help that I needed from their lab. When I finally found Dr. Stork, he was sitting behind his desk, knee deep in paperwork.

"How are you doing today, Doc?" I asked, looking around the room at all the people.

"How do you think?" he said, with a deep Texas drawl.

"What the heck is going on? A bar mitzvah?"

"I wish," he said, running his hands through his already tousled hair. "But there was another murder early this morning—we think it's related to the serial killer."

"How many does that make now?"

"That would be the fourteenth murder in the last six months. Those are the ones we know about, anyway. We're going over the evidence now."

"That's what I'm here for today, Doc. I haven't received any reports concerning the evidence on my murder investigation."

"That's not true," he said. "I just sent over a report this morning...before all hell broke loose." He motioned towards the crowd of people milling about.

"You're right. I did get that. But I need more. It's been almost a week since you've had my evidence."

"I'm sorry. But you see what's going on here. All our manpower is centered towards the serial killer investigation. That order came down from the Governor's office."

"That's not fair."

"I don't like what's going on...any more than you do," he said, trying to soothe my hurt feelings.

"Well, I still need my reports on the evidence. I can't do my job without it. Do you have anything for me, Dr. Stork?"

"Well, let me check," he said. He picked through a stack of reports he had sitting on his desk.

I watched and waited, impatiently, as he looked through manila folder after manila folder. Nearing the bottom of a stack of about fifty manila folders, he finally stopped searching. He had found something. He opened the folder and began reading the file. He also checked the next one in the stack, but then set it back on the pile. He seemed to be satisfied.

"Well, here's something," he said.

"That's it?" I asked disillusioned.

"Hopefully, we'll have more information for you in the next week or so...as soon as things die down a bit," he said, handing me the manila envelope.

"Are you sure about that, Doc?"

"I'll do it myself, if need be," he said, trying to amend our business relationship.

"Is this it?" I asked, glancing through the report. "There's only one report here. I can't believe this."

"Yes, I know. But like I said before, our first priority is the serial killer task force. All our energies are being expunged on that evidence."

"Doc, all I ask is that you promise to do your best. There are other investigations going on besides that task force."

"Detective Hero, I take orders just like you do."

"I'm sorry. I didn't mean to get so uppity. What can you tell me about this report?" I asked.

"Well, we found a number of different fingerprints. However, no bloody fingerprints. As you can read from the report, the fingerprints were introduced into the computer data bank. We had positive identifications on all but one of the prints. That one wasn't found. We are pretty sure that it's a female's fingerprint, though."

"What gender are the others?"

"There were an even number of male and female fingerprints. The names are listed in the report."

I quickly glanced at the names of the people in the report. I would go through it more thoroughly when I returned to my desk.

"Were there any fingerprints on any of the straps or pillow cases or sheets?" I asked.

"The fingerprints that were found were taken from different areas of the apartment. There were no fingerprints found on or near the victim."

"Then where did you find the fingerprints?"

"One fingerprint was found on an ashtray in the living room. One print was found on an end table. Read the report. That's why it's there."

I could see that he was anxious to get back to his work...and wanted me to quit bothering him.

"Doc, please, try to finish my lab work as soon as possible. I would deeply appreciate it. I won't bother you anymore today."

"I appreciate that."

"I thank you for your time." We shook hands.

Then I walked away, heading towards the coroner's office. I wondered if they had checked the knife yet. Evidently, the forensics lab hadn't. It had only been a few days since we had located it. I shouldn't push them, though, I thought to myself.

As I walked to the coroner's office, right next door, I noticed a number of high-ranking political officials standing around.

When I opened the door and entered the Medical Examiner's room, it was the same scene I had encountered in the forensics lab. Milling around were many men in expensive suits. I was sure they were from the serial killer task force.

A group of people that had entered the room with me walked to another group of people on the far side of the room. They were crowded around a dead body—a woman's body. It was the wife of a high-ranking state official. She had been a good friend of the governor. But that was no reason to put my case to the side. I believed my investigation was just as important as the task force investigation...because both involved hunting down murderous villains.

I joined the group and listened as the pathologist talked through his autopsy. But after a few minutes, I left the area to look for Dr. Grady, the director of the coroner's office. I found him a few minutes later, in his office, sitting at his desk.

"How are you, Dr. Grady?" I asked.

"Not too well. The governor has given me a headache over this serial killing spree. What can I do for you?"

"I came by to see if my reports were ready."

"What reports are those?"

"Dr. Grady, are you kidding?" I asked, trying not to show my anger. "I haven't received the autopsy report of my victim...or the report on the possible murder weapon found a few days ago! I'm still waiting for them! It's almost been a week since the body was delivered!"

"Well, you can see for yourself that it's pretty chaotic around here. It's been like this for the last three or four days, since this most recent murder by the serial killer. It's gotten really hectic around here. But I do have a report or two for you lying around here somewhere," he said, scratching the top of his head as if he were waiting for his brain to get into high gear. "Ah, yes. Here it is!" He picked up a manila envelope.

I quickly opened it and scanned its contents. He was right. There were two reports in it. One was on the complete autopsy on the murder victim, Jim Palter. The other was the report on the possible murder weapon.

"So give me the lowdown on the murder victim, Doc."

"The victim died between seven and eleven that Sunday evening."

"Is that the best you can do on the time?"

"We were hoping you could put a tighter time on the murder yourself, through your thorough investigative techniques," he said, trying to inflate my ego.

"Well, I haven't yet. I might have an eyewitness to the murder, though. I'm not quite sure. I have so many suspects. What can you give me to go on? Dr. Grady, what can you tell me about the autopsy?"

"Number one. Whoever killed that man knew him. He was probably a close friend of the victim. The murderer, most likely, was a female. I'm certain that you've concluded that this was a rage killing? Haven't you?"

"Yes. But don't you think a male could have done it just as easily? Maybe an angry ex-lover...or an angry father? Maybe the murderer caught his girlfriend or daughter while they were in the process of having sex. The female either left the room, as the victim was still tied to the bed...or left the apartment all together, when the killer began slicing and dicing his victim. What do you think, Doc?"

"That's possible, but I still favor a female as the killer. We found semen on the victim and fluids from his lover on his body and penis. From the bruises on his wrists and ankles, he was definitely struggling as he was being stabbed to death. And...he was alive when his penis was cut off and his throat was slit."

"How do you know that, Doc?"

"He had blood in his one good lung. He was slowly dying, due to massive blood loss, when the killer began stabbing him in the chest and shoulders...and then directly into the heart. We also found semen in his mouth...as though they shoved the penis in his mouth. But it wasn't found that way at the murder scene. Whether it was male or female fluids or both, we won't know that until we get the DNA analysis report. That is where our problems begin."

"Why? What do you mean?"

"We don't have a contract with any DNA facility. The one we had ran out over thirty days ago, and the city hasn't refunded the project. So, we don't have a DNA lab at all to do our testing for us."

"No DNA information? Great. What about the murder weapon? Was that the murder weapon that we found in the garbage bin at the apartment complex? Do we know yet?"

"Yes. We believe it is. The blood type matches the victim's: AB negative. We didn't find any fingerprints on the blade of the weapon, though. But it fit the victim's wounds perfectly."

"What about fingerprints on the handle of the weapon?"

"There was dried blood on the handle. The knife was sent on to the FBI forensics lab to check for fingerprints. Once the blood is taken off, they use a special laser to lift off any fingerprints that might have stayed on. Hopefully, we should have that information any day now."

"I hope so, Dr. Grady. I've been waiting an awful long time for my information. The forensics lab is still hanging me up."

"I'm sure they aren't doing it on purpose. Since these disgusting serial killer murders, especially after one of the governor's own friends got killed, this place has been a circus. To tell you the truth, I'm getting tired of all the governor's clowns."

"I am, too," I said. "It's interfering with my investigation." I stood up. "Thanks for the reports, Doc. Let me know when those DNA reports come in…or when they go out, okay?"

"Sure thing, Detective Hero."

With that said, I turned and walked out of his office. Then I left the building and walked to my car.

I was glad to get out of that madhouse. I had planned to drive to the address of the victim's ex-business partner right after visiting the coroner's office, but it was lunchtime. Now, I would drive to my favorite café, "Gabrielle's Hoagie Shop," and have my favorite hoagie sandwiches. Once there, I could relax and look over the forensics report. So far, there wasn't one piece of evidence that proved—or pointed to without a shadow of a doubt—the guilty party. Everything had been circumstantial. But I was hoping to get lucky. So far, my luck had been bad.

Ten minutes later, I was at the café, sitting at my favorite back room table. The waitress came over as soon as I sat down. As I ordered my usual hoagie sandwiches, I quickly glanced around the room. My eyes settled on the girl that I had seen before. She was the one that looked like Samantha Manner, but a young Samantha Manner, except with a slightly different hair color. A few seconds later, my eyes turned to the waitress as she delivered my sandwiches.

As I ate, I read the report Dr. Grady had given me. I counted eight different fingerprints found inside the victim's apartment. Seven were identified, but one fingerprint was not found in the FBI's computer database. Evidently, that person had never been arrested or in the military. But the seven that had been identified were people that had a grudge against the victim. His business partner's fingerprints had been found. His were found on an ashtray in the living room...and a hallway wall, as though he had been leaning against it. We didn't find any from the ex-business partner, though.

Another fingerprint found was that of an ex-client. His was found, along with his wife's, on the kitchen table. They were all fairly recent fingerprints—either that or Jim Palter didn't dust or clean his furniture very often. The fingerprints of the young girl that had been supposedly raped by Jim Palter were also found at his apartment...and so were her father's. Hers had been found in the bedroom...on a small jewelry box. Her father's were found on a wall in the living room...and also on an end table, as though he had picked it up for some reason. Maybe to throw at the victim? And Palter's most recent girlfriend, Samantha Manner, also left her fingerprints in his apartment. Hers had been found on the front doorjamb, just as you enter his apartment.

The other person's fingerprint found was that of Rita Margaw. I had forgotten to ask her if she had ever been inside Palter's apartment. I had asked her if she had killed him, but her denial meant that she might never have even entered. I would have to question her again, I thought to myself. Hell, the murderer could have worn gloves. But I was certain that the perpetrator was one of these people in my report—and I was still leaning toward Rita. She could be placed at the scene near the time of death.

I would definitely question Rita again. I would even ask her to take a polygraph test, to see if she was telling the truth about the people she saw entering and leaving that building. But if she were telling the truth, I would especially like to talk to the woman seen leaving the building around nine-thirty that Sunday night. She might be the person whose fingerprint we had no record of? But Rita wasn't sure about that woman. It could have been anyone. She said she didn't get a good look at her.

Anyone could have gone into the victim's apartment. I wondered how many extra front door keys Palter had given to his girlfriends. I wondered if Rita had one. I doubted it. He had lived with Rita, so she wasn't supposed to know about his apartment. He had probably loaned them to other females...or maybe he didn't have any keys made at all. He probably didn't trust anybody.

Looking over the report once again, I noticed that another woman's fingerprint had been found in his bedroom, on the closet door. It was one of the women who had sued the victim in small claims court and lost. It was Carol's print. These fingerprints had been made within the last few days of his life. I was sure of it. Possibly even on the same day of his murder.

I finished my hoagies and paid the check. Now I was ready to find the victim's ex-business partner, Don Cadwell.

Within ten minutes I was standing in front of the receptionist desk of Cadwell's business. "Is Mr. Cadwell in? I'm Detective Hero, and I need to speak with him." I showed the receptionist my identification.

"Yes, I'll get him for you."

I waited for about fifteen minutes before he finally came out of his office to greet me.

"Hello, Detective Hero. I'm Don Cadwell. Can I help you?" he asked, in a deep booming voice, as we shook hands.

"Yes, I wonder if you could come down to the station to answer some questions concerning your ex-business partner, Mr. Jim Palter," I said, looking deep into his eyes, hoping for a spontaneous reaction from him.

"What's this all about?"

"I just need to ask you some questions about Mr. Palter."

"Can't you ask them here?"

"It's better that I interview you at the station so we can get your statement on file."

"Do I need a lawyer?"

"Why do you think you need a lawyer?"

"I don't know. I haven't done anything wrong."

"Well, then…if you don't have anything to hide, why worry about it?"

"I'm not worried. It's just better to be safe than sorry!"

"Relax, Mr. Cadwell…I just need to ask you about Jim Palter. I am investigating a case concerning him."

"What's he done now?"

"Mr. Palter was your business partner at one time, wasn't he?" I asked, not wanting to scare him away.

"Yes, he was my business partner."

"Come on down to the station. Let's get this over with. It'll only take a half an hour. Maybe even less. Why don't you follow me in your car? That'll make it a little easier for you."

"Okay, let's get this over with," he whined, as we walked out of the building to our cars. "I don't know what I have to do with that guy. This isn't over our bankruptcy, is it? They haven't charged me for his crime, have they?"

"Not that I know of."

Once we reached the station, I directed him to the interrogating room, then motioned for him to sit in the chair at the table. Mr. Cadwell seemed very, very nervous...and still hadn't mentioned a word about his ex-business partner's murder.

I left the room for a few minutes to give the suspect a little time to dwell over his situation. I watched him for a few minutes through the mirrored glass in an adjacent room. He kept fidgeting with his jacket. He couldn't sit still. I wondered why he was so nervous.

After letting him sit for a few more minutes, I re-entered the room.

"Is this about the fraud case that Palter ran?" Cadwell asked.

"No, Mr. Cadwell. I don't know anything about a fraud case." I sat down in the chair opposite him. "Why don't you tell me about it? ... But before we start the interview, do you want anything to drink? A cup of coffee or a soda?"

"Sure. I'll have a cola...or root beer. If it's no trouble?"

"It's no trouble at all. I'll be right back." I wanted to bring in a tape recorder to record the conversation.

When I left the room, I looked around for Detective Brenner to help me with this interrogation, but he was nowhere to be found. The department was completely empty of my peers. I was the only homicide detective in the room. But I did manage to find an old tape recorder, which I brought into the interrogation room, along with a soda pop. I set the tape recorder on the table and turned it on, then handed Mr. Cadwell the can of cola.

"Thanks, I appreciate it." He opened the can and then took a long drink. A few seconds later, he let out a big burp...and chuckled. "Sorry!"

"Mr. Cadwell, before I left the room you were going to tell me about your fraud case," I said, wanting to move things along.

He nodded. "I met Jim Palter a couple of years ago. He wanted to buy into my salvage business. He told me he had some money saved that his girlfriends had given him. I asked him, 'Girlfriends...more than one?' Palter said, 'Hell, I got four or five women that give me money.' Then, Palter gave me this big macho rap about all these different women that he kept on the side."

"What did Palter say about the women? Did he mention any names?"

"Palter said the women gave him their paychecks every week. I didn't ask him for names."

"What did you tell him about your company?"

"I explained to him that if he could come up with twenty-five thousand dollars, I would sell him twenty-five percent of my company's business," he explained, before taking a sip of his soda.

"What was Palter going to be, the manager?"

"I told him that I would make him my vice president...and show him the ropes. I must say, Palter was an excellent salesman."

"Why do you say that?"

"Once I showed him the tricks of the trade, he took right to it like a fish takes to water. I mean that guy could talk you out of your underwear, if he wanted them. I mean, he was good. He seemed to be doing even better than I could."

"How so?"

"He was getting deals that were unreal. It seemed every low bid he put in, he won. He never lost one bid. But pretty soon the business began getting out of hand."

"What do you mean?"

"I mean, almost a year and a half after Palter joined my company, his scam came to a head."

"You mean he was pulling a scam on everyone? What kind of scam?"

"Bills weren't being paid. Money from our business account was missing. I soon found out that the Justice department was investigating my company for fraud and grand larceny." Caldwell bowed his head in disgust...or shame.

"Mr. Cadwell, why was the Justice Department investigating your company?" I asked. I thought his story was just becoming interesting.

"Instead of buying salvaged goods, Palter was buying wholesale goods and then not paying the bill afterwards. He had bought merchandise from over fifteen hundred companies. He kept the order to less than four thousand dollars per shipment."

"Why would he do that?"

"That way, it would still be a misdemeanor, under state law. He never figured the federal government would get involved. When the companies demanded their money, they threatened Palter with a lawsuit and said that they would take their evidence to the authorities."

"So what did Palter do then?"

"He would give them some lame excuse about filing bankruptcy proceedings...or he told them that our company was in chapter thirteen. Then he would send the company that complained a small check of one hundred dollars or less—to show 'good faith,' as Palter called it. But even his lousy checks bounced. Then Palter started dipping into our bank account to pay for his expensive way of living."

"You're kidding? How much did he take?"

"I had over fifty thousand dollars in our business account. Now, there is less than a hundred dollars. He sucked it dry. I didn't notice anything was wrong until it was too late. Now, I'm trying to build the company back up."

"Are you having any luck?"

Caldwell shook his head. "Sometimes, I think it's useless."

"Why do you say that, Mr. Cadwell?"

"Palter has destroyed me and my business. He has destroyed everything I have. Even my self-esteem. I started my company with a lot of hard work and sweat. I put in ninety-hour weeks, fifty-two weeks a year. Now, I may be facing federal charges for fraud and/or larceny. That's why I thought you wanted to question me. It is, isn't it?"

"No. I didn't know anything about your troubles. I'm not a fraud investigator."

"What kind of investigator are you, then?" he asked, with a startled look on his face.

"Mr. Cadwell, I'm a homicide detective," I exclaimed, searching his face for a reaction.

"Homicide? What's going on?" He looked shocked, dumbfounded.

"I'm investigating the murder of your ex-business partner, Mr. Jim Palter. Do you know anything about that?" I stared into his eyes.

"No. When did he die?" His body began shaking, as if he had the cold chills.

"I'll ask the questions, Mr. Cadwell. Where were you this past Sunday evening...say between five o'clock and ten o'clock?" I looked deep into his eyes, trying to read his thoughts.

He looked away. "I was at home."

"Are you sure? Do you have someone that can verify your alibi?"

"I don't know? I didn't think I would need an alibi."

"You were pretty angry and upset with Palter for ruining your business, weren't you, Mr. Cadwell?"

"Yes, I was angry and upset with him. You would have been, too, if he had ruined your whole life's work!"

"Were you angry enough to kill him?" I asked, staring into his eyes for his reaction.

"I wanted to kill him, but I didn't!"

I didn't believe a word he had just told me...and he knew it. Again, he tried to convince me. "I didn't kill him," he snapped.

"Then why did you lie about visiting him, that night, at the Admore apartment building?" I asked, watching as his jaw dropped in disbelief. "You were at the Admore Apartments that night, weren't you?"

"Why do you think I was at the Admore apartments that Sunday night? I know for a fact, that I was at home that night. I was watching the *X-files* on television."

"Mr. Cadwell, I just don't believe a word you've told me. What would you say if I told you we had a witness that can put you at those apartments the night of Palter's murder?"

"Who was it? Who said they saw me at those apartments?" he asked. "I don't believe it!"

"Well, believe it. You must have something to hide or you wouldn't be lying about it now."

"I want a lawyer," he said, turning in his chair, not wanting to look in my direction. "I'm not going to say another word until I talk with my lawyer!"

"Mr. Cadwell, why do you want a lawyer if you're not guilty of any crime?"

He thought for a second, then drank the last of his soda pop before shouting, "I still think I need a lawyer!"

"If that's what you want."

"That's not what I want but you are treating me as if I'm guilty."

"And why would I do that, Mr. Cadwell?"

"'Cause you need a scapegoat to solve your case, and it sounds like you picked me."

"Well, I'm sorry to bust your bubble," I told him, as I had Mr. Walters. "But it doesn't work that way. Believe me...that if and when I arrest you, I will do it using hard evidence. Now do you want to waive your rights to a lawyer and answer my questions?"

Cadwell thought for a minute and decided to speak. "Ok, I'll talk. I guess I don't need a lawyer."

"Then tell me who you visited, when you went to the Admore apartments...that Sunday evening? Did you visit Palter that evening?"

"You keep saying that, but I wasn't there," he whined.

He wanted me to believe his story, but I knew better.

"I'm going to give you one more chance to tell me the truth...or you might have to explain yourself to a judge," I said, looking deep into his eyes. "I told you, I have a witness that puts you in front of that apartment building that Sunday evening when Palter was murdered. The more you keep lying to me, the deeper you dig yourself into a hole...so deep that you won't be able to get yourself out of it."

"Get myself out of what? I didn't do anything," he exclaimed, angrily.

I needed to take a coffee break, and I noticed he had finished his can of soda. I stood up. "Mr. Cadwell, would you like another soda pop...or some coffee?"

"Soda pop...if you don't mind."

"While I'm out of the room, why don't you think about what I just said? I have a job to do, and I just want you to tell me the truth. If you have nothing to hide, then you don't have anything to worry about."

I picked up his empty soda pop can very carefully, so I wouldn't get my fingerprints all over it, and walked out of the room without Mr. Cadwell noticing what I had done.

I went to my desk to retrieve an evidence bag and placed the soda can into it. I wanted to take it to the forensics lab to have the fingerprints checked for identification as I had done with Mr. Walters. I wanted to make sure he was the person he said he was. I had a bad feeling about this guy. I still couldn't figure out why he was lying to me about being at the Admore apartments...unless he was guilty of murder.

I handed the evidence bag to a uniformed officer and asked him to take it over to the forensics lab. I hoped to confirm Cadwell's true identity within two to seven days.

When I returned, carrying Don Cadwell's soda, I noticed his somber and sad facial expression. He looked like a beaten man. I handed him the can of soda and sat down in my chair to continue the interview. I had forgotten to shut off the tape recorder before I left the room, so it was time to put in a new, blank tape. I quickly changed the tape, then turned the recorder back on.

"Mr. Cadwell, now that you have had a chance to think about your future, tell me who you went to see at the Admore apartments last Sunday evening. Did you see Palter that night?"

Suddenly, he refused to speak.

"Listen, I can call the witness to come down and pick you out of a lineup. If I have to go to all that trouble, someone is going to jail...and it won't be me."

He straightened up in his chair, took a big swig of his soda, and let out another big belch. Now, he seemed to have a change of heart.

"Okay, you win," he said, as he stared down at the floor and squirmed in his chair.

"Ok then, tell me about Sunday night, Mr. Cadwell."

"I was at the Admore apartments Sunday night. But I swear to you, I didn't visit Palter's place. I went to visit another friend I know that lived in the building. I didn't associate with Palter...not after he destroyed my company...and damn near destroyed my life."

"Why are you telling me this now? Why have you suddenly changed your story? Now you want me to believe that you visited other people at the Admore? I'm sure the friends that you visited can back up your story, right?"

Again, he became a mute. He stared blankly at the floor, not answering my questions. I just waited patiently for him to begin the conversation. Suddenly, he snapped out of his trance.

"What? I'm sorry. What was the question?" he asked, rubbing his eyes.

"Mr. Cadwell, you were going to tell me the apartment number and the names of the people you were visiting that night."

"Well, the first apartment I visited that night was on the fifth floor. The apartment number is 5002. I got to his place about nine or ten o'clock that Sunday evening."

"How long did you stay there?"

"I didn't. No one answered the door, so I figured they may have just stepped out for dinner and would return shortly. So I took the elevator up to the eighth floor to visit another friend of mine."

"What apartment was that...and who lives there?"

"That's Mat Holton's apartment," he said, fidgeting with his hands. "The apartment number is 8122. We went to high school together."

"He can verify your story I take it?"

"Well, not exactly."

"What do you mean, 'not exactly'?"

"He didn't answer his door, either. None of my friends were home that evening...so I turned around and walked back to the parking lot. I got into my car and drove home."

I had the feeling he was lying again...because he looked away from my eyes as he spoke.

"Let me see if I got this straight. First, you lie and tell me you weren't at the Admore apartment building. Then you change your story and tell me that you were at the Admore that night, but the people you went to visit weren't at home. So you decided to drive back home to your apartment. Is that about right, Mr. Cadwell?"

He looked at me with a cold, hard stare and answered, "Yes, that's right."

"Did you know that Palter had an apartment there?" I asked.

"Yes, I knew he had kept an apartment there."

"Mr. Cadwell, have you ever been to his apartment...or in his apartment?" I asked, knowing what the answer was, since we had found his fingerprints there.

He didn't answer right away. He had to think about it for a few minutes. He began to squirm in his seat. He seemed to be very uncomfortable, as he rolled his neck in circles and arched his back.

"Yes, I've been there before," he finally said. "But it's been quite a while."

"How long would that be?" I asked, giving him a cold, hard stare of my own. "And I want the truth the first time."

"I was there maybe four or five days ago," he said, nervously biting his fingernails.

"What did you want to see him about?"

"I wanted to find out when he was going to start his payments for restitution."

"What was the restitution for?"

"Jim and I had made an agreement, but he wasn't abiding by it. He was supposed to pay me five hundred dollars a month for the next ten years...but when the first payment came due, he refused to pay...and told me he wasn't going to pay me."

"So what did you do?"

"What could I do? I took him to court—and the arbitrator came up with the same arrangement. I couldn't put a lean on his property because he had never owned any."

"So, Sunday night, you went over to Palter's apartment and killed him. Didn't you?"

"No. That night, I went to my friend's apartment. Nobody was at home, so I went back to my place."

"Why should I believe you?"

"Because I didn't kill him! I might have wanted him dead. I remember telling him that if I was one of his girlfriends and had found out that he was sleeping around with two or three other women, I would have cut his penis off and shoved it up his rectum."

"You know, Mr. Cadwell, that's a coincidence. How did you know that Palter's penis had been cut off?"

"I didn't! You're turning my words around. ... I didn't kill him," he screamed.

"Okay, settle down. Don't get so upset."

"But you're accusing me of something I didn't do!"

"I'm not accusing anyone. I'm asking questions...trying to find the truth."

This seemed to calm him down. "I'm sorry for getting upset. Please, ask your question."

"Mr. Cadwell, did you happen to see anything out of the ordinary at that apartment building that Sunday night? Did you recognize anyone before you enteredor after you left the apartment building?"

"No, not really," he said. "I did see a few females that I thought I had recognized before. I thought they were headed up to Jim's apartment."

"Do you know them by name?"

"Maybe. One girl was being hassled by the police as I was entering the apartment building. But she was gone by the time I returned to the parking lot. She looked like a woman I had seen before. I believe her name was Rita."

"What did she have to do with Jim Palter?" I asked, already knowing the answer.

"That was one of Jim's girlfriends...once upon a time."

"Did you know her?"

"A little bit. I thought she was a weirdo. Jim thought she was a two hundred dollar a week paycheck. But I'm not real sure if that was Rita or not. I didn't get a clear view of her because she was arguing with two policemen."

"Who was the other girl you saw?"

"When I went up to visit my friend on the eighth floor, there was a young girl already on the elevator. She and I were the only two people on that elevator, and when I pressed the button for the eighth floor, I noticed the number ten button was also lit up."

"So what are you trying to tell me? That she was going to the tenth floor?"

"She was definitely going up to the tenth floor...probably to see Jim. I can't say for sure. But the night I went over to his apartment, four or five days ago, he did have an altercation with one of his girlfriends."

"What kind of altercation?" I asked.

"When I entered his apartment, they were in a heated argument."

"Who was he arguing with?"

"I'm not sure. It was one of his younger girlfriends. I had seen her once before, in court."

"In court? Small Claims or District Court?"
"District Court."
"For what?"
"A young girl's father pressed charges against Jim for statutory rape. Even though the court ordered Jim not to see her again, there she was, in vivid color, standing in his living room. Her father had told Jim, in front of all the people in the courtroom, that if he ever caught Jim around his daughter again he would kill him."

"So the girl's father threatened Jim Palter with death if Jim ever saw his daughter again, is that right?"

"Yes."

"Then what were Jim and the girl arguing about when you walked in on them?"

"When I walked into the living room, where they were arguing, they suddenly became silent."

"Mr. Cadwell, do you know this young girl's name?"

He shook his head. "Jim never introduced me to the girl."

"Why not?"

"I think he was afraid I would try and jump onto his golden rainbow. She was one of his meal tickets. While I was visiting, they acted like lovebirds. When they had stopped arguing, I began speaking."

"What did you tell him?"

"I asked Jim when he was going to start paying off the debt he owed to me."

"What did he say to that?"

"He refused to even discuss the matter with me."

"So, what did you do when he wouldn't talk to you about his debt?"

"I was getting so angry that I got right up into his face. I must admit, I did threaten him if he didn't pay me. But before our argument broke out into a fistfight, I decided to get out of there. I stormed out of his apartment and slammed the door behind me. While walking down the hall, I passed another very young female."

"Do you know her name?"

"No. It looked like another vulnerable female that had fallen for Jim's lies."

"How old did she look to you?"

"She looked less than twenty years old. When I turned around to see which apartment she was going to, sure enough, she had knocked on Jim's apartment door. I wondered what he would say to her to get out of that mess. Both girlfriends meeting each other. I'm sure he'd never planned for that to happen. But before Jim answered the door, I was riding the elevator, heading for the lobby. I sure wished I had stayed now."

"Why do you say that, Mr. Cadwell?"

"I probably would have seen a hell of a cat fight. Then, as I walked out of the apartment building, I ran into another one of Jim's girlfriends. It was his latest gold mine. I had seen her before with Jim, holding hands and smooching, so I figured that she was his latest find."

"Do you know who she was?"

"She was an old hag compared to many of his other girlfriends," he replied. "So, I figured she must have lots of money or Jim wouldn't be going out with her. I was pretty sure she was also going up to his apartment. I just laughed out loud as I thought about Jim's predicament. Each one was supposed to be his 'one and only love.' I just figured it was his Karma catching up to him."

I remembered the photos I had in my jacket pocket. I pulled them out and asked him to look at them. "The women that you saw visiting Jim that night at his apartment...were any of those women in any of these photos?" I asked, as I set the ten photos in a neat pile in front of him.

He quickly picked up the pile of photos and began going through them, one by one. He divided the pile in half, five photos in each pile.

"What is that, Mr. Cadwell?" I asked, tapping my fingers on the two different piles of photos.

He pointed to the pile to his right and said, "This pile is of the women I saw at or near his apartment. This other pile...I've never seen them before." He pointed to the women's photos he hadn't recognized. "Were they also girlfriends of Jim's?"

"Do you know the names of the women that you did recognize?" I asked.

"I know three of their names. But I don't know the other two. But this woman's picture," he said, pointing to Samantha Manner's photo, "looks similar to one of his younger girlfriends. However, the woman in this photo looks much older...I don't know her name. But she does look like the woman I saw entering the apartment building just as I was leaving that Tuesday night."

"Mr. Cadwell, are you sure?"

"Yes. And just recently, I also saw her holding hands with Palter." He had a puzzled look on his face as he continued to stare at the picture of Samantha Manner. "But the woman I'm talking about is much younger than the woman in the photo."

"How much younger?"

"Say about twenty years younger, at least. She was the young lady I saw knocking on Jim's apartment door while I was stepping on the elevator Tuesday night. She was also the woman I saw on the elevator last Sunday night, going up to the tenth floor. Maybe she's the woman's sister," he said, pointing to Samantha Manner's photo. "Or maybe it's just a coincidence and they're not related at all."

I believed Cadwell was talking about the same young woman that I had seen a few times at the cafe. I wondered if she had anything to do with my case. But I didn't know her name. Perhaps, I thought to myself, I'd ask her the next time I saw her. The photo he was looking at was the picture of the woman I'd talked to at the apartment the morning after the murder. She was supposedly Palter's most recent girlfriend...or so she thought. Maybe she was the most recent that he was living with, at her apartment. He had his mistresses visit him, at his apartment. That's how he had planned it, anyway.

Well, I listened as Cadwell told me the other three names of the women in the photos. He mentioned Rita, Carol, and Helen. I didn't have a name or picture of the young girl that we had talked about. I wondered if she was the woman that had left her fingerprint behind in the victim's apartment...of which neither the FBI nor the state had any record.

Now I had two different witnesses that put that young girl at his apartment that Sunday night. It also put his ex-business partner and a few others at or near his apartment that evening. Everyone that I questioned had a motive for wanting Palter dead. Not only that, but I still hadn't heard one good alibi from any of the people I had questioned. I still hoped that the forensic and DNA lab would come up with something that would narrow the field. But when that would be, I didn't know.

"Well, Mr. Cadwell, I think I've asked you enough questions for one day," I said, rising from my chair. "But it's possible that I may want to speak with you again, some other time. However, for the time being, I thank you for coming and talking with me."

"You mean, you're not going to arrest me?"

"No, not yet. But you are still a prime suspect, so don't plan on leaving town anytime soon. I still may need to talk to you."

"All right, but you're just wasting your time suspecting me," he said, biting his fingernails again.

"I will tell you this...if I can break just one of your alibis, I will get you for obstruction or withholding evidence—if not murder," I said. His face turned a deep red as he listened to my words.

Mr. Cadwell rose from his chair and quickly walked through the door, down the hall, to the front lobby and out the front door. He didn't even bother to shake my hand. He just shot straight for the front door.

I put in a call to the forensics lab to see if they had checked the soda can for fingerprints. But lo and behold, they didn't know. They didn't even know if it had come into their lab, yet. I had to control my anger and frustration or I would never get any cooperation from them. I asked Dr. Stork to check their docket to see if my item had arrived and if it had been checked for fingerprints. I asked him to phone the information to me as soon as possible.

While I waited for that, my next method of investigation was to find the young girl's father that had brought charges against Palter for statutory rape. I wondered if the father knew that his daughter had been seeing him again.

I decided I would question him at his place of residence. Hopefully, his daughter would be there, too. I could question her at the same time and kill two birds with one stone—metaphorically speaking, that is.

As I sat thinking, my stomach began to growl from hunger. When I looked at my watch, I noticed it was quitting time. I decided I would go to my favorite cafe for a light dinner. Maybe I would get lucky and see that young girl there—the one that reminded me of a young Samantha Manner. I didn't know who she was, but I was definitely going to find out.

## Chapter 5

I was feeling optimistic—until I walked through the door of the cafe. The beautiful young woman wasn't there. I was a little disappointed, but I knew I would see her again.

I ordered my dinner and showed Bonnie, the waitress, the photo of Samantha Manner.

"Bonnie, have you ever seen a woman that looks like her, but twenty years younger?" I asked, as I held out the photo in front of her face. "She's visited this restaurant a few times within the past couple of days. I've seen her around dinnertime."

She grabbed the photo and looked at it more closely.

"Yeah, I've seen her before...at least I think I've seen her," she said, in her sweet, soothing voice, staring at the photo intently.

"Bonnie, are you sure?"

"Well, there is one girl that comes into the restaurant once or twice a month that looks like the woman in the picture. But the woman in this photo is twice as old as the other girl," she said, handing me the photo. "I'm just not certain. The girl I'm thinking about sure looks like the one in the photo...that is, if she was twenty years younger!"

"If she ever returns to the restaurant contact me as quickly as possible," I said, handing her my business card. "Please keep an eye out for her."

"Why? What's so important about her?"

"Oh, I just need to ask her a few questions concerning a case I'm working on."

"I'll keep my eye open," Bonnie said, as she turned and walked to her workstation.

When I finished my dinner and a cigarette, I left a five-dollar tip, then headed for home. I couldn't get there quick enough. As soon as I walked in the front door, I went directly to the kitchen cabinet and grabbed a new bottle of twenty-year-old scotch.

I figured, if I could drink enough alcohol fast enough, my mind would be too clouded to think about my murder investigation. Unfortunately, it didn't work out. Every time I tried to put the case out of my mind, for some reason it would creep back in.

I awoke the next morning to find that I had slept in my clothes, but I was too sick to change or shower. I just combed my dirty hair and straightened out my wrinkled suit pants and coat.

Instead of driving to the station, I drove directly to the forensics lab. I wanted to check to see if they had fingerprinted the Cadwell soda can. I had a suspicion about that man. I couldn't put my finger on it, but I felt he was hiding something.

When I entered the forensics lab, I sought out the head pathologist and supervisor, Dr. Charlie Stork. He was the person I had spoken with a few days before. I found him near the vending machines eating a donut and drinking a cup of coffee.

"Hi ya, Doc," I said. "Do you have anything for me today?"

"Well, good morning to you, too, Detective Hero."

"What do you have for me today?"

"I've got some good news and some bad news for you," he said, sipping his coffee.

"Like what?"

"Well. We finally sent your evidence to a DNA lab a few miles from here. That's the good news. The bad news is...they won't get to it for at least a few more days...if not longer."

"Doc, what about the soda can? Did you fingerprint it yet?"

"I was just about to do that as soon as I finished my coffee. I will run the report over to you when it's complete."

"How long will that take?"

"Please, I don't like to be rushed. I will have the report on your desk around lunchtime."

"That's fine."

"Oh, yes...and the FBI lab contacted me about the knife," he said. "They just started their analysis, and they should have the findings within a few days. That is, if there are fingerprints to find. They also began work on the pillowcases and bed sheet—looking for semen, fluids, stains and blood type. We're so swamped from the serial killer investigation that we sent much of your evidence to the FBI lab for their expertise."

"I wish we could do the work here, Doc."

"You and me both," he said. "We just don't have the time or personnel to handle this influx of evidence.... Have you found a suspect yet?"

"Yeah, at least six of them. It seems every time I question a witness I end up putting them on my suspect list."

"And why is that?"

"Nobody can give me a decent alibi. That's why I need all the reports from my evidence."

"We'll have your evidence tested when we get to it," he said.

It seemed there was nothing more I could do.

Now it was time to find Mr. Garwood. He had threatened to kill the victim. Now, I wanted to see if maybe he'd gone through with it.

I left the station and headed for Mr. Garwood's place of residence. The address was in the best part of the city. The houses in the area started at five hundred thousand dollars.

They were two and three-story houses with three and four-car attached garages. They looked like mini-mansions.

After driving for more than twenty minutes, I finally came upon the address. I turned into the driveway and continued on for another thousand feet until I came upon a three-story, brick Tudor home with an attached three-car garage. The house was exquisite, and the lawn was completely landscaped and well-manicured. Hell, the circular, asphalt drive had cost more than my house. Palter must have struck a gold mine when he met this young woman. I was sure she had accumulated a few bucks, as rich as her family was, and she probably received an exorbitant weekly allowance—all of which had probably been turned over to her boyfriend, Jim Palter.

I shut off the engine and stepped out of my car, then walked to the front door. Within seconds of ringing the doorbell, a slender and svelte maid answered. I showed her my detective's badge and identification.

"Hello, ma'am. I'm Detective Hero, and I'm here to see Mr. Garwood. Is he here?"

"Yes, follow me," she said.

I entered the home and followed her through a maze of hallways and rooms. The interior of the home was immaculate. Each room had its own crystal chandelier, and every wall was adorned with many famous paintings—Dali, Picasso, and many other famous artists, even Peter Max.

I was escorted to a large room where Mr. Garwood was standing in front of a massive fireplace smoking a foot long cigar. Seconds later, the maid left the room and I introduced myself to my host.

"Hello, Mr. Garwood. I'm Detective Hero."

"Hello, Detective. Please, sit," he said, pointing to a large, black leather couch.

"Thank you," I said. As I sat down, I glanced around the room and noticed that it, too, was filled with very expensive antiques and paintings. Two of the walls contained his library. There must have been five thousand rare and old books. Then I remembered why I was there and got down to business.

"Mr. Garwood, I would like to invite you and possibly your daughter to come down to the station and let me question you concerning a Mr. Jim Palter." He seemed rather startled when I mentioned the name of Palter. "You do know him, don't you, Mr. Garwood?"

"Yes, unfortunately. I know that low-life gutter trash. He raped my daughter. But you already knew that, didn't you, Detective?" He had a very distinctive southern accent.

"I'm here not only to ask you a few questions concerning Mr. Palter's alleged rape on your daughter but also about another situation that might concern you, Mr. Garwood."

"Why do we need to go all the way down to the station? Can't you ask those same questions here in my house?"

"It would be easier for me if we could do this interview at the station. But I guess I can interview you and your daughter here, if you'd like."

"Thank you. Now...what is this all about? Did Mr. Palter rape another young girl?"

"No, not that I know of."

"Then why are you here, Detective? What does Jim Palter have to do with me...or my daughter?" he asked.

"Mr. Garwood, have you visited Mr. Palter in the last few days?" I asked, knowing that he had.

"No, I haven't. But what if I did? What does that have to do with anything?"

"Mr. Garwood, I'll ask you again. Did you visit Mr. Palter at his apartment in the last four or five days?"

"Yes, I did go over to see him at his apartment within the last few days."

"Do you remember what day that was?"

"I believe it was Tuesday or Wednesday of last week."

"What was the reason for your visit? I thought you hated the guy?"

"You know," he said, exhaling a big puff of cigar smoke, "the first time I met the guy was nearly five years ago. My daughter was only fifteen years old."

"So, Mr. Garwood, how did you first meet Jim Palter?"

"I had left work early due to the stomach flu. I arrived three hours earlier than usual. When I entered my home, I walked into my den to find this man, Palter, raping my daughter on the floor, in the middle of the room."

"What did you do?"

He stared down at the floor, rolling his big cigar between his fingers, for nearly a minute before he answered my question. "I was so startled at what I was watching, I stood frozen, as if my feet were glued to the floor. But when the shock wore off, I ran over to them and lifted him off of my daughter. I picked him up by the throat and began choking him."

"I don't blame you. I would have done the same."

"I was like a raving lunatic...I tried to squeeze the life out of him," he said, as he puffed on his cigar. "The only reason he didn't end up dead was due to my daughter's interference."

"Why ... what did she do?"

"My daughter jumped up off of the floor and got between us. She helped him escape my death grip. When I finally released my hands from around his throat, he ran out of my house naked as a jay bird."

"Mr. Garwood, he's lucky he got out alive. I think if I had caught him raping my daughter, I'd have shot and killed him."

"I thought he was raping my daughter," he said, puffing on his cigar and letting the ash fall to the beautiful, hardwood floor. "But I come to find out later that it was supposedly consensual sex. My daughter was only fifteen years old at the time!"

"Did you call the police?"

"Hell yes! I had Palter arrested for statutory rape! He was lucky to still be alive! From that day on, I thought my daughter was through with him. But just the other day I heard my daughter speak to him on the telephone."

"Mr. Garwood, what did you do when you heard your daughter speaking with the man that had raped her?"

"I wanted to find out if he was seeing her again. I told Palter five years ago that if I ever saw him with my daughter again, I would kill him with my bare hands!" Garwood demonstrated by pretending to choke an invisible neck with his massive hands.

"Did you, Mr. Garwood?" I asked, staring into his eyes.

"Did I what?"

"Mr. Garwood...did you kill Jim Palter?"

"No! I didn't even know he was dead." And then he smiled and said, "But I would like to congratulate the killer."

"Where were you this past Sunday evening?"

"What time?"

"Let's say, between five and eleven p.m."

"I was driving in my car," he said, rolling his fifty-dollar cigar between his fingers.

"Where did you drive to, Mr. Garwood?"

"When I get upset, I go for long drives in the country. That's exactly what I did on that particular night."

"Is there anyone that can verify your story? Are there any passengers that can verify your story?"

"No," he said, tossing his half-smoked cigar into the fireplace. "I didn't know I would need an alibi."

"Boy, I've heard that before. Mr. Garwood, are you telling me that you didn't visit Palter on that Sunday evening?" From his nervous reaction to my question, I had a hunch there was something he wasn't telling me. I could sense his tension, and I knew it didn't have anything to do with my questions. He was too confident and shrewd to be rattled by them. But I was sure he was trying to hide something...and I had to get it out of him. I had an idea, so I put it to use.

"Mr. Garwood, what if I told you I had a witness that put you at Palter's apartment on that Sunday evening? What if I told you that a witness also saw your daughter at Palter's apartment that Sunday evening?"

He didn't say a word. He just stared at me intently. I wondered what he was thinking. I couldn't let him stare me down. I had to stand up to him. He was a man that always got his way, and I needed to stay in control of this situation.

Just as I was about to ask another question, he spoke up.

"Well, what if I *was* at Palter's apartment that Sunday evening...so what? That doesn't mean I killed him. Although I wanted to."

"So! You *were* at his apartment on the night he was murdered! You were there that Sunday evening!"

"Yes. You'd probably find out anyway," he said, lighting another fifty-dollar cigar.

"You're right about that!"

"You were also right about my daughter visiting him that Sunday," he said, rolling his cigar between his fingers.

"I followed her to his apartment. I couldn't believe my daughter would go against my wishes and see him again."

"Mr. Garwood, why would you say that?"

"My daughter has a mind of her own. She doesn't listen to me—or anyone—anymore." He puffed on his cigar for nearly a minute before he continued. "The door to his apartment was open, so I let myself in. While I stood in the hallway I listened to my daughter and Palter argue."

"Could you hear what they were arguing about?"

"Yes. My daughter had found a pair of woman's panties. They weren't hers, so she confronted him about it. She was very angry. But when I heard Palter's arrogant excuses for the strange panties showing up, *I* became very angry."

"What did you do?"

"That Jim Palter was a low down, dirty man. I wanted to strangle him right then and there. When he began yelling at my daughter, I couldn't hold back any longer."

"Mr. Garwood, I just want to be sure that you know that you don't have to say anything else. But if you do, I must warn you...anything you say can and will be used against you in a court of law...that is, if I decide to arrest you. Is that understood?"

"That's all right...I have nothing to hide. I told you before, and I'll say it again. I didn't kill that man!"

"Yes, I heard you, Mr. Garwood. But please, continue with your story."

"When I heard that scum yelling obscenities at my daughter, I stormed into the living room and grabbed him by the throat!" Garwood stopped speaking to take a puff on his cigar.

"Okay, so what happened next?"

"We scuffled and then fell to the floor. I landed on top of him, still choking him with all my might. But something came over me when my daughter began beating me on the back with her fists. It was then that I realized I had better stop or I would kill him."

"So what did you do?"

"I immediately pulled my hands away from his throat and picked myself and Palter up from the floor. While he was gagging and coughing, I apologized to him for overreacting."

"So, as far as you know...Mr. Palter was still alive?"

"Yes."

"What happened next?"

"I dusted myself off and left the apartment."

"What about your daughter? Did she leave with you?"

"No," he said. "My daughter stayed behind. She wanted a few minutes alone with him to end it. She wanted to tell him that his gold digging days with her were over."

"So what did you do when she stayed behind in the apartment?"

"I sat and waited in my car for about ten minutes before I finally drove away."

"What were you waiting for?"

"I was waiting for my daughter to show up. I wanted to speak with her. But instead, I decided to confront my daughter at home. I didn't want to make a spectacle of myself out in the parking lot. I figured I would wait until I got home to do that."

"Mr. Garwood, did you see anyone else visit Palter's apartment that night?"

"No. I didn't see anyone."

"How could that be?"

"I came into the apartment building through the back entrance. I walked up all ten flights of stairs to his apartment."

"Why not use the elevator?"

"I didn't want anyone to see me—especially my daughter. I must admit, killing Mr. Palter was on my mind."

"Why do you say that?"

"He had created problems within our family again. I wasn't going to let my daughter throw her life away. And if that meant killing him to do it, I would have. I must say...I tried. But to no avail."

"Mr. Garwood, do you think you daughter had anything to do with Jim Palter's murder?" I asked, watching his body language.

He leaned forward in surprise. "Of course not! She couldn't hurt a flea."

"Who couldn't hurt a flea?" a voice interrupted.

I looked over my shoulder to match a face with the voice to find Mr. Garwood's beautiful, young daughter, Ellen, standing there. She couldn't have been more than twenty years old, and she had the face and figure of a top model.

She walked past me and stood next to her father. Then, as she stood in front of me clutching her big, blue, leather Gucci purse tightly against her body, as if it were her security blanket, she introduced herself to me.

"Hi. I'm Ellen Garwood," answering in her sweet southern drawl, while looking at me with her big, blue eyes.

"Hello. I'm Detective Hero," I said, shaking her hand.

"Hello, sweetheart," said Mr. Garwood, as she turned to him and kissed him on the cheek.

"Miss Garwood, can I ask you a couple of questions concerning Mr. Jim Palter?" I asked.

"About what?" she said.

"It has something to do with your relationship with him."

"Oh, concerning his credit card scams?" she interjected.

"What credit card scams?" I asked.

"I'm not real sure," she said, sitting in a chair next to me. "But one of his female acquaintances confronted him about it one day while I was visiting him at his friend's apartment. She had found some phony identification and credit cards with the same phony names on them."

"Miss Garwood, what were you doing while the woman confronted him?"

"I just stood my ground and stayed out of their argument, until she turned her anger in my direction."

"Then what did you do?" I asked.

"When she began yelling at me, I quickly left the apartment. She sounded just like my mother."

"Well, I'm not really interested in his credit card scams. I'm a homicide detective."

"What does a homicide detective want with me?" she asked.

"Did you know that Jim Palter is dead?" I asked.

She acted as though she hadn't heard me, but she was actually too stunned to speak. Her face went pale. And after a minute of silence, still clutching her purse closely to her stomach, she finally responded to my question. "No," she said. "I didn't know Jim was dead. How did he die?" Tears filled her eyes.

"He was murdered," I said, watching her closely.

"Murdered? I don't believe it," she said, looking at her father.

"Miss Garwood, when did you see Jim Palter last?"

But before she could answer, her father spoke up. "I'm sorry, Detective Hero," he said, staring coldly into my eyes. "I think you should get in touch with my attorney if you want to question my daughter about Jim Palter's murder."

"Please, Mr. Garwood. Let me ask her myself. If she has nothing to hide, she has nothing to worry about."

"I think I ought to contact my lawyer concerning this situation," he said.

"Please, sir. Let me do my job. Let's get this interview over with. Otherwise, it makes it seem like she's got something to hide."

Mr. Garwood thought about it for a minute, looked at his daughter, and said, "It's up to you, sweetheart. If you want to answer his question, go ahead and answer it."

"I don't mind," she said, trying to put forth a brave face. "I told you before, Detective Hero...I have nothing to hide. Now, what was the question?"

"When did you last see Jim Palter?"

"It was about eight o'clock, Sunday night," she said, clutching her purse even tighter.

I wondered what she had in it. I had a hunch she was protecting something important.

"Miss Garwood, did anyone else arrive at Jim Palter's apartment, besides your father, that night?"

"Possibly."

"Oh, yeah, who?" I asked.

"I don't know. As I was walking towards the elevator, I noticed a young woman had just gotten off and walked past me, heading directly for Jim's apartment. But just as I entered the elevator, its doors closed before I could see where she was going."

"Why did you stay behind and not leave with your father?"

"I wanted to finish our argument about a strange pair of lace panties that I had found in Jim's bedroom. We had gotten into a fist fight over that, and I wanted to collect my belongings so I wouldn't have to see him again." Once again, she became teary-eyed.

"I would have been so angry with him about finding those undies that I would have wanted to kill him," I said.

"Believe me, I did want to kill him," she said, dabbing her eyes with the sleeve of her blouse. "He used me for almost two years. I gave him everything I owned. I even gave him my weekly allowance. Then I find out he's out with some old hag, twice my age. You're damn right I wanted to kill him."

As she was explaining her story, she became so intense at telling it that she began throwing her arms about. She lost hold of her purse; it flew out of her arms and landed at my feet. When the purse hit the floor, it opened up. Everything in it spilled onto the floor. But what came out of it wasn't drugs or money—it was a weapon: a big butcher knife. It looked like the same exact knife that had been found in the garbage dumpster near the victim's apartment building. It was the same length, name brand, and the same type of handle.

I was completely startled at this sight. So was Miss Garwood's father. His jaw hit the floor when he saw the knife roll out of her purse. Miss Garwood ran over to retrieve it, but I had already picked it up using my clean handkerchief.

"Miss Garwood, what are you carrying this around for?" I asked, holding the knife up in the air for all to see. "Where did you get it? Did you take it from your kitchen?"

"Maybe you'd better not answer that question, sweetheart," said Mr. Garwood, walking over to me to get a closer look at the butcher knife.

"I've got nothing to hide, Daddy. Jim gave me that knife to carry for protection."

"This knife came from his house?" I asked, still using my handkerchief to handle the knife so I wouldn't get my fingerprints on it.

"That's right," she said.

"If you don't mind," I said, pulling out a plastic bag from my jacket pocket, "I would like to take this knife with me. I want to have our forensics lab analyze it for blood evidence."

"What if we do mind?" asked Mr. Garwood, as I placed the knife and handkerchief into the plastic bag.

"Like I said before . . . if she's innocent, then she doesn't have anything to worry about."

I didn't tell them about the knife we had found in the garbage dumpster because it might come back with the report stating that it was not the murder weapon. I had to have this knife checked out or I wouldn't be doing my job. I had no choice. The blade of the knife had some telltale signs of being cleaned...and I also could detect a small amount of a dark-colored substance—possibly blood—at the base of the handle. I wondered...if it was blood, whose blood was it?

"You don't have any right to take that knife out of my house," Mr. Garwood bellowed.

"Miss Garwood, did you know that it is a felony to carry a concealed weapon?" I said. Then I turned my eyes to focus on her father.

"No, I didn't know that. But I carry it with me for a good reason."

"Why is that?" I asked.

"I was assaulted by some thug. He tried to rip my purse out of my hands. I was scared to death. I thought the hooligan was going to kill me. I feel safe and well protected when I'm carrying the knife."

"Well, it could get you into plenty of trouble," I said. "If you aren't willing to use the knife, the thug could take it away from you and use it against you. How long have you been carrying it in your purse?"

"Just about three months. I was attacked a little over three months ago."

"I just hope there isn't any of Palter's blood on the knife," I said, looking deep into her eyes. "That would put you into a very peculiar predicament. Especially if it corresponds to the murder victim's stab wounds. The district attorney could make a powerful case against you. He could also put you at the murder scene on the night of Jim Palter's murder."

Mr. Garwood didn't like my words and told me so. "You know, Detective Hero," he said, staring coldly into my eyes, "I'm getting pretty disgusted with you. First you accuse me of killing Mr. Palter. Now, you're accusing my daughter...and you're doing it in my home. What kind of man are you!"

"Mr. Garwood. I asked you to come down to the station for this interview, but out of respect for you and your family, I agreed to interview you here. You're the ones that lied to me and then changed your stories."

"We did no such thing," he snarled, throwing his cigar butt into the fireplace.

"Mr. Garwood, if there is no blood evidence on the knife, then she doesn't have anything to worry about. You must admit, it doesn't look good for either one of you."

"Why? We have told you the truth," he snapped.

"Mr. Garwood, you threatened Mr. Palter's life and wanted him dead. You both admit that you visited him on the day of his murder. That's quite a coincidence."

"Get out of my house," he shouted, waving me out of the room with his hands. "I'm tired of your slanderous lies and accusations!"

"Well, I'm taking the knife with me," I said, patting my hand against the jacket pocket that contained the knife.

## MURDER IN THE CITY PARTS I-II

"Do what you want," Mr. Garwood shouted, as he followed me through his house. "We have nothing to hide!"

When I reached the front door, I stopped momentarily to say goodbye to the home's owner. "Mr. Garwood, I'm sure I'll be talking with you and your daughter again."

I drove directly to the forensics lab. As soon as I entered the building, I tracked down the supervisor, Dr. Charlie Stork, and found him standing over his lab equipment. As I walked towards him, he acknowledged my presence and turned towards me. I pulled the Garwood evidence from my jacket pocket and held it up for him to see.

"Dr. Stork, see what you can do with this," I said, handing him the plastic evidence bag that held the Garwood butcher knife. "I want the dark substance on the handle checked out as soon as possible."

"I'm sorry, Detective Hero," he said, shaking his head. "Due to the ongoing serial killer investigation, I will have to send this evidence to the FBI forensics lab. We're still overloaded here."

"Just get me the results as soon as possible," I begged, and then turned to leave the building.

"Oh, by the way," he said.

I stopped in my tracks, then turned to face him.

"You should have the fingerprint results from the soda can you brought in a few days ago. The report should be sitting on your desk."

I didn't say a word. I just smiled, then turned around and walked out of the building to my car.

A few minutes later, I was driving back to the station. I was very interested in the fingerprint results from Mr. Cadwell's soda can. I just had a gut feeling about that guy. I knew when a person was telling the truth or not. I didn't think Mr. Cadwell had been very truthful with me.

The report was on my desk when I got in. It was just as I thought—Don Cadwell was an alias. He was using a phony name. His real name was Paul Donald. He was wanted in another state on a felony charge.

The report stated that Cadwell had parked his car on his front lawn and was ticketed. But evidently, he just disregarded the ticket. When the officer returned to confront him about the ticket, they became engaged in a fistfight. That, in turn, led to the police officer getting pummeled nearly to death. Cadwell was arrested on attempted murder charges and a few other miscellaneous charges and released on his own recognizance. But he left town and never showed up for his court date. He's been wanted ever since...that was three years ago.

I spoke with Captain Blake about capturing the fugitive. He gave me the go-ahead. I also had the use of four uniformed officers to assist in the arrest. Within an hour, I had the manpower, arrest warrant, and had instructed the officers on the arresting procedure. There would be a total of five men at this apprehension—four officers and myself. We drove in three different cars.

All of us arrived within a few minutes of each other and then began walking towards the fugitive's apartment front door together, with guns drawn. I noticed the fugitive hiding behind the curtain, as he looked out of his picture window. He seemed to be very surprised by all the police presence. Once he saw us, he turned away from the window.

We had to climb two long flights of stairs, leading up to his front door. Once there, I immediately beat on it and yelled, "Mr. Cadwell come outside." We received no answer. I yelled again, "Come out with your hands in the air or we will come in and get you." Still, no answer.

Suddenly, I heard a loud thud and bang. The sounds had come from the back of the apartment building. I hadn't deployed any officers to the back area of the residence. We didn't have enough time to deploy them there. As soon as we heard the strange noises, I gave the order to break down the front door. One of the officers kicked it in using a four-foot long steel battering ram. Within a flash, we had entered the apartment and thoroughly searched the place.

Don Cadwell, or Paul Donald, whatever his name was, had escaped from the apartment and the building. He was nowhere to be found. Soon after, we learned that he had also escaped the neighborhood. He was a fugitive from justice, again. We'd lost him. We had screwed up. *I* had screwed up.

I wondered why Cadwell had run. Did he know that we knew his true identity—or had he thought we were there to arrest him for Palter's murder? I was a patient man. I was confident that we would catch him, sooner rather than later.

I immediately put out an all-points bulletin and faxed all patrolling officers a photo of the fugitive. We had over fifty patrol cars searching for him within ten minutes after my call went out over the wire.

I decided to let the patrol units worry about Don Cadwell; I wanted to concentrate my thoughts on my murder investigation.

## Chapter 6

After I signed in at the front desk, I walked directly to my desk. I sat down in my chair and thought about my murder investigation and what I wanted to do next. I definitely wanted to talk with Rita again. But before I talked with her, I wanted to contact Samantha Manner.

On a hunch, I decided to check the local telephone directory. I was certain that it was a waste of my time. I was never that lucky. But lo and behold, with just a few minutes of effort, I was able to find her number. I phoned her immediately, but nobody answered. I wrote down her number and address and shoved it into my shirt pocket.

Over the next few hours, I tried again and again...but without any luck. Nobody answered the telephone on the other end.

I decided to visit her place of residence, but this seemed like another dead end. No one answered the door. I got back in my car and left, but over the next several hours I made repeated trips back—also without any luck. I was anxious to find her. She was an important piece to my puzzle. The many witnesses I had talked with, and the many reports I had read, had stated she was Palter's most recent girlfriend. He had been living with her, at her place of residence...not at his apartment where the murder was committed. He used his address, strictly for his mistresses.

I wondered how long Miss Manner had known that Palter had his own apartment. There were also many other questions I needed to ask her. I had hoped to drop her from my current suspect list. But that wouldn't happen...not just yet, anyway.

I returned to the precinct and to my desk. I decided to try my luck once again and phone Manner one last time. While I was placing the call, one of the technicians from the lab stopped by and handed me a report. I thanked him for it, and he departed. I quickly read the report while I listened to the phone ring on the other end of the telephone line. After waiting for nearly ten minutes, I hung up the phone.

The forensics report stated that the substance on the knife I had taken from Ellen Garwood was blood. It was the same blood type as Palter's. Now they had to send it out to the DNA lab to verify whether it was actually *his* blood. Not only that, but it also fit the knife wounds on the body. It was an exact replica of the knife that had been found in the garbage bin, also with Palter's blood type on it. Now there was the possibility that both knives had been used on Palter. And if that was the case, which one had been used to kill him...or had they both been used? Now, I would have to question Miss Garwood again. This time, I would question her at the station. She would have a lot of explaining to do.

I finished reading the report and tried phoning Miss Manner once again. After nearly fifty calls, someone finally answered.

"Hello?" said a female voice.

"Yes. This is Detective Hero. I would like to speak with Samantha Manner. Is she there?"

"Yes, I am Samantha Manner. What do you want?"

"I don't know if you remember me, but I was at Mr. Palter's apartment investigating his murder the morning I met with you. I had talked with you for a few minutes, but you left before I could finish questioning you. Do you remember?"

"I think so. I was pretty shocked and shook up when I learned of his death."

"Miss Manner, I would like you to come down to the station to get your statement on file. Could you come down this afternoon?"

"I don't know. I'm pretty busy today."

"Please, it's very important that we get your statement on record as soon as possible. You may have some pertinent information that may help solve my investigation."

"Is the station on Second Street?"

"Yes, it is. Come to the front desk and just ask for me. Detective Hero."

"It will take me a few hours to get ready. I will try to be there just after lunch. Say around two o'clock."

"That will be just fine. I'll see you then," I said.

I had a few hours to kill before Miss Manner would arrive to be questioned. I decided to walk downstairs to the women's jail cell and ask Rita if I could question her again. I didn't see any reason why she would turn me down, especially if she didn't have anything to hide.

In the back of my mind, I knew that Rita hadn't killed Palter. But I still had many puzzling questions I needed answered. I wanted to dig deep into her soul. I wanted to look deep into her eyes. I wanted to get tough with her. She knew more than she was telling. At least that was my gut feeling.

I was positive that a jealous woman had killed Jim Palter in a blind, jealous rage. Rita had been near the apartment during the time of his murder. She had been stalking him for nearly a year. She had the means, the opportunity...and a good motive. But if she hadn't killed him, she might have seen the person who had. She had been watching the apartment building for over five hours on the night of Palter's murder.

I thought she might have been protecting the killer. Or maybe she had been involved in the murder. She might have shown one of the jealous girlfriends his apartment—where he was taking his mistresses—not knowing that the woman was going to kill Palter. I couldn't put a finger on it. But I was sure she wasn't telling me the whole story. I was going to find out, though.

As soon as I finished my coffee and cigarette, I walked down to the other end of the building, taking the elevator to the basement where they housed the female prisoners, and had one of the guards escort Rita to a holding cell. There was a glass partition separating us, so I spoke to her through the little screened opening in the glass. She gave me a dirty look.

"Hello, Rita. I would like to ask you a few more questions concerning Jim Palter's murder."

"Go away! I don't want to talk to you! Leave me alone!"

"Please. I think you can clean up a few details that have clouded my mind."

"Like what?"

"I'm hoping you may have forgotten some important details during the time you were standing outside the apartment building. You may have seen the killer and don't even know it."

Rita pulled out the last cigarette from the pack that she had carried with her, put it to her lips, and lit it with a match. She took a long, deep drag, exhaled the smoke, and said, "I told you everything I know."

"Let me decide that," I said. "Rita, don't you want to get out of that dirty little cell for a few hours? Maybe have some coffee and donuts or junk food?"

"Well, if you think I can help," she said. "I want to find his killer as bad as you. I really loved Jim!"

I had the guard remove Rita's handcuffs and leg shackles and release her into my custody for an hour or so. I wanted her to be comfortable. I wanted her to trust me. If she thought I was her friend and wanted to help her, she would open up more when I questioned her.

Within a few minutes, we were back in the interrogation room. I had her take a seat and then I left, returning with a soda and two bags of potato chips for her to munch on. I also gave her a pack of smokes and a book of matches. She liked all the attention she was getting.

Sitting across the table from her, I opened my notebook, which contained the transcripts of our first meeting, and turned on the tape recorder. Before I asked my first question, I waited while Rita opened the pack of cigarettes, pulled one from the pack, put it to her lips, and then lit it.

"Now, let's get down to business," I said. "Rita, I want you to tell me why you were at the Admore apartment building the night that Jim Palter was killed. And I want the truth…and nothing but the truth! Is that understood?"

She nodded "yes" and then took a long drag on her cigarette. When she exhaled, she blew the smoke into my face and then said, "I told you before, I was watching and waiting for Jim to come out of the building. I wanted to see what girl he was dating."

"Why would you still be interested in a guy that had already dumped you and swindled you out of your life savings?" I asked, waving away the smoke.

"I thought I loved him. I guess some part of me is still in love with him."

"Rita, I want you to tell me exactly who you saw leave the building that Sunday afternoon that might have visited Palter's apartment."

"You want me to tell you who I saw leave the building…or enter the building?"

"Both."

"Well, like I told you before, I arrived at the building around two o'clock that Sunday afternoon. ... I think it was about two. But it could have been an hour or so later than that. I wasn't wearing a watch."

"Where were you watching from?"

"I sat near the front entrance under a big oak tree. It kept me hidden so the security guard couldn't see me. The first person I saw enter the apartment building was, ah, Helen. I think that's her name, but I'm not certain."

"Describe her for me."

"She's a young, beautiful blonde-haired girl ... probably in her twenties."

"How did you know she was going to Palter's apartment?"

"I had seen her before with Jim. That's why I knew she was visiting his apartment."

"Who did you see next?"

"The next person I saw enter the building was an older woman. Her name is Manner."

"Samantha Manner?" I asked.

"Yes, I think so. She arrived about an hour after the first woman."

"Was the first woman you saw still at Palter's apartment when Manner arrived?"

"I didn't see the first girl exit the building, so I don't know if she was still in his apartment or not," she said, snuffing out her butt before lighting up another cigarette.

"Rita, did you visit Palter's apartment that night?" I asked, searching her eyes for a reaction.

"No, I didn't," she said, looking away.

"Are you sure? Remember, I want the truth! Did you visit Jim Palter's apartment that night?"

She didn't answer my question right away. I could see from her actions that she was trying very hard to come up with an answer, but couldn't get the words out of her mouth.

"I shouldn't say anything else until I see my lawyer."

I looked deep into her eyes and said, "Rita, the only reason a person needs a lawyer is if that person is guilty of a crime. Are you guilty of a crime?"

She squirmed in her chair and then said, "No, I'm not!"

"Listen...I'm going to help you even if you don't want to help yourself!" I leaned across the desk, getting so close to her face that our noses nearly touched. Then I let her have it with both barrels. "I know you were at his apartment! We found your fingerprints there!"

Her face suddenly turned a very pale white, and she slumped in her chair. She stared at me, not knowing what to say, so I spoke up instead and asked her a very important question. "Now, I want to know why you lied to me."

"Like I said before, I'm not saying another word until I see a lawyer," she said.

"Rita, if you don't tell me what you know I will take my evidence to the district attorney and have you arrested for conspiracy to commit murder," I said, trying to scare her into telling me the truth.

"I didn't kill anyone," she snarled.

"If you're not involved in Palter's murder, then tell me what you know!" I still hoped she would break down and spew her guts. "And if you are involved, you'd better tell me now. Right now, I can help you. But if you want that lawyer, you're on your own. I won't be able to pull any strings for you!"

She took a long, deep drag on her cigarette, exhaled a big cloud of smoke into my face, and then said, "Okay, I'll tell you everything!" She paused for a few seconds and then continued with her explanation. "The reason I didn't tell you before...well, I thought you would think I had something to do with Jim's murder."

"You're right! I wasn't sure, but I had a gut feeling that you weren't telling me everything you knew. Are you sure you don't want an attorney?"

"Yes, I'm sure." She nervously tapped on the tabletop with her sweaty palms, trying to decide how to tell her story. "Let me start from the beginning."

"Please do."

"I saw that young woman enter the building first. Then, about thirty minutes later, I noticed Miss Manner enter the building."

"Did they see you?"

"No, neither one saw me...because I was hidden out of sight, behind the big oak tree. But when I saw Manner, I noticed that she was carrying a small, brown paper bag. And my curiosity got the best of me. I wondered what she was carrying in that bag...so I followed her."

"Rita, weren't you afraid the security guards were going to catch you and turn you over to the police?"

"Sure! I had to be very careful. I tried to stay invisible while I was in the apartment building."

"So what happened when you entered the building?"

"I continued to follow Miss Manner. She didn't walk directly to the elevators. Instead, she walked to the manager's apartment. I waited while she pounded on the door. But no one answered. Then she turned and walked towards the elevator. That's when I bumped into her."

"What did she do then? Did she realize who you were?"

"Not at first. She seemed disturbed with my actions—until she recognized me. Then I asked her what she was doing at the apartment building. That's when she asked me where Jim's apartment was. She told me that she had something to give him."

"What was it? Did she say anything about it to you?"

"Not really. I didn't know what she was talking about—until we reached Jim's apartment. We rode the elevator to the tenth floor. She followed me to Jim's apartment. While we were standing outside in the hall, we could hear two people arguing. The closer we got to Jim's apartment door, the louder the arguing became."

"Did you know who he was arguing with?"

"Before we knocked on the door, we listened intently to the argument. Jim was yelling at one of his mistresses. I figured it must have been the girl I had seen earlier entering the apartment building. I think it was Helen or Ellen that was arguing with him. But just as Samantha was about to knock on his front door, I stopped her."

"Why did you do that?"

"I knew Jim never locked his front door, so I quietly tried turning the doorknob. Sure enough, it opened. So we let ourselves in...and very quietly stepped into the hallway. The shouting was coming from the living room, so we slowly inched forward until we were a few feet from the arguing couple. But they were so engrossed in their loud discussion that they hadn't noticed us."

"So what happened next?" I asked.

"When I saw Jim and Helen, arguing, I couldn't believe what I was seeing. Helen, I think that's her name...or Ellen...was waving a big butcher knife in his face. She damn near stabbed him with it, but just as she was about to plunge the knife into his chest she saw me and Samantha standing there and put the knife to her side."

"I take it this Helen...or Ellen...was angry at Palter?"

"To say the least...she was very upset. But she was startled to see us standing there."

"What did Jim do?"

"Jim looked at us and hollered out, 'What the hell are you doing here?'"

"What did you do then?"

"We didn't say a word. I was waiting for Samantha to answer him, and she was waiting for me to say something. We just looked at each other."

"What did Jim and his mistress do when they saw you?"

"When they saw me and Samantha, they suddenly quit arguing and acted like the best of friends. Helen tried hiding the knife, but it was too late. We had already seen her threaten him with it. Palter came within a few feet of us and asked why we were in his apartment without being invited."

"What did you say to him?"

"Nothing! That's when Manner threw the paper bag into his face. When it hit his face, it exploded...and its contents flew all around the living room."

"What was in the bag?"

"I didn't know, but I wanted to find out. So I bent down and picked up one of the items."

"And what was it?"

"It was an identification badge with Jim's picture on it...but it didn't have his real name on it. It was phony identification. Then I picked up another piece of laminated plastic from the floor. That, too, was phony identification."

"What kind of phony I.D.?"

"The one I picked up last was a phony driver's license. This guy was so stupid that he used his own address—but used someone else's name. The name on the license wasn't Jim Palter; it was Paul James. This guy was a real prize."

"Why do you say that?"

"Without skipping a beat, he looked at me with such a disgusting look I thought he was going to hit me. But instead, he just hollered at me to get the hell out of his apartment before he called the police."

"So, what did you and Samantha do?" I asked, staring into her eyes.

"I just called him a low-life scum ball that was lower than pond scum. I told him that I must have been brain dead to love a person like him. Then I turned and left the apartment."

"What about Samantha Manner?"

"Samantha stayed behind," she said, biting her fingernail.

"Where did you go?"

"I walked back outside and sat under the oak tree again. Luckily, I got past the security guard, both times, without him seeing me. I had to be on my toes all the time."

"Rita, do you know whether Samantha and the other woman knew each other?"

"I don't know. I don't think so."

"Why do you say that?"

"As I was walking out of Jim's apartment, I heard Samantha ask Jim, 'Who the hell is that bitch?' I could hear them yelling and bickering as I walked towards the elevators."

"So, as far as you know, Jim Palter was still alive when you left his apartment. Is that right?"

"Yes...that's right," she said. "I don't know what transpired after I left his apartment. But I know I had nothing to do with his murder!"

"Rita, did you see Miss Manner leave the building?"

"She left, probably twenty or thirty minutes after I left the apartment."

"Did you notice anything strange about her clothing? Were they disheveled? Did you notice any blood stains on them?"

"No, I didn't really notice. I wasn't looking for anything like that. She didn't see me, anyway. She looked pretty upset, though. She walked directly to her car, all the while talking to herself."

As I was about to ask her a few more questions, one of our department's uniformed officers came into the room and whispered into my ear. They had caught Palter's ex-business partner, Don Cadwell...or should I say, Paul Donald. I motioned to the guard that I was leaving so that they could have Rita escorted back to her cell. I excused myself from the interview, shut off the tape recorder, and left the room.

A few minutes later, I saw the prisoner, Cadwell, locked in a holding cell. However, before I went to speak with him, I phoned the state police of Cadwell's home state, where he was a fugitive from justice.

Finally, the state police answered their telephone. But what was to come gave me quite a shock. They no longer wanted my prisoner. All charges had been dropped. He was no longer a fugitive from justice in their state. I just couldn't believe it. I was flabbergasted, to say the least. I had to ask them again...to make sure I had heard correctly. They told me that we had to let him go—that we had to give this guy his freedom. The state police were right. Now, we didn't have anything to hold him on. Now he wouldn't have any reason to answer my questions. But I was going to try anyway.

I walked over to his holding cell. He was sitting all alone on a wooden bench. He was very angry, scared, and disgusted. When he saw me, he gave me very sinister look.

"It's nice to see you again, Mr. Cadwell," I said, grinning. "Or should I say Mr. Donald?"

"My name is Cadwell! ... Tom Cadwell!"

"Do you mind telling me why you ran from the police? What were you thinking? Were you running from your past...or for some other reason?"

"I ran because I was in fear for my life...not because I had something to hide."

"Using an alias for over three years? What do you call that? You wouldn't have to use an alias if you weren't hiding something. Didn't you know that the law would catch up to you, sooner or later?"

He refused to speak to me. He just kept giving me dirty looks. I ignored them and continued talking. Suddenly, he jumped up and walked over to the cell door.

"Are you arresting me for murder or what?" he asked, grabbing the cell bars, trying to bend them wider so he could push his body through the gap.

"Why do you ask?"

"I haven't been told why I've been arrested."

I wanted him to answer my questions first, before I answered his questions. "Tell me, Mr. Cadwell," I said, staring into his eyes. "Why did you run from me when my uniformed officers and I came to your apartment? How did you know that I didn't just want to talk with you?"

"I didn't run from *you*...I ran to stay out of jail," he said, pacing back and forth. "I knew that if you were going to arrest me for Jim Palter's murder, you would take me to the station to book and fingerprint me. And once you had my fingerprints and ran them through the FBI's database, it would have been only a matter of time. It would only take a day or a few hours, perhaps, before you knew my true identity. Anyway, you don't question a person with four armed, uniformed cops in tow. ... So what crime am I charged with?"

"Why do you think we arrested you?" I asked, looking deep into his eyes.

"I guess you think I killed Jim Palter."

"I didn't tell you that!"

"Then why was I arrested?"

"First, tell me what you did to get arrested on a felony charge back in your home state. Your arrest warrant states that it was for attempted murder. Is that true?"

"No! I was framed," he said, stopping to press himself against the cell bars again.

"Boy, I've heard that before," I said, laughing and shaking my head in disbelief.

"I don't care what you believe! I'm innocent!"

"Mr. Cadwell, don't you know that all criminals are innocent."

He gave me a dirty look and said, "Before you call me a criminal, let me tell you what happened."

I nodded my approval and he began telling me his story.

"My ex-wife's boyfriend, who happened to be a cop, was drunk one night and acting like an idiotic jerk. A few months before that night, he had written me out a ticket for some stupid reason. I can't even remember what it was about now. But when I forgot to show up in court, he came over to my place to arrest me. He was off duty at the time and had been drinking liquor."

"He's still a law enforcement officer!"

"But that wasn't the real reason for his insanity. He became jealous, just because I was talking to his new girlfriend, who happened to be my ex-wife. We were standing in my apartment parking lot when the idiot took a wild swing at my head with his fist."

"He nailed you, huh?"

"No! I saw the punch coming out of the corner of my eye, so I stepped to one side. He was so drunk that he swung too hard; his momentum carried him forward."

"What happened to him?"

"He stumbled and fell, flat on his face. His head hit a speed bump, which knocked him unconscious and cut a deep gash in his forehead."

"So what did you do then?"

"After about thirty seconds, I got in my car and sped away."

"What happened after that?"

"The next thing I knew, the police were dragging me out of bed and arresting me for attempted murder. But after spending a few days in jail, I was released on my own recognizance. Just a few days before my court appearance, I ran away and started a new life."

"How did you do that?"

"I came to this town and met Palter. He helped me get phony identification. He knew a fellow that sold me everything I needed to start my new life."

"What did you buy from this fellow?"

"I bought a driver's license and a phony social security card. I thought with new identification I could start a new life. And it worked for a while! I thought Palter was my savior, but instead, he was the beginning of my downfall." Cadwell shook his head in disgust.

"Well, if you were innocent, why didn't you stay and fight the charge?"

"My ex-wife's boyfriend was a cop!"

"So, what?"

"He told me if I ever came back to his jail, I would never walk out alive! That the only way I'd get out was in a pine box! That's why I didn't want to stick around."

"Mr. Cadwell, you could have fought it in the courts."

"Yeah, right! Who are the courts going to believe? Me or a lousy cop? The cards were stacked against me. I wouldn't have had a chance. Either the cop would have gotten to me...or the judge would have thrown me into prison. Either way, I was a dead man!"

"That's not a reason to run away. You could have taken your complaints to a higher authority."

"Yeah, sure! Hey, you never told me why I was arrested. Was it for murder? Do you really think I killed Jim Palter?"

"Why?" I asked, trying to read his thoughts. "*Did* you kill him? Were you involved in his murder?"

"I told you, I am innocent! I hated the guy, sure. But I didn't kill him! Get that through your head! ... Now, would you please tell me why I am locked up, like a hunted animal, in this dirty cage?"

"Mr. Cadwell, when I questioned you almost a week ago, I asked if you wanted to drink a soda pop. Remember?"

"Yes...I remember."

"That's right. You asked for a pop, so I went and got you one. When you finished it, I had it analyzed at the forensics lab for your fingerprints."

"Why did you do that?"

"I wanted to have your identification checked. After working twenty-five years in this business, you tend to read a person. I could read you like a comic book. I knew you weren't telling me the truth."

"How could you tell?"

"There was something about your attitude that caught my attention. When your fingerprints came back as another person's, the computer showed that you were wanted in another state for a felony. So, my officers and I drove out to your place...and we were going to arrest you on your felony warrant, not for any murder. At least not yet!"

Cadwell listened intently to my words and then said, "I told you...if I go back to that jail, they'll kill me!" Then he looked at me with utter contempt. "I told you before that if you couldn't find the real killer, you would try to convict an innocent man. Now I've proven it! I'm just a statistic to help your career!"

"What are you talking about?"

"You don't care if a guy is guilty or not. You don't even care if I killed him or not. Just as long as you have someone to convict! Now you can close your case. My conviction should make you a captain...at least!"

I didn't say a word to him. I let him ramble on to his heart's content. I just let him spew his venom, until he was spent. Even if I had tried, he wouldn't let me get a word in edgewise. So I just stared at him and listened to his mutterings. He began getting so upset that I had to grab him through the cell bars and shake him to get his attention. He seemed to calm down for a few seconds, then he exploded again.

"Mr. Cadwell," I bellowed, "would you please quiet down! You're beginning to give me a headache!" Then I walked across the room and picked up the cell door key.

While he kept ranting and raving, I strode over to the cell door, gently inserted the key into the lock, and opened the cell door. Mr. Donald, alias Don Cadwell, looked very surprised. I just smiled at him and motioned for him to come out of the cell. He didn't know what to think. Then he became very paranoid and yelled for all to hear, "What do you want!"

"Please, Mr. Cadwell, come out of your cell. I promise...I won't hurt you."

After thinking it over for a few minutes, he finally shuffled slowly out of the cell. Then I shut the cell door and directed him to a chair near my desk. Just as he sat down in the chair, he became flippant and cocky once again. "Now what are you going to do? Fingerprint me, then book me to get me into the system? At least let me make a phone call to my lawyer!"

"Not just yet. I need to tell you a few things before you make any phone calls."

"Like what?"

"We called the city where your arrest warrant was issued so they would send the extradition papers, so we could release you into their custody. However, we ran into a little snag."

"What do you mean? What kind of snag?"

"Mr. Cadwell, it seems they don't want you, anymore. They dropped all charges. I don't understand how the police in your state would allow this to happen. Especially on an attempted murder charge! Well, I guess stranger things have happened."

"You're kidding, right?"

"I wish I were! If we'd have known beforehand, we could have saved our state some money...and I could have saved our police officers a lot of hard work. We would never have arrested you in the first place. In fact, you are free to go."

"Are you serious?" he asked, having a hard time believing me.

"Unfortunately, yes," I said, nodding. "And you can start using your true identity again. You don't have to hide any longer. But don't go too far. I may still need to question you again about Palter's murder. Also, someone in our fraud department may want to talk to you concerning the friend that sold you your phony identification. You may become a permanent fixture around here yet!"

Mr. Cadwell was stunned, to say the least. He just sat in his chair with his mouth wide open. A minute later, he stood and turned to leave, but suddenly sat down again and gave me another dirty look. "You mean you arrested me for nothing!" His face turned red with anger.

"No, on the contrary. We arrested you on a valid felony warrant. It was your police department that decided to drop the charges. I guess they were too lazy to claim their prize. Just be thankful that you're a free man."

"Why should I be thankful? You arrested me for nothing!"

"We could be holding you in jail...until we extradited you back to the state where the crime was committed. So, count your blessings. Go home and stay out of trouble. But I'll tell you this," I said, looking straight into his eyes.

"What?"

"Mr. Cadwell, if you're involved in Palter's murder...I'll get you. So if you decide to take a trip out of town, I want to know about it. I want to know your whereabouts at all times until I solve this murder investigation. Understand?"

"No problem."

"Now, get out of my sight," I said, as I pointed to the door.

He couldn't leave fast enough. He bolted from his chair as if it had shocked him with a charge of electricity. I was going to have an officer give him a ride back to his place of residence, but he was out of the building within a few seconds.

A few minutes later, I looked at my watch. It was well past lunchtime and nearly two o'clock. Miss Manner would be arriving very shortly for her interview.

As I sat awaiting Manner's arrival, I decided to call Miss Garwood. I wanted to confront her about the blood on the butcher knife that had fallen out of her purse. But I needed to interview her at the station, not at her home. I also wanted to question her without her father present.

I made the phone call to the Garwood residence. After just one ring, a female voice answered.

"Hello. This is the Garwood residence," said the female voice.

"Yes," I said, speaking into the phone. "This is Detective Hero. I would like to speak to Ellen Garwood."

"One minute, sir."

Finally, after nearly a five-minute wait, someone answered the phone.

"Hello, this is Mr. Garwood, speaking."

"Yes, Mr. Garwood. This is Detective Hero. I would like to interview your daughter, here, at the station."

"What about?"

"Concerning the Palter investigation."

"She told you everything she knew the other day."

"Mr. Garwood," I said, becoming frustrated with his objections, "we have uncovered some new information...and it would be best if she would come to the station so we can get her statement on record."

"What new information?"

"I would rather not talk about that now. I need to speak with your daughter here at the station."

"Why can't you ask her over the phone?"

"I'm sorry, Mr. Garwood, that just won't do! I need to question your daughter here! If she has nothing to hide, she has nothing to worry about."

"Oh, no! You're just trying to put her in jail! I'd bet your questions have something to do with that butcher knife that fell out of her purse, right?"

"Yes, they do," I said.

"You're not saying that you think it's the murder weapon, are you?"

"I'm not saying that at all, Mr. Garwood. Please, sir. It will make it easier on everybody if you could bring your daughter to the station to be interviewed."

"If I do, it will be with my attorney!"

"If that's what it takes to get your daughter down here...so be it. But I would rather question her without her lawyer's interference."

"No way! If you want to question my daughter, my lawyer will be present and representing her during the interview. ... Take it or leave it!"

"I'll take it," I said reluctantly.

"Fine. I'll contact my attorney and he can make the appointment with you," he said, hanging up on me.

That was fine with me, I thought to myself. I still didn't have the analysis report on the blood DNA from the knife anyway. I just wanted to find out how the blood got on the knife. Ellen Garwood could clear it up, easily. She might have a plausible explanation, but her father wanted to make things difficult for me.

Just as I was thinking about Miss Garwood and her father, I noticed that Samantha Manner had walked through the front door of the station. I could see that she was asking the officer at the front desk of my whereabouts. He pointed right at me. I looked busy, reading reports, as she walked towards me. A few seconds later, she was standing in front of my desk.

"Hello, are you Detective Hero?" asked Samantha Manner.

"Yes. And you must be Samantha Manner."

She nodded, and I arose from my chair. "Please, step this way," I said, and escorted her to a chair in the interview room. "Please sit down." We both took our seats. Then I turned on the tape recorder and began the interview.

"Miss Manner, I need to ask you some questions about your former boyfriend, Jim Palter. I tried questioning you the day of his murder, but you got away from me."

"When you told me about Jim's murder, I think I went into shock. I can't even remember leaving his apartment building that day."

"Tell me, Miss Manner, when did you first meet Jim Palter?"

"I first met him more than twenty-five years ago. We were in high school together...and high school sweethearts." Then she stared down at the floor and said, "He also walked out on me over twenty-five years ago. But I thought it would be different this time."

"Why did you think it would be different this time?"

"I thought he really loved me. I thought he had changed from the selfish person I had known before to a sweet, understanding man."

"Did he?"

"For the first six months, our relationship was magnificent. As long as I didn't ask any compromising questions, he was gentle. But if I became suspicious and distrusted him, he would tell me I was becoming too paranoid...or that it was all in my mind. Then he would sit in another room and watch television or just sit and stare out the bedroom window."

"How often did that happen?"

"That didn't happen very often during the first six months of our relationship. As long as my money held up, he stayed close to my side. But he began to spend my funds faster than ever. Around the seventh month, things began to change for the worse."

"Why?"

"I became suspicious of his actions when he wouldn't return home for one or two days at a time. He wouldn't phone me or contact me. So I didn't know if I should call the police or just wait until he returned. I was so mixed up and confused. I remember one time he was gone for more than two days—and finally arrived home eleven o'clock that evening."

"What did you do then?" I asked.

"As soon as he walked into the apartment I began questioning him."

"What did he say?"

"Jim refused to answer me until I calmed down. I was livid. That made me even madder. How dare he tell me to calm down! I thought he was lying dead somewhere! I was so scared and confused. I asked him to tell me what was going on."

"Did he?"

"No! He didn't say anything."

"So, what did you tell him?" I asked her, looking deep into her eyes for a reaction.

She sat silently for a few seconds and then spurted out, "I told him that I loved him and that I thought he loved me. ... I just had to have an answer."

"Did he give you one?"

"No! He refused to say a word about it. He wouldn't even speak to me," she exclaimed, looking at the floor.

"So what did you do?" I asked her.

"I asked him what I had done wrong to make him act this way. I asked him if he still loved me. I just had to know."

"Did he tell you?"

"No," she said, staring at the floor. "He just gave me a dirty look and walked out of the room."

"What did you do?"

"I followed him into the bedroom and repeated my questions."

"What did he do?"

"Nothing. He remained silent. He tried to walk away from me and hide in the bathroom. But I followed him there, too."

"Was he getting angry with you, Miss Manner?"

"Yes. He yelled at me to quit following him and to leave him alone. But then, a few minutes later, he broke down and told me he had been arrested by the police for driving under the influence...and had been held in jail until he could find someone to make his bail. I asked him why he hadn't called me."

"What did he say to that?" I asked.

"He said he didn't want to hurt me or worry me, and he didn't want me to know that he had been arrested."

"Did you believe him when he told you?"

"He could say anything and I would have believed him. I didn't find out he had lied to me until a month ago. But I believed him that night. Then I found out he was seeing not just one woman, but two. Not only that, but one was just a child."

"Did you know who she was? Do you know this young lady's name?"

"I'm not sure. He had been seeing and sleeping with a young girl that he had been accused of raping. I thought there was another young girl that he had been seeing just recently, too, but I wasn't sure."

"So what did you do then? Did you find out the girl's name?"

"I got angry and walked out on Jim before I could ask him about her. I did suspect him of having a new girlfriend. I thought it was that young girl, but I was mistaken."

"Why do you say that, Miss Manner?"

"The young woman had phoned me the day I thought he was with her. But she was looking for him, too. So, he had to be with someone else."

"So what did this young woman tell you about Jim?"

"She said she hadn't seen him in almost a week. That meant she hadn't slept with him in almost a week."

"That must have made you angry knowing that he was seeing another woman?"

"You're right! I was saddened at the thought of sharing him with another woman. I was angry that he was sleeping around. He had spent all of the money that I had saved for my retirement years. He said we would use it for our future. But instead, he used it for *his* future. We broke up over twenty-five years ago for the same reason. But when he contacted me this time, I thought it would be different."

"What made you think that?"

"This time, we actually talked about getting married and settling down," she said, shaking her head in disgust. "He promised to be with me in our golden years!"

"And you believed him, didn't you, Miss Manner?" I asked, looking into her eyes.

"Of course! Otherwise, I wouldn't have quit my job and moved a thousand miles away to be with a man that only wanted me for my money—a man that depleted my life savings and then threw me to the dogs."

"No, I suppose not."

"I had planned to return back east after we were married, just for a little vacation," she said, as tears welled up in her eyes. "But now, when I get the money saved I am going back east to be with my family. I have been hurt enough in one lifetime. This guy has left me high and dry, twice now. Maybe him dying was his karma getting back at him."

"You might be right, Miss Manner."

"They always say," she said, smiling, "what goes around, comes around!"

I'd had enough of the small talk. Now I wanted to get down to serious business. "Miss Manner," I said, "where were you on the night of Jim Palter's murder? Say around five in the evening to around eleven that Sunday night?"

She didn't answer my question right away. Suddenly, she acted as if she was in a deep trance. I could tell she was trying to come up with an answer, but couldn't decide what to say.

"What? ... I'm sorry. What was the question?" she asked.

"Miss Manner," I said, staring into her eyes. "Did you visit Mr. Palter at his apartment that Sunday evening?"

Again, she didn't say a word. The room was completely silent. You could hear her heart beating. She was hesitating, but I just sat and waited patiently for her answer. Suddenly, she broke out of her trance.

"Yes, I saw him that night," she said, clutching her midsection, as though her stomach was twisting and turning in knots.

"At his apartment?"

"Yes. I had found out that he had his own apartment and I went to confront him about it."

"What time did you visit him?"

"I don't know the exact time. But it was approximately five or six that Sunday evening."

"Why did you go there?"

"Two reasons. I wanted to confront him about his apartment...and the bag full of phony identification that I had found hidden behind my dresser. But I had one problem."

"What was that?"

"I didn't know what floor his apartment was on."

"So how did you find it?"

"Just as I arrived at the building, I ran into one of Jim's old girlfriends—a woman named Rita—and she volunteered to show me to his apartment."

"Did you ask Rita why she was at the apartment building?"

"No! I wasn't concerned with Rita being there. I had other things on my mind. Anyway, she had been an old girlfriend of Jim's. And up until a few weeks ago, he had been living with me. But she did escort me to his apartment. And just as I was about to knock on his apartment door, we could hear loud arguing between Jim and a female."

"What did you do?"

"Rita turned the doorknob and found that the door was unlocked...so I let myself in. Rita followed behind me. We stood for a few seconds in the hallway and listened to them argue. Then I peeked around the corner and saw a young female waving a large butcher knife at him."

"Miss Manner, how old would you say the young female was?"

"She was in her late teens or early twenties."

"What was Palter doing while she was waving the knife around?"

"Nothing...just arguing. When the woman began waving the knife in his face, that's when I came into the room. They were both shocked to see Rita and me standing there."

"What did Jim Palter do then?"

"When Jim and the young girl saw the two of us, they quit arguing and acted like great friends. The woman even tried to hide the knife behind her back. It was all a big act. Then Jim yelled at me and Rita to get out of the apartment."

"So what did you do?"

"I didn't say a word. I guess I was in shock. But when Jim put his arm around that young girl, I became enraged and threw the bag, which hit him in his face."

"What did Jim do then?"

"He began picking up the phony I.D. and placed them back into the bag. When his young female friend tried to help him retrieve the items, he quickly grabbed them out of her hands, before she could look at them. He looked at me with disdain and anger. His evil eyes pierced my body and soul. I couldn't even speak. I just began crying."

"Miss Manner, you must have been very upset. So what did you and Rita do then?"

"I turned and ran out of his apartment. The girl that had escorted me to his apartment left a few minutes before I did. I saw her again, outside, sitting under a big tree. When she saw how upset I was, she came over and then walked me to my car. I was very upset. My whole life had collapsed on top of me...and it was smothering me."

"So, he was alive when you left him?"

"Yes, absolutely!"

"Do you remember about what time that would be?"

"No. I only stayed at his apartment for a few minutes. So, it was around five thirty or six o'clock when I ran out."

"Did you return to his apartment that night?"

"No. I didn't return to his apartment until the next morning...when I talked with you. I was going to apologize to Jim for my behavior the day before. I guess his karma got to him, before I could."

"Miss Manner, I don't know if it was his karma that gave him bad luck, but it was a psychopath that killed him! ... I'd like you to stick around town for a while longer. I'll need to question you from time to time."

"Am I being arrested?"

"Why?" I asked. "Are you guilty of a crime?"

"I told you, I didn't have anything to do with Jim Palter's death! Even though he used me and spent my life savings on other women, I am not a murderer! I thought he and I had something special together, but I guess I was wrong! And please, don't worry about me leaving town! It's going to take me a few months to save enough money just for the plane fare to get back east."

"Where will you be staying for the next few months?"

"Well, I'm house-sitting for a good friend of mine. She isn't expected to return for some time to come...at least for the next month. So I'll be running back and forth from her house to my apartment."

"Very good! ... I think I've taken up enough of your time. Do you need a ride back to your apartment?"

"No thank you, Detective Hero. I have a ride waiting for me," she said, and then shuffled out of the station.

I turned off the tape recorder and returned to my desk. Looking at my watch, I noticed it was an hour past quitting time. I was beat. This investigation was taking its toll on my mind and body. I was drinking too much alcohol and not getting enough sleep.

My life was slowly evaporating in front of my eyes—and all because of this investigation or maybe because of my incessant drinking and horrendous nightmares. The other few hundred homicides hadn't affected me as this one had. Maybe it was due to the vulnerable women. What kind of man would play with a woman's heart and soul, tell them that he loved them, and then leave them, after he had squandered and spent all of their life savings? Jim Palter had left more than ten women lonely and destitute. That's not a man, I thought, that is a monster. When I thought about what this monster had done, and all the females he had used as his stepping stones, I become enraged. My blood pressure went sky high; my whole body began to shake and shiver. It hit me personally because my daughter had been in a similar situation with a boyfriend that had used her and abused her until I ran him off.

The man had gotten what he deserved. I wondered how many other women he had used and abused.

When I arrived home, I went directly to my kitchen cabinet and extracted my bottle of scotch. I couldn't pour the drink fast enough. I went into the living room, took off my shoes, and sat down on the couch. I quickly finished a double shot and then poured another...and tried not to think about the case...but it always came popping back into my mind. I couldn't avoid it. I had to solve this case, and soon. My health and peace of mind depended on it.

# Chapter 7

The next morning, after drinking a cup of hot, black coffee, I stumbled out of my apartment to my car and headed to the station.

Once there, with coffee and donut in hand, I walked to my desk and flopped into my chair like a dead weight. I sipped my coffee, waiting for my hangover to subside. My head ached so badly that I could hear a loud ringing in my ears—until I realized it was my phone ringing. It was Ellen Garwood's attorney calling me to make the appointment for his client's interview. They would arrive around three that afternoon. I only had one or two questions to ask Miss Garwood, which would only take a matter of minutes...but with the lawyer in the room, the interview could take an hour or more.

I decided to leave my desk and head to my favorite café, still hoping to see the young woman I'd been looking for.

When I arrived, I noticed Bonnie cleaning my favorite table. She greeted me with a big smile.

"I have a big surprise for you," she said.

"Great, but can I order two steak and cheese hoagies, first?" I asked, as I sat at the table. "Now, what's the big surprise?"

"Just a minute," she said, as she walked behind the counter to retrieve a small, brown paper bag. She returned to my table.

"What is that?" I asked, as Bonnie handed me the paper bag.

"That girl finally came into the cafe yesterday," she said, as I looked into the bag. "I forgot to ask her what her name was, but I did keep her water glass for you."

I was ecstatic. I couldn't wait to get the glass to the forensics lab for analysis. This wasn't really legal but it wouldn't be used in a court of law. I just wanted to see if I could find out her identification from her fingerprints.

"Thank you, Bonnie. But why didn't you call me? I would have liked to talk with her myself."

"Well, I had your business card pinned on the bulletin board, but someone must have taken it down because I couldn't find it. So I didn't know the telephone number to call you. Besides, she was only here for a few minutes."

"Why didn't you keep her here?"

"She ordered her food for take-out. But I remembered you wanted to get her fingerprints, so I gave her a glass of water to drink while she waited for her order. One of the busboys nearly spoiled the day."

"How's that?"

"He almost picked up the glass as he was cleaning the counter. I grabbed it before he could."

"I thank you for that, Bonnie. That was very quick thinking on your part. I really appreciate the help. ... Maybe I should get your fingerprints, so we can match them to the ones on the glass."

"That's not necessary. I grabbed the top of the drinking glass. I made sure not to get my fingerprints on the outside of it."

"Smart thinking," I said, gently patting her hand with mine.

I grabbed my sandwiches and left Bonnie a big tip. I decided to take my hoagie sandwiches back to the station to eat. But first, I wanted to get to the forensics lab and have the glass analyzed.

Within five minutes, I was there—glass in hand—looking for the supervisor. I finally found him, peering under a microscope.

"Good morning, Dr. Stork," I said.

"Good morning, Detective Hero. What do you need?"

I held up the paper bag containing the water glass. "I need the fingerprints from this item analyzed. Can you help me?"

"Of course!" He grabbed the paper bag from my hand and a few seconds later, pulled the glass from the bag with a Kleenex. He held it up to the light to get a closer look. "Who do the fingerprints belong to?"

"That's what I want you to find out, Doc! ... But it may be a waste of time. This person might not have anything to do with my current investigation, but that's what I need to find out."

"You can see we are up to our ears in work. But for you, I should have the report on your desk by morning. ... That is, if I'm not disturbed by someone else."

"I knew I could count on you, Doc. By the way, how is the serial killer investigation coming along?"

"Don't ask!" he snapped.

"Why not?"

"These investigators walk all over each other for recognition from their superiors! They've cluttered this lab with circumstantial evidence!"

"I can see that!"

"After it's tested, they find out it's got nothing to do with their investigation. ... I'm fed up with their crap."

"I don't blame you, Doc."

"They act as if they own this lab. They order me around like I'm dirt. I'll tell you this..."

"What's that?"

"One day, I'm going to tell them to stick their investigation where the sun don't shine!"

"I'm sorry you feel that way, Doc. I hope I haven't done anything to make you feel that way towards me."

"No, you treat me as your equal. ... Not like some dog! That's why I do as you ask. You are a good friend, Detective Hero."

"Thanks Doc. I feel the same way towards you. ... Well, I've wasted enough of your time. I'll let you get back to work...and I better get back to my investigation."

As we shook hands, Dr. Stork added, "Oh! I nearly forgot to tell you...the DNA reports should be in by the end of next week. I should have them within five days, if we're lucky. Plus, the forensic evidence that was sent to the FBI crime lab should be here by the end of next week."

I nodded my approval, then turned and left the room, heading for the parking lot.

I walked away with a smile on my face. This day couldn't have gone any better. The only way it could have was if one of my suspects confessed to Jim Palter's murder.

Just as I got behind the wheel of my car, I remembered that I had an appointment to interview Ellen Garwood. I needed to return immediately to the station to meet with her and her attorney.

Twenty minutes later, I was at the precinct, sitting at my desk, when Miss Garwood and her high-priced attorney, Tom Davis, arrived for her interview. After introducing ourselves, I directed them into the interview room, not the interrogation room. Once they were comfortable in their chairs, I turned on the tape recorder and began questioning my suspect.

"Miss Garwood, the knife I took from you had the same blood type as Jim Palter's. Do you know how his blood got on that knife?"

"Don't answer that," interrupted her attorney with his New York accent. She did as she was told and remained silent.

But I continued my search for the truth and said, "The knife also fit the chest wounds of the victim. This could be the knife that was used to kill Jim Palter. So, I ask you again, Miss Garwood. How did Jim Palter's blood get on your knife?" As I asked this question, I looked deep into her beautiful, blue eyes for a reaction.

Just as she was about to answer my question, her lawyer put his two cents worth into the conversation.

"Miss Garwood, you don't have to answer that!" snapped Davis. "Detective, let me see the DNA report to verify that it's really Palter's blood-type...and his blood."

"Well, I don't have it with me," I said, trying to stall him.

"So, go and get it and then we'll answer your questions!" he said.

"Actually, it hasn't come back from the lab that was contracted to do the testing. But we do have the reports and findings on the testing that *was* done."

"What does that say?" asked Davis.

"It states that the blood that was found on the butcher knife that rolled out of your client's purse was the same blood type as Jim Palter's."

"Yeah, and one million other people in this city!" Davis said. "So, until you have proof that it's Jim Palter's blood, she won't answer any of your questions concerning that knife. Is that clear, Detective Hero?"

"Yes. But, I thought your client could clear this up without going through all this hassle. Especially if she doesn't have anything to hide!" I looked pleadingly into Ellen Garwood's eyes, hoping she would break down and tell me what I wanted to know, but her attorney continued to speak for her.

"Well, Detective Hero, you're wrong!" Davis said. "But don't hesitate to call my office if and when you receive that information. Then I'll set up another appointment for you to interview my client, so she may answer your question. ... Is there anything else you would like to ask my client before we leave this building?"

"Yeah, I have a question! Did she kill Jim Palter...or have anything to do with his murder?" I looked deep into her eyes for an answer, but again, her attorney blocked my efforts.

"Don't answer that, Miss Garwood!" he said. "Detective Hero, I'm disappointed by your actions. When you get the evidence against my client ... Arrest her! Until then, we're history! Let's go, Miss Garwood." Davis helped his client from her chair, and they quickly left the room and building, disappearing into the evening air.

I had gotten nowhere fast with that interview—it was a total washout. That's why I never liked attorneys in the interview room. They tend to make a short interview into a very long one...and sometimes tend to make an innocent person seem guilty by not letting them answer a detective's questions. That made it hard for me to do my job properly. But now, it was quitting time. And I wouldn't have to worry about it for two days. The weekend was here, and I just wanted to go home to meditate and hibernate with my bottle of scotch.

Monday, when I was finally able to lift myself from the couch, I slowly straightened out my wrinkled and disheveled clothes and walked to the bathroom to splash some water on my face. Then I went into the kitchen and warmed up the coffee I'd made a couple of days ago. While I waited for the coffee, I lit a cigarette and nursed my hangover. A minute later, I was sipping my Columbian nectar and lighting another cigarette.

After my third cup, and nearly five cigarettes, I was ready for the day ahead. I placed my empty cup into the sink full of dirty dishes, grabbed my wrinkled, gray suit coat, and headed out the door to my car. As I jumped behind the wheel and started the engine, I had to sit for a few seconds to gather my strength. My head pounded hard enough to split the Liberty Bell. After I lit another cigarette, I put the car into gear and slowly backed out of the driveway. Then I shifted into drive and headed for my precinct.

Ten minutes later, I had parked my car in the station's parking lot and signed in at the front desk. When I finally arrived at my desk, I was a complete mess. I smelled like a gin mill. I stayed away from everyone, including my boss, and for the next few days was totally engrossed in my murder investigation.

But by the middle of the week, my investigation had slowed down, even though I had received the fingerprint analysis report from that young girl's glass. It was just my luck: Her fingerprints weren't found in the database. However, they matched the fingerprints that we had found at the scene of the murder. Somehow, she was involved with Jim Palter. But how? I had to find out her true identity and put a name to that beautiful face.

Now, this young woman was wanted for questioning in the Jim Palter murder investigation. She couldn't be but twenty or twenty-five years of age. And her image began to haunt me. I would visit the cafe every day, to wait for her to return, if need be. I was, perhaps, a little infatuated with her beauty. I thought maybe I had simply overlooked her name. So, I read all the reports again and went through the murder investigation, step by step. But no such luck. I put her out of my mind. At least I tried, anyway.

I still had a few other women to contact and interview. They were some of the women that had sued Palter, but had lost their case. I just had to touch base with these women. I wanted to make sure they weren't involved in the murder. These were nearly all the suspects I could think of to interview that had some contact with the murder victim—and all had a motive for wanting him dead. I wanted to see if they had alibis for their whereabouts on that Sunday evening.

I finally got around to contacting the women later that week. The first woman I talked with was a short, petite, plump, chubby-faced female that wore thick-lens eyeglasses. Her name was Mary Ann. She was the type of woman Palter loved to scam—a woman with very low self-esteem. However, she was the first person with a plausible alibi. And she verified it with her time ticket from a department store's underground parking lot. She had been working at a local department store that day and was driving to her place of residence during the time Jim Palter was murdered. She had definitely hated Palter, but supposedly, she had gone on with her life and married shortly after losing her court battle with him.

Carol, the second woman I suspected and interviewed, also had a valid alibi. She had been working at an all-night diner on the night of Jim Palter's murder. Her boss verified the time she had worked that Sunday night with her time card. It was the first time I didn't have to add suspects to my list. I finally had a few that I could eliminate. For now, I was satisfied that their alibis were true. But there were still over six suspects that didn't have alibis for Palter's murder. And they all had an excellent motive.

While driving across town, to and from work, I had seen Jim Palter's ex-business partner, Paul Donald, wandering about. He was always in the presence of a beautiful young woman, who looked similar to the young lady I was trying to meet at the cafe. But I never really got a clear look at her face. I had to find out if she was the young girl that I longed to know.

The young woman I had seen at the café had left such a strong image in my mind that I couldn't get her out of it. Her image was imprinted in my psyche. When I tried putting her out of my mind, she kept popping up.

I decided to stop by Mr. Donald's place of residence and ask him a few questions about his personal life. For instance, who was the girl I had seen him walking with? Actually, I hoped to catch her at his place, and then I could check her identification.

When I arrived at his apartment, I knocked on the front door. I hoped the two of them would be together. However, he answered the door alone.

"Yeah? What do you want?" Paul Donald, formerly known as Don Cadwell, asked.

"Mr. Cadwell," I said, standing on the balcony, "I need to ask you a few questions about your personal life."

"That's none of your business! And my name is Paul Donald!" he yelled.

"That's true. But murder is my business! And I want to know about that young girl—the one I've been seeing you with lately. Was she one of Jim Palter's ex-girlfriends...or one of his mistresses?"

"I told you ... That's none of your business. Now, would you please get off of my property? That is, unless you're going to arrest me."

I stared into his eyes and just shook my head "no." Suddenly, Donald became enraged. "Next time, you better have a warrant if you come back to this place!" He slammed the door in my face.

*Well, that went well,* I thought to myself. I hadn't gotten a straight answer out of him. But I could tell from his body language that his girlfriend had something to do with Jim Palter. I was sure about that. I would have to keep my eyes on him ... and his new sweetheart.

## MURDER IN THE CITY PARTS I-II

That night, I tried to fight my demons, but I was too weak. It was useless to struggle with my addiction. I sat at the kitchen counter with my hands covering my sweaty face, sulking about my alcohol addiction. It had overtaken my willpower. My excuses ran out...so I fed my demons.

I reached for the scotch and turned to walk to the living room, prepared to drown my sorrows in alcohol, but my eyes fell on a butcher knife on the kitchen counter—one I'd used earlier to cut a hoagie. It was the same type that had killed Jim Palter. That set off a bell in my head. My mind honed in on the two knives that were now out being analyzed for any evidence connecting them to the Palter murder—both supposedly stained with Palter's blood. I couldn't remember if any of the reports had mentioned the origins of the knives. That puzzled me. Ellen Garwood had mentioned that Jim Palter had given her the knife. I wondered where the other knife had come from. Had they both come from Palter's place?

I sat down on my couch and began drinking shot after shot of scotch while thinking about the Palter murder investigation. Only a few more days, and I should have the reports I'd been waiting for. The reports which would, hopefully, wrap up the case.

I decided that in the morning, I would go back to the crime scene where Palter's murder had occurred. I wanted to see if my theory was correct. I believed Palter was murdered with his own knife. That was the last thing I remembered before I passed out, once again, on the couch.

As I headed for the station the next morning, I still had quite a hangover from the previous evening. But that was nothing new. It was beginning to be old hat with me—just another typical morning.

It took a while to come out of the fog, but when I did, I gathered up all the reports and memos from the drawers of my desk and stacked them into a neat pile. It was about two inches thick already. I began looking through them to see if anyone had mentioned anything about the suspected murder weapons and their origins. But none gave me the answer I was looking for—only that the first knife had been found in the Admore Apartment building garbage dumpster.

I decided to take a ride back to the murder scene. I was sure the murder weapon had come from the victim's own house.

When I returned to Palter's apartment, the police tape was still covering the front door. I tore the tape away and let myself in. To my surprise, the door was unlocked. I slowly walked through the clutter on the floor. The apartment looked the same as when I had left it. The once white kitchen floor was still covered in blood. But this time, it was dried blood. It had turned a dark brown.

Remembering how the victim's body had looked, all cut up to hell, I suddenly became light-headed and dizzy. The kitchen began to spin 'round and 'round, as if I were drunk. Maybe I *was* drunk—drunk with rage. Rage for the victim and what he had done to his victims. If he had been a decent human being, he might still be alive today. Suddenly, I remembered what I had come there for.

I glanced around the kitchen, then began looking in the counter drawers. Just as my search began, I noticed a large, wooden butcher knife holder sitting on the counter. I counted twelve slots for butcher knives. Nine of the slots were filled—three were empty. That meant there were three butcher knives missing.

I was sure we had two of the knives at the FBI forensics lab. There was still one out there, somewhere. I looked around the room for the other butcher knife, but no luck. I didn't see one. So, I looked around the apartment to see if there was another knife that we had somehow overlooked. After checking all of the rooms and closets, I still couldn't find it. Maybe there were only eleven butcher knives to start with? I didn't know, but I was going to find out. My gut instinct told me that I was going to catch the killer.

In twenty-five years as a homicide detective, I only had two open murders, not yet solved. And I vowed to find their killers...no matter how long it took!

As I exhausted my search for the butcher knife, I finally gave up the hunt. Just as I shut the front door behind me and began walking towards the elevator, I heard a woman's loud scream coming from another apartment down the hall. I ran to where the screams were coming from. A cleaning woman came running out of the apartment into my waiting arms.

"What's wrong?" I asked, holding the woman away from my body. She was crying.

"The old woman that lives in the apartment is lying on the floor...covered in blood," she said, pressing her face against my chest.

I pushed the cleaning lady away and ran into the apartment. When I entered the living room, I saw an old lady lying in the middle of the room. She was naked, and there were massive knife wounds to her chest. Also, it looked as if her throat had been split. Blood had spurted out from her jugular vein. There was a large pattern of spatter. The carpet beneath her and around her was also stained with her blood. Her clothes were torn and stripped from her body. Clumps of her hair littered the floor near her shoulders. Her right breast was severed and hanging by a thin piece of skin. The left breast had so many stab wounds that it was imbedded into the chest cavity. The knife wounds went from just below the neck area, all the way down to the top of her pubic hair.

As I kneeled down near the body in a state of shock and anger, I wondered what kind of animal could do this to an eighty or ninety-year-old woman. I knew the answer to that question—a rabid animal. This killer was one sick and sadistic individual.

As I stared at the female victim, I became weak in the knees and had to take a few deep breaths. When I turned my eyes away from the corpse, I noticed another blood trail, leading to an adjacent room. I stood up and followed the bloody trail into the bedroom. Lying on the floor, near the middle of the room, was a second frail, old woman covered in blood.

I quickly went to her to check her vital signs. It was too late. She was also dead—and cut up worse than the other one. This one's head was nearly severed from the body—and so was her left hand, which was hanging by a thin piece of skin. It looked as though it had been severed while she held her hands out in front of her body, trying to protect herself—defensive wounds. And both of her breasts were completely cut away from her body. The killer had plunged the weapon, neatly, around each breast. There must have been over forty or fifty puncture wounds from some type of weapon—possibly a large butcher knife. They looked similar to the knife wounds found on Jim Palter.

This scene was just too intense for me to handle. I had to get out of that apartment. In all my years on the force, investigating murders had never affected me that much. But seeing this was too much to bear.

Just then, it hit me. This was the apartment I had visited when I first began the Palter murder investigation. I had questioned these two adorable old women about Jim Palter. I was devastated—so stunned I had to sit down. I sat on the floor, leaning against the wall to catch my breath. That made three murders, in the same apartment building, on the same floor, within a two-week period. Our city murder statistics had just gone up about ten percent.

I had to call the coroner, but first, I wanted the forensics team to go over this apartment with a fine-tooth comb. It looked to me as though the same killer that had murdered Palter had also killed these women. But why? That's what I wanted to find out. What could have been the motive for this horrendous killing? I was sure a woman had killed Palter. But why would she also want to kill these women? Had they known something?

Once I caught my breath, I hurried out of the apartment. I shut the door behind me and called the station on my cell phone. I called in the homicide detectives and asked for the forensics crew. Captain Blake also ordered me to contact the coroner's office to deal with the bodies.

While waiting for the forensics team to arrive, I paced the hallway and thought about the Palter murder investigation. I began comparing the two murder investigations in my head. Only the forensic evidence—such as hair and fiber samples—could tell me if these murders were connected with the Palter murder investigation. Hopefully, they would find the fingerprints of the killer...or maybe the murder weapon. There were similarities to both crime scenes, and their apartments were very close to each other—just a few doors apart.

As the forensics team arrived so had the old women's doctor. He was very upset to find the chaotic condition at his patients' apartment.

"What the hell is going on?" he bellowed, trying to get past the outside guard.

"Ah, please Doc," I said, as I grabbed him gently by the arm and directed him away from the apartment, "let's step over here and talk about it."

"Please, tell me," he begged. "What is going on? ... Has something happened to the Weinburg sisters?"

"The ladies have been murdered." When I told him this, he barged towards the apartment doorway, but I stopped him. "You don't want to go in there right now, Doc."

"You forget, sir. I am a doctor. I might be of some assistance."

"Why were you visiting them now?"

"I give them each a bi-weekly injection of vitamin B-12. They were still suffering from chest colds. If it isn't kept under control, they could come down with pneumonia again."

"Do you know of anyone that would want to kill these lovely old ladies?"

"No ... except maybe Jim Palter!"

"Why do you say that, Doc?"

"He was the only person I ever saw them argue with."

"But they were just arguing, Doc. Why would you mention Palter's name? Anyway, he's dead."

"That's the only person I could think of that might have had it in for the sisters."

"Why do you say that?"

"He was always yelling at the ladies for spying on him. I remember, not too long ago, that him and one of his whores had barged into their apartment and yelled and screamed at them to keep their noses out of their business!"

"Doctor, what were *you* doing while all the commotion was going on?" I asked.

"I was right in the middle of giving one of the girls an injection when Palter and his whore barged into the apartment."

"What happened then?"

"Nothing! We were startled by their actions ... and couldn't do anything but wait until they left the apartment. ... In fact, it's getting late, and I have to get going."

"What's your hurry, Doc?"

"I have many more patients to attend to. ... Do you need me for anything else?"

"No, I don't think so."

"If you won't let me help with this investigation, then I must leave. I'm afraid I have other live patients that need my attention."

"Fine, Doc. If I need you for anything else, I'll contact you...or you can contact me at the station if you think of anything that might help us in our investigation."

I entered the apartment as the doctor walked away towards the elevator. The forensics team was hard at work. They had already found some important evidence—strands of long, blonde hair similar to the hair found at Palter's apartment—and a cigarette butt with lipstick on it. There were also a number of fingerprints found. Now they would have to go through each and every one and exclude all irrelevant fingerprints.

We would have to start another independent murder investigation, unless it was determined that the Palter murder and these murders were linked together. Then I would get jurisdiction for the Weinburg murders. But until those questions were answered, we would have to act as though they weren't connected.

Our investigative teams would also have to canvass the apartment complex and the tenth floor to see if there were any witnesses to these most recent killings. We would have to cover the same exact ground as we did in the Palter investigation.

The serial killer investigators were also on the job. They were investigating these murders to see if the case belonged in their jurisdiction.

I was going on the assumption that a woman killed Palter. But I wasn't at all sure that a woman had committed these murders.

We had just started this investigation, so we had a long way to go before we could draw a logical conclusion. After seeing those two lovely, old ladies butchered and lying in their own blood, I vowed not to retire until I caught their murderers. That was my mandate. I wanted to leave this job with a near perfect record, and I meant to do just that. But the serial killer investigation was making it a lot more difficult on me. They had first priority for everything—money, investigators, lab work, and anything else that was needed to do a complete job.

I wondered if these murders could have been the work of the serial killer. Possibly. But the serial killer investigators weren't too anxious to talk about it. Even though I had been on their staff at one time, my brother detectives refused to speak with me about their investigation. I was totally miffed by their attitude. I thought that maybe it was because of my drinking, although I hadn't heard any rumors concerning my extracurricular activities.

Suddenly, my mind stopped thinking about my brother detectives and began thinking about these two most recent horrendous murders. I would have to do a serious background check on the two sisters to see who would benefit the most from their deaths. Perhaps the killer was a relative looking for an inheritance check. That would be a good motive for murder.

I stayed with the forensic and coroner investigators late into the night. The serial killer investigators left after only a few hours. The coroner team left the scene first. The coroner said the females were brutalized and cut up, lying down: one on the couch, the other on her bed. But they were both thrown from there to the floor, where they were found. There, the killer or killers finished the job. They continued to stab the victims and mutilate their bodies. Their throats were also slit while they lay on the floor. It was quite a messy situation.

These weren't killers ... they were savages. I just couldn't understand what would make a human being do such a disgusting and sickening act. The more I thought about it, the more enraged I became.

Once the forensic team departed, I followed right behind them. However, before leaving, I fastened the crime tape across the front door so nobody could get into the apartment except law enforcement officers.

I finally arrived home just before midnight. I was too tired to change into my pajamas or even to eat. But, I wasn't too tired to drink. I needed a couple of shots after the day I'd had. If I didn't have a drink or two before bedtime, I wouldn't be able to fall asleep.

I flashed back to the clumps of hair that had been cut from the two female victims' heads. Usually, women cut the hair of their victims. Men don't, generally speaking. But whatever theories I came up with, I still came to the same conclusion: I would have to wait until all the evidence was gathered. This investigation had just started. All I had to go on right now were opinions. Mostly...my own.

I finally fell asleep on the couch, still in my suit clothes. I tossed and turned thinking about this new murder investigation, wondering if the evidence would point to the same person that had killed Palter.

# Chapter 8

I awoke in my work clothes. That was nothing new. I quickly shaved and washed up. I had to iron my suit jacket before I left for the station. I was hoping the Weinburg investigation would be assigned to someone else. I had enough work to do on my own.

Within ten minutes, I had arrived at the station. I quickly signed in at the front desk and actually walked to the snack room instead of stumbling. I poured a cup of black coffee and drank it in two gulps.

When I finally reached my desk, I began sifting through a stack of reports and interviews on the Weinburg investigation. Why? Because first thing, Captain Blake had assigned *me* to investigate the Weinburg murders. Every other homicide detective was working on the serial killer investigation. I didn't like it, but my captain gave me an order, so I couldn't refute or refuse it. He seemed to think the Palter murder and the Weinburg murders were linked. I disagreed with him, at first.

But as I went through and read the reports, it became evident that the same killer had murdered both Palter and the old women. But why? Why would the person responsible for the Palter murder want to kill those frail old ladies? What possible motive could they have? One report stated that there was only one person, a woman, that would inherit the Weinburg fortune—and that was a good motive to kill them, or have them killed. She was my first logical suspect.

The two old ladies didn't act or look like big spenders, but they left behind quite a sum of money, jewelry, stocks, bonds, and real estate that they had accumulated over their eighty years of existence. The ladies' niece was the only known relative still alive to inherit their estate—her name was Precious Diamond.

No one in the apartment complex saw or heard anything suspicious. The old women were killed in the early morning hours. According to the coroner's report, they had been dead at least three to five hours before I found them.

I had to take a little break. My eyes were beginning to see double. I started getting the shakes, and my body began to shiver due to a lack of food. I walked over to the snack area and grabbed a donut out of the box, then poured a cup of black coffee. I had to get something into my stomach to get rid of the shakes. That's one of the side effects of my alcoholism. My drinking was starting to interfere with my work.

While I ate and drank my coffee, I noticed that one of the forensic investigators had stopped at my desk and placed something on it. He continued on his way, so I wasn't able to ask him what he wanted. I slowly walked back to my desk to find out what he had left on it. It was a report from the lab. I thought maybe it was the finished autopsy report from the coroner's office.

I quickly glanced through it. It was a preliminary report from the DNA lab. The complete report wouldn't be finished for another week, if not longer. But this report wasn't the one I had been anxiously waiting for. It was the blood analysis report of the butcher knife, which had fallen out of Ellen Garwood's purse.

I sat down at my desk to read the report more closely. It was short—only three pages long. The report stated that the dark substance at the base of the handle, where the blade began, was definitely the blood of Jim Palter.

Now there were two identical butcher knives with Palter's blood on them. But which one was the actual murder weapon? Now, I wanted to find out that answer. I decided to call Miss Garwood's attorney so we could set up an appointment for another interview with his client. I only had one question to ask her.

I began looking for the attorney's telephone number. I finally found his business card in one of my jacket pockets. I punched in the number and waited for an answer. The secretary called him to the phone.

"Hello. This is Tom Davis. Can I help you?" he asked.

"Yes. This is Detective Hero, Mr. Davis. I would like an interview with your client, Ellen Garwood."

"Did you receive the DNA report yet?"

"Yes. It's sitting here on my desk. You can look it over when you arrive at the station."

"I would just like to know if you think my client is a suspect in your murder investigation."

"Yes, she is. She doesn't have an alibi during the time of Palter's murder. She is one suspect out of many."

"I think you're wasting your time investigating my client for a murder she didn't commit," he said. "But that's my opinion. ... We'll be at the station tomorrow at three o'clock. Is that all right?"

"That'll be fine," I said, and hung up the phone.

I went back to reading reports on the Weinburg murders. But I still felt queasy ... and my energy was drained.

I visited Gabrielles Hoagie Shop for lunch to eat a hoagie and managed to get one down without it coming back up. I had to sit there an extra hour just to digest my food. I had hoped that the mysterious female would have showed up, but no luck. I even returned there for dinner. It had been almost a week since I had eaten dinner there.

I had spent the whole day at my desk going over all the reports on the Weinburg murders. I expected there to be more with time, but after thoroughly reading all of the investigative reports I'd received so far, I was still under the opinion that two different had people killed my victims. My captain disagreed.

I kept thinking about the strands of long, blonde hair and the cigarette butt that pointed to a woman as the killer—just as in the Palter murder. Then there was also the hair that had been slashed from the victim's head. I imagined that only a woman would cut another woman's hair.

I spent the rest of the afternoon reading reports and comparing similarities and discrepancies between my two murder investigations while waiting for Ellen Garwood and her attorney to arrive for the interview. As I looked up to take a little breather from reading reports, I noticed them walking through the front door of the station. I met them halfway and directed them to the interview room. Once we were all seated comfortably, I turned on the tape recorder and began my questioning.

"Hello, Miss Garwood. How are you, today?" I asked, trying to break the ice.

"Miss Garwood," said her attorney, "before you start answering questions, I would like to see the DNA report. I would like to read it over before we begin with this interview. You do have the report, don't you, Detective Hero?"

"Yes, I do," I said, and pushed the report across the table into the hands of the attorney.

We waited in silence for a good minute or two while the attorney read the report. When he had finished reading it, I began to speak. He held up his hand, cutting me off.

"Excuse me, Detective Hero," interjected Davis, "but you did say my client was a suspect in your murder investigation, didn't you?"

"Yes, she is, Mr. Davis! Along with five or six other people."

"Did you read Miss Garwood her Miranda warning?"

"No, of course not! She's not under arrest...she's just here for questioning. I'm hoping she can clear up some cloudy issues."

"Fine! Ask your questions," snarled Davis.

"Now, Miss Garwood," I said, staring into her big blue eyes. "A dark substance was found on the butcher knife that fell out of your purse. The DNA analysis report states that the substance is Jim Palter's blood. Do you know how that blood got on your knife?" She didn't answer. She just sat slouched in her chair and stared blankly across the room—as if in a deep trance. But I ignored her behavior and continued with my questioning. "Miss Garwood, the knife had Jim Palter's blood on it! And it's the same type of knife used in at least one murder that we know of. You were seen at the victim's residence near the time of his death. You were also seen arguing with him. And you threatened him with the butcher knife. Then you stayed behind, as the other women left the apartment. Now, I ask you ... how did Palter's blood get on that knife?"

Before she could say a word, the attorney interrupted.

"Miss Garwood, you don't have to answer that!" he snapped.

She did as she was told and remained silent. She seemed to be very frightened of me. But her attorney seemed to frighten her even more. I had to calm the situation or I would never get her to answer my questions.

"Please, Miss Garwood," I said, looking into her eyes. "I'm sure there has to be a reasonable explanation for the blood. Just tell me what it is." She remained silent, so I pressed on. "You'll answer the question, Ellen, if you don't have anything to hide."

"Don't answer his question, Ellen!" Davis said, as he stood up. "If you have nothing more to ask my client, then we'll be leaving!"

"Mr. Davis, I was hoping to clear your client's name! I was hoping to wipe her name off of my list of suspects. But now, you're making her look guilty. The next time I question your client, I may have to arrest her first. Is that what you want, counselor?"

"Let's go, Ellen!" Davis said, motioning for her to rise.

As the attorney took a few steps towards the door, Ellen Garwood just sat in her chair, stiff as a board. She looked like a robot with a dead battery.

"Miss Garwood, are you all right?" I asked. I waved my hand in front of her eyes to snap her out of her trance.

Finally, Ellen started to speak.

Davis interrupted her before she said two words. "Miss Garwood, you don't have to answer him if you don't want to. I suggest you don't."

"But I want to!" she said.

"Remember," Davis said, pleading with his client, "anything you say, can and will be used against you in a court of law. But most of all, the police can use it against you. Even though you are innocent, *they* think you are guilty. Especially if they need a scapegoat!"

"I don't need a scapegoat!" I snapped. "If the evidence points in her direction or in someone else's, we use the evidence to convict the guilty culprit!"

"Yeah? Even if all the evidence you have is all circumstantial?" Davis asked.

"Well, I'm not going to argue about it with you, counselor. She may have a reasonable explanation for the blood being on the knife."

"I don't have anything to hide!" Garwood said, not letting her lawyer silence her this time. "I just hope you believe me!"

"Then tell me what happened at Palter's apartment," I said.

"I went there to confront him about a few things concerning his lying and infidelity."

"So what happened?"

"We were arguing and yelling about my concerns when all of a sudden, he began to push me out of the apartment. I couldn't believe what he was doing!"

"What do you mean?" I asked.

"He was shoving me out of the apartment that I'd paid the rent on! Hell, I paid all the bills! That made me very angry. And when he pushed me into the kitchen that made me even angrier. That's when I saw a big butcher knife lying on the kitchen counter."

"So, what did you do then?"

"I grabbed it and waved it in front of him. We ended up back in the living room. Then, two women walked into his apartment and saw me threatening him with the knife."

"Miss Garwood, did they say anything when they saw you two arguing?" I asked.

"No. Everyone was more or less too startled to say anything. In fact, Jim and I stopped arguing when we saw them standing there."

"What did you do with the knife?"

"I tried hiding it behind my back...but they had already seen me with it. So Jim and I acted like nothing was wrong—just to make a good impression in front of his mistresses. I was really steaming by then!"

"Miss Garwood," I said, staring into her eyes, "I bet you that made you madder and madder seeing those women at the apartment—the apartment you had paid rent on! You must have hated Palter for embarrassing you like that."

"Well, I didn't mind paying the bills," she said. "It was his lying and infidelity that I didn't like!"

Just as she was about to open up, Davis tried to muzzle her. "I'm sorry, Miss Garwood ... but as your attorney, I must warn you not to say another word about the matter."

"But I want to get it off my chest!" she snapped, leaning back in her chair. "I want to clean up this mess that Jim has caused."

"Then tell him ... if you must," said the attorney.

So she began telling me her side of the story, saying, "When the two other women stormed out of the apartment, Jim and I began arguing again. And I still had the butcher knife in my hand."

"Miss Garwood, why did you have the knife in the first place?" I asked.

"I used the knife to defend myself, so he wouldn't attack or hit me. ... But I'm getting ahead of myself. I forgot to mention about the paper bag."

"What paper bag?"

"Before the two women stormed out of the apartment, one of them threw a paper bag at Jim...and the stuff inside the bag went all over the room."

"What did Jim do?"

"He began picking the stuff up off the floor while yelling at the woman to leave his apartment. He was like a madman!"

"Did the women leave?" I asked.

"Yeah. But before they did, they yelled a few obscenities. And when Jim finished picking up the items that flew out of the bag, he had become enraged. I thought he was going to take it out on me!"

"Why?"

"Sometimes, he couldn't control his anger and would strike out at whoever was in his direction. So, when he tried pushing me out of the apartment, again, we began arguing. That's when I began waving the knife in front of him, to make a point."

"What did Jim do?"

"He grabbed me and tried pushing me out of the room. When I tried to push his hands away ... when I did that, the knife accidentally cut him on his left hand. It cut a little vein, so it bled quite a bit."

"Miss Garwood, is that when you left the apartment?"

"No. When I saw him bleeding, I put the knife in the kitchen sink and we quit arguing, so I could wash and clean his wound. When I began bandaging his hand, he told me to stick the knife in my purse for protection."

"Why, if you had just cut him?"

"He didn't want me to get robbed or assaulted again. So, after I mended his wound, I cleaned and dried the knife and then placed it in my purse. That's when my father entered the apartment."

"So, your contention is that you cut Mr. Palter on the hand. Was that the right or left hand?" I asked.

"The left hand. No, the right hand. Yeah, that's right. The right hand."

"Are you sure it was the right hand?"

"No, it was the left hand. I'm all mixed up. I'm so nervous. Now, I'm certain, it *was* the left hand. Yes ... I cut him on the left hand!"

Her conflicting statements gave me a headache. I had to take a short break.

"Please excuse me for one minute," I said, then left the room to get a cup of hot, black coffee.

I didn't want them to know what I was doing. I wanted Miss Garwood to sit and think about what she had said. I wanted to watch her body language as she sat and thought about her interview. I could tell she was wondering what I was doing. I still had my doubts about this woman. She wasn't completely innocent.

"I'm sorry about the inconvenience," I said, re-entering the room. "I just have one more question for you, Miss Garwood."

"And what is that?" she asked, as I sat down in my chair.

"Would you take a lie detector test?" I asked. Just then, I watched her face turn a pale white. Her jaw dropped to the floor. She seemed very surprised by my question.

The lawyer seemed perturbed. "I take it, Detective Hero, you don't believe her story?"

"I didn't say that," I told him. "Let's put it this way ... The lie detector test will help prove her story."

"Well, when she's arrested," Davis said, "or when I think it's imperative that she take one, then I'll let you know. But until then, we'll decline your offer. Now, if there is nothing more, we'll be leaving."

"Okay," I said. "If that's your attitude. Just remember...I tried to be nice. I tried to help you."

Davis stood up. "She answered all of your questions," he said. "Just because you refuse to believe her story is not her fault. This interview is over!" He helped his client up from her chair and directed her out of the room.

I watched them leave. I thought Davis was right about one thing: I could make a good circumstantial case against his client if I thought she was guilty.

However, I did happen to lift a few blonde hair samples from her sweater, which I placed into an evidence bag after I had left the room. I would drop them off at the forensic lab to see if they matched the other blonde hairs that had been found at the crime scene.

I got the evidence to Dr. Stork. He promised to test it against the other hair fibers within a day or two. So if it matched the evidence that we already had, that would be some powerful evidence against Ellen Garwood. But until then, I would have to concentrate on my other suspects. And I still had to contact the Weinburg sister's niece.

I drove from the forensic lab to the cafe. About a block away, I noticed a young girl walking. I was sure she was the lady I'd been looking for.

I quickly sped up to reach her before she got away. But traffic was heavier than usual. Once she turned the corner, I lost track of her.

When I reached the café, I parked my car and ran after her—but I was too late. She was nowhere in sight. I even ran all the way around the block, checking all four streets. But she had disappeared, like a ghost in the night.

By the time I returned to the café, I was tired and out of breath. Not only that, but my gut ached like crazy. I guess I wasn't in the best of shape anymore. As soon as I entered the café, I looked to speak with Bonnie. She must have had the same idea because she met me at the door.

"Your girlfriend was just here," Bonnie said. "She left just two minutes before you came in."

"I know. I just saw her leave here. But I lost her in the crowd. Why didn't you call me the second she came in?"

"I did! But you weren't at your desk. They said you had left for the day. You must have been on your way here."

"Damn," I said, pounding my fist into my forehead. "I should have given you my cell phone number, too!" I quickly wrote down my cellular number on a scrap of paper and handed it to her. Then I asked her the magic question: "You didn't happen to get her name, did you?"

"No," Bonnie said, shaking her head. "She just stopped in to use the phone. She made a phone call and then left.

She was only on it for about thirty seconds. I don't think anyone answered because I didn't see or hear her talking, and when she left she seemed angry."

"Why do you say that?"

"She left in a big huff."

"Well, Bonnie, you know what they say. If at first you don't succeed, try, try again," I said.

Once home, I grabbed my bottle of scotch and danced into the living room, plopping down onto the couch. I poured a shot and drank it, then chased it with another.

I still couldn't get the Weinburg murders out of my head. When I finally fell asleep, I kept waking up from the same nightmare. It had a strange twist from the others. I was the one holding the knife this time, stabbing the victims in the chest, then cutting their throats and yanking their heads from their bodies. But then, the mouth on the severed head begins to suck me in. That's when I wake up, just when the beast nearly consumes me completely.

I tossed and turned for an hour before I finally fell back to sleep. And then, sometime later, I had the same nightmare again. But this time it was Ellen Garwood holding the knife, stabbing and butchering the victims. It was then that I realized how the blood had gotten onto Ellen Garwood's butcher knife.

I heard a loud buzzer. I looked at the killer and then at the buzzing alarm clock. The clock's time read six a.m. The crazed woman was standing over the butchered old lady with bloody knife in hand, laughing and staring at the alarm clock, with eyes so big I thought they were going to pop out of her head.

Six o'clock was the time the Weinburg murders had taken place. There, I had the case all wrapped up, I thought. I was ready to handcuff the culprit and take her back to the station. But first, I had to shut that loud buzzer off. It was so loud it was shaking the furniture in the room. The killer covered her ears with her bloody hands, trying to block out the loud noise. But it did no good. The noise just kept getting louder and louder, until I thought our eardrums were going to burst. I ran across the room, then reached out to shut off the loud noise. But just as I went to shut off the alarm clock, I realized I was dreaming and it was *my* alarm clock that was ringing.

It was time for me to get up and get ready for work. I was anxious to get to the station. I wanted to read the rest of the reports on the Weinburg murders, and I wanted to contact the only known living relative who was to inherit the two sisters' fortune—Precious Diamond. I believed her to be the prime suspect in their murders, even though my captain thought otherwise.

No matter what, I ran my own investigations. I worked them the way I wanted to, not the way someone else wanted me to. But, I had been wrong before. Not many times, though, in over twenty-five years with the homicide department. I could only remember two or three times in my long and distinguished career that my gut instinct had been wrong—that had been over ten years ago. That's not a bad average. If I were wrong again, I'd take responsibility for my actions. That's just how I am.

After I signed in at the front desk, I quickly walked over to the snack counter and grabbed a fresh, jelly-filled donut, then poured a cup of hot, black coffee.

As I walked up to my desk, I was ecstatic to see a few new investigative reports sitting on top of it. I quickly glanced through them and noticed that the background check of Precious Diamond was among them. I was anxious to read about her. I wanted to see what kind of skeletons she kept hidden in her closet. There was also a photo of her stapled to the report, but she must have been a teenager when the photo was taken—she looked about seventeen or eighteen years old.

The more I glanced through her report, the more interested I became. It seemed Precious Diamond had quite a few skeletons in her closet. She had lived out of state up until about three and a half months ago. Then she moved to our fair city. She was nearly thirty years old, had a rap sheet over three pages long, and had been arrested over forty times during her lifetime. And the report didn't include her criminal record for her teenage years—only from the age of eighteen till the present.

She had been arrested for many different reasons. Ninety percent of them were misdemeanors and minor offenses, which included obstruction of justice, assaulting a police officer, prostitution (more than a couple of times), drug possession, grand theft, joy riding, D.U.I. (twice, in a three-year period) and burglary. But the worst charge was for murder. She had allegedly killed her own mother. And that was only four years ago.

During the murder trial, Miss Diamond lucked out when a few of the jurors had reasonable doubt and voted to acquit, so the judge ordered a mistrial. Then, the district attorney decided not to retry her due to a lack of evidence. So she walked out of the courtroom a free woman. That's when she decided to move near her aunts' residence—but she hadn't acted on the idea until four months ago.

She had received almost a quarter of a million dollars from her mother's insurance policy, but she went through it within a one-year period. She seemed to be addicted to money. Another good motive for murder.

The report stated that she was a twenty-nine-year-old, five feet-ten inch, blonde-haired, blue-eyed beauty, with a number of tattoos on different parts of her anatomy—some were visible...others were not.

Her hobbies were riding Harley motorcycles and mud wrestling. In her younger years, she was a "gangster wanna-be." She was never a member of any gang, but she hung around with gang members from three different gangs.

I couldn't believe it. More than forty arrests and she'd never spent a night in jail. The charges were always either dropped or she received a few months of probation. And once her probation was completed, her record was expunged.

This lady seemed to be very lucky. Now, she was going to inherit another fortune. How lucky can one person be? Well, maybe her luck was about to run out. Maybe luck didn't have anything to do with it. She had a good motive for the killings. Now, all I needed was some decent evidence against her.

The only other suspect that I had was dead. That was Jim Palter. He had had a few altercations with the old ladies, but there was nothing in his past to indicate that he would kill them. Anyway, he was dead long before they were. Maybe the old ladies saw the killer or killers of Jim Palter, and they returned to quiet any witnesses. That would be a clear motive for murder.

As I neared the end of the report, my stomach began to growl. I looked at my watch and saw that it was way past lunchtime, so I decided to snack on junk food. I would raid the vending machines today.

After eating a quick lunch, I decided I would drive to Miss Diamond's dwelling. I didn't have a telephone number, but I did have her address. I hoped to interview her today. That is, if she was at her abode. If I could, I would talk her into coming to the station for the interview. I wanted to confront her in unfamiliar surroundings. I wanted to test her patience.

I had planned to hop into my car and drive to her residence once I'd read her report; however, the report following Miss Diamond's background check was the coroner's autopsy report of the Weinburg sisters. I wanted to read it before visiting my female suspect.

The autopsy report stated that the old lady found in the bedroom was first stabbed in the chest as she lay on the bed. Then she was thrown to the floor, where she was found lying in a pool of blood. The killer cut her throat, then stabbed her repeatedly, and then mutilated her breasts. Her chest was so mutilated that she had two six-inch long, three-inch wide holes where her breasts had been.

However, Mira, the other female victim, was a different story. She was found lying naked on the floor in the middle of the living room. She had to be alive and breathing when her throat was cut because her blood had spurted more than four feet onto the adjacent wall. So the heart had to be pumping. Her body was also stabbed repeatedly and mutilated—one breast was imbedded in her chest cavity. And once the blood had drained out of her body, the hair on her head was hacked away and placed neatly around it.

Their bedclothes were stripped and ripped from their old and deformed bodies and strewn all over their rooms. They were clothed while they were being stabbed and butchered because cloth fibers were found stuck to the bloody sides of their flesh, inside the many deep stab wounds in the chest cavity and other parts of their bodies.

There were also two long blonde hair fibers found in the hand of one of the old ladies, which were to be analyzed at our forensics facility. But instead, they were sent out to the DNA lab for final analysis because our lab had been overwhelmed.

The Weinburg sisters' autopsy photos were hideous. I had investigated plenty of horrible murders, but this one made my blood boil. The bodies were so mutilated you couldn't tell if they were male or female.

The forensics lab had completed the fingerprint analysis. They identified many of the people whose fingerprints were found in the sisters' apartment—and a couple were suspects in the Palter murder, such as Ellen Garwood, Samantha Manner, and Paul Donald. Rita Margaw's were also found there, but she had been sitting in jail when the Weinburg murders were committed. However, there weren't any bloody fingerprints found. Most of the ones that were identified were taken from the hallway walls, the front door, and the living room wall near the hallway entrance—as if someone had been leaning against it. None of these fingerprints were any good as evidence. We couldn't distinguish the timing. It could have been the morning of the murder or two weeks before...or even longer.

However, there was one set of fingerprints that wasn't identified by name. But they matched the ones lifted from the water glass that I had gotten from Bonnie. These were the fingerprints of the young girl from the café—the girl whom I believed had been one of Palter's more recent girlfriends. They were found in the hallway, near the front doorjamb—left there, probably, when she opened the door to leave the apartment. She must have been there with Palter, or possibly the Weinburg sisters may have invited her in. Whatever the reason, I still needed a name to go with the young woman's fingerprints. I wasn't worried. I would learn it in time. And I was sure that our paths would cross in the near future.

Once I received the rest of the DNA reports from the Palter murder, that should narrow down my suspect list and direct me to his killer—or killers—and hopefully, help me prove whether or not they were also involved in the

Weinburg murders. And those reports should be here any day. They were actually past due. I was very anxious to learn which woman had made love to Palter just before he was murdered—or murdered as they were making love. Maybe Palter hadn't made love to her properly...or to her liking. So, she'd killed him. Or maybe she was jealous at him for his infidelity. I still didn't know the motive, but I was going to find out.

    I decided I needed some fresh air, and it was time to find my new suspect for the Weinburg murders.

    While driving to Precious Diamond's address, I drove slowly past the residence of Palter's ex-business partner, Paul Donald. Just as I approached the street on which he lived, I noticed he was outside washing his car with that young, blonde beauty. She had her head tilted as she washed the car, so I couldn't get a very good look at her face. I wanted to stop, but I didn't have time. The Weinburg sisters' niece was more important to me. Once I had interviewed her, then I would have the time to visit Donald and his new girlfriend.

# Chapter 9

I had been driving for more than twenty minutes, and I found myself surrounded by beautiful homes. Precious Diamond lived in the most expensive part of the city—and not far from the Garwood home.

I finally found the address I had been looking for. There wasn't a gate blocking the driveway, so I drove straight up to the house, which was hidden from view between two massive rows of Weeping Willow trees and a thick blanket of foliage. The house seemed out of place, being so little and hidden as it was, while the houses nearby were massive and in plain sight. But to get to Miss Diamond's house, you had to walk about one hundred feet from the driveway to reach it.

Before I knocked on the front door, I pulled out the photo that I had brought with me of Precious Diamond. What an unusual name, I thought to myself. A beautiful girl answered the door, but it wasn't the one I had expected.

"Hello, I'm Detective Hero," I said, showing her my badge and police identification. "Is Miss Precious Diamond at home?"

"I don't know. Wasn't she at home?" asked the young woman.

"Doesn't she live here, in this house? This is the address I have for her."

"Are you kidding? This is the maids' quarters. Miss Diamond lives in the big house," said the young woman. She pointed in the direction of the house.

"Where is it? I didn't see any other house on this road."

"Just keep following the drive. It will take you right to it. It's just over that hill."

"What's your name? You said you were the maid. Is that right?" I asked.

But before she could answer my question, a young adult male, possibly her boyfriend, walked up behind her and interrupted our conversation.

"What does he want?" the man asked.

"He's a police officer and he—"

"Does he have a warrant?" the man snapped.

"No, I don't have a warrant. I just—" Before I could get out another word, he slammed the door in my face.

I shook my head in disgust. I didn't take kindly to being yelled at by a young, tattooed thug. I wondered whether he'd had anything to do with the Weinburg murders. He looked and acted the type. Miss Diamond could have hired him to do the killings.

I calmly climbed back into my car and continued up the driveway. I followed the drive for a good quarter mile before reaching the top of the hill. Then I saw it. In the gully stood a brick mansion. I couldn't believe Miss Diamond lived in such a luxurious house. It had to be a million-dollar home—maybe more. I wondered how she paid for it.

With that thought in mind, I parked the car and walked up to the front door. Before I could knock on it, the door suddenly opened.

"Yes, may I help you?" asked the female, dressed in a maid's uniform.

"Yes, I'm Detective Hero. I would like to speak with Miss Precious Diamond. This is her place of residence, isn't it?"

"Yes, it is. But I'm sorry. She isn't here at the moment."

"Do you know when she will arrive home? Do you know where she is now?"

"Just a minute," said the maid. She walked away to another room of the house.

I waited patiently outside on the steps for two or three minutes before she returned and handed me a business card.

"This is where Miss Diamond is at the moment," she said.

I looked the card over. It had the address and phone number of a nudie bar. I had heard about this club but never visited it. The bar catered to a more affluent clientele, but sometimes the biker-type also showed up. The patrons that visited this bar were not just losers, perverts, and sex maniacs—they were *rich* losers, perverts, and sex maniacs.

"Does Miss Diamond work there?" I asked.

"Yeah, she owns the place," the maid said.

I thanked her for her time, then walked back to my car and drove away. For the very first time, I was going to visit a nudie bar.

Fifteen minutes later, I arrived on the adult entertainment scene. The building from the outside was quite exquisite—architecturally speaking, that is. Inside, however, the interior decorating lacked "good" taste. But what did I know? I couldn't see too much anyway. The place was dimly lit and filled with cigarette smoke. Red and blue colored lights adorned the walls and tables. I also noticed many nude females dancing in different parts of the club. Others were shaking and slithering their nude bodies against the clientele seated at their tables. The couples did everything but fornicate right there in the middle of the room.

Watching the girls' naked bodies and flirtatious actions, I began to get hot and sweaty in the smoke-filled room. I wanted to leave as soon as I entered, but I had a job to do.

I walked over to the closest bartender and asked him the whereabouts of Miss Diamond. He turned away from me and walked into another room. As he walked away, I glanced around the club. The place was full of male patrons. The only females, including the waitresses, were completely nude.

Then, I got quite a shock. I saw Paul Donald, alias Don Cadwell, sitting at a small table near the stage. I couldn't believe what I was seeing. I had just seen him not more than forty minutes before, washing his car with his girlfriend. I wondered why he was at this club. Did his girlfriend work at this place? Or was he a close friend with Miss Diamond? Maybe he helped Diamond in the Weinburg killings.

Just as I was about to walk over to his table and speak with him, I had another surprise. A very tall, slinky, beautiful, blonde-haired woman came up to me. She introduced herself flirtatiously.

"Hello, I'm Precious Diamond. Can I help you?" she purred, in a low sultry voice.

I quickly looked at my photo to see if she resembled the young girl in the picture. She did. Looking into her big, beautiful eyes, I completely forgot about Paul Donald and introduced myself.

"Hello, Miss Diamond, I'm Detective Hero. I would like to talk to you about your two aunts. They were murdered a few days ago."

"We can go into my office and talk there," she said. She led me between tables into a room in the back.

"Miss Diamond. If it's all right with you, I would like you to come down to the station this afternoon. If you're not too busy?" I asked, not realizing that her beauty was blinding me to the matters at hand.

"I'm always busy," she said, laughing. "But I'm always happy to help the police. I have to take care of a few things though, before I leave. I could meet you there, say by four o'clock. If that's all right?"

"That would be fine," I said. "I'll see you then." With that said, I turned and walked out of her office.

After speaking with Miss Diamond, I decided to question Mr. Donald about his relationship with his girlfriend and Miss Diamond. But when I looked for him, I couldn't find him. He had gone.

I walked out of the club and got back into my car. But just as I put the car in gear, I thought I saw Palter's business partner, Tom Walters, enter the club. I wondered whether this place was just a watering hole for him, or did he, too, have a close friendship with Precious Diamond? My suspicions got the best of me.

I shut the car off and jumped out. Entering the club once again, I walked around for a couple of minutes before I gave up. I didn't see any sign of the guy.

I looked at my watch. It was getting late, and I needed to hustle back to the station for the interview with Miss Diamond. I had a lot of questions to ask her. But before I interviewed her, I wanted to call the insurance companies that had issued the life insurance policies on the Weinburg sisters and on Palter. I wanted to find out if there was any link between them. I also wanted to contact the insurance company that had issued Diamond's mother's life insurance policy. I wanted to get their side of the story as to why they had paid out the money.

I exited the club again, glad to be out of that unholy place. My whole body was soaked with sweat. Seeing all those naked bodies at one time was too much for an old man to take.

I arrived back at the station around three o'clock. When I reached my desk, I phoned the insurance company mentioned in one of my reports and spoke with a Mr. Dean. He was the person that had issued the insurance policy to Diamond's mother.

"Yes, Mr. Dean. My name is Detective Hero. Could you tell me why your company decided to pay Precious Diamond the money from her mother's life insurance policy if you thought she was the one responsible for her mother's murder?"

"We did refuse to pay her the money," Dean said, "but she petitioned a judge to make our insurance company pay up. We had no other choice. We would have been held in contempt of court. The minute the district attorney admitted he wasn't going to retry her because of a lack of evidence, we lost any chance of voiding the contract."

During this phone call, I also learned that the Weinburg sisters carried life insurance policies with Dean's company. But the sisters' benefactor hadn't been paid yet—and Dean refused to say why. When I asked him the name of the benefactor, he refused to tell me, stating confidentiality laws. But I was already well aware of the name of the benefactor. I was going to have an interview with her in about an hour.

I thanked the insurance agent for his time and insight, then hung up the phone. After lighting a cigarette, I went back to reading over the investigative reports. I continued this until I saw Miss Diamond enter the building. I watched as the officer at the front desk directed Miss Diamond to my area. I thanked her for coming, then escorted her directly to the interview room. I walked slightly behind her and picked a few long, blonde hairs from her blouse without her knowledge before quickly sticking them into a small, plastic bag I had in my jacket pocket. I then placed the bag of hair fibers into my shirt pocket to have analyzed at a later date.

Once we were in the interview room, I helped her to her chair, then sat across the table from her and turned on the tape recorder.

"Thank you for coming today, Miss Diamond," I said, smiling. "You do know why I've asked you here for an interview, don't you?"

"No, not really," she said. "Something to do with my aunts' murders, I presume." She put a cigarette to her lips, lit it and blew the smoke into my face as Rita had done.

I acted casually, as though the smoke and her belligerent attitude didn't bother me. I wanted to show her kindness and understanding. I knew, sooner or later, I would question her again, before my investigations were completed, so I wanted and needed her cooperation. I watched as she took another drag or two on her cigarette before speaking again.

"Miss Diamond, I called you here to question you about your aunts' murders. Where were you on the day your relatives were killed?"

"I don't know? What day was it?"

"It was last Tuesday morning."

"I was at home in bed sleeping, at six in the morning," she said, as she smoked her cigarette. "I didn't wake up until ten—just like all my mornings. Then I get ready for work. I'm usually out of the house by eleven. Does that answer your question?"

"Miss Diamond, I didn't tell you what time the murders occurred. How did you know that?"

"I didn't. I just surmised the time of their deaths. The police told me that my aunts were murdered. They telephoned me in the early afternoon, and the officer said they had been dead for quite a few hours. So, I just figured, it must have happened around six or seven that morning." She suddenly snuffed out her cigarette, then lit another.

"You do have somebody that can verify your story, don't you, Miss Diamond?" I asked.

"If I need to, I'm sure I can. Even though Tuesday was the maid's day off, I'm sure I can get someone to verify my alibi. You didn't ask me if I had someone in bed with me."

"Did you?"

"That's for me to know and for you to find out."

"Miss Diamond, what time did you get home from your club Tuesday morning?"

"I think it was about five or six in the morning. Usually, I'm home by four, but I had some extra work to do."

"Like what?"

"The books didn't add up. I had to find the mistake."

"Do you own the club?"

"Yes I do. I bought it more than 6 years ago."

"Miss Diamond, do you know that biker thug that lives with the maid at your little cottage?" I asked.

She nodded. "Yes, I know him."

"Do you know his name?"

"His name is Ron Black. He has helped me many times."

"Doing what?"

"I have paid him to do odd jobs and errands for me."

"What kind of guy is he?"

"He's not such a bad guy, if he's sober. But you're right. He is a biker. ... I don't know what my maid sees in him."

"I saw a couple of other people at your club today that you might know."

"And who is that?"

"Miss Diamond, do you happen to know a Mr. Paul Donald? He goes by the alias Don Cadwell. Do you know him?" I asked.

"Yes, I know him. He comes into my club every now and then."

"Do you know a guy by the name of Tom Walters? I believe he visits your club, also."

"Yes. He's been a patron of my club for nearly two years."

"Now think, Miss Diamond. Did he ever come in with his business partner, Mr. Jim Palter?"

"Yes, I knew Jim," she said. "He was a regular—until he was killed." She paused to blow cigarette smoke in my face again. "He was always trying to pick up my girls at the club."

"Do you know anyone that would have wanted Jim Palter or your aunts killed?" I asked, looking directly into her eyes, through the thick haze of cigarette smoke, trying to see her reaction.

"No," she said, shaking her head. "I don't know anyone who would want to kill any of them. Why, do you think there's a connection with Jim's murder and my aunts?"

"I don't know for certain. I'm just rounding all the bases? How well did you know Palter?"

"I didn't know him that well. Only from seeing him when he visited the club. And as far as my aunts are concerned...they didn't have an enemy in the world."

"Well, now I know you're lying."

"What do you mean?" she asked, staring at the floor.

"They had at least one enemy," I said. "Miss Diamond, did you know that you were in your aunts' will? Did you know that you would inherit their estate when they died?"

"I never thought about it." she said, as she squirmed in her seat and seemed upset with my questions. "I loved my aunts. They were the only living relatives that I had left on this planet." She gave me a look of disgust.

"Miss Diamond, do you know if your biker friend knew either of the guys that we just talked about? Did he know Palter's business partner, Tom Walters, or Palter's ex-business partner, Don Cadwell? Did you ever see or hear them discuss any business at your club?"

"Ron Black and some of his biker friends would visit the club when those guys were there. But ... I don't know if they knew each other or not. You'll have to ask them."

"I just might do that. But Jim Palter won't be able to answer my questions, will he, Miss Diamond?" I asked.

She gave me a cold, hard stare. I didn't let it bother me and pressed on. "Let's get back to your aunts' investigation. Did you know that they had bought life insurance policies, and you were the beneficiary?"

"No," she said, again blowing cigarette smoke into my face. "I didn't know about any life insurance policies, but I knew about the will. I mean, I was the only living relative. Who else would they leave their inheritance to?"

"Miss Diamond, when was the last time you visited your aunts' apartment?"

"Well, I don't know," she said, flicking her lit butt to the floor. "But I drove by there about a week ago. I had planned to visit them that day and called them on my cellular phone as I was driving to their place, but they told me not to come up. They were still very ill and didn't want me to catch their illness."

"What did you do?"

"I stayed away. Then, a day or so later, they were murdered. Why did it happen?" she asked, pounding her fist on the table top. "Who would do such a disgusting thing?"

"I don't know yet," I told her. "But, I promise you, Miss Diamond, I will catch the killer—or killers."

"I hope so. I want the death penalty for the person responsible for my aunts' murders," she said, as she lit another cigarette and crossed her legs.

"Let me ask you this question, Miss Diamond. Do you think that biker, ah, Ron Black, could kill someone for money or out of revenge?" I asked, watching her closely for a reaction.

"What a question to ask me," she said. Then, after taking a long drag on her cigarette, she added, "I suppose anyone could kill, if they had a good enough reason."

"Well, a million dollars would be a good reason, wouldn't it, Miss Diamond?"

"I guess it would. But if you're suggesting I killed my aunts for their insurance money, you're very mistaken."

"Well, did you? Did you kill your aunts?" I asked, getting right to the point. She didn't answer me, just casually continued smoking her cigarette right down to the filter—then threw it to the floor and lit another. She was a smooth cookie. Nothing seemed to rattle her. She was going to be a challenge. But I was up to it.

"I want to know why you killed your aunts. Or did you hire someone to kill them for you? You definitely had a good motive for wanting them dead. Come clean, now," I said. "You know I'll find out, eventually."

She jumped up from her chair. "If you're going to keep asking me these same ridiculous questions, I'm going to leave." She began heading towards the door.

"Please, Miss Diamond," I begged. "Please, come back and sit down. I only have a few more questions to ask you."

"Ask my lawyer!" She stormed out of the interview room...and out of the station.

I didn't have any solid evidence to hold her. And I needed more than just circumstantial evidence to get an arrest warrant. I needed a witness. Maybe Ron Black, the biker, knew something. That was just conjecture on my part, but I wouldn't put murder past him. I had to dig up something on Mr. Black to put his butt in jail, that way, he might want to trade some helpful information about Diamond—such as what skeletons she kept hidden in her closet. For a lenient jail sentence, he might even give me the perpetrator's name in the Weinburg murders. First, I would have to do a background check on him before making a decision one way or another.

Now I wondered, with everyone knowing each other, maybe they'd helped each other in killing the victims. Miss Diamond knew Black and Cadwell, and maybe some others that could have helped in the murders—and also had a connection with Palter. Maybe Black or Diamond had helped Cadwell kill Palter, and then helped Diamond kill her two aunts. But why? Well, if I were a betting man, I'd say they did it for the same ageless reason—money. Sooner or later, I would find out.

Before I could head home, I had to drop off the hair samples I had taken from Miss Diamond's clothes.

I signed out and drove directly to the forensics lab. When I arrived, all was quiet. I found a lab worker and explained to her what I had in the plastic bag, then handed the evidence over to her. She promised to turn it over to the supervisor in the morning. He would be responsible for the analysis of the hair samples. I wanted them to be matched against the ones we had found at the two crime scenes.

Once I had completed my business at the lab, I drove directly to Gabrielles. I was starving. When I entered, Bonnie was standing there waiting for me with coffeepot in hand. She was about to seat me at my favorite table when I spied the Weinburg sisters' doctor sitting alone at a table. I casually walked over and introduced myself.

"Hello, I'm Detective Hero. Remember me? I was investigating the Weinburg murders and we met and talked in the hallway of their apartment building. Do you mind if I join you for dinner?"

"I don't mind. Have a seat." As I sat down at his table, he said, "Have you caught the murderer yet?" he asked in a gruff, rough voice.

"Not unless you can tell me who did it," I said. "You said murderer. Why not murderers?" I asked.

"Well, I think the niece killed them."

"Why would you say that, Doc?"

"When I learned of the murders, I thought to myself, who would want them dead? Who had the most to benefit from the old ladies' deaths? That's when I thought of the niece. I had been the sisters' family physician for over thirty years. We were like family. We discussed many things together, including their only living relative. Their niece." He paused to take a bite of his hamburger.

"Dr. Rhodes, if you have time, I would like you to come down to the station for an interview so I can get your statement recorded and on file."

"Why don't you ask me whatever it is you need to ask right here? I'm too busy with my elderly patients to take time away from them for some frivolous interview that can be done right here, right now."

"Yes, but I would like to record the interview, and I can't do that here."

"You could have if you would have brought a tape recorder with you, like the one I carry," he said, pulling out a small, portable, hand-held tape recorder from his jacket pocket. He set it in front of me and then turned it on.

"All right, Dr. Rhodes," I said, laughing. "You win. We'll do the interview here while we eat our food." He nodded his approval.

The waitress stopped by with my two steak and cheese hoagies and placed them on the table in front of me. I thanked her as she walked away, and then began questioning the doctor in between bites.

"Doc, what can you tell me about the sisters' niece? I know she was tried for the murder of her mother, but she beat the rap. Tell me why you think Precious Diamond killed her aunts?"

"Well, the sisters and I discussed their niece many times recently. The sisters had a falling out with her. They stayed by her side all during the trial of her mother's murder. But once she was acquitted, they became disgusted with her attitude and lack of morals."

"Why do you say that?"

"Miss Diamond became addicted to money. She squandered her mother's life insurance money and her estate. She spent money like she was a billionaire. The sisters really hit the ceiling when she invested in that den of inequity."

"You mean the nudie bar?"

"Yes. They didn't want her in that disgusting business. They told her that if she didn't get out of that dirty business, she would be written out of their wills. When the niece refused to sell the club, the sisters made up their minds and decided to leave all of their worldly possessions to various charities."

"Dr. Rhodes, did Miss Diamond know about that?"

He nodded. "When the niece found out about their plans, she became enraged and vowed to see them in hell. That's what the sisters told me of that situation, anyway. I don't think they ever got the chance to change their will."

"You're right about that. Do you know any other time that the niece and the sisters argued over money—or the club?"

"Yes. One time she wanted to borrow money from them but refused to say why she needed it. When the sisters found out what the money would be used for, they refused to discuss the matter with her."

"How long ago did that happen?" I asked.

"That was just a week ago. I know, because I was over at the apartment checking on them."

"Dr. Rhodes, let me ask you a serious question."

"Go ahead."

"Do you really think Miss Diamond could kill her aunts?"

He thought for a moment, then said, "Yes, I do. I hate to say it, but I really think she killed them—or hired someone else to do the killing. Now it's your job to catch her."

"Thank you, Dr. Rhodes. You've been a big help to me. I guarantee that if the evidence points to her, I will put her in jail and throw away the key."

"I hope so," he said.

"But I need hard evidence. I can't put her in jail on hearsay or circumstantial evidence."

"Well, you know best, Detective. But please, don't hesitate to contact me anytime, day or night, especially if I'm needed to help in your investigations."

I nodded in agreement. "I will. I promise."

"You know, Detective, when I first started medical school, I moonlighted doing work in the coroner's office. And I did it without authorization or money."

"Why?"

"I did it to learn … Hoping it would help me in medical school. Which it did. I did autopsies for the state for nearly two years without being paid for my troubles."

"Why would you do that, Doc?"

"The coroner was a good friend of my father, so he let me work there. He taught me quite a bit. More than what I had learned from medical school. Of course, that's when I was a very young man."

I had heard enough. It was getting late, and I was very tired, so I thanked the doctor for his time.

# MURDER IN THE CITY PARTS I-II

"Thank you, Dr. Rhodes. I've enjoyed our conversation. And you've been a big help," I said, standing up to leave.

Before we went our separate ways, we shook hands and he handed me the tape out of his recorder. I placed it in one of my jacket pockets so I wouldn't forget to take it into work with me in the morning. I left a decent tip and walked out of the cafe to my car.

Driving home, I kept thinking about my investigations. Many different theories and suspects raced through my mind. This new information I had just learned about—and the people I had talked with and seen in the past few days—made me think even harder about a conspiracy theory. This web could possibly entangle three or four different people in the murders of Jim Palter and the Weinburg sisters. But then I thought, wait until the DNA reports on the hair fibers, semen, fluids and other forensic evidence are completed. That should narrow down my list of suspects.

When I reached my place, I was ready for a good, stiff drink. As soon as I entered my apartment, I went directly to my bottle of relaxation. The second my butt hit the cushion of my couch, I began exercising my arm. I drank shot after shot until my thoughts became one. I passed out.

When I reached my desk the next morning, there was a new pile of reports sitting there. The first one that I picked up was Miss Diamond's financial statement. I was so anxious to read it that I set the others aside to read at a later time.

As I began reading the report, I soon learned that what the doctor had told me at dinner the night before was true. Precious Diamond seemed to be in quite a financial mess. Her adult entertainment business was barely afloat, her credit rating was dismal, and she had been in debt for more than six months. And there were big discrepancies in her financial accounts. She had been doctoring the books for months to make it look as though the nudie bar was still turning a profit—but it was actually losing money big time. She had hoped to have her financial problems straightened out before anyone found out about it. But the bottom line seemed to be that if she didn't come up with some big bucks—nearly four hundred thousand dollars—the bank would foreclose on her business, mansion, and anything else she owned. Of course, now, with the inheritance of her aunts' estate, plus two large life insurance policies, I would say she had more than enough money to pay off her debts.

This report was a gold mine of information. It showed that Diamond had a very good motive indeed for killing her relatives—because they'd refused to loan or give her the money she needed to get herself out of trouble. But, as of yet, we still didn't have any forensic evidence to connect her to the crimes. Everything was circumstantial. That's why a witness to the crime was crucial. Especially if we had no murder weapon to present at trial.

I believed Miss Diamond had been involved in the murder of her aunts. She seemed the type of person that could kill someone when she didn't get her own way. Or maybe she thought that her aunts owed it to her because she was family—or because she was going to get the money anyway, after they were dead. When the Weinburg sisters still refused to give into her demands, she either killed them or had them killed—possibly using Palter's ex-business partner or the biker to help in the killings. That was a plausible scenario, but my scenarios were driving me in circles. There were just too many suspects, too many people without alibis, and too many people with a good motive for murder. I needed hard evidence.

I set the financial report to the side and began reading the next one in the stack. As I quickly glanced at the report, I nearly choked on my tongue. It was the DNA analysis report on the semen and fluid stains from the bed sheets and pillowcases. I was ecstatic. This should point to a suspect.

As I read, I tried to make sense of the findings. According to the report, the blood on the sheets and pillowcases all belonged to Jim Palter. No one else. The report stated that the DNA samples were that of Jim Palter and his female offspring. Unbelievable! He had been making love with his daughter? This report had to be wrong.

Palter didn't seem like the type of guy to want or have children. He only had feelings for himself. He was in love with himself. He wouldn't have the time for kids. And the idea that if he did have a daughter, he would have committed incest seemed unbelievable. I just couldn't believe this analysis report. None of the background reports on Palter mentioned anything about children.

I got on the phone and asked Dr. Stork, the supervisor of the lab, if this DNA analysis report on Jim Palter was correct. As far as Dr. Stork knew, it was. He told me that the lab did the test three different times. So, it had to be correct. I thanked him for his time and hung up the phone.

I still couldn't get over the fact that Jim Palter had been having sex with his own daughter. I wondered if he had known about it. If he had, he was a very sick individual. When I thought about that, it made me hate the guy even more. I was happy the bastard was dead.

Now I would have to contact his business associates and ex-business associates and anyone else that could tell me about his offspring. Then I remembered that the closest person I knew to talk with was right below my feet in the women's jail cells in the basement. I decided to ask Rita about any kids Palter might have had. This news was mind-boggling.

I quickly walked down to the basement and had the guard bring Rita to the visiting room. Rita seemed to be in another bad mood. As she entered the room, she gave me such a dirty look that it could have muddied the city's water reservoir in an instant.

We both took our seats at the small table.

"Hello, Rita," I said. "I hope you're in a good mood today."

She didn't answer me. So I pulled two packs of cigarettes out of my jacket pocket and set them on the table in front of me. Then I told her, "You can have these cigarettes, if you answer one more question about Jim Palter."

She thought about my proposition for a few seconds and then said, "Okay, what's the question?"

"Rita, do you know if Palter had any children?"

She laughed. "Hell, no. He hated children. He never wanted to have kids. What gave you the idea he had kids?"

"I got the DNA analysis report and it stated that the semen and fluid stains contained his offspring's DNA."

"Are you sure the tests were right?"

"I was told that the tests were analyzed three different times. Each time, they showed the same results. The DNA proved to be Jim Palter's offspring, which would be his daughter. Did Jim Palter ever mention a daughter? Did it ever come up in any conversations that you and he might have had?"

"When I talked with him about having a baby, he told me he was sterile and couldn't have children. He told me explicitly that he didn't have any kids and never wanted any. Then he said, 'Besides, I'm still a kid at heart.'"

"You're sure about what you're saying?"

"Yes. I don't believe he had any children. He told me he didn't. And I believed him."

"Well, thank you Rita. I'll give your cigarettes to the guard. You can get them from him." I stood up, waved goodbye to her, and then handed the packs of cigarettes to the guard.

I walked back upstairs to my desk and put the reports away in a desk drawer. I was very confused over this recent situation over the DNA reports. I had to sit down and think this out. I sat for nearly an hour, thinking about what I wanted to do next in my investigation. Then I finally decided. I would drive to Tom Walter's place of business and ask him the question. If this report were correct, Palter must have told one of his friends that he had children.

I drove across town to Walter's place of business. I was there within fifteen minutes. I anxiously walked into his building and was stopped by the receptionist.

"Yes, may I help you?" she asked.

"Yes, I'm Detective Hero. I would like to talk to Tom Walters. Is he available today?"

"I'm sorry. Mr. Walters is out of town until tomorrow afternoon. Would you like to leave your phone number? I'll have him contact you as soon as he returns," she said.

"He might already have one of these, but let me give you another one," I replied, as I handed her my business card.

I thanked her and decided to go to Cadwell's home. He might know if Palter had any children. I also wanted to ask him about his girlfriend and his friendship with Precious Diamond. If I was lucky, his girlfriend might even be there with him. Then, I could see if it was the same girl that I had seen at the cafe.

I had to drive back the way I came. Cadwell's residence was at the opposite end of town. I was there within twenty minutes. After walking up two flights of stairs, I was feeling my age. By the time I reached Cadwell's front door, I had to stop to catch my breath. That's when I noticed that the door was ajar.

I yelled Cadwell's name but received no answer. I stepped inside. I had barely taken two steps before I saw the body. I stopped in my tracks and immediately got on the phone to call the precinct and coroner's office. Palter's ex-business partner was lying naked and dead on his wooden floor, in the middle of the living room, in a pool of blood. His throat had been slashed from ear to ear and his chest was full of large knife wounds, similar to the other victims I had been investigating.

Once I had completed my phone call, I decided to wait outside the residence until the forensic investigators and coroner's staff arrived. I didn't want to contaminate the crime scene.

The coroner was the first to arrive. I showed him to the body. It was then that I noticed that besides the stab wounds, the victim's penis had been severed and placed in his left hand. After viewing the body, I believed the person that had killed this man had also killed Jim Palter. The similarities were just too perfect.

The blood trail started in the bedroom doorway, continued down the hallway, then ended in the middle of the floor of the living room. The victim's throat had most likely been cut while he was lying there because the blood spurted from his juggler vein a good five feet across the living room floor, nearly hitting the wall. And his penis was severed at the base, then placed in his left hand within a few inches from his mouth. His eyes were open and staring at his organ. This was definitely a sick scene. And there were no bloody footprints or fingerprints, which were also absent at the other murder scenes I had been investigating. However, we did find some long, blonde hairs lying near the pool of blood.

I wondered if I would be stuck with this murder investigation too. It looked like I might have a serial killer of my own. Although, I still thought Precious Diamond had killed her aunts. But I didn't think she had killed Palter.

While I investigated inside the house, I had uniformed officers canvass the neighborhood. They would have to ask questions to everyone in the immediate area. The forensic investigators had already begun collecting evidence. The coroner used special tape to outline the body, then placed it into a body bag. He placed the murder at about ten to twelve hours before I had arrived. But he said he would know more after the autopsy was performed.

I continued to look around. It looked as if nothing of value had been taken from the premises. This was the same as in my other murders. There were never any valuables stolen. In fact, this victim had had a two-carat diamond ring on his left hand and a two-carat ruby ring on the other. And his wallet contained two hundred and thirty-two dollars, along with all his credit cards—all still in his pants pocket. This definitely wasn't a robbery gone awry.

I wondered where Cadwell's girlfriend was, and if she'd had anything to do with his murder. I still didn't know who she was or even what she really looked like.

As I looked for a murder weapon, I received a call on my cell phone. It was Captain Blake. He wanted to see me immediately and wouldn't explain why. I took one last look around and then headed out, leaving the investigative teams and the coroner to work the murder scene.

## Chapter 10

By the time I walked into the station, my head was pounding. As soon as I signed in at the front desk, I went directly to Captain Blake's office. I tried shaking the pounding out of my head, but that didn't work either. Standing at the opened door, my captain invited me into his office.

"Come in, Detective Hero," said Captain Blake. "Boy, you look like crap...if you'll pardon the expression."

"Yeah, I haven't been getting much sleep, lately, working two investigations simultaneously."

"Three."

"What? No, I'm only working two murder investigations...but yes, there are three murder victims. Is that what you meant, Captain?" I asked.

"No. Now you're working three investigations," he said, looking me coldly in the eyes. "I'm letting you investigate Don Cadwell's murder."

"Why me, Captain? Why don't you take one of the other detectives off the serial killer task force so I can concentrate on my two investigations?" I asked, holding back my anger.

"You know the score. That investigation has first priority. They need all the detectives working that as they can get. I've already pulled my best detective off of that task force because I knew he could solve these murders by himself. And I know he won't let me down."

I nodded. "You're right, Captain, I won't let you down."

"I spoke to the coroner, and he believes that two, if not all three cases might be connected. He's not positive, but he's fairly certain that they are somehow linked together."

"Is that what you think, Captain?"

"That's beside the point. You are my best detective. And I want my number one investigator on this murder investigation. You'll continue working on the Palter and Weinburg murders. Is that clear?"

"Yes, sir, very clear," I said. "Thank you, sir."

"I have the utmost faith in you, Detective Hero." Before I could respond, he gave me another cold look and said, "Now get back to work."

I left the room feeling angry. But what could I do? My captain had given me an order. I sure didn't need another case on my docket. It was bad enough that I was working on two different murder investigations, alone. Now it would be three.

I still had to go to Samantha Manner's residence to talk with her about Palter's possible daughter. But right now, I needed to get back to the crime scene of Paul Donald, alias Don Cadwell. I also needed to get some fresh air to cool down.

I walked out to the parking lot and jumped into my car. I roared out of the station's parking lot and headed back to Donald's residence.

I had hoped that investigators might have found the murder weapon, but no luck. The murder weapon wasn't on the premises. The coroner's team had left for the morgue, with the body in their possession. If the coroner began the autopsy that day, I would have their preliminary report on my desk by morning. The complete autopsy report wouldn't be finished for at least two days or maybe longer. The forensic reports would take even longer. They had found a bit of evidence. They had found many fingerprints, but no bloody ones. They'd also found more long, blonde hairs.

The main witness I wanted to talk with was the victim's girlfriend. But before I met with her, I wanted to talk with Samantha Manner. It was already late. That interview would have to wait until morning.

The next morning, I woke up feeling as if I were a dirty carpet—muddy, smelly...and matted. To hide the smell of my alcoholic body odor I drenched myself with after shave lotion and cologne so my fellow detectives wouldn't notice.

I managed to get to work on time, but barely. I stumbled up the stairs to the station, then to the front desk. My eyes were still blurry, and I couldn't stay between the lines on the paper when I tried signing in. I was a mess. But a hot cup of black coffee and a stale donut would straighten my body out. I hoped so, anyway. At least the donut settled the queasiness in my stomach and the coffee woke me up a little bit.

When I finally reached my desk, I noticed that it was conspicuously absent of new reports. The reports on Don Cadwell's recent homicide investigation hadn't come in yet. We had only left the residence less than ten hours ago. It would take our investigators at least twenty-four hours to type the reports. But I still had five or six reports yet to read from the other murder investigations I was conducting. So I pulled them out of my desk drawer and set them on my desktop with the ones I had already read.

I didn't bother to sit down. I just set the reports aside and walked to the parking lot. I decided to drive to Manner's address. She would be there or house-sitting at her friend's residence, I hoped. I had to find out about Jim Palter's possible daughter. I still believed that the DNA analysis report was wrong. I didn't believe a guy like that would have or want kids. He was too much in love with himself.

I lucked out for a change. Just as I pulled up to Manner's address, I saw her unlocking her front door. She entered before I could get her attention. I quickly parked my car, then walked to her front door. I knocked on it and waited for Manner to answer. Two minutes later, she finally came to the front door.

"Good morning, Miss Manner. How are you today?" I asked, as she opened the door.

"I'm fine. What can I do for you?" she asked, stepping aside so that I could enter. "Would you like a cup of coffee while we talk?"

"That would be fine." I followed her into her kitchen and sat at her table.

"Now, what is it that you want to ask me? Is it about Jim's murder?"

"I just need to ask you a few more questions about him in light of some new developments. Miss Manner, did you know if Jim had any children...or talked about any children that he may have had?"

I watched as her faced turned a pale white, as though she had just seen a ghost.

"Why do you ask that?" she said, turning away.

"We have some information that leads me to believe that he may have had children. Did he ever mention anything about children?"

"No, he never spoke about having children. He didn't know he had children."

"What? What do you mean 'he didn't know he had children'? Miss Manner, what did you mean by that?"

"Did I say that? It must have been a Freudian slip. You know ... a slip of the tongue. I meant to say...he didn't like children. Anyway, why are you so interested in his kids?"

"Well, we have reason to believe that his offspring might be involved in his murder. The DNA analysis showed that the fluid stains on the bed sheets were that of his female offspring. If that's true, he was having intercourse with his own daughter."

"Oh, no. I don't believe this." She began sobbing.

"What's wrong, Miss Manner? What is it? Did you know he was having relations with his own daughter? Is that what's making you so upset?"

She shook her head. "No, I don't think he knew that the female he was supposedly having sex with was his daughter. He didn't know he had a daughter."

"Why do you say that? How did you know he had a daughter when he didn't even know?"

"She was *my* daughter!"

"What? What are you saying, Miss Manner? You and Palter had a daughter together? Is that it?"

She nodded. "Yes. Twenty-five years ago, Jim Palter and I were high school sweethearts. While we were going steady, I became pregnant with his child, but I never told him. He never knew I was pregnant."

"Why not?"

"I had taken my savings out of the bank so we could get married and get our own place to live. Once we had found our love nest, then I was going to tell him that I was pregnant. But then I found out...he only wanted me for my money."

"Why do you say that, Miss Manner?" I asked.

"When my money ran out, Jim ran all the way to California, then to Missouri, without ever knowing that he was going to be a father."

"So, what did you do?"

"I stayed behind and had the baby. I didn't have any money or know how to raise a baby, so I did the best thing for the baby and gave her up for adoption."

"Did you get to see your baby, or was she taken away immediately?"

"When she was born, I was allowed to hold my daughter for about two minutes before she was taken away from me.

I never again got to hold her." Tears streamed down her cheeks.

"Miss Manner, couldn't you get visitations to see your daughter?"

"No. I wasn't able to contact her or know who had adopted her. Nor was I allowed to know where she was living."

"Why not? Couldn't the adoption agency help you?"

"The records were sealed for life and couldn't be opened. Not even by an act of god. So I never had any reason to tell Jim about her birth."

"Were you ever going to tell the father that he had a child?"

"If we had ever gotten married, I might have mentioned it. But my mother made me push the birth out of my mind."

"Your own mother didn't want you to remember that you had a daughter?"

"Yes. That was the first thing my mother made me promise her. That I would never say a word about my baby. After a while, her birth had become just a dream."

"Was Jim Palter a dream, also, Miss Manner?"

"Yes. When Jim left me and ran to another state, I didn't hear from him again for almost twenty-five years, and I had forgotten him. Then a few weeks ago, I was with him, once again. But our recent relationship didn't last too long, either."

"Did you tell him about his daughter, then?"

"No. I never got up the nerve."

"Why?"

"I didn't want to cause him any more problems than we already had. He didn't want kids. He had told me that...many, many times during our relationship. Whenever I mentioned having a baby, he wanted no part of it. That's why I believe he never knew he had any children."

"Well, he might have."

"What do you mean?" she asked.

"Miss Manner, I mean, your daughter may have found out that she was having sex with her own father. When she realized this, she stormed into a rage and killed him."

"So you actually think my daughter had something to do with Jim Palter's murder? I don't believe it." She remained silent for nearly a minute and then blurted out, "Maybe neither one knew that they were related. Isn't that a possibility?"

"That is possible. But my gut says otherwise. The way Palter was killed, the murderer was filled with rage...and lots of it."

"I just don't believe the DNA results. It must be an error. They should test the evidence again. I don't believe any of this."

"Neither did I at first. That is, until I checked with the lab. They tested the evidence three different times. The tests don't lie."

"Well, you should still ask for confirmation, again. I still say they are wrong," she snapped.

I changed the subject to calm things down. "Miss Manner, is it true that your daughter would now be approximately twenty-five years of age?"

"Yes. She will be twenty-five on the twenty-eighth of this month. But, I haven't seen or heard from her since she was born, and I never knew my daughter's adopted parents. But I really thought my daughter was dead," she said, drying her eyes with a Kleenex.

"Well, you answered my questions, so I guess I've taken up enough of your time."

"Does this mean that I'm no longer a suspect in Jim's murder?"

"It seems that way for now, Miss Manner. The evidence seems to be pointing in another direction. But I'll keep in touch with you."

I let myself out.

Once home, I was relieved to be able to pour myself a drink. And then another. And another.

I slept straight through till morning and had just enough time to drink a cup of hot, black coffee before leaving for work. I could barely see straight. My head pounded from the night before, but I had to find the strength to delve back into my three murder investigations. There were still many, many questions to be asked and answered.

When I finished my coffee, I decided to read the rest of my investigative reports. I had just picked up the stack when my desk phone rang. I answered it.

"Hello. This is Detective Hero of Homicide."

"Hello, Detective," said the female voice on the other end of the telephone. "Right now, my name isn't important. I don't know if you are the right person to speak with, but the operator transferred me to you. I'll explain my situation, and then you can decide if I should speak with you or someone else. Is that all right with you, Detective?"

"That's fine. Continue."

"It might take a few minutes to tell my story, so just bear with me and be patient. I won't take any longer than I have to," said the mysterious female voice.

"Very well."

"My name is Mrs. Marion Weltman. My story begins when a young girl had a baby girl. In fact, she was a baby having a baby—and too young to care for a baby. The director of the girl's home, where she had given birth, talked her into giving the baby up for adoption. He had found a very affluent and rich, infertile couple that wanted to adopt a healthy baby. The nurse allowed the young mother to hold her child for two minutes and then she was taken away from her. Then the doctor shot the birth mother up with morphine for six consecutive days so her pregnancy would seem like a dream to her...and it worked."

She continued telling me the story. She talked for nearly an hour before I was able to get a word into the conversation, but I listened with great interest.

The couple had given the doctor twenty thousand dollars for their gift of love. Then, the doctor had a friend, who happened to be the local judge, seal the records of the girl's adoption. It would be almost impossible for anyone to unseal the records. You would need a special court order to get the file reopened, even now.

The adopted parents never told their daughter that she was adopted. They told her that they were her real parents. The court had the adoption files sealed, but the doctor that was involved in the adoption gave the adoptive parents the child's real birth certificate and one that was a counterfeit. The phony certificate had the adoptive parents as the birth parents. And it was up to them to decide what they would tell their child, if and when that time ever came. It was the couple's responsibility to destroy or not to destroy the true birth certificate. But, they couldn't decide, so they kept both certificates hidden under lock and key—or so they thought.

The child grew up to be a spoiled but bright young woman. She was given anything and everything she wanted, within reason, of course. She had been a brilliant high school and college student and graduated third in her class from an expensive and well-known Ivy League college. She got along well with her parents—or so said the adopted mother. But then everything changed the day her daughter found a locked metal box while cleaning out a closet, which contained both birth certificates and other papers. She also found the adoption papers, plus a letter that the birth mother had written while at the hospital stating the name of the father, and the receipt for the twenty thousand dollars that the adopted parents had paid the doctor.

The adopted parent's whole world turned upside down from that day forward. Their daughter fretted around the house day by day, becoming very upset and very angry. She just couldn't get the adoption out of her mind. She kept ranting and raving about how her birth mother sold her, as if she were a piece of meat. The young girl kept referring to her biological mother as a "monster." Saying, only a monster could give her away. She became so angry that she could no longer hold it within.

According to Mrs. Weltman, the day her daughter found those papers was the day her daughter's personality and attitude changed—completely opposite of her quiet and nice disposition. She became someone they didn't know anymore. She dropped out of graduate school. She became distraught and uncontrollable. She began cursing and talking back to her adopted parents—something she had never done before. It was like she had turned into an evil twin. Her adopted parents tried to reason with her, but she just lashed out at them with profanity and violence. And she threatened them, daily. She also threatened to find her birth mother and kill her. And her birth father, too, if she could find him. I continued to listen to Marion Weltman's story.

"I was beginning to worry that she might actually do what she was threatening to do. She was going to find her birth mother and father. She was going to hunt them down, then kill them," she said.

"Mrs. Weltman, do you really think she will keep her promise? You really believe she has it in her to kill?" I asked.

"I'm not real sure. But the more she ranted and raved about killing her birth parents, the scarier she became. Then one day...we got into an argument. I can't remember now what it was about. But she stormed out of the house and never returned."

"Did you hear from her again?"

"I thought she would have phoned to let me know that she was all right. She has been gone now for over a month. I never thought she would put her crazy idea into motion."

"Mrs. Weltman, what is your daughter's name?"

"Elaine. Elaine Weltman."

"So, why do you think she's going to kill her birth mother?"

"Because I found her diary in her jewelry box, and it detailed her whole plan. She found out that her birth mother had moved a thousand miles away, to Missouri."

"How did she find that out?"

"From her biological grandmother. Elaine had found her name in the letter her birth mother had written while in the hospital and called her. The woman gave her an address and other information, inadvertently, not knowing who she was or why she wanted it. I'm fairly certain the old woman didn't know who was calling her."

"So then what happened, Mrs. Weltman?"

"My daughter took all her life savings out of her bank and closed her account. I'm afraid she has gone to Missouri to look up her birth mother and possibly her birth father, if she can find them. Then she plans to kill them both."

"What is your daughter's birth mother's name ... And are you sure she traveled to Missouri? This is quite a big state."

"Her birth mother's name is Samantha Manner. And the birth father's name is Jim Palter. They both live in your city." The woman paused, then said, "Please find my little girl and stop her before she does something stupid—something she'll regret for the rest of her life."

She was pleading for her adopted daughter's life. But it may have been too late. She may have already killed her birth father. But it wasn't too late to warn Samantha Manner.

"Excuse me, Mrs. Weltman. I will need you to fax me a recent photo of your daughter. Please leave your name, address, and phone number where you can be reached if an emergency arises. I'm going to transfer this call. Give the information to the person who answers. He will also give you the fax number for sending the photo of your daughter to our precinct. This is very important, so don't hang up until you give someone that information. Right now, I need to make an urgent phone call to your adopted daughter's birth mother, to warn her to be on the lookout for her daughter."

"You mean you have the birth mother's telephone number? Do you know her?"

"Yes. I have interviewed her in an investigation that I'm working on. So please, I must go now. I must make the phone call to Samantha Manner," I said, and then transferred the call.

Once I was done with the transfer, I quickly dialed Miss Manner's telephone number, but the line was busy. I decided to drive over to her residence to tell her in person. Five minutes later, I was sitting behind the wheel of my car heading straight for Samantha Manner's address to warn her about this ungodly situation. I had to tell her that her own biological daughter was looking to find her and kill her.

I had a gut feeling that something was wrong. I didn't know what, but I just didn't feel right. But I thought that if the phone was busy, she must still be alive. She had to be alive; she was talking on the telephone. This thought and many others, not as optimistic, were running through my mind.

I raced to her address, weaving in and out of heavy traffic. Fifteen minutes later, I was standing at her front door. I knocked on it and waited for her to answer, but nobody came.

By this time, the neighbors had gathered in front of Manner's house to see what all the commotion was about. I shouted to the crowd that I was a detective. After waiting five more minutes with no answer, I decided to try the door to see if it would open. Sure enough, it was unlocked. I opened it and peeked inside.

"Samantha? Samantha Manner," I called out. "Are you in there?" Still no answer...so I entered the premises.

I took about four steps into the hallway, then looked to the left. I stopped in my tracks. Someone—whom I assumed to be Samantha Manner—was lying on the floor, in the middle of the living room, in a large pool of blood. She seemed to be dead, her body frozen into position, but I didn't check because I didn't want to contaminate the crime scene. I was certain, however, that she was dead and had been dead for quite a while. Then I noticed something quite odd. This body had no head—at least not one that was attached to its shoulders. Then I saw it just sitting a few feet away on a small table. That was it. I had seen enough.

# MURDER IN THE CITY PARTS I-II

I quickly turned around and left the room. I walked outside and used my police radio to call the crime into dispatch, then used my cell phone to call the boys at the lab. This was getting to be a habit. First, I contacted the forensic investigators, then made another call to the coroner's office. Once they were notified, I sat outside on the porch and waited for the investigative teams to arrive, along with the uniformed police officers.

A few of the patrol units that were in the vicinity had heard the call over their radios and immediately headed to the crime scene. Within ten minutes, the first of six police cars arrived at the scene. After briefing them, the uniformed officers began canvassing the immediate neighborhood, interviewing some of the neighbors standing in the victim's front yard. A few minutes after the first police car arrived on the scene, the coroner and forensic investigators arrived.

I entered the victim's residence with the coroner and showed him the body. It was so mangled and bloody that it was hard to tell if the body was that of a male or female. It had been slaughtered, like a steer that had just been butchered at a slaughterhouse. The murder scene made one want to regurgitate. It also made me very angry. I couldn't believe one human being could do this to another.

I figured I would be assigned to this murder investigation, also. This one seemed to be connected with the Palter murder case. Now, I would be investigating five murders. I had a feeling I would rap this murder investigation up in a hurry. As soon as I received the photo of the young girl, I would put an APB out for her for questioning. She was now the primary suspect in at least one murder, if not two or even more.

The coroner found long, blonde hairs at this murder scene, too—this time in the closed hand of Samantha

Manner. The investigators worked around the clock. It was déjà vu all over again. We had just played the same game two days before. But, there was one main discrepancy between this murder scene and the last. This murder victim's head had been completely severed from its body and placed upon a small end table with its eyes looking down at its headless body. The chest was covered in stab wounds, just like my other victims. This killer—loved to mutilate. The one responsible for this murder was one sick, sick individual.

I continued to watch as the coroner lifted and turned the headless body of the female murder victim. The breasts were sunken deep into the chest cavity...because the chest was one big open hole. There were knife wounds all the way from the shoulders to the pubic mound. Each leg had been stabbed numerous times, also. Two of the victim's toes from her left foot were cut off, with just a small stump showing. Both hands had deep cuts—which resulted from trying to fend off her attacker's knife blows—and one finger on her right hand was hanging by a thin piece of muscle.

The coroner's assistant picked up the victim's head from the end table and placed it into a black plastic bag. Then he placed the rest of the victim's body into a body bag. The body had been dead for nearly eight hours. She had been killed sometime during the night or early in the morning. The coroner could tell me more once he completed the autopsy. He had just completed the last murder victim's autopsy a few hours ago. Now, he was doing another one. Boy, I just hoped these murders didn't continue. If not for the coroner's sake, at least, for mine.

I stayed behind at the murder scene with the forensic investigators and the photographer, while the coroner's team left for the morgue. By the time we had bottled up the crime scene, it was well past midnight. I didn't get into bed until nearly two in the morning. I drank two quick shots of liquor before I finally retired to bed. And I went to sleep in my bed for a change. However, I was dead tired when I awoke in the morning.

It was getting late, so I quickly showered, dried myself off, and then dressed for work. I didn't shave. Being this tired, I might have cut my own throat. But I did have time to make some toast to go with my cup of black coffee. This was my miracle day. It was a miracle that I wasn't waking up with a hangover. I felt like a new man. I drove to work and entered the station with a big smile on my face instead of fighting a pounding headache.

I was able to sign my name in the correct area on the sign-in sheet at the front desk for once. Then, instead of stumbling to the snack table, I walked in a fairly straight line. I poured myself my second cup of black coffee and grabbed a jelly donut to eat. I carried them to my desk without spilling a drop of my coffee or picking my donut off the floor.

As I sat in my chair procrastinating, my thoughts crept back to Samantha Manner's murder investigation. I hoped the photo of my murder suspect had been faxed by now. I still had three reports left to read on the first two murder investigations.

Twenty minutes later, I checked for the photo of Elaine Weltman, but it still hadn't come over the fax machine. I needed a face to go with the name. If the photo didn't come in by lunchtime, I was going to phone Mrs. Weltman to remind her about sending me the photo of her adopted daughter. If, for some reason, she didn't have a fax machine, I would ask her to go to the closest police station in her city and send it from their fax machine. However, I'd give her a few more hours.

I began reading the last of my investigative reports on the first two murder scenes. The first report was the DNA analysis of the long blonde hairs found at the Palter murder scene. They matched the DNA of the semen stains found on the bed sheet and pillowcases. The next report stated that the DNA from the hairs found in the Weinburg sister's hand also contained the same DNA as the semen found at the Palter murder scene, as did the cigarette butt found at the Weinburg sisters' murder scene. In my mind this connected the cases to one killer.

Just as I was about to read the last and final investigative report, Captain Blake stopped by and told me that I had been given the Manner murder investigation. Not because he thought the same killer had committed the murders, but because the serial killer task force was too overwhelmed with their investigation and he couldn't afford to take anyone off of that crew. In return, I thanked him for the honor and for being such a nice guy.

When he left, I went back to reading my last report on the Palter murders. It was the one I had been waiting for—the FBI lab report. They had found one partial fingerprint on the butcher knife found in the garbage Dumpster near the Admore apartments. The partial fingerprint was found on the bottom of the handle. The rest had possibly been wiped off. The technicians had to use a special type of laser to find the print. It matched the fingerprint found at the Palter murder scene...but it wasn't found in their database. They couldn't identify its owner. This person, evidently, had no criminal history.

Just then, the fax machine lit up and spit out the photo I had been waiting for. Now I had a face to go with a name. The woman in the photo was the same girl that I had seen at the cafe. I had been right. There was a connection to the Palter murder. Possibly the Weinburg sisters as well.

She was also the main suspect in Samantha Manner's murder. This girl had allegedly just killed her biological mother, her biological father, and possibly the Weinburg sisters. Now, I had to check the reports to see if she could also be a suspect in the Cadwell murder.

I figured the girl had gone berserk when she found out she had been given up for adoption. In a way, I felt sorry for her. Now, I could put an APB out for her. She was wanted for questioning in at least one murder...and possibly others. The evidence seemed to point that way. But what could be her motive for the Cadwell murder? That question and many, many more were running through my head, such as why were there only a few hairs in the hands of these victims? If I had grabbed the hair of my killer, I would have pulled out a big chunk of it, not just a few hairs. But, I didn't dwell on it for very long. I was glad to have any hairs for evidence.

I sat back to relax and reflect on the past few weeks of investigating. I was quite happy with myself. I knew I had at least one murder investigation wrapped up, if not more. But, I didn't want to seem too arrogant and excited. The other detectives in my department were already avoiding me. I wasn't one of the gang anymore. I wasn't in their task force, so I was off limits. And now that I was about to nab a very bad and evil criminal, they still neglected my presence. I just ignored them. They acted like little children. And I was just doing my job.

My thoughts were suddenly interrupted when an investigator from the Forensic Science department stopped by and handed me a new stack of reports. I quickly glanced through them. Included were the crime scene analysis reports on Cadwell and Manner. However, I didn't see any more reports on the Weinburg or Palter murder investigations. That was fine with me...because I had narrowed down my search for their murderer—which I now believed to be Elaine Weltman. And I felt fairly certain that Cadwell's murder had also been committed by her. Heck, if I could get enough circumstantial evidence to go along with the fingerprint and hair fiber evidence, she could probably be charged in all four of my murder investigations. But what could her motive be for killing a guy like Cadwell—or the Weinburg sisters? I knew the motive for Palter and Manner's murders—hatred—that is, if I could prove that Weltman was their killer. And maybe, if we got lucky, we'd find the knife that had killed Manner, hopefully in Weltman's possession. That would really close the lid on her coffin.

What a misguided child, I thought. By now, every patrol car should have had the photo of Elaine Weltman. I had put out an APB. Now it was just a matter of time before she was picked up.

Suddenly my thoughts were interrupted once again, but this time by hunger—my stomach was grumbling. I decided to head down to the cafe. Maybe I would get lucky enough to run into my suspect. But that would have been too easy. Naturally, Elaine Weltman wasn't there.

I sat at my usual table and ordered my steak and cheese hoagies. I finished my meal and then waited around the cafe for an extra hour, hoping that Weltman would show up. But it just didn't happen. I waited as long as I could before I had to return to the station. I reminded Bonnie to phone me immediately the minute my suspect entered the cafe.

I returned to the station in a happy mood. That was a rare occasion for me. I sat at my desk and read more reports. I began with the preliminary autopsy reports. But after reading a paragraph, I had to pick out a different report. My stomach couldn't handle it—especially the words telling about the degradation and mutilation of the victims. I read the fingerprint report instead.

Many of the fingerprints that were found at the residences of Palter, Cadwell, and the Weinburg sisters also showed up at the Manner residence. But there were never any bloody fingerprints—or bloody footprints—found at any of the murder scenes. But one thing was for certain...we had the murder weapon that killed Jim Palter, with Elaine Weltman's fingerprint on the handle. Now, I hoped to find the murder weapon she used on her birth mother.

But I still wondered about the motive. What could have angered Weltman enough to murder and mutilate the Weinburg sisters? Or Cadwell? Then I wondered if Weltman had tried to kill anyone else. Like, maybe Palter's business partner, Tom Walters. Did she go after him—and he just got lucky and missed her bloody wrath of terror—or did she want to hurt him at all?

I tried putting all the pieces of the puzzle together. But the question of a motive still kept popping up in my mind. I kept asking myself ... Why? When we caught her, I would ask her that question and many more, I thought to myself.

I needed a breath of fresh air, so I walked over to the snack table to stretch my legs. I grabbed a custard-filled donut and poured myself a cup of black coffee. I was in one of the best moods I had been in, in quite a long time. I couldn't remember the last time that I'd smiled or laughed. I was definitely happy. Why? Because I honestly believed that one or two of my murder investigations were about to come to a close. I was elated as I thought about arresting the murder suspect, jailing her, and then throwing away the key.

I drank my coffee slowly, using it to wash down another donut. My body deserved the short time away from my desk. All the gory details in those reports could make a man shiver in his boots. I needed time to relax my overworked and overtired brain. It was near quitting time, anyway. And I really didn't feel like reading those disgusting reports any longer.

I decided to leave work early and take in an early dinner at my favorite cafe. I would continue reading the reports in the morning, when I could get a fresh start at it. I just had to get away. So I left the station and then drove to the café, which took about ten minutes.

As I opened the café's front door, a tall, lanky, beautiful, blonde-haired female was exiting. We bumped into each other. I looked at her, beginning to apologize, and in that moment I recognized the woman for whom I had been searching. She was my murder suspect, Elaine Weltman.

I grabbed her by the wrists and twisted her arms behind her back. As she screamed for help, I handcuffed her hands together. She continued to yell and scream as I read her the Miranda warning. I tried calming her down, but it was of no use. She was very upset. She couldn't understand why she was being arrested.

Using my cell phone, I called for a patrol car. The uniformed officers would take her back to the station for booking, where I could question her more thoroughly. I wanted a confession from her. I wanted her to confess to the Palter murder...and any others that she may have wanted to get off her chest.

Within just a few minutes, the officers were leading Weltman to a waiting patrol car. I watched as they drove away, all the while my suspect screaming obscenities. I thought I would have been happy with the outcome, but I was actually saddened. I had wanted to meet with her for weeks and now, when I did finally meet her, I had choked up; all I could say to her was: "You have the right to remain silent, and anything you say, can and will be used against you in a court of law."

I decided to let my suspect cool her heels for the night in our beautiful jail—and think about her predicament. I would go home and think about her predicament, too. But I'd also be exercising my arm by drinking shots of scotch. For me, this was a night of celebration. Or was it?

I hugged the bottle of scotch close to my bosom as I carried it into the living room. Once on the couch, I poured shot after shot and tossed them down my gullet just as fast as I poured them. When I reached twenty-five, I quit counting. I emptied one bottle and then another. Soon after, I passed out.

Once again, I awoke with a splitting headache and little time to waste. If I didn't hurry, I would be late for work.

I gulped down a hot cup of black coffee as I washed up and straightened out the wrinkles in my disheveled clothes. I had expected to be fresh and lively for this morning's interview with my female suspect, Elaine Weltman. But instead, I was running in slow motion. Footsteps sounded like pounding jackhammers. But like the old soldier that I was, I would pull it all together by the time I had my interview—or should I say my interrogation—with my female suspect.

# Chapter 11

As I walked into the station, I noticed my peers staring at me. Suddenly, a few of the homicide detectives volunteered to be my partner in the interrogation. Now I was the center of attention. Before, I had been the butt of their jokes, or they had ignored my presence. Now, they were acting as though they were my best friends. I took a lesson out of their book and just ignored them. I was going to get this collar on my own.

I walked over to the snack table and grabbed a jelly-filled donut, then poured myself a cup of black coffee. As I walked to my desk, I felt the eyes of my peers upon me. I wallowed in their envy. Now, it was my turn to gloat.

I geared my mind to the present situation. I still had a lot of hard work ahead of me and a big job to do. I had to get a confession out of my female suspect using my charm and intelligence—not by force or aggressive behavior. I wanted her to like me. I wanted to be her friend.

By the time I finished my coffee and donut, I had become re-energized. Now, I was ready to interrogate my female suspect. I was both eager and anxious to question her. Two weeks ago, I had wanted to talk with her, to get to know her, but not in this fashion.

While sitting and gathering my thoughts, a uniformed officer walked up to me and handed me a large object in a clear, plastic evidence bag. When my bloodshot eyes finally focused on the object, I noticed that it was a large butcher knife, similar to the murder weapon found in the garbage bin near the Admore apartments. The officer told me that they had taken it from my suspect's purse while they were booking her.

I thanked him and had him take it to the forensics lab for final analysis. The report should be completed in a day or two, depending on their workload. I hoped it was the actual murder weapon used in Samantha Manner's murder. No wonder the guys were falling all over me; they thought I had my murder investigations all wrapped up. Now, they wanted some recognition for themselves. *Sorry*, I thought. *This is my show.*

I telephoned the jailer and told her to have Elaine Weltman escorted to the interrogating room.

When I saw her, she was already wearing an orange jump suit, given by the county to all new inmates. I couldn't understand why her hands were handcuffed in front of her chest and chained to leg irons. She hadn't been convicted, yet. And she didn't seem to be much of a threat. She couldn't have weighed more than a hundred and ten pounds, soaking wet. And the leg shackles stifled her movement; she didn't walk, but shuffled along. She didn't look so beautiful, now. And she seemed angry rather than frightened. Seeing her this way...saddened me.

I stood in silence as she was directed into the interrogating room. I watched as she shuffled past me, the chains clanging together in a song of despair and sorrow. The female guard showed her where to sit, then pushed her into the chair. I questioned the guard concerning the leg irons and handcuffs. I explained to her that the female suspect hadn't been convicted yet, and didn't seem to be much of a threat. But the guard maintained that she had been ordered by her superiors not to let the suspect escape, under any circumstances.

I asked the guard to unlock and remove my suspect's handcuffs and leg irons, but the guard at first refused my request. However, after a little prodding, she at least agreed to remove the handcuffs. I didn't want to argue or cause any problems, so I let the leg irons stay on. Then the guard and I left the room.

I watched my suspect's reaction from the mirrored window in the adjacent room. She looked like a scared little girl. I stood and watched her for a few minutes before returning to the interrogating room. And I interrogated her alone. Even though I had a number of fellow detectives offering their expertise and help in interrogating the suspect, I declined. I wanted to do this job alone.

There was a dead silence as I entered the interrogating room and walked to my chair. Before I sat down, I turned the tape recorder on to record our conversation and hopefully, Weltman's confession. Then I began my questioning.

"Hello, Miss Weltman. Your name is Elaine Weltman, isn't it?" I asked.

"Yes, that's my name. ... Now can you tell me what I've been arrested for? I've never been arrested in my life," she said, tears coming down her cheeks.

"We're holding you for suspicion of murder."

She snapped, "Suspicion of murder? I don't know what you're talking about."

"You've been given your Miranda warning, haven't you?"

"Yes, I know my rights. But I haven't done anything wrong." She slapped the tabletop with her hand.

"You know, Miss Weltman, you are allowed to have counsel with you during questioning. You do know that, don't you?" I asked, wanting to do everything by the book.

"I told you, I didn't do anything wrong. So I don't need a lawyer. ... I just want to leave here and go back east," she exclaimed, wiping away her tears with her hands.

"Miss Weltman, I just need to clear up a few things to clarify some important issues. You want to help me clear them up, don't you?"

"Of course. I want to help any way I can. ... And please, call me Elaine," she said in a calm, soothing voice.

"Elaine, would you like a soda or a cigarette before I begin the questioning?"

"I don't really smoke, but yes, I would like a cigarette."

I pulled the pack from my shirt pocket, gave her a cigarette and lit it for her. She took a long drag and suddenly began coughing.

"Are you okay?" I asked her.

She nodded and replied, "See, I told you I don't smoke much."

"Okay. Elaine, my first question I need to ask is this: When did you arrive in our beautiful state?"

"I came out here over a month ago."

"Where did you start your travels from? ... Why did you come out here?"

"I came out here ... for a vacation. I have friends out here."

"Your vacation is a month long? Are you on a paid vacation from work?"

"No, I came out on my own. I paid my own way."

"Boy, I wish I could afford a month long vacation," I joked.

"I just started looking for a job. And then you arrested me."

"What state did you start your journey from, Elaine?"

"I traveled from back east—more than a thousand miles north of here."

"Why the sudden urge to travel? Why not go somewhere warm, like Florida? Why pick our state?"

"Well, I told you...I have friends out here," she replied, then took a long drag from her cigarette. "I was in the process of looking for them when you arrested me."

"What are their names? I'll help you locate them," I told her.

"That's all right. I'll find them myself," she snapped.

"I don't think you'll have the time. At least, not for a while." Suddenly, the room became silent. Weltman stared at the floor. She seemed to be deep in thought, so I broke the silence.

"Elaine, would you like something to drink or eat? Can I offer you another cigarette?" I asked, just as she put hers out. I handed her a pack of filter cigarettes from my coat pocket, the same brand as the butt that was found at the Weinburg murder scene. I wanted to see if she smoked that brand.

She looked at the pack, pulled a cigarette from it, and said, "This is the kind I smoke. That is, when I feel like a cigarette. How did you know what brand I liked?" Then she placed the cigarette between her lips and waited for me to light it for her.

I just smiled and lit her cigarette. "What else can I get you, Elaine? Would you like a sandwich from the vending machine?"

"Yeah ... Egg salad, if they got it. And a root beer soda and bag of potato chips." Then she took a deep drag on her cigarette and coughed once again.

I left the room to get her some food and a drink. I had the female guard keep an eye on her while I was gone.

Weltman's eyes lit up as I returned with an armful of goodies—everything she had asked for. I handed her a soda, an egg salad sandwich, and a small bag of potato chips. I even allowed her to eat her meal before I started the questioning again.

That didn't take long. Within two minutes, she had consumed it all. Then she pulled another cigarette from the pack and put it to her lips...so I lit it for her. She took a long, deep drag while I waited patiently until she was ready to talk.

"Thank you," she said. "I hadn't eaten since yesterday afternoon. ... Just before you arrested me. Now I would like to know, why have I been arrested?"

"I told you. Suspicion of murder."

"I can't believe I'm in here on suspicion of murder. ... Is that why I'm in leg shackles and handcuffs?"

"Miss Weltman, I mean, Elaine, you're right. We're actually holding you for murder, not suspicion of murder," I said, looking deep into her eyes.

"Tell me. Who am I supposed to have killed? I've never been arrested for anything in my life."

"Well, I guess there's always a first time."

"Do I need a lawyer?" she asked, in between sips of her soda.

I quickly changed the subject. I wanted to control this interrogation and ask *her* the questions, not some lawyer.

"When was the last time you talked with your family?" I asked.

Before she could answer, I heard a loud commotion outside the interrogation room. I apologized to Weltman and went to find out what was happening. As I exited the room, I looked to the left and saw a large crowd of nosey detectives. They were crowded around the mirrored window so they could look in on my interrogation without being seen. This pissed me off.

"Come on, guys, let me do my job," I pleaded. "And you guys should be doing yours."

Reluctantly, the detectives gave into my demands and slowly walked back to their desks.

I returned to the interrogating room with at least one victory. And was about to get another one, shortly—that is, if I played my cards right.

As I took my seat, I apologized once again to my suspect. "Elaine, I'm sorry for the interruption. ... Now let's get back to the interview. I still have a few questions to ask you. Like ... when did you last talk with your family?"

"I don't have a family," she snarled.

"Do you know that your mother is worried sick about you?" I said, shaking my head. "She doesn't want to see you throw your life away. ... But it's too late for that, isn't it?" I asked her, trying to get a reaction.

"My real family gave me up for money."

"What do you mean?" I asked, already knowing the answer.

"I was worth twenty thousand dollars to my birth parents. I guess that's what a baby was going for on the black market in those days."

"Elaine, are you saying that you were adopted?"

"Yes," she replied angrily. "But...no one ever told me that I was adopted. My parents let me live a lie—my entire life."

"What are you saying?"

"They let me believe that I was their natural born child. They tried hiding the truth from me."

"So how did you find out you were adopted?"

"Fate intervened!" she replied in a rather loud and angry voice. "I found the adoption papers and a phony birth certificate. I also found my real birth certificate with the names of my birth parents on it. They didn't want me, so they sold me for a measly twenty thousand dollars. So, I left my adopted parents and came out here to find my friends."

"Elaine, are they the only ones you came out here to see?"

She nodded. "Yes. Between looking for a job and looking for my friends, I didn't have the time to look for anyone else."

"Your adopted mother seems to think otherwise," I told her, sympathetically.

"Why? Did you talk with my mother?"

"Yes, I did. We had a rather long conversation."

"What did my mother have to say?" She seemed genuinely concerned.

"She said you came out here to find your birth mother. Is that true?"

"What if it is?" she snapped. "There isn't a law against it, is there?"

"Only when it includes murder," I said, leaning forward.

"I told you. I didn't kill anyone. ... I'm innocent!" she ranted.

"Okay. Let's get back to your biological mother. ... You did say you came out here to find her, didn't you, Elaine?" I asked, as she blew cigarette smoke into my face.

"Yes, I wanted to find her. But not for the reason of killing her." She lit another cigarette from the butt of the other, then quickly threw the butt on the floor.

"What were you going to do once you'd found your birth mother? Were you going to take her into your arms and hug her to death?"

She shrugged. "I just wanted to talk to her. I wanted to see what she looked like. ... But what I really wanted was to ask her why she'd sold me." Weltman took another drag from her cigarette.

"Do you really think she sold you because she needed the money?"

"Yes, I do. I found the receipt, along with some other adoption papers."

"Elaine, you said you found your birth certificate. Did it have your father's real name on it? Did your mother use his true identity when she signed the name of the father?"

"Yes, she signed a name, which I presumed was my real father's. Because that same name was also mentioned in a letter given to my adopted mother from the doctor, who had gotten it from my birth mother."

Now I was getting to the real nitty-gritty. "What was the name of your birth father that was written on your birth certificate and mentioned in the letter?"

She didn't answer immediately. Instead, she stared at the floor, puffing away on her cigarette. But then, a minute later, the silence was broken. In a barely audible voice, she said, "The father's name signed on my birth certificate was Jim Palter."

"Elaine, did you know your father was living out here, too, when you decided to leave your home state to find your birth mother?"

"No, I didn't know he was out here."

"Come now," I said, leaning back and eyeing her skeptically. "We found your fingerprints in his apartment."

"Yes, but I just found out his last name."

"Why is that?"

"When I met him, he was going by another name. He wasn't using the name of Jim Palter."

"What do you mean? What name did he go by?"

"I didn't know him as Jim Palter. I knew him as Jim Webber," she stated matter-of-factly.

"So, you just learned about his fraud?" I asked.

"Yes. But I didn't know about it until I found a bag full of phony identification, sitting in his commode drawer. He had a number of driver's licenses, showing the same photo but different last names. He also had other phony identification cards—from the gas company to the phone company."

"So how did you find out his true identity? How did you find out his name was Jim Palter?"

"I'll tell you...if you'll stop interrupting me and let me finish," she snapped.

"I'm sorry, Elaine. I won't interrupt you again. So please ... Continue."

"Like I said. I knew him as Jim Webber, not Jim Palter. When I found his phony identification cards, I also found, in that bag, Jim's wallet and his real driver's license."

"How did you determine that the driver's license in his wallet was his real one, with all the other phony driver's licenses he had?"

"It looked professionally made. At least at the time, I figured it was his true identity."

"So it was *then* that you found out his true identity?"

"Yes. And I believed his real name was the one on his driver's license—the one I found in his wallet."

"Which was?" I asked.

"The name that was signed on that driver's license was Jim Palter. That's when I put two and two together and figured out that he had misled me," she said, taking her last drag from her cigarette before lighting another.

"When was that? Elaine, do you remember what day that was?" I asked, looking deep into her eyes.

"It was the last day I saw him," she replied, looking down at the floor.

"What day was that?"

"I believe it was on a Sunday evening, but I'm not sure about that," she said, nervously, biting her fingernails. ... "I do know, a day or two after I left him, I found out he was dead."

"You mean, when you put two and two together, you knew then that the man you thought was your boyfriend was actually your father. Isn't that what you meant to say?" I asked, leaning across the table, our faces nearly touching as I looked into her eyes.

"No, not at all," she replied, moving her face back, away from mine.

"Elaine, when you found his wallet and driver's license and saw his last name was really Palter and not Webber, you knew then, that he could be your birth father, didn't you?"

She turned her head away from my prying eyes, then, speaking in a soft, low voice, she said, "I suspected he might be."

"I'm sorry Elaine, I can't hear you. Would you repeat the answer into the tape recorder, please?"

"I suspected he might be my father," she said, staring at the floor.

"You found out that you were having sex with your own father, didn't you?" I asked.

"No. That's not true," she whined.

"I believe your birth father was as shocked as you were, at the thought of making love to his own daughter. He was as sick to his stomach as you were, wasn't he, Miss Weltman?"

"No, that's just not true."

I pressed on. I didn't want to let up. I didn't want to give her the time to think about her answers. I wanted to break down my suspect's willpower, until she confessed to at least one hideous murder, if not more.

"Elaine, I believe, when you learned the true identity of the man with whom you were sexually involved, that you became enraged, disgusted, and angry over this bizarre and sick situation. So, while Palter was still tied to the bedposts, due to your strange ways of lovemaking, you picked up the butcher knife that you had used to cut the ropes with...and you killed him. You stabbed him over and over. Tell me the truth, Elaine. I know you did it!"

I threw the autopsy photos of Palter in front of her so she could see the utter destruction she had brought upon her very own birth father.

But she wanted no part of them. She pushed the photos away and onto the floor.

"I told you," she said, angrily, "I didn't kill anyone."

"Elaine, are you telling me that you didn't plan to kill your birth mother when you found her?"

"That's exactly what I'm telling you. I didn't know what I was going to do.... But I know I wasn't going to kill her."

"Then why did you want to see her?"

"I told you...I just wanted to speak with her." She continued to look at the floor as she answered my questions.

"That's not what you stated in your diary—the one your adopted mother found in your jewelry box at home. You wrote that you wanted your birth mother dead."

"I might have felt that way at one time, but I changed my mind. I just wanted to find out who she was and why she did the things that she did. I'll admit that I was angry at her for abandoning me, but I wanted to know the real reason behind it," she said, as tears fell from her eyes.

"Elaine, when did this sudden change of heart take place?"

"I guess I've always felt that way."

"So, what you wrote in your diary was a lie?"

She shook her head. "Not at the time I wrote it, but I was in a lot of pain at the time."

"Elaine, how did you feel about your boyfriend when you learned that his real name was Jim Palter and not Jim Webber...and that he was really your birth father?"

"I was angry at him, too. I really did want to kill him. I wanted to strangle him. I felt dirty and humiliated. I wanted him to feel the same pain that I was feeling."

"Well, you did a good job."

She snapped, "I'll tell you, again. I didn't kill him or anyone, for that matter."

"Come now, Miss Weltman. We have the murder weapon with his blood all over it. It also has your fingerprint on it."

"I don't believe it."

"It was used not only to cut the ropes that were tied around Palter's wrists, which were tied to the bedposts, but it was also used to kill him."

"Well, I didn't do it."

"Miss Weltman, we have your fluid on the bed sheets from the murder scene. Your fluid is also mixed with the victim's semen. The DNA analysis showed us that you were screwing your own father!"

"But I didn't know he was my father. ... When I did, I left him."

"Yeah, you left him all right. Dead!"

She yelled, "I didn't."

"When you found out he was your father you flew into a rage. You picked up that big butcher knife off of the carpeted floor and killed him with it."

"That's a lie," she snapped.

"This was the same knife that you had just used to cut the ropes to their correct length, so you could tie his wrists and ankles to the bedposts."

"Yes, that's true. We used a butcher knife to cut the ropes."

"Then, you held that knife over his naked, outstretched body and began stabbing him over and over," I said, as I got right up into her face.

"You're crazy," Weltman snarled.

"Did you know that you plunged the knife in so hard that it went all the way through your father's body, nearly an inch into the mattress?"

"I didn't! I didn't," she screamed, covering her ears with her hands.

"Then," I said, not letting her get away, "when you cut his ropes and dragged him from the bedroom into the kitchen, you stabbed him again and again so hard that the knife went through the body and into the hardwood floor. Isn't that right, Elaine?"

"No! It isn't so. But yes, I did use a knife to cut the ropes. ... But that was before we had sex. And long before I even knew that he was my birth father."

Just then, my questioning of the suspect was interrupted when a uniformed policeman came into the room and handed me an evidence bag. It was the butcher knife in question. I had asked him to retrieve it for me when I left the room to confront my peers.

I pulled the knife from the bag and showed it to my female suspect, then asked her the important question.

"So, you do admit that you used this knife?" I asked, holding it in front of her.

She looked at it very closely. "Well, it looks like the one I used to cut the ropes with. But Jim used it, too. We both used the knife for that purpose. And yes, it looks similar to the one that I had in my purse. However, the one I had in my purse, I used strictly for protection. In fact, Jim helped me pick it out when we went shopping one day. But I didn't use it to kill him...or anyone else for that matter."

She was upset. "Settle down, Elaine. We'll know more about that when the forensic testing is completed on it. But we know that the knife found in your purse isn't the murder weapon that killed your birth father. We have that knife. It's the one I'm holding now. *This* was the knife that you used to cut the rope and kill your birth father," I said, setting the butcher knife on the table in front of her.

She seemed startled by what she had just heard. "Wait a minute. The knife I used to cut the pieces of rope to correct lengths, I dropped to the floor. Once I was finished cutting the rope, I never used it again. I never touched the knife after that," she said, throwing her cigarette butt to the floor, then lighting another one.

"Elaine, are you sure you never touched that knife again?" I asked, looking deep into her eyes.

"I'm positive. I swear, I never picked it up again," she said, as she stared at the floor. But seconds later, she reversed herself. "No, I take that back. I did pick it up again. ... I shouldn't tell you this, but I have nothing to hide."

"So, if you have nothing to hide, spit it out."

"I used it to threaten him," she whispered.

"Threaten him, how?"

"While Jim was tied to the bed, I used the knife so he would tell me his true identity. I wanted to know his real name. That's when I told him about the bag of phony identification I had just found in the bathroom commode."

"Did he tell you his real name?"

"He told me immediately when I started waving that big butcher knife around. Actually, he tried stalling me, until I grabbed hold of his penis and threatened to cut it off if he didn't tell me the truth the first time. And I meant it. And he knew I meant it."

"Elaine, do you remember what day that was?"

"No. I told you before. I can't remember," she replied, taking a drag on her cigarette.

"You were seen at Jim Palter's apartment that Sunday evening. You were seen exiting the building on the night Jim Palter was killed. The bloody murder weapon had your fingerprint on it. Now you tell me that you threatened to whack off his penis with it. And that you threatened his life with the butcher knife for the sole purpose of getting the truth out of him. Isn't that true?"

She bellowed, "Yes. I threatened him...but I didn't kill him."

"How did you feel when you found out that you were making love and had been making love to your own father? The father that gave you away? The father that didn't want anything to do with a daughter he knew nothing about," I said, looking deep into her teary eyes. "Miss Weltman, how do you explain that?"

"I can't."

"You said you threatened to cut off his penis if he wouldn't tell you the truth."

"That I did."

"The funny thing is, his penis was severed...completely. How do you explain the coincidence?"

"I don't know," she shouted. "I can't explain it, other than it's just a coincidence. You'll just have to take me at my word and believe me." Her eyes were pleading with me to stop badgering her.

"Elaine, when did you start dating Paul Donald?" I asked, changing the subject.

"Who? I don't know any Paul Donald."

"You might know him by his alias, Don Cadwell."

"Yes, I know Don Cadwell. I didn't start dating him until I broke it off with Jim, that Sunday night."

"Miss Weltman, I just caught you in a lie. Earlier, you stated that it was two or three days before Sunday. Now, which is it?"

"No," she said, shaking her head, "you said I was there Sunday. I couldn't remember what day it was. So I'm taking your word on it. But you called Don, Paul. Was he using a phony name, too?"

"Yep. Paul Donald, alias Don Cadwell, was running from the law."

"You're kidding? Why would he run?"

"He decided it was smarter to run than it was to face up to his responsibility."

"Then why isn't he in jail?"

"Luckily, he outlived the charge. For a while, anyway. That is, until someone caught up with him. Now, he's dead. By some strange coincidence, Miss Weltman, everyone you meet...ends up dead."

"It seems like that, doesn't it?" she stated matter-of-factly.

"What did you have against Cadwell?"

"Nothing. I just found out, two days ago, that Don was dead. ... We dated a few times, sure. But our relationship wasn't that serious."

"Did you two ever fight or argue?"

"We argued, but what couple doesn't? Gee. What are you trying to do, clean up your work docket? You're trying to hang every unsolved murder on me, aren't you?" she asked, as she blew her cigarette smoke into my face.

"No. We don't charge anyone with anything unless we have the evidence. And we have overwhelming evidence that points directly to you, as the murderer in one, if not two or more recent murders," I replied, giving her a cold look.

"I told you and I'll say it again. I didn't kill anyone. If you arrest me for any of those murders, you will be letting the real murderer run free. First you say I killed my birth father. Then you say I killed my birth mother. Now, you accuse me of killing my new boyfriend. Why, in god's name, would I want to kill him? If anything, I was only angry with him."

"Then why were you mad at him? What transpired between you and Don Cadwell that made you angry? Maybe even angry enough to kill him?"

"You're right," she said, nodding. "I was angry with him. Damn angry. He forced me into making love with him. I tried fighting him off, but he was too strong."

"Maybe he thought you consented to having sex with him? Sometimes when a woman says no, she really means, yes. ... Are you saying he raped you?"

"What do *you* call it when a man forces himself on a woman?"

"What did he do?"

"He held me down, against my will, while he tore my clothes away and forced himself on me. ... There ... Are you satisfied, now?" she asked. I noticed a tear running down her cheek.

"What did you do after he raped you?"

"I ran out of his place, practically naked. I couldn't even think straight. I had just gotten over my hideous ordeal with my last boyfriend, who turned out to be my birth father. Then, I had to deal with this terrible ordeal with my new boyfriend. I felt betrayed."

"So betrayed that you killed him?"

"No, I didn't kill him. ... After going through that catastrophic event with my birth father, I felt like I never wanted to have sex with anyone again. I thought Don understood me. But I don't think he really cared about my feelings being hurt. He only cared about his own feelings. So, when he forced himself on me—"

"You killed him," I said, finishing her sentence.

She smiled and said, "I must admit, I did feel like killing him. I don't know. I must not be living right or something."

"There. You just gave me a motive for Cadwell's murder. ... You killed him because he raped you. That's understandable. In fact, your attorney might be able to plead that case to a manslaughter charge. But what I can't understand is...what could possibly be your motive for killing those two dear old ladies?" I asked, trying to control my anger.

"Are you talking about those two dear old ladies a few doors down from Jim's apartment? ... They were killed, too?" she asked, shaking her head in disbelief.

"Yes, and I think you were somehow involved. Maybe with the sisters' niece? I haven't figured that one out yet, but I will in time," I said, staring into her teary eyes.

"What are you talking about? I talked with those two old ladies many times. I even bought them groceries, using my own money. I considered them friends of mine."

"Then what were your long, blonde hairs doing in one of their dead hands?"

"I don't know! I think someone is setting me up. I think I'd better get an attorney." She threw her cigarette butt to the floor, pulled another out of the pack, and lit it.

"Okay, we'll get back to the Weinburg murders in a little while. Let's talk about your birth mother. That is, if you want to talk about it. ... Elaine, we can end this interview right now if you would like an attorney."

"I think I need one," she said, nodding her head.

"We'll get one for you. But once we do that, we can't help you. An attorney won't let you speak with me. So change my mind and make me believe someone else killed these people. It's all up to you now. ... What do you want to do?"

"I told you. I have nothing to hide. I haven't killed anyone. So go ahead and ask your questions."

"When was the last time you saw your birth mother, Samantha Manner?"

"I can't remember exactly. I think it was just two or three nights ago."

"Your mother was killed three nights ago. And more of your physical evidence showed up at her murder scene, also. I'm sure that by the time we're through with this interrogation, the district attorney will probably charge you with a number of heinous murders and other sadistic crimes, so you might as well help yourself and come clean."

"How can I come clean if I'm not dirty?"

"You're not funny, Elaine. If you come clean now, I'll be able to help you with the district attorney. But right now, you're facing the death penalty. You do know that, don't you?" I asked, trying to get a reaction out of her.

"I told you, I'm innocent. I can understand how you could make one mistake in a murder investigation. But now, you're accusing me of three or four murders. I just can't believe it. And I'm not responsible for any of them. But yet, you're going to hang me and not bother to look for the real killer. ... I'll even take a lie detector test."

"Elaine, we don't make up the evidence that we gather at the crime scene. When the hairs from your head are in the grasp of a dead woman's hand, that's pretty damning evidence."

She slapped her hand on the tabletop. "I told you, someone is setting me up!"

"We have your fingerprints from inside the Weinburg sisters' apartment. We have your cigarette butt from inside their apartment. And we have even better evidence at the Palter murder scene."

"I don't believe this." Shaking her head in disbelief.

"We also found similar evidence from the Manner murder scene. Hey, if it walks like a duck and it quacks like a duck, it must be a duck. Well, if the evidence points to you, then you must be the guilty party."

"Of course my fingerprints would be there," she shouted. "I was in every one of their apartments. That's why my hair was found at the different murder scenes. I have a logical answer for every one of your questions. I mean, what motive could I possibly have to kill these people?"

"Are you kidding? You have a strong motive for wanting Palter and Cadwell dead. You said so yourself."

She looked at me in disdain. "Well, I guess I did have a motive for some of the murders, but why would I want to kill those dear old ladies?"

"Maybe they saw or heard you kill Jim Palter? I don't know for sure. But believe me, before I'm finished...you will tell me everything you know and then some."

"I can't tell you what I don't know," she whined. "All the evidence you have against me has to be circumstantial."

"Why is that?"

"Because I'm innocent. I haven't killed anybody. How many times do I have to say it?"

"Miss Weltman, the evidence shows otherwise."

"It's true. I might have wanted to kill my birth parents at one time, but I forgave them. Even though I had a much harder time forgiving my birth father. ... I still can't comprehend or understand why this is happening to me."

"The evidence brought you to this place."

She took a long drag from her nearly finished cigarette, exhaled a large cloud of smoke, and said, "This must be my karma getting back at me. And if you charge me with these murders, you are putting an innocent person in jail."

"I know. You said that before. However, Miss Weltman, you will be sent to jail only if the evidence warrants it. Tell me. What did you do the minute you found out that you were making love to your father?"

"I wiped myself. And then, after going to the bathroom, I confronted him about the bag of incriminating evidence. ... Didn't we go over this once already?" she asked.

"We'll go over this until I decide otherwise. And I'll keep asking questions until I get the truth."

"I am *telling* you the truth. Somebody else killed those people. If you'd done your job properly, you'd know!"

"Miss Weltman, when the facts dictate the answers...there is no reason to investigate further. But if I think there is another suspect and more investigative work needs to be done, then I'll do it. But I have to justify my time. Elaine, if I thought you weren't guilty of these crimes I wouldn't have arrested you."

"But I'm innocent!"

"Elaine, I interrogated and interviewed many other suspects before I arrested you. But I arrested you on one murder. Now, it will be up to the district attorney to decide what other murders to charge you with."

"Great. You're going to send me to jail when the real criminal is out there somewhere, still committing murders. I don't know when, but one day you are going to find out that I didn't commit any of these crimes that you are accusing me of doing."

I shook my head. "I don't think so."

"When that day comes around—and it will—just remember my words. Then, I hope that your conscience haunts you till the day you die. I hope your conscience will remind you that you sent an innocent woman to prison." She stared at me with hatred in her eyes.

"Like I said before, Miss Weltman. The evidence points to the guilty culprit and a jury decides whether a person is innocent or guilty. ... But let's get back to your birth mother. Did she know you were coming to visit her...or did you surprise her?"

"No, she didn't know I was coming. I never spoke with her until that day—the day you say she was murdered. When she answered the door, I told her who I was and then introduced myself."

"What did she do?"

"She invited me into her home. We sat in her living room and talked about her past. When we started talking about *my* past, I became upset. I had to leave before I said something that would cause either her or me pain. I just stormed out of the house. That was the last time that I saw her or talked to her," said Weltman.

"Was Samantha Manner still alive when you stormed out of the house?" I asked.

"Of course she was. And to tell you the truth...when I first entered her place...I thought about using the knife on her."

"What knife are you talking about?"

"The knife that I carried in my purse. But after we began talking, my birth mother suddenly broke down and apologized for ruining my life. Before my rage built up and exploded, she had asked me to forgive her for her reckless behavior and idiotic actions."

"So, you talked with your birth mother for five minutes and then you completely absolved her of any responsibility for ruining your life? Is that what you're telling me?"

"But she cried for my forgiveness for her past sins...and made no excuses for her reckless behavior. ... Then, we both broke down and cried. We cried and hugged each other for what seemed like hours. She said she had never forgotten me...but had no way of finding me because the adoption file was sealed."

"Tell me what she said to you."

"My birth mother explained the whole situation. She was very young and immature when she became pregnant with me. She counted on her boyfriend to care for her and the child. But instead, he ran out on her before she was able to tell him that she was with child. She explained to me how her mother made her forget about me. She couldn't say a word about me, especially while living at her mother's house. The more she told me the story, the more I felt sorry for her."

"So, what did you do?"

"I suddenly forgot about my hurt feelings and felt a change of heart. Before I met her, I wanted to kill her. But after we talked...it was a different story."

"Why? What was different about it?"

She thought for a moment, took a long drag on her cigarette, and then said, "When I looked into my birth mother's eyes, it was like looking into a mirror. I looked exactly like her. Just much younger. And then something came over me—my hatred for her suddenly disappeared. I no longer felt that inner rage; it melted away, like the snow does on a sunny day. And at that moment, I felt closer to her than anyone else in my short and confused life.... But then, I remembered why I had traveled over a thousand miles. I was so upset and confused, I had to get away and think about my situation. I had to clear my confused head."

"What did you do, then?"

"I didn't say a word to my birth mother. I just stood up and ran out her front door." Tears welled up in her eyes.

"Did she come after you?"

"She didn't move from her seat. I guess she was just as dazed and confused as I was. I wanted to turn around and go back to her, but I had to get away. I needed time to myself...to think things out. I wanted to visit her again, but I wasn't sure when."

"What about your birth father, Elaine? Did you want to visit him again?"

"No. He made me sick. Just thinking about him made me want to regurgitate. He never knew about me...and I wish he had never seen me...or ever met me. But that's water under the bridge, now."

"Elaine, why don't you just come out and admit that you killed your birth parents? It will help clear your conscience. You'll feel better about yourself. ... Be honest with yourself."

"You want me to say I did it, when I didn't. Do you want me to plead guilty, when I'm really innocent?"

"I don't want you to do anything you're not happy with."

"What's wrong with you? I told you I'd take a polygraph test."

"I told you, a polygraph test isn't completely reliable."

"Well, let me see if I understand you correctly," she said, blowing cigarette smoke into my face. "You have evidence against other people...but because you have more evidence on me, you're sticking me with murders—that I didn't commit—just so you can close your investigations. Is that about right?"

"No. That's not true."

"Hell, if you're charging me for those murders, bring up some others that you haven't solved, yet. Hell, hang them all on me. That way, you can close all your open and unsolved investigations. ... I guess, I'm your scapegoat."

I ignored her sarcasm and studied her face and body language as she sat and stared at me, blowing clouds of cigarette smoke into my face. She had smoked so many cigarettes, and the room had become so smoky, that my eyes had become irritated and started tearing. But I persevered and continued on with my interrogation.

"Let's get back to the interview. When Don Cadwell forced himself upon you, how did that make you feel? Did you want to strangle him, too?" I asked.

"As a matter of fact, I did," she snapped. "I wanted to cut off his penis and shove it down his throat. ... Let him see how it feels to have it shoved into him."

"Boy, Elaine, you are really one tough lady. Why this sudden urge to whack off his penis? You were going to whack off Jim Palter's penis, too. Isn't it a funny coincidence how both of those individuals had their penises chopped off? ... Then I hear from my number one suspect, that you 'wanted to do it.'"

"I might have wanted to do it...but I didn't."

"What if you did? Maybe you just blacked out and can't remember doing it. Have you ever experienced any seizures or blackout spells before? Are you a crack addict, Elaine? They tend to have seizures all the time."

"No. I'm not a crack smoker. I don't do drugs. I've never had any seizures or blackouts. I would know if I killed someone or not...and I haven't. I told you I'd take a lie detector test."

"And I told you they are unreliable."

"You know, we've been at this now for over two hours. When are you going to give up? You won't change my mind. Just because I was at the wrong place at the wrong time doesn't mean I killed these people. I will tell you until I'm blue in the face. I am innocent. I haven't killed anyone. ... Please," Weltman begged. "Give me a lie detector test."

"How many times do I have to say it? Lie detector tests aren't reliable! We go strictly by the evidence. I don't care if we stay here for thirty-six hours. We aren't going to leave this room until you tell me the truth...." I softened my voice. "Elaine, I am here to help you. The judge will go easier on you if you take responsibility for your actions. If you confess, that would probably save you from the executioner."

"Look. What do you want from me? Do you want me to say something that's not true? Do you want me to say, 'yeah, those two nosey old hags got what they deserved? They stuck their noses into another person's business and their nosiness got them killed when they saw me kill Jim Palter, so I had to kill them to quiet them from telling the police. And Jim's ex-business partner raped me, so I killed him for it. My birth mother saw me as a spoiled piece of meat and didn't care that she destroyed my life, so I didn't care when I destroyed hers.' Is that what you wanted to hear? Is that what you want me to say? ... There, I've said it. Does that make you happy now? ... It doesn't matter what I say. I can't seem to change your mind."

"Why doesn't it matter what you say?"

"You still think I'm guilty, so you're still going to prosecute me...and keep me in jail. I can't fight the state. I don't have the money to prove my innocence. If you guys think I'm guilty, then it doesn't matter what I say."

"It does matter, Elaine. Why do you think differently?"

"You'll twist my words and you'll twist the facts to correspond with your theory and evidence. ... That's why I didn't want an attorney."

"Why not?"

"What could he do? The only thing I have going for me is the truth. It's up to you and the jury to believe me or not," she replied, seeming to give up.

"That's true."

"I can't twist your arm to believe my story. You believe in your theory. The evidence might point in my direction, but like I said before, it's all circumstantial."

"Not all of it."

"It has to be. I'm innocent. I'll say that again and again until I'm blue in the face. You won't change my mind, and I know I won't change yours. So, do what you will." She flicked a lit cigarette butt against the wall.

Just as I started to question her again, the district attorney, Bob Dent, came into the room and interrupted the interrogation; he wanted to speak with me. I apologized to Weltman for the interruption, then followed the D.A. to the viewing room, where he had been watching my suspect and listening to her every word for more than two hours. He had heard enough...and made a decision on my case.

"Detective Hero, I've decided that we don't need Weltman's confession to get a conviction," he said. "I have heard enough. I believe I can use her words from this interrogation against her in a courtroom. She has just confessed, as far as I'm concerned. I can fit her words to the evidence."

"Bob, what do you mean by that?" I asked.

"In order to understand her confession, you have to read between the lines," he said.

The district attorney believed Weltman was guilty beyond a reasonable doubt. In fact, he believed she was guilty as sin...and was going to charge her with at least three counts of first-degree, premeditated murder, and second-degree in the others. He believed she knew, before she even found her birth parents that she was going to kill them. That's why she came to our city in the first place. Her adopted mother even told us so.

The district attorney was going to charge Weltman with first-degree murder in the premeditated death of her birth mother and the Weinburg sisters. And second-degree murder for the Palter and Cadwell murders. He believed that Weltman freaked out when she learned that she was having sex with her own father, and she killed Cadwell for raping her—allegedly, of course. Cadwell wasn't here to defend himself, and we only had Weltman's word that he raped her. But the district attorney was going to give her the benefit of the doubt in that case. Still, she had the means, motive, and opportunity. Plus, the evidence so far backed up the theory that she'd killed them.

So, the district attorney had heard enough. I could wrap up the interrogation right now, as far as he was concerned. But I wanted that confession more than anything. I was becoming more and more frustrated over Weltman's insistence of innocence. She wouldn't budge, even when confronted with the massive amount of hard evidence against her.

But with the tape recording of the interrogation and the accumulation of hard and circumstantial evidence, the district attorney felt he had a very strong case against her— and he showed just how strong it was when the case finally went to trial.

Six months passed before the trial got underway. It lasted a little more than three weeks before it went to the jury, who came back with a verdict within nine hours. They found Elaine Weltman guilty of first-degree murder against three of the victims and guilty of second degree murder against the other two victims. The district attorney got everything he had wanted. The defendant, however, didn't agree with the outcome—and shouted her innocence as she was being led away to jail. She would have her sentencing in two weeks.

There was something about the way she reacted that didn't sit well with me. I began to question my investigative instincts. My gut now, for some reason, told me that we were putting the wrong person in jail—even though all the circumstantial and hard evidence pointed in Weltman's direction. There was just something about her insistence of innocence that had me believing in her story. She just might have been in the wrong place at the wrong time. What did she say about the hard evidence? It had been planted.

I questioned that premise myself early on in the investigation. I wondered why there were just four or five blond hairs in the victims' hands instead of a whole handful. There should have been more hair found if it had been pulled out of the killer's head. A good defense attorney could have made a strong case for his client on that assumption. But a good prosecuting attorney would have an answer to any theory in response. That's his job.

If the D.A. thought he had enough hard evidence for a conviction, he would go ahead and prosecute. If not, he would plea bargain with the defendant or wouldn't prosecute at all.

The district attorney on this case, however, thought there was a sufficient and substantial amount of evidence to warrant a trial. If the jury didn't believe the prosecution, they would acquit the defendant. Those were the checks and balances built into our justice system.

The jury thought Weltman was guilty of the murders...and at that time, so did I. But as the months passed, I had become more and more disillusioned with our justice system. Just before the trial, I wanted to give Weltman a lie detector test, but the district attorney refused my request. He refused to allocate the funds for the test. He felt it wasn't necessary. It wasn't allowed as evidence; therefore, it wasn't necessary. He said he had more than enough pertinent evidence to warrant a conviction for the death penalty.

That's why I had become disgruntled. The lie detector would have given us a clear indication of whether or not she was innocent or guilty of the crimes of which she had been accused. I wanted to use every tool that law enforcement had at their disposal. I didn't want to put an innocent person behind bars, but evidently my district attorney didn't feel the same way. In his eyes, he had the evidence that proved beyond a reasonable doubt that Weltman was guilty of crimes against the state...and it was his job to prosecute.

That's when I vowed to find the real killer to those murders—if there was one—and get Weltman released from prison before she walked the path to the deathbed and saline drip. I vowed to win her freedom before I retired, which was less than fourteen months away. I knew I had some hard work ahead of me. Even if Captain Blake ordered me to close the investigation, I would keep it open on my own. Even if it meant that I had to investigate on my own time, I'd work twenty-four hours a day, seven days a week, if I had to. If there was a way, I was going to save Elaine Weltman from the death penalty. I promised myself to right the wrong that had been committed by all of us in the law enforcement community. If I had made a mistake, I would be the first to admit it.

## Chapter 12

Now that I had wrapped up the Weltman murders, I was suddenly a big hero around the station. Sure, I had cracked a big case, but I wasn't happy about it. I now firmly believed that the person that was arrested, charged, prosecuted, and convicted was possibly an innocent victim. Basically, she was convicted on circumstantial evidence. Although we did find her partial fingerprint on the murder weapon, my gut instinct said we had the wrong person in jail for the murder of one, if not five different victims.

I was determined to find the guilty culprit. However, now that my investigation was closed, I had been reassigned to the serial killer task force once again. My peers now greeted me with kindness, which was a complete change of heart from days past. They had completely ignored me after I had been taken off the task force and assigned to another murder investigation, which I had solved—or so I thought. But the more I began to tumble the evidence in my head, the less certain I was that I had the right killer.

Later in the day, while driving slowly across town, I passed a nearby park and heard what sounded like gunfire—approximately six to seven loud "pops" in succession. I quickly turned my car towards the exploding sounds and drove down a long, one lane dirt road. Even though dusk was just setting on the park, I could make out three figures lying on the ground about eighty to one hundred yards directly ahead of me. The closer I got to the area, the more it reminded me of a bloody battlefield.

When I finally arrived at the scene, I stopped the car and jumped out to see if I could be of some help to the fallen victims. But the moment I saw the carnage, I froze in my boots. This bloody scene shouldn't have bothered me at all, especially after what I had seen from the murders that Elaine Weltman was convicted of. I am a weathered and hardened homicide detective with over twenty-five years of experience. But this scene made no sense. It was inconceivable to me why such an act would occur.

    I walked hurriedly to check out the victims. Coming up to the scene I saw three figures lying dead on the ground. There were two males and one female. One male was lying face down, with his head sunken into the soft, red mud. The other male was lying face up, with the female lying somewhat on top of him. The top half of her body was lying on him and the other half, from the waist down, was lying in the soft, red mud. All the bodies were covered in blood.

    I walked over to the couple first, then knelt down and felt their bleeding and battered bodies. They were still very warm. Whatever had transpired, it had happened within the last few minutes. I checked their pulse to see if they were still alive. They weren't. I had to take a couple of deep breaths before I could continue.

    I looked over the dead couple's bodies—neither looked to be more than thirty years of age. I couldn't do any more for them, so I walked quickly to the other male victim, then bent over and checked for a pulse. He was also dead. He seemed to be a very old man. But his body and face were lying in a puddle of soft, red mud, so I wasn't sure about his age—although I could see a partial plume of gray hair on the back of his head. He lay about fifteen feet from the young couple.

    As I stood up to survey the scene, I noticed a very strange object lying on the ground nearly twenty feet away from the old man. I went to investigate—and found a large necklace of plastic phallic symbols. That's what I thought it was anyway, until I picked the object up and looked at it more closely. I nearly shit my pants when I realized that the objects weren't made of plastic; they were the real thing. There were a total of nine penises strung onto a long piece of string, then tied to make a necklace. It was a sickening sight. Who would carry around such an item? This object de art—or whatever it was—made me ill. Each penis had been threaded through at its base—where it had been severed from its body—and attached to the string.

Once I had thoroughly examined this mass of one-eyed monsters, I returned it to where I had found it, then stepped back to catch my breath and calm my nerves. While I was standing there, I noticed a huge object lying about twenty feet from the penis necklace and approximately forty feet from the murdered couple. It was another dead body. Closer inspection revealed it to be another male victim—approximately thirty years of age—lying face down on the ground.

I quickly checked for a pulse, but he had none. His body was also still quite warm to the touch. Then, for some strange reason, as I was deciding my next course of action, that penis necklace popped into my mind—which made me wonder about this victim's penis. Was it still intact...or had it been severed? I didn't want to move the body until help had arrived, but I just had to know. Gently, I lifted the body onto its side to take a look. Sure enough, his penis had been severed at its base.

I placed the body back into its original position and then looked around in the immediate area to see if the guy's penis was anywhere in sight. It was. As I followed a small blood trail to the item of suspense, I found the victim's penis lying in a small pool of its own blood, in the brush, near a small clearing of young Evergreen trees. This victim must have been killed first, I thought to myself, but by whom?

My mind was speeding faster than a speeding bullet. Many questions needed answers. Just what the heck had I stumbled upon? Nearly ten minutes had passed since first arriving on the crime scene, and I was so dumbfounded by the atrocious deaths that I had forgotten to call the paramedics, coroner, and fellow investigators. I must admit, I was in a state of shock. This was by far the most gruesome murder scene I had come across in a very long time.

After some soul-searching, I finally got my wind back and called the proper authorities. Within a few minutes, the investigative team and coroner had arrived at the crime scene. The area was cordoned off, and the investigation began. The photographer was busy shooting pictures of the murder scene while the forensic investigators were picking up any pertinent and relevant evidence—including two large caliber hand guns, which were found lying on the ground near the young male victims. It looked as though they might have shot each other in self-defense. But to know more, we would have to wait for the coroner's report.

There were also two empty vehicles sitting near the murder scene.

The next five or six hours, hopefully, after gathering up all the forensic evidence, would tell us the story of what had happened here. But I was very tired and upset over this horrendous situation. I needed to go home and relax—and I needed a drink very badly. I wanted to clear my mind of the hideous picture I had seen there. This murder scene hounded me with unanswered questions.

When my captain arrived at the murder scene, he began to chew me out for not calling dispatch immediately. He stopped in mid-sentence when he saw the angry expression on my face. I was pale as a ghost. He knew I was in no mood to listen to his guff and wasn't going to let him take his frustrations out on me. Thankfully, he backed down a bit and soothed my hurt feelings by allowing me to leave the murder scene and return to my home. Of course, not before assigning me the murder investigation. I was the detective that had stumbled upon the victims, so he wanted me to finish what I had started.

When I arrived home, I walked directly to my kitchen cabinet and grabbed my bottle of twenty-year-old scotch. After the first shot, I found that I needed four more before I had the strength to move my numb body into the living room to relax on the couch.

I wallowed in self-pity and continued to pour shot after shot of scotch down my gullet. I wanted my mind to stay numb to all of this insanity. But no matter how much liquor I consumed, the questions still seemed to pop up and boggle my mind. One question in particular was ... What were these people doing in that park...and who were they?

The next morning, I arrived at the station to a near empty department. Many of my peers were still working on the serial killer task force, which still hadn't been solved in nearly a year. Nearly a dozen police officers were assigned to this new murder investigation, trying to find witnesses and searching the crime scene and were to report directly to me. I quickly signed in at the front desk and stopped off at the snack table. As usual, I poured myself a cup of black coffee and grabbed a jelly-filled donut. I carried the items to my desk and was surprised to see a few investigative reports already sitting there in a neat pile.

Sitting down in my chair, I quickly glanced through about a dozen different reports concerning the park murder scene and its victims. Just thinking about the carnage of bodies made my skin shiver. So I put the reports to the side and lit a cigarette. As I sat back eating, smoking, and drinking my coffee, I thought about the horrendous scene I had stumbled upon the day before. But after a few minutes of daydreaming, I began reading the reports and made notes about the subject until late in the afternoon.

I needed some air and decided to drive back out to the murder scene. The bodies had already been removed from the area, but I wanted to see what the scene would look like in the daylight. And there were only a few hours of daylight left.

I left the reports sitting on the desktop and headed to the park. Within fifteen minutes, I had arrived at the crime scene. I parked my car and sat there, thinking about what must have transpired the night before. But my mind had suddenly become clouded and confused. I had to get out of the car and look over the area more closely.

During my inspection of the crime scene, a homicide detective from another state arrived on the scene and introduced himself to me.

"Hello, I'm Detective Banner," he said, showing me his identification and then shaking my hand. "I'm investigating a serial killer from the West Coast. ... Can you direct me to the senior investigator on this case?" He had a deep distinctive voice with no accent.

"You're looking at him," I said. "I'm the senior investigator working this crime scene. In fact, I'm the *only* investigator working this crime scene. Most everyone else is on our serial killer task force. ... By the way, I'm Detective Hero."

Just five minutes into our conversation, another out-of-state vehicle arrived on the scene. The license plate showed that it came from the Northeast coast, nearly fifteen hundred miles away. Detective Banner had traveled a similar distance. The vehicle's driver parked the car, and then a minute later walked up to Detective Banner and me.

"Hello, can I speak with the lead investigator on this crime scene?" asked the tall, robust fellow.

"You're talking to him," I said. "What can I do for you?"

"I'm Detective Stanton," he said, showing me his identification. "I've been following the trail of a murdering son of a bitch—a serial killer from the northeastern part of the country. And his trail led me to your doorstep. I think he's one of your victims?" He seemed to have a Bostonian accent that sounded like Ted Kennedy.

"Our department has been hunting for a serial killer in this area for nearly a year. How long have you been chasing your killer, Detective Stanton?" I asked.

"He's been on a murder spree for over two years, and that's just about the length of time I've been searching for him," said Stanton. "I think my prayers have been answered and the killer finally got what he deserved. ... I guess you could say 'he reaped what he sowed.' If it's all right with you, Detective Hero, I'd very much like to take part in this homicide investigation. I want to wrap up any loose ends...and make sure that the victim is really the person I've been hunting for the last two years."

"I will have to get the authorization from my captain, but I have no problem with that," I said.

"How about me, Detective Hero? Can I also work this investigation with you?" asked Detective Banner. "Because I believe the killer I've been stalking all of these years might also be involved in your murder case."

"Excuse me, Detective Stanton, this is Detective Banner," I said, as I introduced everyone to each other. "I know you guys are anxious to help, but I will have to get approval from my captain before I can give you an answer. I'm sure there won't be any problems. I can use all the help I can get."

"Good. I'm anxious to get started," said Stanton.

I made a suggestion to my two brother detectives. "There's a little cafe right down the street. Why don't we go there and have a cup of coffee? We can talk over the crime."

"That's fine with me," said Banner.

"Ditto," said Stanton. "I could use a cup of coffee...and something to eat."

"Fine. You can follow me in your own vehicles. It's just a mile and a half east of here," I said.

During my drive, I kept thinking about my captain's reaction and what he would say, now that there would be three investigative detectives working my case. I thought it was quite a coincidence that three homicide detectives—all from different states—would converge at this crime scene at the same time looking for answers in three different homicide cases. I wasn't quite certain how the two out-of-state homicide detectives figured in to my homicide investigation, but undoubtedly I would find out soon enough. I didn't have any idea what information they had or how much they knew concerning the deaths of the four park victims. But I figured there was at least one perpetrator, if not more, involved in those four deaths.

I still didn't have much to go on. But once I had received all of the forensic and investigative reports, the pieces of the puzzle should start falling into place.

I still had to run over to the coroner's office for their analysis of the crime scene and also for the autopsy information. The fingerprints taken from the victims would also be helpful in determining their true identity. The identification that these victims carried with them could have been phony. That is, if they had any at all. The reports I had read so far didn't mention anything about identification found on the victims. That's why we liked to check the fingerprints, just to double check.

There were at least three different weapons found at the crime scene lying on the ground—some, near the victims. It was still undetermined if the weapons were used or fired. Maybe my new comrades would have some missing parts to the puzzle.

We had come from different parts of the country, chasing a deliberate, maniacal killer. Detective Banner had traveled over two thousand miles from the state of Oregon. Stanton had traveled nearly fifteen hundred from the state of Maine. How did it happen that all three of us would converge on this spot in the great state of Missouri? We had never met before this day. And I had never expected to run into other detectives working similar murder cases...especially from far away states. But I was mystified by the fact that my investigation would be intertwined with their murder investigations.

We finally arrived at the little cafe. When we entered, the place was as dead as those victims in the park. We were the only customers. That was all right with me. The less noise, the easier to have a conversation. I was anxious to find out just how much the two detectives knew about the park victims. Or were they victims at all?

The two out-of-state detectives followed me as I walked to my favorite table in the far corner of the dimly lit cafe. The darkness and emptiness of the small room seemed befitting to the moment. We were all in a somber mood as we took our seats at the table and quickly ordered alcoholic drinks. While waiting for the spirits, we became acquainted. And then, once we had a few drinks in us, we began to loosen up. It took me three stiff drinks before I felt comfortable around them enough to open up and talk from my heart. Soon after, I began telling them how I had been assigned to this case. Normally, I was a shy person, so it took the numbing of my body before I could really speak my mind.

I let them start the rap session. I decided I would rather listen to their stories than tell my own. I didn't have anything to tell them, anyway. I hadn't even been to the coroner's office yet. I wanted to see what they knew about my case.

Detective Banner spoke up first.

"I have been traveling from one state to another for more than three years, chasing after my crazed female killer," he said. "She was leaving bodies everywhere...which brought me to this state. In fact, I met Detective Stanton at the St. Louis coroner's office. But the coroner was in the middle of an autopsy, so we didn't get too much information out of him. We were told to come back in two days, then he should have some pertinent information for us.... They are analyzing the fingerprints as we speak. So we should know something by the end of the day, hopefully."

"Detective Banner, how do you know that your suspect is among the victims at the park?" I asked.

"The reason I'm fairly certain that I have the right person is by the fact that there were severed penises made into a necklace found at the murder scene...and I believe they belonged to the female victim."

"The penis necklace was lying near one of the male victims. And he was a good twenty to thirty feet away from the female victim.... Why do you think it was the female's necklace?" I asked.

"By the fact that all of her male victims had their genitals cut off. The DNA from those penises found on that necklace needs to be checked and matched against the victims that she has left in her wake."

All this talk about that penis necklace was making me nauseous, so I changed the subject and said, "Banner, you look as though you could have been a professional football player. You look about the same height and weight as me.

I would say you are a good six feet two inches tall and must weigh a good two hundred twenty . . . maybe thirty pounds. The only difference is you have hair on your head and I don't."

"Hero, you look like you could have been a football player too. So what? What does this have to do with our investigation?" Banner asked.

"It doesn't have anything to do with our investigation," I replied. "I was just wondering how long you've been a homicide detective. You look fairly young. I was just wondering how much experience you've had in homicides."

"I'm old enough!" snapped Banner. "And I've got plenty of experience."

"Please don't get angry," I said. "I ask this question in the most respectful way... Hell, Detective Stanton looks even younger. In fact, you two look as though you just got out of high school. What's your story? How do guys stay so young?"

"By staying single," Stanton said.

Banner nodded. "I'll agree with that."

"Now, on a more serious note. Banner, why don't you tell Stanton and myself a little bit of your background and why you became a cop," I said.

"I can do that," Banner said.

"When you're finished telling us your story, we'll do the same," I said. "That way, we'll feel more comfortable working with each other if we know what makes each other tick."

"Well, I grew up in an Italian family and neighborhood," stated Banner. "My father passed away nearly two years ago. My mother is still with me, and I have only one sibling, a younger brother, who is two years younger than me. We're complete opposites. As kids, one of our favorite games was cops and robbers. I always played the cop...and my brother always played the robber. I grew up wanting to be a cop...and my brother grew up wanting to be a gangster. I guess it must have stayed with us because his dream came true, as did mine. He became a made-member of a Mafia family...and I became a hard-working police officer. After a few years of hard work, I was given my gold badge as lead homicide detective."

"Detective Banner, isn't there a little bit of conflict of interest with your brother being in the mob? Better yet, isn't the pressure you receive from your peers relentless?" I asked.

"You can say that again," he quipped. "Some days I wonder if it's worth all of the trouble and aggravation. Especially working a case for more than three years without anything to show for it...except an ulcer. That's when I want to throw in the towel. But I always tell myself, 'there's always tomorrow.'"

"Thank god for tomorrow," I quipped. "But with your brother in the mob, you'll never get respect from your fellow detectives."

"I really don't care what they think of me," Banner said. "I only wanted my family to be respected and honored. My brother makes that wish impossible. He has besmirched our family name. He actually thinks he's respected in our neighborhood. He doesn't understand that our neighbors are afraid of him. They don't respect him...they fear him. But what can I do about it?"

"You can arrest him and put him in jail," I said.

"But he's my flesh and blood. I love the guy. So I try to stay out of his business...and he stays out of mine."

"But you have a job to do. ... Why would you just ignore him and let him get away with murder?" I asked.

"We do this out of respect for my mother. But I have told him many times that if he gets out of hand, I will bust him in a minute."

"What did he say to that?" asked Stanton.

"He thinks money will buy him out of trouble. He thinks the mob is going to make him a rich and powerful man. He doesn't understand that he's only an expendable soldier to his boss. They would kill him in a second if they thought he was a danger to their organization."

"You can say that again," I said.

"My brother is just a sacrificial lamb. And I'm determined to help victims. That's why I became a law enforcement officer. The war in Vietnam helped me in my quest," said Banner.

I spoke up, exclaiming, "Most of the people I know that lived through Vietnam are delusional and not playing with a full deck, if you know what I mean. How could the Vietnam War help you in your profession?"

"I'll tell you how," Banner answered. "My four-year hitch in the marines helped mold my instincts to protect and serve the people of this nation. Fifteen years ago, I received my gold shield and became a homicide detective in the Eugene police department. The last three years, I have been hunting a female serial killer."

"Why did you think it was a female and not a male?" I asked.

"All the evidence pointed to a female. But I didn't know that right away. I came to that conclusion after investigating three similar murders over an eight month period."

"What was so similar about the murders?" I asked.

"Every victim's penis was severed."

"Say that again. Did you say their penises were severed?" Stanton asked.

"Yeah. Why?"

"I just closed a case where two of the victims had their penises severed," I said.

"Maybe Banner's suspect committed those crimes," said Stanton.

"I don't think so," I mumbled.

"Did you find the killer?" asked Stanton.

"Yeah. The woman that committed the murders was found guilty and sentenced to death and two consecutive life terms." I shook my head.

"Detective Hero, you act as though you convicted the wrong person," said Banner.

"No, not really. But I'd be lying if I said it hasn't crossed my mind at one time or another."

"Were the severed penises ever found?" asked Banner.

"Yeah. They were in the hands of the victims," I told him.

"The penises were never found at any of my murder scenes," Banner replied. "That is, until now. I'll know for sure in a couple of days if the string of penises is related to any of my victims. Then maybe I'll be able to close the book on my investigation after all these years. I think I'm going to sleep great tonight."

"Detective Banner, I'll keep my fingers crossed for you," I said.

"Thanks. I need all the help I can get."

"So Detective Stanton," I asked, turning to him, "what's your story?"

"My story is similar to Banner's," he said, shrugging. "I wanted to be a cop from the age of five. But I have a few more siblings than him. And they are all female. I have six older sisters."

"Oh my god. Six older sisters and no brothers," I said, shaking my head in disbelief.

"I've been bossed around by females all my life," said Stanton. "I always longed for a brother."

"That's your mother's fault. You should have bugged her about it," I kidded.

"I did. I begged her to go out and get me a brother but she never did. I come from a very strict catholic family. I was an altar boy until the age of fourteen. At the age of ten, I joined the Boy Scouts. Then, over the years, I graduated to eagle scouts. Then I earned a scholarship to the local university and received my bachelor's degree and then my masters in criminology. I wanted to join the FBI, but I couldn't pass their physical."

"Why? What happened?" I asked.

"The federal government told me I had high blood pressure. But my blood pressure was low enough to pass the physical for my local police department. I was hired in as a detective in the homicide squad and have been with the department for almost eight years. Two of my sisters are also in law enforcement."

"Do they work for your police department?" I asked.

He shook his head. "No. They work for the FBI. They passed their physicals. And they tease me about it all the time. But it's all in fun," said Stanton. "I wish I could say the same thing about my murder investigation. Once I knew I was on the trail of a serial killer, I couldn't get the killer out of my mind. He was in my dreams. He was in my nightmares. He was in my head every second of every day."

"I have the same problem," I said.

"Me, too," said Banner.

"I can't believe that it ended this way," said Stanton. "I always expected to capture him dead or alive. I didn't care. I just wanted the killing to stop. We *had* a general task force set up for the first few years. But when this maniac left our state, the task force was dissolved."

"I wish they would do that with our task force," I said. "So what happened after they shut it down?"

"I was ordered to follow up and investigate the case—which led me to St. Louis. And, Detective Hero, I'm happy to say I believe my serial killer is one of the males found dead in the park. I think he's lying in your morgue right at this very moment. But I will know for sure when the medical examiner finishes his report."

"Well, like I told Detective Banner...I'll keep my fingers crossed. You know...this is unbelievable. What are the odds that two serial killers would end up dead at the same murder scene?" I asked.

"I don't know, but it must be in the millions," said Banner.

"What the hell was going on in that park that night?" I asked my two comrades. "I wonder if the two serial killers knew each other. Maybe they were partners in crime. Maybe they came to the park to murder their victims but were killed themselves when their victims defended themselves. Or maybe there was another shooter that escaped before I arrived."

"Well, the investigative reports should clear things up," said Banner. Then he looked at me and asked, "When do you think the reports will start coming in?"

I really didn't have an answer, but I gave him one anyway. "Well, the officers have to canvass the area. The medical examiner has to finish the autopsies, latent has to check the prints, and the forensics lab has to do the tests and analyze the results on any forensic evidence that was found at the crime scene. Then the automobiles that were impounded from the scene have to be checked, and rechecked, for fingerprints and any other evidence that might seem relevant to the investigation."

Banner didn't seem to like my answer. He gave me a quizzical look and said, "Yeah. So how long will we have to wait for the information we need to close our investigations? We have to tell our superiors something. At least I do. I have to have a very good reason to charge expenses to my department, especially if I'm gone for days. We are on a very tight budget. In fact, my captain may order me back and have you fax me the information. I can stall him for a day or two, but anything over that and I have to give him a very good excuse or my ass is grass. So, Detective Hero, what do you think? How many more days before the pertinent information becomes available?" Banner finished his second drink and ordered another scotch and soda.

"I already have a few reports on my desk, but they are only interviews with a few bums and derelicts that were in the area. None of them saw anything. Hey, guys, before we get too loaded I think we better order something to eat. What do you say?"

"Okay," replied Stanton and Banner in unison.

We called the waitress over and we each ordered two steak and cheese hoagies. Gabrielles was famous for their hoagies. Once we had gotten a few bites into our stomachs we continued with our conversation.

"How long before you get the autopsy reports?" asked Stanton, after lighting up a cigarette.

"I should have them within a couple of days," I said. "We'll stop by the morgue in the morning and you can ask the coroner yourself. But like you said, Detective Banner, we can always fax the information to you. You'll still have to come back to retrieve your perp's body."

Banner nodded his approval, and then Stanton spoke up.

"Okay, Detective Hero, you know our life stories, how about yours? Why did you join the police force?" he asked between bites of his hoagie, sips of his drink and puffs on his cigarette.

"Gee, it was so long ago I really can't remember," I replied. "I've been in the homicide department for over twenty-five years. It's taken over my life. I'm a single divorcee—tried marriage three times. I would have two more under my belt if I had married the broads. When I joined the force, I didn't drink alcohol or smoke tobacco. Now, I'm addicted to both." With that said, I took a drag on my cigarette and finished my fourth drink.

"That's not good," Banner said. "You should get help if you need it. What's the problem?"

"I hate to say it, but this job has made me an alcoholic. It's taken me a long time to come to that conclusion. But it's the truth. I just hope it doesn't happen to you."

"It won't happen to me," Banner said after finishing his third drink.

"It won't happen to me, either," said Stanton, also finishing his third drink of alcoholic beverage.

I laughed and told them how it is. "When you've been in this business as long as I have, it tends to take the enjoyment out of life and the pursuit of happiness. This job takes over your life if you let it. Each and every murder scene that you investigate takes something away from your soul. It'll make one older, sooner than later. That's the way it's been for me, anyway."

"Boy, what a pessimist," Banner said. "I hope I never let this job get to me like that. I'll hang-up my badge before I'd let it ruin my life."

"I hope you don't have to," I said. "But enough of the small talk. Let's get back to business at hand.... Are you guys certain that two of the people killed at that park were your suspects?"

"Yes," said the detectives in unison.

"Well then, I still have two victims to investigate. Maybe even another shooter. Your investigations are nearly ending, but mine is just beginning.... Boy, I envy you guys," I told them. "But one thing I don't understand is how you can investigate a case for years and not become annoyed with it...or grow tired of it."

Stanton answered first. "I don't know about Detective Banner, but believe me I have become very annoyed at times. Many times I wanted to give up and leave the work to other jurisdictions to find the killer. Yeah, it's eating me up inside and has taken its toll on my mind and body, but I'll keep pushing forward. I will say one thing though...it is a never-ending job with very little satisfaction. But then again, I wouldn't trade it for any other profession. This is my life."

"My view's similar to Stanton's," Banner said, nodding his head. "But I keep my options open. If this job became too possessive and traumatic, I believe I would resign my position and look for another job."

After finishing our meal, we ordered another round of drinks and continued our conversation.

"Detective Stanton, I'm curious. What is your nationality? We know that Banner is Italian, even though the name doesn't sound Italian. But what is yours?" I asked.

"I come from an Irish background. My family came to America in the early eighteen hundreds from Northern Ireland. Ever since our family arrived in America, there has always been a Stanton in law enforcement."

I looked at Banner and said, "Now I have a question for you, Detective Banner. How did the name Banner ever get to be Italian?"

He gave me a cold look and replied, "If you must know, the name Banner used to be Bannero. My grandfather changed it to Banner when he was always being teased about being a dirty immigrant. He got tired of hearing all the name-calling and took off the 'O' from our last name. That's how my name became Banner. Now you guys know about my name. What about yours, Hero? That's an unusual last name. Where did your family originate?"

"Well, my family tree originates from England," I said, and then gulped down my sixth double shot of scotch whiskey. "Near the area of Wales. They came from the city of Hero. That's where I got my last name. They came to America about twenty years after the Mayflower landed."

"Your family sounds like it has a lot of history behind it," said Stanton, smoking away on his cigarette.

I shrugged. "I guess so. I'm not a big history buff. But as far as my nationality goes, I'm a Heinz kind of person: Fifty-seven varieties. I have a little English, French, Armenian, and I'm told a little Native American in me. But I have the thirst of an Irishman. In fact, whose turn is it to buy the drinks?"

"I guess it's my turn to buy," said Banner, letting out a loud belch.

We ordered another round before continuing our conversation.

"Okay," I said. "In the morning, we'll all meet at the coroner's office. I know the coroner said two days, but he told you, he didn't tell me. We'll stay out of his way. If he becomes agitated by our presence, we'll just leave the building."

"That sounds good to me. How about you, Detective Banner?" asked Stanton.

"That sounds like a winner. I was hoping that we would meet here, have breakfast, then all ride together to the coroner's office. Then, if you don't mind, Detective Hero, I was hoping we could all go out to the crime scene and go over it with you. You were there just minutes after the killings occurred, right?"

"I'm sure the victims' deaths occurred only five or ten minutes before I arrived. I'd bet my life on it." I sighed. "You know, it's really funny. We have a task force set up with over fifty detectives to investigate a serious serial killer in our area. Over a dozen similar killings in a sixty-mile area have been giving our detectives ulcers—and they don't have one piece of pertinent information to go on."

"That sounds like our serial killer task force," Banner quipped.

"But it's not, it's ours," I said. "And they've been beating their heads against the walls for over a year now. They've had the forensics lab and the DNA lab tied up for months, checking and rechecking what little evidence they've found. All this time and money wasted and nothing to show for it. And when I need the forensics lab to check my evidence, they act like I don't exist."

"Why is that?" asked Banner.

"They are only concerned with the serial killer investigation. Everything else is put on the back burner. I was even a member of that task force until I was kicked off the investigation and out of their fraternity. I suddenly became the outcast of our department. You noticed I don't have a partner to work with..."

"I wondered about that. Why did they dismiss you from their task force?" Banner asked.

"Are you kidding? I was never given a reason. I'm just no longer one of the boys. They act as though they are better than I am." I took a sip of scotch. "Maybe it's because I drink and smoke too much."

"I don't believe that. There's got to be another reason," said Stanton.

"Hell, I don't know," I said, tossing back my drink. "But I got news for them... I may have just closed two serial killer investigations at one time. They should give me a medal. Instead, they give me a kick in the rear.... Oh, well. Such is life. I just do my job as best I can, under the circumstances." I added a belch to the end of my sentence.

"Ah, don't let it get you down, Detective Hero," said Stanton. "If you let it get to you, it will eat you up inside."

"No, it won't. I numb my body with this," I said, holding up my drink. "Scotch whiskey is my favorite drink. Sometimes with ice, but most of the time, without. When I'm down and out, this stuff always gives me a new outlook on life."

"Does it work?" asked Banner.

"So far, so good," I said, with a wink of my eye.

"Well, I'll pat you on the back," said Banner. "I think you've done a hell of a job. If it wasn't for you, I wouldn't be here now hoping to close an almost three-year-old case." He raised his glass into the air and toasted me, and then ordered another round for everyone at our table.

"And I owe you a debt of gratitude, too," said Stanton. "I don't want to sound too corny, but I always say there is a reason for things happening the way they do. I don't know why. Some say it's fate. Others say it's luck. Sometimes it comes down to just plain hard work—which is what you were doing when you came upon the killing field. If it wasn't for your investigative instincts, someone else may have just kept driving to their destination and not have been so inquisitive. Luckily, due to your work habits, you were. All I can say is that you've been very helpful to me. And if you ever need a letter of reference, don't hesitate to ask. You are number one in my book."

"Here, here!" said Banner. All three of us raised and clinked our glasses together, toasting each other for good luck.

"Okay, guys, flattery will get you everywhere. Just don't overdo it," I kidded. I looked down at my watch. "Gee, look at the time. I bet you guys want to get back to your hotel rooms and get a good night's sleep. We've been here for quite some time. But if you guys want to stay and keep drinking or have something else to eat, I'll stay with you and have one last drink. If not, I'll let you guys relax and enjoy yourselves."

Banner looked at me and said, "Man, I've never seen one guy drink so many shots of scotch and not be passed out by now. I would have been passed out after the third one. Detective Hero, you handle alcohol very well."

"I'd hate to break your bubble. But you should see me when I'm at home, alone, when I don't have to get behind the wheel of a car to drive myself home. Boy, I can sure put it away. And I drink only twenty-year-old scotch. That's a man's drink."

"I'm sure you know your limit. You're a big boy," said Banner.

"I do know my limit. If I ever got behind a wheel while I was drunk and then killed someone, I could never forgive myself. I would make sure I couldn't drive again. I'd end it myself," I told them.

"You know, I don't even know your first names," said Stanton, looking at Banner and me for an answer.

Before I could say a word, Banner said, "Just call me Joe, which is short for Josepie."

Then Stanton spoke up. "My first name is Allen. But I use my middle name. My father and I share the same first name, so I go by my middle name, Edward or Eddy. Either one is fine." Then he looked at me and asked, "What's the name you go by, Detective Hero?"

"Well, I go by Detective Hero. But you guys can call me Detective Hero or Mr. Hero. Whichever you prefer." I told them this with a straight face. At first they weren't sure if I was pulling their leg or serious—that is, until I smiled. We all laughed, then I told them something that very few people knew. "If you guys must know, my first name is Baxter. Just don't say it too loud."

This talk bored and embarrassed me, so I changed the subject. "I'll tell you what. Instead of going to the coroner's office and meeting there in the morning, why don't we do as one of you suggested? We'll meet here, have our coffee and breakfast, and then we can either ride together or take separate cars to the coroner's office. What do you guys think?"

"Can we stop by the crime scene after we stop by the coroner's office?" asked Banner. "I would like to get a better picture in my head of what went on. There has to be another shooter that got away. I'd bet my life on it."

"You might be right," I said. "We should start receiving the photos and sketches of the crime scene tomorrow or the day after."

Both Banner and Stanton said that they hoped so.

"The investigators are probably still collecting evidence and interviewing people in the nearby area," I said.

"Did you see anyone in or near the park while you were driving to the crime scene?" asked Stanton.

I thought for a minute—back to the night of the killings. I took a deep drag on my cigarette, then said, "You know, now that I think about it, I did see two bums walking on the sidewalk, very close to the park's entrance. It didn't dawn on me until now. If they were in that park that night, they might have seen or heard something. I'll have to find those guys."

"Did you get a good look at them?" asked Banner.

"Yeah, I saw two dirty, scraggy men. I better tell the patrol units to keep an eye open for them. They could be important witnesses. Or worse...the killers."

"You should make up a composite drawing of them," Stanton suggested.

"Yeah, but I'm going to have to think hard to remember what those guys looked like," I replied.

"Why is that?" asked Banner.

"As I drove past them, they turned and walked away from me. And now that I think about it...they walked away fairly quickly. But I really didn't have any reason to look at them, other than that they stood out as bums."

"But did you see their faces?" asked Banner.

I leaned back in my seat before answering. "I saw more of their clothes than their facial features. I'm going to have to think more about this when I get home. Once I'm relaxed and breathing the stale air that flows throughout my house, I think much better."

Stanton nodded and said, "I know what you mean. I think better at home, too."

I retorted, "Until my eyes burn, sting, and water, I don't feel quite at home. Any place else is foreign to me. In fact, I do my best work at home. But enough of that. I'd like to hear your theories on the incident at the park. What do you think happened out there? Maybe you guys can help me close the rest of this crazy investigation."

"Sure, whatever you want," Banner said. "We're here to help."

Suddenly, all the drinks that I had consumed during my conversation with my two new friends hit me, and hit me hard. Without drawing attention to my predicament, I nonchalantly said, "I'll tell you what. Why don't we leave the discussion about the park killings until tomorrow? I'm afraid if I stay here any longer I won't be able to drive home safely."

"You're right. What time do you want to meet us here?" asked Stanton.

"I'll meet you here tomorrow morning, at eight. We'll eat breakfast, drink our coffee, and then drive over to speak with the coroner." With that said, I stood up and shook their hands. "I'll see you in the morning."

"Drive safely," said the detectives in unison, as I walked out of the cafe and into the dark night.

# Chapter 13

The next morning, traffic was miserable as I drove my old clunker through the morning dew. After a thirty minute drive that should have taken fifteen, I made it to my destination. As I pulled into the cafe parking lot, I saw the two out-of-state detectives, Stanton and Banner, smoking cigarettes while awaiting my arrival. I parked my car and then walked over to where they were standing.

"Good morning, fellows," I said to my new friends, smiling. "What do you say we go into the cafe and have some coffee and eat a hearty breakfast?"

"That sounds good to me," said the two detectives in unison.

"Seriously, I have to get something into my belly or I'll get the shakes. I guess it's from old age."

"I'm going to eat light this morning," Banner said, as we entered the café. "I don't know if it will stay down. I have a massive hangover."

We walked to the back of the room, to my favorite table in the smoking section. Now we would be able to talk without speaking over all the peripheral noise.

I looked out the window and noticed drizzle falling from the sky. This was the sixth day out of seven that it had rained. The murder scene was muddy enough from last night's rain. Today it would be even more difficult to walk around in that area.

I was quickly brought back to reality as the waitress came over to take our orders.

While waiting for our food to arrive, we smoked numerous cigarettes, drank lots of coffee, and tried to get the cobwebs out of our heads. I was still very weak and very hung over, as I was sure my brother detectives were. I was positive they felt just as bad as I did. Their faces sure reflected it—the pain from too much alcohol. Their noses and cheeks were puffy and red, and the rest of their faces looked a very pale white. Banner and Stanton seemed too dazed to speak, so I started the conversation.

"What did you guys do after I left you last night?" I asked.

"Not much of anything," exclaimed Stanton. "We ate another hoagie, then returned to our hotel rooms—which, by the way, are in the same hotel. But boy was I plastered. As soon as I got into bed and placed my head on the pillow, I went out like a light."

"Not me," interjected Banner. "When I lay down on the bed, the room began spinning out of control. I tried to get up to go into the bathroom, but I couldn't move. It was as if a large magnet was holding me down. I ended up throwing up on myself, right there in bed. It was disgusting. I passed out in my own vomit."

"Oh, please. Don't talk that way at the breakfast table," snapped Stanton. "Why don't we change the subject before I start throwing up?"

"I'll say one thing," continued Banner. "I had never been so drunk in all of my life. Not even at my brother's wedding. I drank more alcohol last night than I did all of last year."

"You're kidding?" I asked.

Banner bowed his head in shame and said, "No I'm not. Last night I drank my limit ten times over. I don't drink much, unless it's for a very special occasion."

"What kind of special occasion?" I asked.

"Like a very special wedding—or closing a serial killer investigation after nearly three long years. That's what I call a special occasion," he said.

"Amen to that," said Stanton.

I nodded and said, "I second the motion."

Just then, our meals arrived. I wasn't really in the mood to eat, but I knew I had to get something into my stomach or I would get the shakes.

"Gee, I hope the coroner has some good news for us," said Banner, looking directly at me. "Better yet, I hope he's got some answers for us. Baxter, do you think the fingerprint analysis reports will be in today?"

"I hope so."

"Me too," said Banner. "I'm anxious to close my investigation and erase it from my docket. It's been one big headache. But now I hope to get rid of my headache and my investigation at the same time."

"I know what you mean," I said. "I just cracked a lulu of a case involving the deaths of five innocent people."

"Did you find the ones responsible?" asked Banner.

"Yeah... And the perp was convicted for all five murders. But for some strange reason, my gut instinct tells me the person wasn't involved in all five murders...and maybe not any of them."

"You're kidding, right?" asked Banner.

"I wish I were," I said, shaking my head. "Although I can't say for sure that the person is innocent because I don't have the proof yet. Actually, I don't have *any* evidence proving the killer's innocence. In fact, all the evidence we have accumulated up to now points to this person's guilt. But after being in this business for as long as I have, my gut instincts really mean something to me."

"By the way, was the killer a man or woman?" asked Banner.

"A woman...in her mid-twenties...who was convicted on three counts of first-degree murder and second-degree for the other two. She got the death penalty, plus four consecutive life sentences without the possibility of parole.

She has never shown any remorse for the murders. She has always maintained her innocence."

"All convicted felons say they are innocent," said Stanton. "The prisons are full of them."

"You may be right," I replied. "But I now believe at least two, if not three of the murders were committed by someone else."

"What did the evidence tell you? Is that the reason you asked me about the penis being cut off?" asked Banner.

"No," I replied. "I was just curious and trying to find the reason behind all of these severed penises. I believe Loraine Bobbitt is behind the phenomenon that started these people cutting off their partner's private parts. And as far as the evidence, it was basically all circumstantial—even though the killer's alibis never held up under questioning. But she has always maintained her innocence. Right at this moment, I can't prove anything. But my gut instinct never lies."

"You have to just let it go," said Stanton. "Put the case behind you and start another. It sounds to me like you did some good police work. So, forget about it. I know that sometimes, it's hard to do. It's hard to get it out of your head. We are only human. But you can't let it eat at you. I don't know why I'm telling you this... You're the senior investigator. You helped write the book that I learned from."

"That's nice to hear," I said with a smile. "But like I've said before. I'm just doing my job. I might drink a little too much, but it *never* interferes with my police work. In fact, I take my work home with me. And as I'm pouring shot after shot of scotch down my gullet, I'm constantly thinking about my current investigation."

"Let's not talk about alcohol right now," Banner said. "My stomach can't take it. Instead, while we're eating our breakfast, why not have Baxter tell us how he happened to arrive at the park just minutes after the killings occurred. That way, we kill two birds with one stone. And when we see the coroner this morning, we'll have our questions ready for him to answer."

As I started explaining what I had stumbled upon that morning, their faces turned pale.

"Well, I guess I was wrong," quipped Stanton. "Why don't you tell us after breakfast? I want my food to stay in my stomach."

I guess I had been a little bit too explicit. That's all right. I could wait another twenty minutes.

Once we were finished eating, sitting back smoking cigarettes and drinking our coffee, Banner said, "Okay, Baxter, now tell us how you happened to come upon this gruesome murder scene. How did you find the victims?"

"Are you sure you want to know?" I said. "I don't want you guys to lose your food."

"I just want to visit the area sometime today," said Banner. "That is, if the forensic investigators have searched the area thoroughly and completed their work."

"That's what I expected us to do," I replied. "After we had stopped by the coroner's office to see if his report is finished yet. But I doubt that Doc Grady had the time to finish it. Still, there is no harm in trying."

"So come on, Baxter, tell us what happened," said Stanton, anxiously.

"Well, if you really want to know. On that particular evening, while investigating another case on my own time, I just happened to be driving past the park entrance—it's adjacent to the highway. You've seen the place..."

"Yeah, for a couple of minutes...with you and Banner," Stanton interjected. "I didn't see much though."

"Well, as I was saying, I was driving past the park entrance when I thought I'd heard what sounded like a car backfiring behind me. But when I looked in my rearview mirror, I didn't see another car in sight. Then I thought about gunfire."

"You must have good hearing," kidded Banner.

"Believe me, I know the difference between a gunshot and a car backfiring, although at the time I wasn't expecting to hear anything, let alone gunshots.... Anyway, I heard a number of muffled 'pops' as I drove past the park entrance. Then my conscious got the best of me, so I decided to make a U-turn and investigate the situation."

"About what time did this happen?" asked Stanton.

I took a long drag on my cigarette and continued. "The sun was setting at the time of the incident...and just as I turned onto the park's entranceway, I saw two bums leaving the park. As I said before, at the time, I didn't think too much about them and continued driving down a steep incline until I came upon the crime scene."

"How many bums did you say you saw leaving the park?" asked Banner.

"As I told you before, I'm sure it was only two, but unfortunately I didn't get a look at either one of their faces. I did, however, get a good look at the way they were dressed. And they were definitely dressed like bums. But at the time, I was only concerned about where the popping noise had come from."

"What was the weather like that day?" asked Banner.

"There was a slow drizzle coming down, so visibility wasn't perfect. And then, approximately a hundred yards and to the left, I noticed what seemed to be piles of garbage. But the closer I got to the area, the more I could see that it wasn't garbage; it was three large piles of something..."

"What was it?" asked Stanton.

"At that moment, I really didn't know what it was. But I had my suspicions, and boy did I begin to sweat. My breath became shorter and faster, and my heart was pumping like I had just run the one hundred-yard dash. I became so excited I damn near pissed my pants in anticipation. It was as if I were a rookie cop all over again." I stopped and took another long drag on my cigarette.

"Okay, Baxter. Come on... Tell us what happened.... What were those piles you saw?"

"You know what they were. I told you yesterday. But if you want me to tell it again, I will."

They both nodded.

So I continued with my story. "Ok, you guys asked for it. As I came upon the crime scene, I couldn't really tell at first what I was looking at. And then the rain began falling faster and harder, which made it more difficult to see—that is, until I got within ten yards of the scene. That's when I could see that there were at least two figures lying on the ground. But I didn't stop, immediately. I drove slowly past the scene, thinking that the perpetrator could still be in the area. I also noticed two cars parked nearby, one behind the other, as though the people driving them might have come to the park together. But that was total conjecture on my part. So, I tried to be as quiet and discreet as I could. I acted as though I was just another person visiting the park and parked my car about fifty yards away. I wasn't sure exactly what was going on or what had transpired, so I wanted to look over the scene from a short distance. I felt it was better to be safe than sorry."

"Then what did you do?" asked Banner.

"Then, I slowly walked through the mud and found two bodies lying on top of each other. I saw a female lying on top of a male. Both were bleeding so profusely that there was nearly twenty pints of blood lying at my feet."

"Didn't the rain wash the blood away?" asked Stanton.

"Yeah, it was still raining...but the blood was so thick and there was so much of it that it stayed in a big puddle."

"Were the victims alive or dead at that time?" asked Banner.

"I checked for a pulse without moving them. But they had already expired. Then I hurried over to another victim, who was lying face down in the mud."

"Was this guy completely submerged in the muck?" asked Banner.

"The back of his head and half of his ears were the only things showing," I said. "The rest of his body had sunk about two inches into the mud."

"I know what you mean," interrupted Stanton. "When I met you at the crime scene and stepped into that red mud, I damn near sank a foot deep."

I nodded. "Well, when I kneeled down to check the victim's pulse, I knew he was dead already because he was lying in a lake of blood. I was sure he had also been shot, but I couldn't tell where. If he hadn't been shot, he'd have suffocated from being face down in the mud. And when I stood up to walk back to the couple, that's when I noticed another large clump lying near two picnic tables about fifty feet from the couple and thirty feet to the left of the man lying face down in the mud."

"What was it?" asked Stanton.

"When I walked closer to it, I could see it was another male victim. He seemed to be about twenty-five to thirty-five years of age, and was lying face down in the tall grass, while the other three victims were lying in the mud. I'll tell you this much," I said. "Seeing all that carnage had a horrendous effect on me. It put me in a state of confusion."

"Why do you say that?" asked Banner.

"Because when I first arrived on the scene, I had overlooked two large-caliber handguns. When I did notice them, I just left them where they lay. I was too busy checking the victims for a pulse to see if they were still alive. But just as I was walking towards the last victim, I got the shock of my life. I damn near crapped my pants, if you'll pardon my French."

"Why? What was it?" asked Banner.

"That's when I saw the large, round necklace of severed penises, all strung on a long piece of string, then tied at the top to make it into a necklace—as though someone actually wore it."

"Oh, that's gross. Why would anyone want to wear a penis necklace? Stanton asked.

"It was definitely one of the sickest sights I had ever witnessed to this day," I replied. "I couldn't believe a person in their right mind could do or even wear something as hideous as that."

"What did you do then?" asked Stanton.

"When I saw it lying a few feet from the male lying face down in the tall grass, I immediately wondered if his penis was still intact or if it had been severed. But I didn't want to turn him over and disturb the crime scene. Eventually, my curiosity got the best of me, and I took a quick peek. Sure enough, it was gone. So I began looking around the immediate area to see if this guy's penis was lying on the ground."

"Was it?" asked Stanton.

"Sure enough, a few feet behind him was a bloody, severed penis. It was lying near a rock hidden by the tall grass. I damn near stepped on it and squished it."

"I think I'm going to be sick," said Stanton.

"Evidently, she didn't have time to finish threading her necklace of phallic symbols," I kidded.

"Where did you find the guns?" asked Banner. "Which victims used them...or did they?"

"I was just coming to that," I replied. "After I discovered the guy's manhood lying in the tall brush, I walked back over to the couple to see if that guy's manhood had also been severed, but—"

Stanton interrupted me. "Why don't we talk about another subject?"

My talk about severed penises seemed to upset Eddy, so I agreed to his request. "Okay, we'll talk about the guns that were found. One gun was lying by the male with the severed penis. It was just out of the reach of his right hand, and completely hidden by his body."

"Where was the other gun found?" asked Banner.

"That one was lying near the right hand of the male that was lying beneath the female. His gun was completely hidden by both their dead bodies."

"Was his manhood still intact?" asked Banner.

"Yes and no. His penis had also been severed, but not completely. It was dangling from his body by a thin piece of skin."

"What did she do, bite it off?" Stanton joked.

"No," I said. "She used a knife—probably a twelve-inch long butcher knife. It was found lying in the mud within reach of her outstretched right hand. It seems that when the two finally collapsed from their wounds, the female fell on top of the male.... It was a crazy scene to stumble upon."

"Good god," exclaimed Stanton. "What a scene to have to witness. It's too much to put into words."

But that's exactly what I was doing—putting it into words. So I asked them, "Do you want me to continue?"

"Yeah, please," Stanton said. "I didn't mean to interrupt you. Sometimes I put my foot in my mouth."

"All right, I saw the weapons that the couple had. Then I walked back to the guy lying face down in the puddle of mud to see if he had a weapon, but there wasn't any to be found. I looked all around the victim, but nothing. Then I walked over to the male lying in the tall grass and checked around his body and found his gun."

"So, how many weapons did you find?" asked Banner.

"There were at least two guns and a large butcher knife found at the scene of the crime. But the guns were completely hidden by the dead bodies covering them. That's why I overlooked them when I first arrived on the scene."

"What about the two guys you saw leaving the scene?" asked Banner.

"I don't know if the two bums I saw at the park's entrance had anything to do with the killings or not. But they should be questioned."

"How many people do you think were involved in this crime?" asked Stanton.

"There were too many footprints to tell just how many people were in that area. And then, with all the rain, the mud covered up most of the evidence. The place was a mess."

"I could imagine how bad the grounds were while it was pouring down rain. It was bad enough there today," said Banner. "So what did you do after you had checked the pulse of the bodies?"

"I finally got around to calling the paramedics, the coroner's office, and the homicide investigators. I was really too pooped to participate. That crime scene took everything out of me. So, I just returned to my car and sat and waited for my captain, the coroner, and the rest of the investigative team to arrive."

"What did you do when they finally got to the crime scene?" asked Banner.

"When they finally arrived, I was allowed to leave the murder scene and return home. After stumbling on that crime scene, I was just caught by surprise. I never let death get to me like that, ever."

"Never?" asked Stanton.

"Even my last murder investigation was hideous, but this one was hard to beat."

"Why do you say that? What happened in your last murder investigation?" asked Stanton.

"There were two victims with severed penises. Plus, there were two wonderful old women that had their breasts mutilated and their throats sliced open so far you could see their spinal column. These were very sick and hideous scenes. But I kept my cool. I didn't let that murder scene get to me. But at this murder scene, something happened to me when I saw that penis necklace. I suddenly lost my composure."

"Why? What happened?" asked Banner.

"What do you think happened?" I replied.

"I don't know. That's why I asked," said Banner.

"When I bent down and picked up that phallic necklace, I didn't know what the damn thing was at first. I just thought it was a bunch of cheap plastic costume jewelry. But when I held it in front of my eyes, I quickly found out differently. And nearly threw up my lunch!"

"That would have turned my stomach, Baxter. Didn't it turn yours?" asked Stanton.

"You can say that again, Eddy. In fact, my knees became so weak that I had to kneel down for a minute or so to get my wind back. I just couldn't comprehend the object I had just held in my hands. It was utterly disgusting."

"That's putting it mildly, Hero. I don't know if I could have handled it as well as you," said Stanton.

"You won't know that until it happens to you. But I hope it never does. ... And I'm not sure I handled it all that well anyway. In fact, I felt like leaving the scene. I didn't want to stay in that bloody carnage another minute. But then, a sudden cool breeze blew across my face, and it seemed to bring me back to reality. That's when I got on my cell phone and called the station and the medical examiner's office."

"Did you look for the killers?" asked Stanton.

"No, not really. I had to wait until the investigative teams arrived. I should have looked around for the perpetrators, but for some reason I was just too stunned to move."

"It sounds to me as if you were in shock," said Banner.

"I could have been," I replied. "This had never happened to me before. I didn't know what had come over me. All I could think about was getting out of there as quickly as possible."

"I would have done the same," said Banner.

"This wasn't supposed to happen to a weathered, experienced, old detective like me. I'm supposed to be immune from this sort of thing...and shouldn't have had any feelings at all. But I did," I said.

"I suppose we all go through one or two investigations like that in our lifetime," said Banner.

I nodded in agreement, and then said to Banner, "Let me ask you a question about your investigation."

"Go ahead."

"What in god's name was wrong with your suspect, that she collected her victim's private parts?" I asked, shaking my head in disbelief.

He smiled and replied, "I don't think she was carrying a full deck of cards. If you know what I mean."

"Yeah, I guess she wasn't," I quipped. "She must have been a real nut case if she collected her victim's penises. And what did she do with their testicles?"

But Banner didn't answer my question. "I wonder if the forensic investigators found her testicle necklace to go along with her beautiful penis necklace." I kidded. "Didn't you know, it's all the rage in fashion this year."

Banner didn't seem very amused or happy about my attempt to make a joke. So I got serious and asked him, "What did she do with the rest of her victim's private parts?"

"What private parts do you mean?" asked Banner.

"You know, what I was just talking about—the victim's testicles."

"We believe she ate them."

"Are you serious?" Stanton said. "That is the most outrageous, sickening thing I've ever heard."

"Well, we believe it to be true. And so do her psychological profilers," said Banner.

"What else did the psychological profile say about your murder suspect—or should I say, serial killer?" I asked, as I smoked my cigarette.

"Lots... But before I get to that, Baxter, I want to ask you one last question."

"Go ahead. Ask away," I said.

"When you arrived at the murder scene, did you get a clear picture of who shot or stabbed whom that night?" asked Banner.

I shook my head. "I don't think so. There was too much to take in. To be honest, I think I was totally dazed and confused by the things I had seen. Why do you ask?"

Banner replied, "I want to know what transpired that night at the park—at the killing field. Were those people friends? Did they know each other? Did they come to the park together, in separate cars? I need to know what the hell happened out there."

"Me, too," said Stanton.

"I don't think we'll ever know what happened for sure, unless we capture the shooter or shooters or find an eyewitness. That is, if there are any," I said.

"How many guns were found at the crime scene? Three or four?" asked Stanton.

"I told you before, Eddy. Haven't you been listening? There were only two guns found at the crime scene. And there must have been at least ten to fifteen bullets fired. But I could be mistaken about that. That's why we need to speak to the coroner today. The autopsies should tell us most of the story."

"Then we should be leaving now so we can talk to the medical examiner," said Banner. "I'm really anxious to learn the identity of the victims. I can't tell you how bad I want to close my investigation. It's been a long time coming!"

"I'm pretty well pumped up myself," Stanton said. "I'm hoping to close my case today, too. Believe me, it's been hell chasing this guy. He's been like a shadow—until now."

"Which male do you think was your perp, Eddy?" I asked. "The one lying face down in the mud, the male with the severed penis, or the male lying underneath the female?"

"I believe it was the male lying under the female."

"Are you sure?" asked Banner, as he put out his cigarette.

"I could be wrong, but I'm pretty sure. Two of the males are very close in age, height, and weight. So their fingerprints should tell me which one it is."

"What about the victim's driver's license?" I asked.

"Well, when I asked the coroner for their identification, he stated that there wasn't any—no wallets, registration, credit cards . . . nothing that could identify them. At least, that was the answer I received when I asked about those items," said Stanton.

"They probably hadn't checked yet," I said.

"Well, you could be right," replied Stanton. "Maybe they've found something by now, but as far as I know there wasn't any identification on any of them."

"You're right," I said. "There wasn't any identification on any of the bodies. Either they didn't carry any or someone—possibly the shooter—robbed them of their valuables. But the fingerprint analysis will give you the answer you want. That should tell you which male is your perp."

"To tell you the truth," said Stanton, "I don't care which male it is as long as it's one of 'em. I've been waiting too long to catch this guy and put him away. Now, hopefully, we can save the taxpayers some money."

I checked my watch for the time. We still had some time to kill before we visited the coroner's office. I was only on my third cup of coffee and Banner still hadn't described his suspect's psychological profile. I mentioned this to him. "Joseph, you still haven't told us about your serial killer's psychological profile...so why don't you give us the low down? We have about thirty or forty minutes before we have to leave...and I'm dying to hear why a person would cut off their victim's private parts, keep the penis as a souvenir, and then eat the testicles as if they were M & M candies. So please tell us. I'm curious."

"Well, when the psychological profile was taken, neither the psychologist nor the police investigators knew that the person we were seeking was female. The consensus between our investigators was about three to one in favor of a male committing these grotesque, atrocious murders."

"Why did your investigators think it was a male that was committing the murders?" I asked.

"Basically, the main reason was that many of the victims were big, strong men. Hell, one of the victims was three hundred pounds and over six and a half feet tall. At one time, we even thought there were two perps. But after another half-dozen murders occurred with the victim's penises severed, we came to the conclusion that the suspect was a female and had taken the victims by surprise."

"Just from that?" I asked.

"At first, we thought the perp was a gay male. But not all of the victims were gay or involved in the homosexual world. The psychological profile report completely exonerated males from the killings."

"How so?" I asked.

"The report stated that the killer or killers were female, between the ages of twenty-five to thirty-five, with a long history of incest or sexual molestation, which had probably continued right up until the time of the killings."

"Who sexually abused her?" asked Stanton.

"The sexual abuse was probably at the hands of her father or another close male relative," replied Banner.

"How old was she when the sexual abuse began?" asked Stanton, puffing on his cigarette.

"The incest or sexual molestation probably began at a very early age—probably around the age of three—and continued into her adult years."

"Man, that's sick," I said.

"The report also stated that after each sexual encounter, she was most likely beaten to a bloody pulp. And then, after a day or two of healing, the episodes were probably repeated time after time. So she grew to hate and despise men ... all men. Especially those that reminded her of her father or the molesters who had tormented her for all those years."

"Is that the reason she only killed men?" I asked.

"Every time she was with a man, she would explode into a rage as they were having sex. Then her demons would take control of her mind. ... She was reliving those moments from her dark past. That's how she would get rid of her anger and rage."

"What? By killing them?" asked Stanton.

"The report stated that by slicing up her victims and keeping something from each one of them, it would remind her of the relationship they had had. She loved those objects just as if she had loved her victim. Instead of keeping the victim's ring or wallet or some other material object, she picked the victim's most prized possession: his private parts and manhood. If she could have carried the victims with her, she would have. Evidently, the victim's manhood was enough."

"What about that phallic necklace? What role did that play in her sick mind?" I asked.

"By wearing her souvenirs around her neck, in her mind, she was actually keeping her lover close to her heart and with her at all times. That way, he could never leave her. By eating the testicles...she thought her lover would be with her until death. But I'm not a psychologist. That is really conjecture on my part. But the other investigators came to the same conclusion. We knew we were dealing with a nut case."

"I want to say something, but I don't know if I should bring it up right now. I don't want anyone to get sick," I said.

"My breakfast has settled. I don't mind," said Banner.

"Go ahead. I can handle anything," said Stanton.

"Okay, you asked for it. Don't say I didn't warn you. But when I picked up that foul, horrendous-looking penis necklace, they weren't rotten or decaying. Why were they in such fresh shape? They looked as if they had been cut off yesterday, not two years before."

Banner gave me an answer, but I wasn't sure I believed him.

"Although I didn't get the chance to see that necklace, and I can't say that I'm over anxious to even look at it, I might know one reason why it's in such good shape."

"Yeah, so tell us," I pleaded.

"Well, when we first learned my killer's name, we began investigating her, and one of the things we found out was that she had learned the taxidermist trade from her sexually abusive father."

"You mean, he taught her something other than sex?" I joked.

Banner ignored my insensitivity, gave me a dirty look, and continued with his explanation. "It seems when her father wasn't sexually molesting her, she was working in her parents' basement helping her father and uncle in the family business. She wasn't allowed to go to school and get an education like the other girls her age. Supposedly, the family was very spiritual."

"In what religion? Satanism?" I asked.

"No. They studied from the Bible. That's what the father told the investigators, anyway," said Banner.

"But how did she manage to keep those victims' penises so fresh?" I asked.

Before Banner gave me an answer, he thought for a few seconds, took a long drag on his cigarette, exhaled, and then gave me his best explanation. "I would say that she somehow cured them in some type of chemical and used her taxidermy experience and skills to keep them fresh in order to cherish them. I know it sounds sick, but that's the way it is."

"When you went to the coroner to see the victim, didn't you see her face? You don't need her identification if you have a picture of her."

"That's the problem. This female never liked to have her picture taken. Because most of the time the state was taking the pictures—of her bruised, swollen, and beaten body—and usually the face was unrecognizable. The last one taken was at age fifteen. So I don't have a recent photo of her. That's why I have to wait for the fingerprint analysis. Even if she had identification, I would still have to verify her identity by her fingerprint analysis."

"Well, Joseph, from what you've told us so far about your serial killer, she definitely wasn't a stupid person," I said. "In fact, it seems to me that she was fairly intelligent. I mean she had gotten away with her crimes for quite a few years. And I know she knew the difference between right and wrong...especially having to study the Bible every day."

"You're right. The psychologist report stated that the serial killer was a female with a very high I.Q. But the report also stated she would probably be an independent and educated woman. She was educated all right, but educated in sex and abuse."

"What else did this report have to say?" I asked.

"It stated the female suspect would be a dominant, bossy person and show very little emotion. And that she would use her female qualities and attributes to get her way. Especially with men, even though the report stated she was most likely a lesbian, with male tendencies. Furthermore, she was like a chameleon that could change her personality in a split second—like a person with a split personality."

"How would she do that?" I asked.

"She would reach a point, then suddenly something would snap in her head and she couldn't control her actions, as if there was someone in her head telling her what to do and what not to do—telling her to kill those victims."

"It's a shame that she didn't get the psychological help when she needed it," I said. "It might have saved a few innocent lives."

"Why? What would the psychiatrists have done for her? Give her shock therapy?" asked Stanton.

"I'm sure the doctors could have given her medicine for her chemical imbalance," I said.

"That's true. You know we had her a few times. But in every instance, she somehow fell through the cracks."

"What do you mean, you had her a few times?" asked Stanton.

"Just what I said. She was being held in a county jail, a few states away from mine, in the state of Utah. By the time we found out about it, she was gone," said Banner, shaking his head in disgust.

"Gone? How did she get away? Did she escape?" I asked.

"She didn't have to escape. The guards opened the door and let her walk away."

"Incredible," I quipped. "I can't believe it. They had the fugitive sitting in their jail and they let her go? What did they arrest her for? Jay walking?"

Banner smiled and said, "Just about. They picked her up for shoplifting some clothing at a local department store and then transported her to jail to fingerprint and interrogate her. But she had no identification and gave the arresting officers a phony name that didn't have any priors. They let her out on her own recognizance."

"Why did they release her?" I asked.

"She was arrested on a Friday afternoon, and within a few hours the holding cells began filling up with drug abusers and other violent, hardened criminals, so they began releasing the nonviolent and misdemeanor offenders to make room for the overflow of new prisoners...and my serial killer was one of those released."

"Don't feel so bad, Joseph," I said. "We do the same thing here."

"What happens if they find out that they had released a serial killer into their own community?" asked Stanton.

I thought for a second, then said, "If it's learned later on that a wanted criminal had been turned loose back into the community, the 'Brass' would try to cover up their mistakes, until the situation is forgotten." Then I turned my attention to Banner. "But as far as your serial killer is concerned, Joseph, all I have to say is that she lucked out when the guards released her."

"Yeah... I'll say she lucked out," said Banner. "Because twenty minutes after the guards had released her back into an unsuspecting community, one of the detectives called down to the jailers to congratulate them about the serial killer that they had captured and told them to hold her until further notice. That's when he was told the awful news—that they had released her."

"Most likely to kill again," I said.

"Which she did, shortly after her release from that county jail," said Banner.

"I can tell a similar story, but it's not something I like to talk about," exclaimed Stanton.

"Eddy, don't tell me it happened to you, too?" I asked.

"Yep. My suspect was found, arrested, thrown into jail, and then let free. Not once, but twice," he said, shaking his head in disgust.

"Well, I got you beat," exclaimed Banner. "It happened three different times to me, within an eighteen-month period. It was enough to give me an ulcer."

"When did you find out about your killer's second arrest?" I asked.

"I guess it was about four or five months after the first one. I received a call from a detective from a little town called Ely, Nevada—which was a few hundred miles south of the city that had first released my killer. He also had the jailer, who was guarding my suspect, on another line so we could all listen in on the conversation."

"So," I quipped, "you were on a three-way phone conversation. You, the detective, and the jailer could talk all at the same time. Right?"

"Yep," said Banner, "but when the detective asked the jailer about my female suspect and mentioned her real name and the alias she had been using, the phone became silent. The jailer didn't answer the question for nearly a minute. Then, he gave us the bad news—that she had been released two hours earlier."

"That's incredible. I can't believe this," said Stanton.

"The system again, released her on her own recognizance," said Banner. "She had given the arresting officer the same phony name that she had given the officers at her last arrest. And that's when I found out that she had slipped through our fingers once again."

"What did the detective from Nevada say about it?" I asked.

"He was as angry about the mishap as I was," Banner said. "He couldn't believe that the jailer had allowed a killer to go free."

"What had she been arrested for?" I asked.

"She was being held for the same exact crime as before—shoplifting."

"I think she ought to go into another line of work. She's not too good at that job," I joked. "Of course now, she'll be working in hell."

Banner ignored my statement and said, "It just so happened—by coincidence—that at the time of my serial killer's arrest, the chief of police had received an order from the courts to release all nonviolent prisoners charged with minor offenses."

"What was the judge's reaction when he learned that he had released a serial killer into his own community?" I asked.

"He used the excuse that his docket and courtroom were overburdened with too many mediocre cases...and that he had too many important and long trials coming up and didn't have the time to deal with unimportant and inconsequential cases. And then complained how the judges in his county were overworked and underpaid."

"They should hang that judge," I said.

Banner nodded in agreement and said, "If the chief of police hadn't obeyed the judge's orders he would have been jailed for contempt of court. ... However, before being released from her holding cell, my suspect was warned not to shoplift in their city and had to sign a release form promising to return to the courts at a later date."

"But it was the judge who had the serial killer released into society to kill again. Which, I'm sure she did," I said.

"You're right. In fact, the day after she was released, they found a dead adult male with his penis severed and missing. And I believe one of the penises found on that necklace will turn out to be that victim's."

"It's a shame that these so-called judges have immunity from prosecution," I said. "Because the families of those poor victims who were killed after the judge had released the killer back into their communities aren't allowed to sue him for monetary damages. And the government should also do away with that immunity clause for unscrupulous prosecutors, and then we might not have innocent people in our prisons. ... I think that judge just wanted to get rid of any excess work that he thought wasn't up to his standards and issued that order for his own selfish reasons. And most of these judges nowadays only work a twenty-hour week as it is, if that!"

"You're right. All this particular judge did was have the prisoners sign an affidavit that they would show up in court on a certain date to pay a monetary fine."

"That's all the judge did?" I asked.

"That was it. Except the female prisoner never fulfilled her promise to show up in court to pay her fine. I don't even know if she had to sign a court summons."

I could feel the anger in Banner's words. "There should be a law that the criminals should be held until their fingerprints are cleared," I said. "When the computer search shows that the prisoner isn't a fugitive from justice or doesn't have any warrants...*then* let them walk. But not until then."

"Yeah, but if it's not done within a reasonable amount of time, you'll have the ACLU suing the city and department for some ungodly reason. Probably for violating the person's civil rights," said Stanton.

"So, what happened? Did anyone get reprimanded—or fired from their jobs—for letting a serial killer go free?" I asked.

"No. We ended up just gritting our teeth and biding our time. We knew we would catch up to her, sooner or later," said Banner.

"I wonder if that judge was reelected." I asked.

"No, he wasn't," Banner said, sounding satisfied. "The people voted him out of office. His political career is *finished*!"

"So what was your next move?" I asked.

"I drove to Ely and the surrounding area and checked the lesbian bars and other queer hangouts she had been known to frequent. We depleted our resources tracking that woman." Then, nervously rubbing his sweating palms together, he said, "I've even interviewed some of the girlfriends she had while on her killing spree."

Finally, Stanton jumped into the conversation and asked Banner a question. "When was the first time you knew you had a serial killer on your hands? Better yet, where and when was the first killing that you tagged to her?"

"Wait a minute!" I barked, giving Stanton a cold look. "Before we get to that, *I* want to know more about Joseph's serial killer. He told us that his suspect was released from jail three different times." Then I looked at Banner with questioning eyes and said, "You told us about two of them. But how did she slip through your fingers the third time?"

Banner changed the subject. "Baxter, isn't it getting late? Shouldn't we be heading for the coroner's office?"

I wasn't going to let him get off that easy. Before I answered, I looked at my watch, sipped my fourth cup of coffee, lit another cigarette, and then said, "No, we still have a few minutes. Why? Are you guys in a big hurry?"

"I guess not," said Banner. "I just hate bringing up the past. Especially when talking about a ruthless, senseless serial killer that used her victims' private parts for lunch. Take your pick." Then he added, "But I *am* anxious to see the coroner."

Just then, I remembered something he had told us earlier. "Wait a minute! I just thought about something else you said. You told us before that you didn't have a photo of your suspect, except one from her younger years. Why didn't you get one faxed from the jails where she had been staying? They did take her mug shot, didn't they?"

"That's a good question," he replied. "In each separate occasion, except for the D.U.I. arrest, the police were only holding her until they were certain that the stores where she had shoplifted were going to press charges. But the stores never did. So they had to release her. And not one of the police officers had taken her photo or fingerprints."

"Never?" asked Stanton.

"They only took her fingerprints one time out of the three times that she had been arrested. And I believe that the people responsible for releasing her were lying about that...just to save their own skin."

"Why do you say that?" I asked.

"I don't know," replied Banner. "It's just a hunch.... I don't think she was ever photographed or fingerprinted by any of the precincts that detained her. I think they just stuck her in the holding cell for a few hours, then when they found out the stores weren't going to press charges...they released her. It's as simple as that."

I took my last drag off my cigarette, snuffed it out in the ashtray, and said, "Okay, Joseph, now that you got that off your chest, why don't you tell us about the third time you lost your killer?"

"This time, we thought we had her for sure," he said, smiling. "She had been arrested in the state of Arizona for D.U.I. after being stopped at a weekend roadblock set up to catch drunk drivers."

"Did they fingerprint and photograph her this time?" I asked.

"Yes, but let me explain," replied Banner. "When the officer asked for her I.D., she had none and gave him a phony name—her lesbian lover's name—but at the time she didn't know that her girlfriend had a warrant out for her arrest. And when the name was run through the computer and came back showing an outstanding warrant, she was carted off to jail. Once they had booked her, they ran her prints through their database, and it came back as a hit for my serial killer. So they contacted me."

"So they finally held onto her?" I asked.

"Yeah ... For a while. But the jailer made one mistake."

"What was that?" I asked.

"He put my killer into a cell with another female."

"So what does that have to do with anything?" asked Stanton.

I spoke up, asking Banner, "Why didn't they place her into a cell alone?"

"Being the weekend," he said, "the jails were overflowing with all different types of offenders. They were overwhelmed. And with so many new prisoners coming in...the violent ones were sometimes moved to other cells...away from the nonviolent ones."

"Don't tell me. They released her because of overcrowding jails, again," interjected Stanton.

"No, not exactly," replied Banner. "When my killer's cellmate was being bonded out, the two female prisoners quickly exchanged wristbands—they were easily slipped off when lathered with lots of soap."

"What are you talking about... Wristbands?" I asked.

"That's something new that a few different jails are trying out on a trial basis," said Banner. "That way, the guards, when releasing a prisoner, can check out the prisoner's name from their wristband instead of searching through stacks of paperwork.... That was all there was to it."

"Why didn't the guard know what his prisoner looked like?" I asked.

"Because a new shift had just started working...and anyway, they didn't need to know their faces because they relied on the prisoner's wristband for identification. And when my killer answered to the name the guard had called out, he thought she was the person that had been bonded out...especially after checking her wristband I.D. Then he ordered the female to get out of 'his cell' and 'never return.' And without a second thought, she obliged him."

"So where did she go?" asked Stanton.

I gave Stanton a blank look and replied, "Where do you think she went?"

Banner snickered at my remark and then told Stanton, "The minute she was released from jail, she headed to Hero's neck of the woods."

Banner then gave me a look...like it was my fault that she'd come to Missouri.

"When did you first find out about your killer's escape?" I asked.

"Not until the next afternoon, while my partner and I were waiting to take her back to Oregon."

"You mean to tell me that you had gone to pick up your prisoner and she wasn't there?" I asked.

"Yep. We flew over a thousand miles to get there and then found out that we would be going back empty-handed."

"I bet you were pissed off over *that* foul-up!" I exclaimed.

"That's putting it mildly," Banner said. "But I was definitely angry. My partner was even more livid. But that's not the worst of it."

"Why? What happened?" asked Stanton.

"When I asked the person in charge for the photograph of our suspect, all hell broke loose. Him and his fellow workers acted like I was the criminal."

"Joseph," I interjected, "if they had given me any hassles, I'd have gone immediately to their superiors. Did *you*?"

"I did," Banner replied. "I must have talked with ten different law enforcement officials, from the arresting officer, to the desk Sergeant, to the chief. Not one of them would give me a straight answer to my question."

"Why? What did they say?" I asked.

Banner didn't answer immediately. Finally, he said, "They somehow lost the paperwork and photographs of my killer, but they didn't say how. That's why we were never faxed the photo.... They had lost the paperwork before we even left our airport."

"So what happened?" asked Stanton.

"After the crazy mix-up and after arguing with those law enforcement officials, my partner exploded in rage."

"Why? What did he do?" I asked.

"He kicked in one of their vending machines that served hot lunches."

"What did they do then?" I asked.

"Boy," said Banner, shaking his head in disbelief, "we nearly didn't get out of their station. I thought there was going to be a riot between us and their uniformed officers."

"Why?" I asked.

"They wanted my partner's blood! They must not get much action in that area of the country. I believe they would have arrested my partner, but I finally talked them into believing that it was their fault that the incident had happened in the first place."

"You mean to tell me that they thought it was *your* fault that they'd lost the paperwork and photograph?" I asked.

"That's right. We ended up leaving their station empty-handed, with our tails tucked between our legs. That was one of the lowest points of my entire life. My partner and I flew back and didn't say a word to each other during the entire flight. We were utterly disgusted by the sudden turn of events."

"Why? You knew you would catch your killer sooner or later, didn't you?" I asked.

"To tell you the truth, I wasn't sure. We figured this was our third strike. And my optimism turned to pessimism. I'd never been a pessimist in my life—until that dreary day. When we returned to the station, then we did what we were good at."

"What's that?" asked Stanton.

"Waiting and biding our time," replied Banner. "We knew that sooner or later we would get another chance at bat." Then he looked into my eyes. "And thanks to Baxter here, I think I've hit a home run. That is, if that female in the park is my serial killer. And I have a feeling that she is—and the one I've been hunting for the past couple of years."

I wondered where Banner's partner was, so I asked him. "Where's your partner? Why didn't he tag along with you?"

"My superiors heard about the hassle we had with the Arizona police officers when we went to pick up our suspect, so they didn't want it to happen a second time."

"You wouldn't have had any trouble here," I said. "Law enforcement officials in my city are all professionals."

"But that's not the only reason my partner isn't here," said Banner. "Our budget would only allow one of us to fly this far. Since I was the senior and lead investigator, I got the call."

"Why do you think your killer came to St. Louis? Do *you* have any theories about the incident in the park?" I asked.

"If I do, I'm keeping them to myself," he replied.

"Then let me ask you this... If your killer was a lesbian, was the guy lying underneath her a john...or just somebody she could rob and kill?"

"I'm not sure. But if she was with a man, she only had only one thing in mind—to kill him! I don't think robbery was an issue with this particular serial killer."

"Why do you say that?" I asked.

"She didn't want to *rob* her victims... She wanted to kill the demon that had been haunting her since childhood.... When she met the guy in the park...in her mind, she probably thought that she was with her father. Then, when she realized that she was being used sexually, her inner rage exploded and her terror began all over again.... That's when she usually kills her victim—which have all been men. As far as I know, she hasn't killed any females...probably because she doesn't fear them like she does males. And that goes back to her childhood...and the abuse she experienced by her father."

"I don't believe that. A psychopath will kill anyone," I said.

"You could be right, Baxter," said Banner. "But there could be another reason."

"Like what?" asked Stanton, finally getting into the conversation.

"She might kill out of rage or jealousy...or maybe over her torment from years of torture and sexual abuse.... There were times when I felt sorry for this woman."

"Why would you feel sorry for a psychotic psychopath?" I asked.

Banner thought for a minute, took a long drag on his cigarette and exhaled, then said, "I wondered how she could live with herself knowing that she has killed over and over again. I'm sure she had a hard time looking into the mirror in her normal state of mind."

"I disagree. A psychopath has no conscience," I said.

"She had one, though. I'm sure of it," replied Banner.

"I doubt it," I replied.

"It's when she's in her abnormal, mental state that she turns into a psychotic, psychopathic maniac," opined Banner.

"But if that's the case, Joseph, why would she carry around that penis necklace...if she was in her normal state of mind?" I asked.

"To keep her victims close to her heart," replied Banner.

"I don't buy it," I snapped. "I think she was totally wacky. I think she was in her own fantasy world. Possibly started, then festered into wicked rage only after years and years of sexual abuse. If she had gotten the proper help when all of this abuse first began, she would have been able to control that rage."

"So whose fault is that?" asked Stanton.

I thought for a few seconds, then said, "Society let her down.... By letting her family educate her instead of the state. This should never have happened."

"It shouldn't have," interjected Banner, "but it did.... And we found out why."

"Why?" I asked.

"Because the father was a member of the church where the girl's principal worshiped. And he told the principal that his daughter was much slower than other children her age, and that she was slightly retarded. So the principal agreed and allowed her to study at home."

"Then that principal should be jailed for his part in her damaged life," I said.

"Him and many others," said Banner, nodding his head. "Everyone seemed to be against her—even her close friends. In fact, they knew her as a 'reject.' That's the label they put on her—and many others that were less tasteful...like retard, dopey, and P-brain just to name a few. She grew up not wanting to go outside—wanting instead to remain behind darkened windows. She preferred the night so she couldn't be seen."

"You know," said Stanton, in between sips of coffee. "I'm not sure that she would have been found guilty in a court of law. She might have been acquitted by reason of insanity."

"Are you kidding!" exclaimed Banner. "She killed more than ten people, and they all had their private parts severed and missing. She was guilty as sin."

"You may be right," answered Stanton. "All I'm saying is that she may have been mentally incompetent. It's like a brand new puppy. Depending on the owner, the pup will turn out to be gentle and loving…or vicious and mean. It's all in the way they are brought up."

"That's true," said Banner.

"Same thing with kids. They learn what is taught to them," said Stanton.

"You may have a good point, Eddy," I said.

"You're damn right!" exclaimed Stanton. "And I say Banner's killer knew right from wrong…and has to take the responsibility for her vicious actions. And to atone for her sins, she must make restitution to the state where she has committed her dastardly crimes."

"If Joseph's killer is in our morgue, I think she has paid the ultimate price," I said. "What does the Bible say? 'Ye who reaps by the sword shall parish by the sword.' And we will soon know whether those words are prophetic."

"She reaped all right," Banner said. "Hell, she has left bodies all over the country. In fact, Baxter, I'm surprised that there aren't more detectives from other states knocking at your door. They'll catch up to you sooner or later. They always do!"

I acknowledged Banner's prophetic words with a nod and smile, then said, "I'm sure I'll be hearing from them sooner or later. I'm not looking forward to it, but if other detectives do come here, I'm sure they'll be happy to learn that their city won't have to make the funeral arrangements or be charged for returning the body to their jurisdiction. Unfortunately, my city is now responsible for that." But this talk didn't interest me. I wanted to know more about Joseph's killer. I tried again. "Joseph, when did you first realize that you were looking for a serial killer?"

"Oh, that's easy . . . the second murder scene that I visited where the victim's manhood had been cut off and was missing from the crime scene. That's the first time I knew we had a serial killer on the loose."

"So what did your department do?" I asked.

"We started our own task force. We wanted to get the suspect off the street as quickly as possible. As you can see, it took a little longer than expected."

"If you thought you had a serial killer after the second 'missing penis murder,' who did you think was the suspect in your first murder?"

"We suspected the ex-wife or his girlfriend. Neither one had a reliable alibi. Also, they each had a very good motive. But that second similar murder was the kicker. We knew then that we had a real nut case on our hands. So we came up with a good name for our suspect."

"What was that?" I asked.

"The 'missing manhood murderer,'" said Banner, smiling.

"How many victims do you think she killed?" asked Stanton.

"We believe at least ten, if not more," replied Banner. "Now, we'll never know. The amount could be much higher. Hell, she could have left bodies all over the country, besides the ones that we know about. What we should be asking is *when* did she start killing people? Maybe she began her killing spree without leaving her signature."

"What do you call cutting off a person's manhood? *That's* her signature. And that's something that you don't overlook," I said.

"Cutting off the person's manhood might have just been a hobby for her. I don't know," said Banner. "We'll probably never know. Hell, she may have been killing for the past five years, seven years…maybe even for the past ten years. I don't know. We'll probably never know. Hell, some poor police detective may be looking for a serial killer that doesn't exist anymore."

With that said, we took a short break from our conversation while Bonnie refilled our cups with coffee. As I lit a cigarette, I looked out the café window and noticed rain pouring down from darkened skies. I knew we weren't going anywhere as hard as the rain was falling, so I started up our conversation again. "What about your suspect, Eddy? You stated he was given his freedom twice. How did that happen? How did he get away?"

"That's not important," he replied. "The important thing is to get to the coroner's office and talk with him. I'm still not sure if that guy at the morgue is my suspect."

"Why do you say that?" I asked.

"'Cause I'm not sure what my suspect looks like. I don't have a recent photo of him. The only photo that I have of him was taken when he was committed to the juvenile home at the age of thirteen. And that was quite a few years ago. So the only way I can tell if he's my suspect or not is from the fingerprint analysis."

"Didn't any other police department send you or fax you a photo of your killer?" I asked.

"No," replied Eddy. "I was never faxed a photo from any police agency. I don't even know if your medical examiner has taken the fingerprints yet. But I'd like to find out."

"I know you would," I said.

"Don't you think we should be leaving?" asked Stanton.

"We will. But look at the weather. It's pouring cats and dogs. And I didn't bring an umbrella with me. Did you?" I asked.

"Evidently not," said Stanton.

"Let's wait awhile until the rain slows. Then we'll head for the coroner's office."

"Why wait? It's getting late," said Stanton.

"But the coroner probably isn't at work yet," I said.

"He should have started work a few hours ago," exclaimed Stanton.

"He's getting up in years," I explained, "so the city cuts him some slack. He doesn't have the same hours we do. Most of the time, he picks his own hours."

"We should still head over there," said Stanton.

"Don't worry, we'll leave in a few minutes. I'll drink one more cup of coffee and *then* we'll take a ride over to the coroner's office. Maybe then the rain will subside," I said

"I hope so," said Stanton.

"So Eddy, why don't you tell us how your suspect slipped through your fingers, not once but twice," I asked, lighting a cigarette from my second pack.

"There's not much to tell," he replied. "He was picked up at the bar for drunken and disorderly—for fighting with the bouncer. The bouncer wanted to put him out like a cigarette. But instead, he called the police."

"What did *they* do?" I asked.

"They held him in a patrol car for a few minutes."

"That was it?" I asked.

"No," Eddy said. "Before they let him go, they gave him a ticket and court summons. They didn't even take him to jail. He gave them his real name. And when it came up for a hit in their computer a few hours later, my suspect was long gone."

"A few hours!" I exclaimed. "It usually takes only a few minutes to check for outstanding warrants. At least in our department it only takes a few minutes—that is, if the person we're checking is a citizen of this state."

"Yeah," said Stanton, "it should only take a few minutes, which it usually does except when the computers are down. And our department has been updating our computers ever since the Y2K problem, so they have to shut down the computer every so often, for hours at a time."

"We also have that problem," said Banner.

Stanton interjected. "We never know when our computers are going to shut down. Sometimes it's once a week or once a month. Lately, it's been once a day. And that's what *their* problem was. Their computers were shut down when they ticketed my killer."

"What did the cops do when they found out that they had released a killer back into society?" I asked.

"What could they do?" replied Stanton. "They put out an APB on him. But he split town for parts unknown ... Just like Banner's killer."

"When did it happen the second time?" I asked.

"Five weeks later, he was picked up again."

"What did they get him on this time?" I asked.

"Vagrancy. And this time he was fingerprinted *and* photographed. But they couldn't run his prints due to their own computer mishap. And then the photo they took of him didn't come out."

"Why not?" I asked.

"It seems a drunk that had his picture taken right before my suspect was to have his taken began fighting with the arresting officers. In the commotion, the camera was knocked to the floor. When they tried to take my suspect's picture, it wouldn't focus. I guess they had broken the lens."

"What did they do?" I asked.

"They had to get a new camera, but couldn't buy one until the next morning. So they put the guy in a cell and then let him out that very next morning. So he never had his photo retaken."

"Incredible. What fine police work," I joked.

"Yep! They wrote him a ticket and let him go," said Stanton, shaking his head in disbelief. "And he never paid the fine. Or showed up for court. Instead, he split town—again. Just like Banner's killer did."

"What did *they* say when they found out that they had released a serial killer?" I asked.

"Their police department called us a day or so later once the fugitive warrant had showed up on their computer. They felt worse than we did."

"I bet he killed again, didn't he? Probably the same night they released him," I said.

"You're right," replied Stanton. "He did kill again...and that same night. Ten hours after they released him into society, he strangled a young, twenty-year-old female."

"How did you know it was your suspect that killed her?" I asked.

"That's easy to answer. My suspect left something at each one of his murder scenes," said Stanton.

"Like what?" Banner and I asked in unison.

"A Bicycle playing card," replied Stanton. "He always left an ace of spades near the victim's body."

"Why would he do that, Eddy?" asked Banner.

"I have no idea why he picked the ace of spades. I was hoping to ask him when he'd been apprehended. But I don't think that's possible now."

"Only if you can talk with the dead," I joked. "Eddy, did you think your investigation would end up like this?"

"Never," he said, shaking his head. "I was like Joseph. I figured we would get him...in the long run. We always do. The criminal's luck usually runs out sooner rather than later. Just as it did here. But I thought we would apprehend him alive...not dead. "

"At least you have him in custody and he can't escape," I said.

"Yep. Two months after he was thrown in jail, he turns up dead. At least I hope he's dead," said Stanton.

"Eddy, criminals have a bad habit of getting caught. And your guy sounds like a career criminal. Am I right?" I asked.

"You sure are—one hundred percent. This guy was a crook from the age of five. His father tried to make him the best in *that* profession—using him to sneak into homes after the occupants went to bed."

"That's insane," I exclaimed.

"The kid elevated from shoplifter to burglar by age six," said Stanton, as he finished his third cup of coffee. I was on my seventh.

"He was weaned on crime. Is there any wonder that he would make his way up the criminal ladder and commit murder? I think not."

"Where were the social services people? Why didn't they intervene on the kid's behalf?" I asked.

"Who knows?" replied Stanton. "Isn't that the way it usually is? Social services usually only interferes in innocent people's lives. Never the guilty ones—that is, until it's too late."

"Isn't that the truth," I said.

"Yeah. And Lawson and his siblings were either starving, beaten, or dead by the time the social services employees got off their butts to investigate the situation," said Stanton. "By that time, Lawson's future had already been molded. And when his parents weren't teaching him the tricks of the trade, he had many tutors to further his criminal education. He also had tutors to further his education when he was on vacation visiting juvenile hall. In his mind, he wasn't there to receive a decent, normal education—just a criminal one."

"Did he have a very high I.Q. or was he like most of the criminals—brainless?" I asked.

"No, he definitely wasn't brainless. In fact, he was quite intelligent. He was able to keep one step ahead of law enforcement for nearly two years until he stepped into your town."

"He picked the wrong town to visit, I guess," I said.

"That was one of a few mistakes that he had made while running from the law," said Stanton. "But the reason we had such a hard time catching him was that he left very little forensic evidence, if any at all, at his crime scenes—except for the playing cards, of course."

"We've been talking about this guy and I don't even know his name," I said. "Do you know his real identity? What's his name?"

"The suspect's name—the name he was given at birth—is Jerry Lawson," replied Stanton.

"How is it that he didn't leave any evidence at his crime scenes? Actually, now that I think about it, he didn't leave much evidence at this crime scene either, except for a weapon and his severed penis," I joked.

"This guy, believe me, was well disciplined while committing his crimes," said Stanton. "He even wore gloves so he wouldn't leave prints. Were any gloves found at this crime scene, Baxter?"

"I don't know," I replied. "I didn't see any while I was checking the bodies for a pulse. Although I wasn't really looking for a pair of gloves. Remember, I had overlooked the guns when I first arrived there."

"I'm sure that when the medical examiner checks my suspect he'll find that his whole body has been completely shaved. He did this so he wouldn't leave any hair fibers behind at his crime scenes."

"This guy doesn't sound stupid," I said.

"No, this guy was no dummy. He was sharp. That's why I'm so anxious to hear the coroner's report. I want to find out how that guy died."

"It was fate," I said.

"I would like to know," said Stanton, "if Lawson was at the park that night to kill one of the other victims, or did he go there with something else in mind? Did he go there alone? Or did he arrive there with one of the victims?"

"I don't know," I said.

"I want to know which person shot him," Stanton added. "I would like to find out why he was at the park in the first place. Was he there for pleasure...to rob...or was he there to kill? What the heck was on Lawson's mind that day? I'm very curious about that. But I'll probably never know for certain."

"We all want to know those details," Banner said.

"When we hear the report from the medical examiner, he'll probably have his own theory about the killings," I said.

"I'm sure he'll have his own take on the murder scene," said Stanton. "But my suspect was very street wise. After raping and sodomizing his vulnerable victims, he made them shower or bathe—to wash away any semen or DNA evidence."

"You're kidding?" I said.

"I'm not," replied Stanton. "Once he was happy with his victim's cleanliness, he would allow her to dry off and smoke a cigarette before strangling her to death. Then he would mutilate the body. This guy was an evil seed from birth, then grew into a bully. And his parents condoned his vicious behavior."

"Then they are as guilty as their son," I said.

"Before the age of five," Stanton added, "Lawson cornered two little puppies in a vacant house, poured gasoline over their tiny bodies, and lit them on fire—then roared with laughter as he watched the little puppies run around in circles, yelping in agony."

"That's sick," I said.

"The burning animals eventually caught the litter in the place on fire and burned the house down to the ground."

"Too bad Lawson wasn't in it. I guess it's a good thing that he finally got what he deserved," I said.

"Just not soon enough," Stanton said. "I just hope that the fingerprint analysis that's being done at your lab proves my killer's identity. Because we won't be able to identify him from his teeth—he never went to a dentist."

"Not ever?" I said.

"Never. His parents didn't believe in dentists or doctors. They believed in laying of the hands," said Stanton.

"What do you mean by the laying of hands?" I asked, after lighting a cigarette.

"It's the art of faith healing," said Stanton.

"What happens if he had a toothache and the faith healing didn't get rid of the pain? Then what would he do?" I asked.

"If his teeth became rotten, he would pull them out himself," replied Stanton. "His father did it for him during his childhood years. The problem is...he never had any xrays done of his teeth, so we have nothing to go on in that regard. But I'm sure we'll get a match off his fingerprints."

"Lawson's childhood was something else," I said, shaking my head.

"I told you," said Stanton. "At six, he was burning animals and houses. And at the age of ten, he was capturing lost and abandoned animals to play his most favorite game."

"What was his favorite game?" I asked.

"He would take his magic hammer with a big, blunt head and smash their brains in. Then he would spread the dead carcasses on the neighbor's lawn."

"What did the neighbors do about his vindictiveness?" I asked.

"They spoke to his parents about it."

"That's it? That's all they did was speak to the kid's parents?" I asked, shaking my head in disgust.

"Yes. They wanted his parents to punish him...but they never did."

"Why didn't his parents discipline him?" I asked.

"They said he would grow out of it. Like it was just something all kids did."

"His parents should have been responsible for his actions. They should have been thrown in jail themselves and had that kid taken away and put into a normal home setting," I said.

"To get his revenge against those neighbors that had told on him, Lawson kidnapped *their* pets and smashed in their heads with his trusty hammer," said Stanton, as he put out his cigarette.

"If I ever saw him doing that to my pets, I would have taken the hammer away from that kid and used it on *his* head," I said.

"Please, let me finish what I was saying," said Stanton.

"I'm sorry, Eddy... I didn't mean to interrupt you. So what did Lawson do next, after he had bashed in their little heads with his trusty hammer?" I asked.

"He placed the dead animal parts on his neighbors' front porch or in their expensive cars. ... He was the *real* animal!"

"You can say that again. He was the devil in disguise," I said.

"And as he grew into his teens," Stanton continued, "he became bolder and focused his rage towards kids instead of animals. He especially liked torturing kids smaller than he was...because he was small, too. In fact, the psychological profile stated that my killer was a small, stout male. Which was correct. He's just under five and a half feet tall."

"Was the psychological profile on the right track?" I asked.

"Definitely," replied Stanton. "But the rest of the answers will come from the medical examiner. Then, I can check one report against the other. But from what I've heard and seen, our psychological profile was dead on. It couldn't have been any better unless it was written by the perpetrator himself."

"Eddy, do you know if your perpetrator ever killed anyone as a juvenile?" asked Banner.

"I don't know for sure. I wouldn't put it past him. What we do have on record, however, is close to murder."

"What age did that start?" I asked.

"When he was a mere twelve years old," replied Stanton. "Because he didn't particularly like one of the younger kids that played in the neighborhood. And when the kid came near Lawson's yard, Lawson grabbed him and threw him to the ground. He put a wrestling hold on the scared youngster." He took a long drag on his cigarette, then added, "When Lawson began squeezing and bending the kid's legs, the kid started screaming. So Lawson placed his hand over the terrified youngster's mouth to muffle his screams, and just at that moment, the little kid's bones broke."

"The psychopath must have known that he was hurting the little kid. Why didn't he let him go?" I asked.

"Lawson refused to release his hold until the bones had completely snapped. He laughed as the little kid screamed in agony. But he wasn't quite finished yet," said Stanton.

"Why? What did Lawson do?" I asked.

"He jumped up from that kid . . . Then jumped another— and placed his hands around the terrified kid's head and twisted it...with amazing force. Luckily, he didn't break the kid's neck and kill him. Which, I'm sure he tried to do."

"Man, Eddy ... Lawson was a real bully. Did he hurt that kid?" I asked.

"This time, instead of legs breaking, it was the kid's collarbone. When the maniac finally released him, the little kid fell to the ground writhing in pain and agony, while Lawson danced around both kids, taunting and teasing them. He had no conscience, whatsoever."

"Did he ever apologize to the people that he hurt that day?" I asked.

"No. He had absolutely no remorse for the revolting things he had done."

"What about Lawson's parents? Didn't they get him any psychological help?" I asked.

"When the maniac's parents were notified about what their son had done, they only made excuses for him. They would never scold him or correct his evil ways for hurting others. They only beat him when he wouldn't listen to *their* commands," said Stanton.

"Why didn't the police department do something about that crazy kid?" I asked.

"They did," Stanton replied. "But when they took him away, they would return him to his parents a day later. And the parents were unsympathetic to law enforcement demands. They used the excuse that their kid was hyper and would grow out of it, in time."

"You know, it's too bad euthanasia isn't legal in this state. Lawson would have been a perfect candidate," said Banner.

"It is, Joseph," I replied. "We give the ones who win the prize a lethal injection. No more electric chair—where the body is fried to a crispy brown—it was deemed too sadistic. And they've practically outlawed the gas chamber...because it eats the guts from the inside out. And very few states allow public hanging, anymore. ... Society thinks it's more humane to kill the criminal by lethal injection because they look as though they are fast asleep."

"Yeah, they just never wake up again," exclaimed Stanton.

"That's fine with me," said Banner. "I believe in being compassionate if they have to die. Why make it any more painful than it already is? I mean, they are never going to wake up and hold another conversation or eat another meal. They are gone forever. But in the end, they will be judged by god."

"But a horrible, crazy person deserves to suffer and feel pain," I said. "And Lawson wielded enough of it on his victims. Why shouldn't he get some of his own medicine? ... I wonder if his parents ever punished him when he played wrestler and broke those kids' bones."

"I don't think so," replied Stanton. "I remember looking through his juvenile report. A few minutes after that episode, the police were called to the scene. They immediately carted him off to juvenile hall. He was there, off and on, until the age of eighteen."

"They should have kept him and never let him out," I said.

"They wanted to keep him longer but they couldn't," said Stanton. "They *had* to release him. And that's when his murderous crime spree began."

"He was *born* a criminal," I said.

"You could be right, Baxter," replied Stanton. "But Lawson was given a very lenient sentence each time he committed an act of violence. The state thought they could rehabilitate him. But he didn't want to be rehabilitated."

"Why not?" I asked.

"He liked the life of crime," replied Stanton. "He thought he was good at it. I guess he was...to a certain extent."

"Why do you say that, Eddy?" I asked.

"He didn't spend one full day in jail," replied Stanton. "Many different police agencies brought him in for questioning on many different crimes, but they always had to release him for lack of evidence."

"But he didn't start out as a killer, did he?" I asked.

"No. Like I said before, he started as a petty thief and graduated on to bigger and better things, until his luck ran out."

"You can say that again," I said.

"Breaking into empty houses when the owners were on vacation just wasn't good enough for him. He wanted something more," said Stanton.

"Like what?" I asked, leaning back in my chair, while lighting another cigarette.

"Something that would give him a rush. He found it when he added violence to his repertoire."

"How is that?" I asked.

"Instead of breaking into *empty* houses, Lawson waited until the owners returned home and then confronted them...with a loaded gun. He would then place the gun to the head of the spouse and threaten to blow her head off her shoulders. Then, he would pistol whip the husband and make him watch as he raped the man's wife. Lawson was one vile and sick individual."

I noticed the rain was no longer coming down in a torrential downpour.

"Hey guys," I said, "look out the window. The rain has nearly stopped. Why don't we finish our coffee and head on down to the coroner's office?"

"That sounds good to me," said Stanton. Banner agreed.

"Well then, let's go and see what Doc Grady has to say," I said.

We finished our coffee, left our tips on the table for our waitress, and then walked up to the cash register and paid our bills. Then, we all packed into my car and headed for the coroner's office. I hoped Doc Grady would have some good news for us. ... But any news would help, I thought to myself.

# Chapter 14

"I hope the coroner can put this case into perspective," said Stanton, during the drive. "Maybe, he'll be able to fit the right pieces into this jigsaw puzzle. I want to close the case today. It's been one heck of a chase and one big headache for me and the victims' families."

"I know what you mean," I said. "My last case was one big jigsaw puzzle. Every time I thought I had a piece in the right place...another seemed to fit better. It was driving me crazy. I had well over ten different suspects, and they each had a good motive for murdering the victim. Plus, their alibis couldn't be substantiated."

"But you eventually found the perp and put him away, didn't you, Baxter?" asked Stanton.

"Oh, yeah," I replied. "As I said before, my perp was guilty and sentenced to the death penalty, plus five life sentences with no chance of parole. ... But I really feel sorry for her."

"You feel *sorry* for the killer? Why?" asked Banner.

I took a long drag off my cigarette and then said, "Once I began my investigation, I found out that the dead victim wasn't completely innocent—he brought the episode upon himself. ... To put it mildly, the victim was an out and out scumbag. He deserved what he got. ... That's my opinion, anyway."

"Why would you say that, Baxter?" asked Stanton. "How could you possibly say that? Nobody deserves to be murdered by some thug."

"Well," I said, "if anyone deserved to die, he did. His name was Jim Palter, and he played with vulnerable women's feelings... And with their hearts. Then he left them—broke and destitute—for someone else."

"That's nothing new. He was a player," said Banner.

Listening to Banner say that made my skin boil. So I set him straight. "Many of the women he conned had to file for bankruptcy. A few of them were even evicted from their homes. Because of this 'player,' those poor women were left broken-hearted and penniless. What kind of person does that to another human being?"

"A scumbag, just like you said," replied Banner. "But did he deserve to be murdered?"

"I think he did!" I exclaimed. "And to tell you the truth, I'm glad he's dead. Now he won't be able to hurt any more people. The murderer put a stop to that. Not only did she kill him, but she severed his penis and slit his throat."

"But why did she have to mutilate him like that?" asked Stanton.

"I don't really know. I guess to make a point."

"Now I remember that case," said Banner. "In fact, when I read the fax about the severed penis, I thought I had another victim to add to my list. That's when I called your department to see if your case had any connection with mine. But I was mistaken. It was a rush to judgment."

"Yeah, but you ended up here, anyway," I said, adding, "So why didn't you think my case had a connection with yours?"

"Because...when I learned that the penis was still at the crime scene, I knew we were on the wrong track and that it wasn't my perpetrator's work—just the work of a copycat killer."

"How did you come to that conclusion?" I asked.

"We kept quiet about the missing penis from our crime scene," replied Banner. "Your killer left them *at* the crime scene. *Ours* took them as a keepsake."

"What did you tell the media?" I asked.

"The reporters were only told that the victim's manhood was severed, not missing. So we continued to hunt for our particular killer...and didn't think about your case again," said Banner.

"We'll have to talk about this subject again, you guys," I said. "I'm curious to learn about your hunt for your killers and where your search took you. You've already said that some of the murders were committed outside of your jurisdiction. How did that play out with those law enforcement officials that were involved in their own investigations?"

"They didn't like it," Banner and Stanton said in unison.

"I don't blame them," I said. "I don't like outside police agencies stepping on my toes either.... No offense to you guys, of course."

"No offense taken," Banner said.

"At least the murders I investigated in my last case were all within our city limits," I retorted. "The victims were killed within a ten-mile radius. ... And three of the victims were actually neighbors."

"It sounds as if your killer stayed close to home," said Banner.

"Well, at the time I had no idea who the perp was. Like I said before, I had over ten possible suspects that wanted Palter dead."

"It sounds like your victim didn't have too many good friends," Stanton joked.

"You're right, Eddy," I replied. "But that's not the half of it. ... When I first began the investigation, I was only investigating one murder. But as *that* investigation progressed, other murders occurred around the city, which, I later learned, were connected to my original murder investigation. And within a month, I was investigating five murders—all killed by the same perp."

"Were you looking for a male or female suspect?" Stanton asked.

"In the beginning, we were looking for a male perp. Even the psychological profile stated that the killer was a male and most likely, one of the women's husbands or boyfriends—or even his business partner."

"So, you were looking for a male perp then?" asked Stanton.

"When I first entered the victim's residence and saw the murder scene, I thought the killer could only be a man. But then we found evidence to the contrary."

"But wasn't a woman convicted of the murders?" asked Banner.

"Yes. A young woman," I said.

"What evidence did you find that made you think a woman had killed the victim?" asked Banner.

"Well, for one thing, we found long blonde hairs all around the murder scene. We also found evidence of semen and fluid on the bed sheets."

"Did the DNA tests confirm your suspicions?" asked Banner.

"Yep. The DNA tests proved the hairs and fluid to be female. Plus, there was other evidence that proved the killer was a woman."

"Like what?" asked Stanton.

"We had the perp's fingerprint on the murder weapon, for one. But what really was the kicker—that really nailed the lid on the perp's coffin—was the DNA evidence. My perp was there at the time the murder was committed, having sexual intercourse with the victim."

"Why didn't you arrest her before the other murders were committed?" asked Banner.

"Joseph, you asked the perfect question. ... I told you. We have a serial killer task force set up."

"So? What does that have to do with anything?" asked Banner.

"Their evidence had first priority. I couldn't get my evidence tested in time to exclude my other suspects," I said, shaking my head in disgust.

"That's not right," said Stanton.

"Then," I continued, "the city didn't renew their contract with the company that does our DNA testing. All the evidence that the forensic investigators found wasn't tested for many weeks. Some for nearly a month."

"How do your superiors expect you to conduct a decent investigation?" asked Banner.

"Talk about hitting your head against the wall," I said. "Every time I tried to push my testing, the medical examiner would just set it aside and work on the task force evidence."

"So what did you end up doing?" asked Banner.

"I concentrated on interviewing and interrogating the suspects...until I had the report on all of my forensic evidence. Remember that the psychological profile stated the perp to be male. So that's what I went with. In fact, the first couple of male suspects I interviewed had absolutely no credible alibis...and had very good motives for wanting the victim dead."

"What kind of motive?" asked Stanton.

"Like a two hundred and fifty thousand dollar life insurance policy."

"Yes. That's a very good motive to kill someone, especially if you don't like the person," said Stanton.

"Another suspect also had a good motive," I exclaimed. "The victim had raped his fifteen-year-old daughter."

"Yeah," interjected Banner, "that's another good reason to kill the guy. Boy, you were right, Baxter. That guy Palter was a scum bag!"

"Yeah ... I know!" I replied. "But to get back to what I was saying about my suspects. I've only mentioned two of them. A third gave me a phony name...because he had an attempted murder arrest warrant out for him in another state. But I didn't find out about that until days later. Then, when I went to arrest him on the warrant, he escaped on foot. ... I could go on and on."

"Baxter, when you said you had a lot of suspects, you weren't kidding," said Stanton.

"You're right about that. Every time I interviewed a witness in that case I ended up placing them on my suspect list."

"So what made your perp kill the guy?" asked Stanton.

"I really don't know for sure," I replied, "although I *think* I know. The perp swears she didn't kill anyone. But then again, she's never shown any remorse or sympathy to the victims' families."

"She sounds like a cold-blooded killer to me," said Banner.

"I wonder what made *her* into a killer?" asked Stanton.

"I don't know for sure," I replied.

"Was she abused as a kid?" asked Stanton.

"Well, she was abandoned as a baby...and adopted by a strict Lutheran family. But basically, she had a normal childhood. And by that I mean her parents used a belt or coat hanger to beat her with. But they punished her out of love...or so they said," I said.

"That sounds like abuse to me," opined Stanton.

"Even if she was abused, that's no excuse to kill," said Banner.

"But abuse had nothing to do with her murdering ways," I said. "In fact, she had been the perfect daughter for her adopted parents...but then, one day out of the blue, her attitude completely changed. She began rebelling."

"If I had been beaten every day, I think I would have disobeyed adults, too," said Stanton.

"That's not the reason she changed," I said.

"What was it then?" asked Stanton.

"She had learned the truth...about being given away at birth," I said.

"How did that happen?" asked Banner.

"One day, while looking for her mother's diary, she came across her adoption papers. Then she confronted her parents and asked them why they hadn't told her that she had been adopted at birth."

"What did her parents tell her?" asked Stanton.

"They couldn't give her an explanation that she would accept."

"So what did this young girl do then?" asked Stanton.

"She began searching for her biological mother, but she had nothing to go on because the papers had been sealed and the adoption company refused to help her."

"That's probably what started her hatred towards authority figures," Stanton opined.

"Then," I continued, "a few weeks later, she found a letter written to her adopted mother from her birth mother. That's when she found out her whole life story of why she was abandoned and adopted. At that moment, her young life was shattered, in her eyes."

"Can you blame her?" asked Stanton.

"Not really," I replied. "But besides being angry with her adopted parents, she also became enraged at her birth mother...for throwing her away like some dirty garbage. So then, she left graduate school and went to find her mother—to either confront her or kill her. She finally did both."

"What? She found her birth mother and killed her?" asked Banner.

"Yep," I replied. "That was the last murder I investigated concerning her case. ... She was found guilty of killing both her birth mother and father."

"That's a shame," said Stanton.

"It certainly was," I said. "Because when she first learned of her true birth parents, she only wanted some type of relationship with them. But then she learned that her real mother wanted nothing to do with her...and her birth father had never been told that he even had a daughter. In fact, she was one of his new prospects."

"What do you mean by 'prospects?'" asked Stanton.

"I mean that my perp and Palter were boyfriend and girlfriend. You know...getting it on!"

"You mean to tell me she was having intercourse with her own father?" asked Banner, looking confused.

"That's right," I replied. "But at the time, neither knew that they were related."

"Then why did she kill him if she didn't know he was her father? You mean...she thought she was actually killing her boyfriend?" asked Banner.

"No ... not exactly," I said. "Let me explain. One day while she was at Palter's apartment, she found a bag full of phony identification that Palter had used to scam vulnerable people out of their money. She also found his real identification, which had a name that she was familiar with. Up to that point, she had known Palter by a different name."

"What did she do then?" asked Stanton.

"We believe that she confronted him about his real name and phony identification. That's when he finally broke down and admitted his evil deeds. And it was during that conversation that she learned of his real identity and that he was actually her father."

"So what did the victim do?" asked Banner.

"Not much of anything. He was more surprised than she was. He had never been told that he had a child. We also believe that he was tied to the bedposts as she asked him the questions."

"Why was he tied to his bedposts? I don't understand." Stanton said.

"They were evidently playing a sex game where he was tied up to the bedposts while she tortured him using sex. The only thing he was able to do was moan with pleasure."

"So what did she do then?" asked Banner.

"That's when she took a bathroom break. It was during her restroom visit that she found the bag of phony identification that Palter had hidden," I said.

"Is that when she confronted him about his true identity?" asked Stanton.

"Yeah. And when she found out that the person she was making love to was her father, a person that she had extreme hatred for, I believe that's when she flew into a murderous rage."

"I think that would have made me mad enough to kill," said Banner.

"Then," I continued, "she picked up the butcher knife—the one they had used to cut the pieces of rope—and severed his penis. After that, she stabbed him more than thirty times in the chest. And then she cut loose his bindings and somehow dragged him into the kitchen where she took his severed penis and placed it into his left hand near his mouth."

"Why did she do that, Baxter?" asked Stanton.

"To make a statement, I guess. And while Palter was lying on the kitchen floor she slit his throat from ear to ear—his chest was one big, open wound. His blood nearly covered the kitchen floor. ... It was a mess."

"All murder scenes usually are," said Banner. "I must say though, the five murders that your perp was convicted of were pretty much overkill."

"Joseph, why do you say it's overkill?" I asked.

"Why? My typical homicide is a normal killing. You know, one shot to the chest with a three-fifty-seven magnum—or from being choked to death," said Banner.

"Well, I'll tell you guys one thing," I said. "I had never come across that type of psychopath before. Not until I investigated those five grisly murders."

"I know exactly what you mean," said Banner. "Until I began my serial killer investigation three years ago, I hadn't seen such gruesome murders either."

"Joseph, you must live in a very big city to be used to psychopathic murder scenes like the one I just described," I said.

"Well, after hunting a psychopath for nearly three years...it kind of grows on you," he said.

"It doesn't grow on me, that's for sure," I said, shaking my head.

"Believe me, I could go the rest of my life without looking at another killing like the ones my perp committed," said Banner.

Finally, we arrived at the medical examiner's office.

"Well, we're here, guys," I said. "First, let's talk to the coroner and forensic lab investigators. Then, if we must, we'll visit the murder scene. ... And once we're finished with our few little chores, we'll go back to the cafe for a late lunch or early dinner. ... It's up to you guys, though."

"That sounds like a good idea to me," said Stanton, as I parked the car. "I like that cafe. They give you large portions of food and vegetables. Plus, their food is delicious. Not only that, but the price is right."

"I second the motion," Banner said.

We jumped out of my vehicle and walked to the coroner's office.

We visited the autopsy room first. The place was very busy. All the specialists were busy testing different types of evidence. Then I noticed Dr. Bradly, the medical examiner's assistant. He noticed me at the same time, so I walked over to him with Stanton and Banner.

"Dr. Bradly," I said. "What's going on? Why are you guys so busy? ... You guys can't be working this hard on *my* case."

"You're right," he replied. "This morning the serial killer task force added another murder to their list."

"I didn't hear anything about it over the radio," I said.

He shrugged. "Maybe you were away from your car."

"I was entertaining two important guests for our police department," I replied. "This is Detective Banner and Detective Stanton. They've come from different parts of our great country to pick up their suspects."

"I'm glad to meet you," said Dr. Bradly, shaking their hands. "You guys are a long ways away from home, aren't you?" he asked, turning away to peer back into the microscope on the table next to him.

"You can say that again," said Stanton.

"Enough of the small talk," I said. "Dr. Bradly, I need some information concerning my investigation. What have you got for me?"

"Just a minute," he said. He looked up from his microscope, then walked to the other side of the room.

At that moment, Dr. Grady, the coroner, walked into the autopsy room. To get his attention, I called out to him. "Hello, Dr. Grady. What are you doing in this part of the building?"

He turned and then headed towards me. "Hello, Detective Hero," he said. "How are you doing?"

"I'm doing fine. How are my autopsies coming along?"

"I told you to give me two days. You will have the report on your desk when I'm finished...and not before."

"I don't mean to get your dandruff up, Doc, but my two detective friends," I said, pointing to Banner and Stanton, "are here as guests of the city. They are also involved in my investigation."

"Oh, how's that?" asked Dr. Grady.

"Well, it seems that two of the park victims may be serial killers that they have been hunting for quite some time. Detective Stanton has been on the hunt for over two years...and Banner for nearly three. So they are very interested about the case. They hope to close their investigations. Dr. Grady, if you can help them verify their suspect's identities, they would really appreciate it."

"Well, Detective Hero, as you can see I'm up to my ears in work. When the task force finds a body that they think has been killed by their serial killer...I have to stop everything else and work on their investigation. They want their autopsies done immediately. And they also want their forensic evidence tested immediately."

"Tell them to stuff it," I said.

"I'll tell you, Hero, I'm at my wits end," said Grady. "I can't take it anymore. They order me around as if I'm something to wipe their shoes on. I'll tell you, I'm sick of it. I damn near quit this morning."

"Well, please don't get mad, Doc, but do you have anything to help me with my investigation? Have any fingerprint analysis reports come in yet?" I asked.

"Hell, I don't know," he replied. "Why don't you ask Dr. Stork at the lab? They helped my technicians lift the prints from the victims. See if they have run them through the computer for identification. I don't think any of the victims had identification on them, but I haven't been out of this room since I came in early this morning."

"Can you tell us anything that would give us a direction to go in?" I asked.

"Like what? What do you mean?"

"Did any of the park victims commit suicide?" I asked.

"Suicide?" he replied. "I've found no evidence to support that conclusion."

"Well, tell me this, Doc," I asked. "Do you know who shot whom? Two guns were found. I believe a forty-five and a three-fifty-seven. Do you know which victims were shot with which guns?"

"Let's see ... I've completed two of your autopsies. ... I was nearly finished with the third last night. But I had to quit from exhaustion. I had planned to finish it this morning, until the task force interrupted me. Since then, we had to stop work on your investigation."

"Which autopsies have you completed, Doc?" I asked.

He thought for a few seconds, and then said, "We have completed the autopsy of the female...and the male she was lying on. But we are still waiting for the drug tests and the fingerprint analysis reports to come in."

"So tell us, Doc. How did they die?" I asked. Stanton and Banner drew closer.

"Well, I can tell you one thing," he replied. "There are three guns, not two. You guys have to find the third gun. Did you?"

"No, not that I'm aware of. I only saw two guns. ... Doc, what were the caliber of the spent bullets?"

"Well," he replied, "the female was shot once with a three-fifty-seven caliber bullet. That bullet went from under her chin, through her mouth—smashing nearly all her teeth and jawbone—then traveled up through her frontal lobe. ... She also had a forty-five *and* a twenty-two caliber bullet lodged in her upper back. But the twenty-two caliber bullet hit bone and exploded."

"What about the male?" I asked.

"The male, on the other hand, was shot with a twenty-two caliber only and that bullet also exploded. The victim was also stabbed numerous times, and his penis was nearly severed. Actually, it was only hanging by one thin piece of meat."

"Dr. Grady, how do you know the female stabbed him?" asked Detective Stanton.

"The knife was found near her right hand ... so *she* evidently stabbed him in the chest and severed his penis."

"Then how do you know that she didn't shoot him, too?" asked Detective Banner.

"We know she didn't shoot him because the twenty-two bullet had to be fired from at least twenty to thirty feet away and to the right of where she died," said Grady.

"What about powder burns?" asked Banner.

"The female *and* the male lying under her had powder burns," Grady said. "But I believe the female had her hands around his as he shot her. ... So he must have shot her as she was stabbing him."

"Then when did she sever his penis, Dr. Grady?" asked Banner.

"She more than likely sliced off his manhood while he wasn't expecting it, then began stabbing him in the chest. When he felt the searing pain, he pulled out his gun and fired one shot up through her chin. The bullet traveled through the mouth and out through the forehead."

"Then where does the twenty-two come in?" I asked.

"The twenty-two," replied Grady, "was fired in the approximate area of where the old man's body was found lying face down in the mud. And seeing that a gun wasn't found on or near him, the shots had to be fired by another person, either standing next to the guy that was found lying face down in the mud or just a few feet behind him."

"Are you sure?" I asked.

"The gunman," he replied, "could have been standing next to one of the cars that were parked nearby. So you definitely have another perpetrator running around able to kill again. Once you find that twenty-two caliber pistol...you've got the killer that got away. If we had the gun we could, hopefully, match it to the exploded bullets."

"Dr. Grady, do you know how the male that was lying in the high grass died?" asked Stanton.

"Well, we aren't completely finished with his autopsy, but we do know that his penis was severed," said Grady.

"We know that," I said.

"He also was stabbed repeatedly in the chest...and stabbed in the face at least four or five times. Also, he was the first, out of the four, to die," said Grady.

"What about the gun that was found under his body?" asked Stanton.

"It looks like he fired it at the female ... who, I believe, had severed his manhood. He died from his wounds."

"Are you sure about that, Dr. Grady?" asked Stanton.

"I'm fairly certain, but we'll have his report along with the others, most likely, tomorrow morning—unless something else happens with the task force. ... And *they* have pushed me to my limit."

"Don't let them push you around, Doc," I said.

"If they order me about anymore...I'm going to quit this job," he exclaimed angrily.

"Doc, can you tell us anything about the man lying face down in the mud?" I asked.

"Well," he replied, "we know he's an old man...and that he was shot a number of times in the chest and face. And we can't use his dental record either to prove his identity."

"Why not?" I asked.

"One of the three-fifty-seven caliber bullets hit him square in the face and blew half of it away, including his nose, mouth, chin, and right eye. Then, he fell face down into the mud."

"How could a bullet do that much damage?" asked Banner.

"Evidently, he turned his head to the side as the bullet hit his face," replied Grady. "And when the bullet hit the jawbone, it exploded and fragmented into many pieces of shrapnel. But I haven't taken all the bullets out of him yet. ... And that's about all I can tell you for now. Except that we still haven't identified the victims."

"Is it all right if we take a look at the park victims?" asked Banner with his fingers crossed. "We might be able to tell our suspects' identities from looking at their faces. ... What do you say, Doc, can we take a quick peek?"

"Just for a minute," replied Grady. "But I don't think you'll have any luck. Only one body out of the four has its face intact and can be readily identified—that is, if you know who you're looking for."

"That's all right. We still need to see them," said Banner.

"Come on then, I'll take you to see them."

Grady led us to the morgue.

The room was ice cold. Dr. Grady quickly pulled out the two different compartments and showed us the couple—the male and the female that were found at the murder scene, lying together. Detectives Banner and Stanton checked their suspects. ... Stanton wasn't sure. And neither was Banner. They would have to wait for the fingerprint analysis report.

A few minutes later, we returned to the autopsy room to look at the other two male victims—the old man and the one with his manhood severed—only to find that the room was still littered with detectives from the task force. We just ignored them...and quietly stood around the table where the old man was lying, all the while drawing dirty looks—as if *we* were interfering in *their* business.

While looking at the old male cadaver, I noticed something about him. I couldn't quite put my finger on it. I thought that I had seen this person before. I tried to think where, but it just wouldn't come to me. My memory wasn't as good as it used to be. So I put it out of my mind. I decided to wait for the fingerprint report.

Suddenly, a thought came over me. I decided to check the cars that had been impounded from the park to see if there was anything of importance in them. Maybe the victims had carried their car's registration in the glove box. If they had, that should help us identify their corpses.

First, I wanted to check to see whether the reports had come in.

I could tell that my two new friends, Stanton and Banner, were anxious to close out their investigations. If I could do anything to hasten or help their quest to find the identification of these four victims, I would.

"Listen, you guys," I said, "I want to stop by my desk. I want to check to see if any of the reports from the investigation have come in yet. They might have the answers you are looking for."

"Well, *I* need to get the fingerprint analysis reports," said Banner. "A name won't help me. My suspect's face was so damaged I couldn't make it out."

"She did look quite hideous, didn't she," I said.

"What do you expect," said Banner. "There was only one eye, part of her nose, and a piece of forehead left. Both her and the old man had similar facial deformities due to the gunshot wounds."

"Joseph, I wonder if one of those cars parked at the park belonged to your victim." I asked.

"She didn't own a car," said Banner.

"Are you sure?" I asked.

"Yes. ... She had always lived with women who had them. She just used theirs."

"Maybe we'll have the answer when we check out the cars that were impounded from the crime scene," I said. "Let's hope that the forensic investigators dusted them for prints because it's possible that your suspect rode in one of those cars."

"I'm sure she did," replied Banner. "But I need the fingerprints of my suspect analyzed. I need a name to go with her blown away face so I can verify that she is, in fact, my suspect."

"I couldn't tell if either male corpse was my suspect," exclaimed Stanton. "The photo I had to identify him with wasn't good enough."

"Why not?" I asked.

"The male victim is older than the photo."

"How come?" I asked.

"I told you before...the photo I have of him was taken when he was just a young teenager. But, luckily, we were able to find out his name from a partial print that we lifted from one of his later murder scenes. So the fingerprint analysis will tell the tale. But if we have trouble with the fingerprints...we always have his DNA to use."

"Good luck trying to get your suspect's DNA tested within a reasonable time period," I said. "It took me more than a week to have my suspect's DNA tested."

"Well, we have our own DNA lab to do our testing," said Stanton. "And I plan on taking some of my suspect's DNA with me...so we can have our own forensics technicians test it...and hopefully use it to close open murder cases. Plus, I'll need copies of all the reports that come in on this case."

"Why would you need all of that?" I asked. "Once you have the identification of these victims and you know for sure that it's your suspect, you'll be able to close your investigation. Am I right?"

"Yeah," he replied. "But I need the information to help write my report. I'll need to write something in my report to verify my being here for three days."

"That goes for me, too," said Banner. "I will also need copies of those reports. I don't want to return to my captain empty-handed."

"Well, you guys," I said, "let's leave from here and drive over to the station to check out my desk. Who knows, we may get lucky and find the reports you need."

We didn't get lucky. When we got to the station, it didn't take long to determine that there wasn't a single investigative report waiting for me to read. It was disheartening to see the disappointment on the faces of Banner and Stanton. They would have to wait around at least one more day.

"Baxter, what do you want to do now?" asked Banner.

"Well," I replied, "let's drive out to the murder scene to see if we can salvage *something* from this day."

Banner and Stanton nodded in agreement.

"I also want to stop by the impound yard to see if there was any identification in the glove box of the cars found at the park. It might not help you guys—I know you need the fingerprint analysis reports—but it might help me."

Within fifteen minutes, we were at the murder scene. I parked in the same spot as one of the victims had, about ten feet from where the old man had been found lying in the mud. The car's rear end would have been in line with the victims. So, the shooter could have been hiding behind the vehicle, firing his weapon: a twenty-two caliber. That would have put him about ten feet behind the old man—which would have put the two victims about thirty feet away...*if* the shooter was firing from behind the car. And that's about the distance the coroner stated.

Stanton, Banner, and I stepped out of the vehicle and walked over to the crime scene. The ground was still wet—but not nearly as muddy as the day before. Although I was sure the crime scene had been picked over with a fine-toothed comb by our forensics investigators, we still wanted to search the area again. We hoped to find something that the forensics team had overlooked—like that third gun. Where could it have gone?

Once we finished searching the immediate area, we fanned out even further. We decided to search a ten-yard radius around the murder scene in case the shooter had dropped the twenty-two-caliber pistol while running away—or thrown it away.

While searching the high grass and bushes, I thought I heard laughter and then yelling, but I couldn't quite make it out. I stopped and lifted my head, trying to find out where the noise was coming from. I heard it again. The sound of men talking and laughing.

Looking through a forest of trees and dense bushes, I saw the two young males that I had seen at the park entrance the day of the murders. They were wearing the same worn and tattered clothes that I had seen them wearing before...including old, long, flannel full-length coats...and one had added an extra dimension to his wardrobe—a floppy, multicolored hat. There was no doubt about it. I was sure that they were the same two young men that I had been looking for.

Just as I focused my eyes, I saw them staring right back at me—and then they took off running. Without hesitation,

I ran after them through the dense forest, cutting my forearms and hands in the process. The two young males were running up a steep incline towards the city streets and buildings, then they disappeared over the hill.

I knew that if I didn't catch up to them soon, I would lose them. So I turned around and ran back to my car. Out of breath, I jumped into my car without telling my two friends anything. But then, as I put the car into gear and was about to drive away I yelled out to them, "Wait here, you guys, I'll be back."

I exited the park and quickly turned onto the highway, heading towards the area in which I'd seen them run. I was certain that the two males I was chasing were the same two guys that I had seen leaving the park on the day of the murders.

I finally reached the area where the two vagabonds should have come out of the park. But they weren't anywhere to be seen...and I was angry with myself that I had lost them. In fact, I slapped the steering wheel with my hand so hard that I strained my wrist. I acted as though these two people were my killers. But in actuality, they were only wanted for questioning concerning the park murders—and as possible witnesses ... Not as suspects. At least, not yet.

Vagabonds don't like anything to do with law enforcement. They feel that the police won't help them, only harass them. And usually these kinds of guys have no job. They steal to eat...and urinate in public. They are a stain on any decent neighborhood. When we do try to help them, they refuse our help. So you can't win.

Finally, frustrated, I turned my car around and headed towards the park to pick up Stanton and Banner. I had been searching for those two vagabonds for over twenty minutes. I just hoped my two friends weren't angry with me.

They were sitting on a picnic table, smoking cigarettes when I arrived. I parked the car near them. Just as I stepped out of it, a patrol unit showed up.

"It's about time you answered my call," I said. "But I lost the two people I was looking for...over *fifteen minutes ago*."

"What call?" asked the uniformed police officer sitting in the driver's seat. "We aren't answering any call. We're here to clean up the yellow tape from the murder scene."

"We aren't finished searching the area," I said.

"Well," replied the officer, "we were ordered by our captain to clean up the tape. The forensic supervisor told us that the investigators had searched the area thoroughly."

"Well, we thought we would search the area one last time for the missing gun," I replied. "But I guess we have completed our search. Go ahead and take the tape down. But, officer, tell me, who answered my call for backup?"

"I wouldn't know," he said, as he and his partner stepped out of the vehicle. "We were pulled away from our desk jobs and ordered by our captain to perform this little task."

"Officer, aren't you supposed to patrol this region?" I asked, as I watched them tear down the yellow crime scene tape surrounding the area.

"Not this week," he replied. "We were sitting at our desks, writing up victim's reports, until our captain got a bug up his butt and decided we weren't working hard enough. He didn't like us sitting on our butts, drinking coffee all day, so he sent us here to play in the park."

"Officer," I asked, "do you know if the patrol units are keeping an eye open for the two vagabonds? They are wanted for questioning in these four homicides."

"What vagabonds are you talking about?" he asked. "Are they suspects? I didn't know there were any suspects to the park killings. We thought they killed each other. Didn't they?"

"We don't know for sure," I said. "But I saw two young males leaving the park entrance at the same time these murders occurred. That's why they are wanted for questioning...and I thought we had put out an APB on them. ... You didn't hear that go out over the airwaves, officer?"

"I'm sorry," he replied, "I didn't hear anything. But like I said...until today, I hadn't been in a patrol car for a week. My partner and I have been sitting at a desk. We don't know who answered your call. ... Maybe the center didn't receive it?"

"I don't know, but I'm sure going to find out," I snapped. "I hope Dispatch responded to my call 'cause I need to question those two vagabonds. They could have all the crazy answers to these four murders. I'll have to have a composite drawing done of them to give to the patrol units."

"Make sure we get one," said the officer, as he and his partner jumped into their patrol car.

"I will," I said, as the officer and his partner drove away from the crime scene.

"What do you say, guys," I asked, turning to Stanton and Banner, "do you want to check out the two cars that were found at the murder scene? I'm sure we'll find something of importance to help us with our investigations."

"I'm ready. All I got here was muddy shoes," said Banner.

"Hell, *I* got a soaker!" exclaimed Stanton. "My right foot sank into that wet mud damn near ten inches. I thought I had stepped in quicksand!"

We jumped into my car and headed for the departments impound yard. We saw the victims' cars as soon as we entered the compound, all parked next to each other. A few minutes later, we were standing near them ready to begin our search.

The first thing that I noticed was that the car doors weren't locked—which meant that anyone could have been in those cars corrupting the forensic evidence. Stanton, Banner, and I decided to go through the cars ourselves—even *if* the forensic investigators had already gone through them. There was still a lot of junk lying on the floorboards and back seat.

When I opened the glove box, I found that it was full of the owner's possessions: napkins, a screwdriver, a padlock, and a few other little trinkets—nothing of real importance. But Banner and Stanton hit the jackpot. Sitting in the back seat was a large cardboard box containing two pocketknives, a sixteen-inch-long Bowie Knife, and a small ax—which should have been packaged and delivered to the forensics lab and tested for fingerprints. But instead, the evidence was in the car, collecting dust.

And with the doors unlocked, anyone could have touched those items in the box—which meant that they could be contaminated if anyone other than the police had handled them. Thinking about this really pissed me off. Hell, the shooter could have owned one of these cars. And all this evidence may have had his fingerprints on them—enough evidence to send him to the death house. But now, whatever we found would most likely be inadmissible in a court of law.

I loaded the box of evidence into the trunk of my car anyway to take it to the forensics lab. Whether they tested the items would be up to them...and the district attorney.

But we didn't find a wallet or anything that would have given us the identification of the four park victims. We would still have to wait for the fingerprint report to give us the answers.

However, I still had a trump card in my pocket. So I played it. Using my cell phone, I ran the cars' plates through dispatch and discovered that one of the cars had been stolen in another state from a parking lot more than ten days ago, and the other was registered to a woman a few miles away. Although her name wasn't one that Stanton, Banner, or I recognized, we still thought we had a good lead—one that could possibly help identify at least one of the park victims, if not more.

We were still trying to locate the owner of the stolen car. A message was left on his answering machine, but he hadn't contacted the department.

Now that we had searched the vehicles, we decided to check in with one of the owners. It was just a few minutes away from the impound yard. It was in the best part of town.

My two friends waited in the car as I walked up and knocked on the front door. An old lady in her seventies or eighties answered.

"Yes, can I help you?" asked the old women, speaking through the glass door instead of opening it.

"Yes, ma'am. I'm Detective Hero," I said, showing her my police identification. "I would like to ask you about a car that you own, which was found in the park a few nights ago."

"I'm sorry," she said, her voice cracking, "I don't own any vehicle."

"Aren't you Pat Dawner?" I asked.

"No, I'm not. She was my roommate."

"May I speak with her?"

"I'm sorry. She's not here. But she never owned a car...as far as I know."

"Do you know when she'll return so I can speak with her?"

"I'm sorry. She's dead. She died over a year ago."

"Do you know of anyone that might have used her car?" I asked.

The woman gave me a puzzled look and then said, "I told you, she didn't own a car."

"But ma'am, we found her name through DMV by running the license plate numbers of a car that was found in a park not too far from here," I said. I showed her a piece of paper with the plate numbers. She opened the door and took the paper from me, but she seemed to be having a hard time reading the small print.

"I'm sorry, I don't know anything about that," she said. "We always called taxis to take us or bring us home. Pat never had any car."

The woman's answers puzzled me. "Do you know if she has any living relatives in the area that might have used her car?" I asked.

"She didn't have any living relatives that I know of," she said. "She was also a widow. As far as I know."

"Ma'am, how long had she been a widow?"

"Oh ... for quite a few years. But she didn't like to talk about it. In fact, she had thrown all of her husband's pictures away. She told me she didn't want anything to remind her of him."

"You're sure then, ma'am, that she didn't have any living relatives?"

"I never met any. I told you. She said she was the last of her family."

"Ma'am, if you remember anything else, would you give me a call at the police station?" I handed her my card.

As I turned to leave, she called out to me. "One minute, detective. I have something that might be of some help to you. Wait one minute while I go and get it."

She returned carrying two small books in her hands, then opened the glass door just far enough to squeeze them through. I grabbed them and thanked her for her time, then turned and walked back to the car.

"Detective Banner, see if there is anything of importance in these books," I said, opening my car door and tossing them into his lap.

"What the heck are these?" he asked.

"You tell me," I replied, starting the engine and pulling away. "They have something to do with the lady that owned that car."

"What did she say, Baxter?" asked Detective Stanton.

"She's no longer living...and has no living relatives. So we still don't know the identity of the driver of that car."

"You mean the owner of that car is dead?" asked Stanton.

"Yeah ... That's what 'not alive' means," I quipped.

"No, I didn't mean that," said Stanton. "I mean...if she's dead, maybe she's one of the park victims."

"I don't think so," I said, as I glanced over at Banner looking through one of the old woman's books. "I think the person who owns that car is over seventy-five years old and female. ... And there weren't any park victims that match that description."

Just then, Banner yelled out, "Hell, this is a woman's diary! What the heck kind of information are we going to find in a couple of diaries?"

"Maybe nothing," I said. "But we need to find a living relative—one who can help us find out who was driving that car at the time of the murders. Maybe Pat Dawner mentions a name in her diaries."

"I'll see if I can find one," Banner said, glancing through the pages.

"Man, I'm getting hungry," said Stanton.

"I'm pretty famished myself," interjected Banner.

The guys were getting hungry so we decided to swing by the lab to drop off the evidence, then head to the café for lunch.

Once at the lab, I carried the box to Dr. Stork's office.

"Here is the evidence from the two cars that were found in the park near the murder scene," I told him. "Your team must have forgotten to take it with them."

"Where did you get that stuff?" he asked.

"They were left in an unlocked car, collecting dust. I'm wondering...did your guys dust the cars for fingerprints?"

"Of course they did," replied Stork. "Don't disrespect my technicians. They've been overworked ever since the serial task force was put together. And they've been putting in fourteen to eighteen-hour days, six and seven days a week, for nearly a year now. So please, Detective Hero, have a little respect."

"Don't get angry with me, Doc," I said. "I just asked because I didn't see any graphite powder residue anywhere on the cars. I wondered if your investigators had tested for fingerprints on or in the victims' cars. I thought that if they hadn't checked for fingerprints *yet*, they might want to do it sometime soon."

"I told you," snapped Stork, "don't rush me. We get enough of that from the serial killer task force."

"But Doc," I pleaded, "we need to know the identification of the victims and who was driving those cars. It could help with my investigation and the identification of the shooter. Right now, the only thing I have to go on is... nothing."

"Well," Stork said, "the answers will be in our reports. ... Give us a chance. I'm sure all your questions will be answered in time."

It was useless to argue with the guy. I didn't feel like arguing, anyway. That would just hinder my investigation. If I made him angry, he might never give me his reports on the forensic evidence. So I had to keep my mouth shut and kiss his feet from time to time. And this was one of those times.

With nothing more to say, I turned and walked out of the building. Soon after, I was sitting behind the wheel of my car, driving towards my precinct, along with the two out-of-state detectives.

I signed in at the front desk and then walked to my desk. I wanted to retrieve any analysis and investigative reports that were there waiting for me. Then I wanted to talk to the dispatcher to find out why my radio call—the APB on the two vagabonds—hadn't been broadcasted to the working patrol units.

But my desk was bare—no reports had been delivered.

I left my desk to visit the dispatcher. At one time, our precinct had three or four dispatchers working full-time. But now, with our sickly budget, the department couldn't afford even *one* full-time dispatcher—only part-time help...and most of those people worked the night shift. Only one person worked dispatch during the day. It was a four-hour shift, then they were relieved with a volunteer patrol officer.

I walked into the dispatch center and quickly found out why my call didn't go out over the airwaves. The voice behind the microphone was an enemy of mine. Actually, this person was jealous of me—a jealousy that has lasted for over twenty years. He was turned down for his detective's shield and *he* thought I had been hired in his place. That couldn't have been further from the truth, but he'd held a grudge against me ever since. Even so, I couldn't say for certain that he had refused my call on purpose because my radio *had* produced a lot of static interference during my call. But my gut feeling told me that the dispatcher, Tommy Minnow, just didn't want to answer my call.

I walked up to his desk and confronted him. "Tommy, did you get my call for backup this morning?" I asked.

"What call? Are you talking about that call that came over the radio all garbled and full of static?"

"Did you hear it or didn't you?" I snapped.

"No. I couldn't make out your words."

"But you knew it was me, didn't you?" I asked, looking him straight in the eye.

"You act as if I ignored your call on purpose!"

"Well, you've held a grudge against me for years," I snarled. "What am I to think?"

"Believe me, Baxter, when I say this. I didn't respond to that call because I couldn't hear it clear enough to understand it. Your radio must be out of whack. You should have one of the technicians look it over."

"I guess I'll have to. I needed backup for a suspect search earlier today and my damn radio went out in mid-call."

"That's what it sounded like to me, too," said Tommy.

"Well, I just wanted to check on that. I'm sorry if I was out of order," I said. I walked out of the room and headed to my car.

"So were there any reports waiting on your desk?" Stanton asked, as I got back into the car.

"No. The cupboard was bare. But mark my words ... by tomorrow morning I'll be flooded with reports. And I'm sure that with the information from some of those reports, you'll be able to close your investigations."

"I hope so," said the two detectives in unison.

"I just wish I had the right information to close mine," I said.

While driving to the café, I decided to drive by the area where I'd last seen the two vagabonds that were wanted for questioning in the park murders. I hoped that I might catch them off guard. But if I did see them I couldn't call for backup because my car's police radio was dead. My portable radio was also broken and our department's budget for the year didn't have any money left in it to buy new ones. Plus, my old and cheap cell phone refused to transmit in many parts of the inner city, especially around its tall office buildings.

Suddenly, my mind switched to another problem. A few minutes before, I had thought about finding the two vagabonds...and just as I had hoped, at that moment, the two young men walked out from between two apartment buildings, which was part of a huge, one-block square apartment complex.

"Hey, look… There they are," I shouted. Banner and Stanton turned to look where I was pointing, excited.

"Those are the two bums I've been searching for… I'm sure of it. All right, you guys … when I park the car, you two chase the one on the left. I'll go after the guy in the hat. You got it?"

I crept up behind them, pulled the car over, and got out.

By that time, the two vagabonds were already crossing the two-lane street and heading towards a row of dilapidated and condemned apartment buildings. They were maybe forty yards ahead of us, near a group of homeless vagrants congregating in front of a small, church-like store, waiting to get some free food.

# MURDER IN THE CITY PARTS I-II

We had to move fast before my two young vagabonds were lost in the crowd. We quickened our pace. We didn't want to give ourselves away, but our wardrobe did that anyway. We had "cops" written all over us.

When the crowd noticed us, someone yelled "Five-O," and the crowd quickly dispersed—including the two vagabonds. They ran into a huge apartment complex containing three buildings: two were condemned and adjacent to each other—the other was behind them and had occupants.

And, of course, I had no radio to call for backup. If I'd had one, I would have called for the police dogs. But now, it was like looking for a needle in a haystack. Instead of two people that dressed alike, there were fifty. And I couldn't recognize the vagabonds by their faces, only by their clothes. But their clothes, I remembered. Especially the crazy hat.

As Stanton and Banner searched one of the four-story, vacant and condemned apartments, I searched the other. Inside, the apartment buildings were dark, smelly, and filled with human waste and garbage. The fumes made breathing difficult.

Detectives Stanton and Banner combed through at least fifty or sixty rooms before they gave up the search. I searched for nearly thirty minutes in the stench-filled apartment building before I finally gave up. My two vagabonds were nowhere to be seen.

As I exited the apartment building, I saw Stanton and Banner...they were waiting for me at the back of the apartment complex. The three of us walked to the last apartment in the complex to ask its occupants about my two vagabonds. Once there, we saw a few women and their small children sitting outside.

"Did any of you ladies see two rough-looking, poorly-dressed characters run past here?" I asked. "They were wearing long flannel coats...and one had on a multi-colored floppy cap."

"No, we didn't see anyone come past here," said one of the women, rocking in her chair.

"I saw them," mumbled one of the male children.

"Who did you see, son?" I asked.

"I saw those two men with the long coats. One had a gun in his waistband."

"Are you sure it was a gun, son?" I asked.

"Uh, huh. Yep," said the boy, who couldn't have been more than eight years of age.

"How do you know it was a gun?" I asked.

"'Cause I saw my brother's gun. His is shiny, too."

"Your brother showed you his gun?" I asked, looking at his mother with disgust. "Son, do you know which way the two men ran?"

"They went that way," he said, pointing towards another row of vacant, condemned apartment buildings directly across the street from us.

"Thank you, son. You've been very helpful," I said, patting him on his head.

Detectives Stanton, Banner, and I continued our search for the two vagabonds, heading for the apartments across the street.

"How long are we going to look for these guys, Baxter?" asked Banner. "You don't even know what they look like."

"That's true," I said, as we walked across the street. "But I'll recognize them immediately if I ever see them again."

"We talked to a few people in the apartment building we searched," Banner said, "but we didn't see anyone that matched the description of the guy in the hat."

"We'll check this side of the street, but this time we won't search inside the condemned apartments. We'll just look around the area. I know you guys are eager to get something to eat."

"You know, this is a job for your patrol units, not us," exclaimed Banner.

"Don't tell me you're getting tired already, Joseph?" I asked.

"No ... that's not it," replied Banner. "But we're searching for two guys when we don't know what they look like."

"You saw them as well as I did," I said.

"Yeah," replied Banner. "But all I had to go on was a long, dirty coat and multi-colored, floppy hat. Twenty other people looked the same. And I felt like a fool asking those people questions inside that apartment building."

"You're right, Joseph. It's not much to go on. But we gotta find them. Especially if one of them has the gun I think he has. He's got it for one reason. And he's gonna use it on somebody. I just hope it's not used on some innocent bystander."

We searched the area for over twenty minutes before Stanton said, "Baxter, we're not doing any good here. We've lost them by now."

"You're right," I replied. "We're just wasting time. I guess I'll have to catch those guys another way. What I'll do is have composite drawings made of them and then give copies out to our patrol units. It might take me a little longer to catch them, but I will...sooner or later."

## Chapter 15

By the time we entered the café and were seated at my usual table, it was well past lunchtime. The minute I sat down, I ordered my usual double scotch. I also brought with me the two diaries that the old woman had given to me. I wanted to read them as I relaxed over a drink or two. I didn't know if it was wishful thinking or not, but I was hoping they might give me some good information to help in the park murder investigation. The diary entries were short, well written, and straight to the point.

In the diary the woman talked about how she married a young man she had met while in graduate school when both were only twenty years old.

She had come from a very sickly family and was an only child ... not by choice. Her siblings died one by one, until she was the only child left in her family.

Once the young woman and her boyfriend married, she quit school to raise a family, and he continued on to medical school. Eventually, he got his medical license and opened a small clinic.

However, soon after, they had become man and wife, she noticed a change in his personality—a change for the worse. She was madly in love with the guy, but he sometimes frightened her, especially during his mood swings when he would become withdrawn and unpredictable. So as the years went by, she learned to stay out of his way when he was in these strange moods, which she believed was due from the stress of his job. But then he began staying away from the house for long hours, if not days, at a time. When she tried to reason with him, he just ignored her. She couldn't talk to him or understand his moody ways anymore.

The more I read of this diary, the more I felt sorry for this woman.

During a period of doubt, this woman had become suspicious of her husband. She began searching his den and bedroom for anything that could give her an answer to his strange behavior. But she could never get up enough courage to leave him...because she was still madly in love with him.

She thought that when she became pregnant with their first child, he would change for the better. But his moods had become even more unpredictable. So, once the baby came, she spent all of her time with her daughter, hardly ever seeing her husband. Then, when her daughter was almost an adult, the girl became very ill and died. She believed her husband had hastened her daughter's death by injecting her with some type of experimental drug, which he had concocted out of the vials tucked inside his black bag.

When her daughter died, she became withdrawn and depressed. She began searching her husband's rooms again—and found what seemed to be a dark stain splattered on the right leg of a pair of his pants. When she tried to wash out the stain, she noticed that it was actually blood. She didn't know whether it was human or animal blood. She believed it to be animal blood, at the time, because her husband had been teaching anatomy at the local university a few days a week, where they demonstrated different surgery techniques to his students using live animals. But then, when she read about a murder on the campus where he taught, she again became suspicious of him. That was the end of Pat Dawner's first diary.

While drinking my fourth double scotch, and after the two detectives had ordered their dinners, I began reading the dead woman's second diary, still hoping for information that would lead me to the identity of the driver of her car.

It turns out that her love for him had grown cold since the death of their daughter. It was easy for her to believe that her husband might be involved in the local murder, and she began searching his rooms once again for anything that looked suspicious. When she searched his den, she found his black bag and searched it, finding surgeon's slippers drenched in blood, rubber gloves, and a woman's angora sweater covered in hair and blood. She wondered what he was up to now. She thought he used the stuff during his surgeries and didn't want to believe anything else, as she had always made excuses for his odd and strange behavior. She knew that he acted strangely at times, but she refused to believe that he had broken the law or damaged his family name. Some would say that she was in denial.

She had written that many times her husband had come home demented and talking to himself, and while in this mood, he would run from room to room, throwing and breaking valuable objects as he went. She would stay away from him when he was in these unpredictable moods.

She began keeping track of his erratic behavior—and would read through the newspaper to see if there were any murders in the area on the nights that the doctor had thrown his demented tantrums. With that information, she began to correlate the killings to his unpredictable, erratic behavior.

She stayed with him for nearly fifty years. And then, nearly a year ago, she moved into a house with her childhood friend...but she continued her vigil of tracking and dating all the local murders.

But then, something must have happened. She suddenly stopped writing about the murders—and her husband. She wrote in big letters that her husband was

DEAD in her eyes, and she wasn't going to his funeral. So, I figured her husband must be dead. But being a homicide detective, I would have to do a little investigative work during my free time to verify her story and to run a background check on her dead husband. I presumed his name to be Dr. Dawner. It was an intriguing story, but one which would have to wait while I investigated real murders. I was disappointed that the diaries had not revealed information about the owner or driver of the car. However, I did jot down a few of the dates mentioned and the names of the three victims that she believed had been killed by her husband.

By this time, my two detective friends had just finished their meals. I was still drinking. I still didn't have a good appetite, so I called Bonnie over and ordered my fifth double scotch. I set the two diaries aside, prepared to listen in to the conversation between my two friends, but they suddenly turned their attention to me.

"Well, Baxter, was there anything of importance in those two diaries that will help us in your investigation?" asked Detective Banner, lighting a cigarette.

"No ... I struck out. But I did read some interesting material. This lady thought her husband was killing people as he masqueraded as a doctor."

"You're kidding, aren't you, Baxter?" asked Detective Stanton.

"No. That's what I read in her diaries. ... She even kept dates, time and places of the murder victims, and how she related it to her husband's demented behavior. When she became suspicious of his strange actions, she began searching and going through his things. I believe she found some incriminating evidence, but she never confronted him about it."

"I wonder why?" asked Stanton.

"I guess you could say she was in denial," I replied. "She didn't want to believe her husband, a doctor, could be a cold-blooded killer. But when she became pregnant with her first and only child, she became even more disenchanted by his strange actions."

"What did she do then? Did she confront him with her suspicions?" asked Stanton.

"No. She cut herself off from him and concentrated on giving her love and affection to her daughter instead," I said.

"So what happened? Did the guy ever get caught?" asked Banner, yawning.

"I don't know. She doesn't say in her diaries."

"Was he ever a suspect in any of the murders?" asked Stanton.

"I don't know about that either," I replied. "But just for the fun of it, I'm going to check our files on a few of these names and dates that she mentioned and see if they correspond to any of our investigations. It's not like I don't have anything to do."

"Why didn't she turn him in if she thought he was up to no good?" asked Stanton.

Before answering Stanton's question, I took a quick puff on my own cigarette and downed the rest of my drink. "She relates in her diary that she was very afraid of him," I said. "He was like a time bomb ready to explode. She knew he was set to go off, but never knew when."

"What is the doctor's name?" asked Banner.

"She doesn't say. She refers to him only as her husband. I'm going to check for a Dr. Dawner. If that's his real name."

"Do you think it's his real name?" asked Stanton.

"That could be the woman's maiden name," I replied. "When I get around to checking this out, I'll go and question the woman who gave me the diaries. She would know if

Dawner was her married or maiden name. But right now, the park murders are the most important on my agenda."

Suddenly, the quiet of the café was disrupted by a scuffle in the front lobby. I stretched my neck to see what all the commotion was about, but the crowd surrounding the arguing patrons blocked my view. I stood up to get a better look at the two men who were arguing.

When I finally had a clean line of sight, I saw two men clenched in a wrestling hold. But when one man spun the other man around, I saw something in the hand of the thinner man. It was a gun. My heart began to race. I pushed my way through the crowd of customers, yelling for the two men to stop their fighting.

When I came face-to-face with them, I was startled to see that the man was now pointing the gun at his adversary. I jumped in the melee, not to break up the fight, but to grab the gun out of the man's hand. Just as I put my hand out to grab the gun, I heard a loud pop that damn near shattered my eardrum. I felt the wind of the bullet as it passed directly overhead. As I fell backward, out of the way of the bullet, I heard two more pops and saw the flash of the bullets leave the barrel of the gun.

Suddenly, one of the patrons standing in the crowd of onlookers fell to the floor. I wasn't sure if a bullet had hit him or if he was just dodging them. A few seconds later, I found out. Blood began seeping out of his chest and onto the cafe floor. By the time I had jumped back up with my weapon drawn, the shooter had already gone. He had finally shaken the hold of his captor and fled the cafe with a bag of loot in hand.

I ran to the front door. "Bonnie," I yelled, "call the police! Tell them there's a robbery in progress and Detective Hero needs backup." Just as I opened the door and ran outside, I noticed that my two detective friends were behind me, guns drawn and ready for the hunt.

The shooter was well ahead of us. We didn't dare shoot our guns, as there were too many innocent people out on the streets. We were in the industrial part of the city. But a few blocks away were the tenement apartment buildings. Many of the dilapidated and abandoned, condemned buildings were firetraps. They should have been torn down twenty years ago, but they stand as a monument to the poor and unfortunate.

I had to stop the chase to catch my breath, as did my two detective friends, Stanton and Banner. The shooter was at least thirty years younger and at least a hundred pounds lighter than I was. The only problem was that all my weight was in my gut.

After a few seconds of rest, we continued the chase. We could still see the suspect's coattails flying in the wind as he ran towards an old and condemned apartment complex, similar to the ones we had searched earlier that day.

The complex spanned nearly one square block. It was a massive sight. I thought they would fall and crumble to the ground at any moment—and there were many homeless and unfortunate people living in these buildings. Why? Because they had at least five hundred rooms from which to choose—rent free.

When my suspect ran past a crowd of homeless people, they began following him. Many of them were also running—away from us, the law. We saw at least thirty people scatter in every direction as we ran towards them and were still able to see in which direction the shooter had gone. He ran right into one of the condemned apartment buildings, which had at least twelve stories and hundreds of rooms.

When the shooter ran into that foul-smelling, urine-soaked building, many of the unfortunate and homeless ran out of their only living quarters. We could hear screaming and yelling as the occupants warned each other that the police were on site. Once we finally reached the apartment building, we stopped and waited for our backup to arrive. One by one, patrol units began filling the streets. We directed them to surround the apartment complex.

It had only been five or ten minutes since we had seen the shooter run into the apartment building, so we were fairly certain that he was still somewhere in the complex. We were anxious to catch this guy. And my two friends looked as though they were enjoying themselves and the action.

Finally, the apartment complex was surrounded by law enforcement, and we were ready to search this huge, garbage-filled, giant of the past.

My team, along with nearly fifty uniformed police officers and a few trained dogs from the K-9 department, began slowly searching the huge building, room by room. This was going to take quite a long time to complete. Everyone involved was given a description of the perpetrator and the color of the clothes he was wearing. We also had the hat that was torn from his head; he lost it while he was wrestling with one of the cafe's patrons. We held it to our dog's nose so it could get the perp's scent to track him down.

We then ran up all twelve flights of stairs, weaving and wading through tons of garbage and human waste. Each group of officers was to search four floors. There were about forty apartments to each dark and foul-smelling floor, with each apartment having three to seven rooms. Detectives Stanton and Banner, plus a few uniformed officers and myself, were to search the top four floors.

The dark and foul-smelling rooms were very difficult to search. If you fell to the floor, you would most likely land in human waste and rotting garbage. Some rooms were stacked to the ceiling in litter and maggots.

Wild rats, field mice, and cockroaches were also occupants of this building. They shared it equally with the drug-infested degenerates and the unfortunate homeless. Many of these unfortunate people were once mental patients in state mental institutions. But due to state budget cuts, they had been released into the streets. They couldn't fend for themselves in the state setting; how were they going to care for themselves in the real world? I could never understand how a government agency—run by so-called rational human beings—could be so cruel and inhumane. We don't even treat animals as cruelly as we do those who are declared mentally incompetent. We are no longer a compassionate people.

But today, we were searching for a degenerate robber and killer. Every room we searched turned up empty. And we were having difficulty breathing and seeing. The foul, putrid-smelling air had turned into a gaseous mixture of methane. Our eyes and throats burned with each step we took.

Detective Stanton thought that the shooter had fled the area. But I was sure he hadn't slipped through our net and was somewhere in the building. We checked and double checked every room, sifting through every pile of garbage and stacks of junk that we came across. We searched under old and discarded urine-soaked mattresses and box springs. Anything that could hide a body, we checked. We left nothing to chance. We wanted this guy, and we wanted him badly. We had lost two fleeing subjects earlier today, and we didn't want to lose this one.

While searching the last few rooms of our four floors, I found something. I pushed two dirty, foul-smelling, battered and torn queen-size mattresses and box springs away from the wall and discovered two decomposing dead bodies—one male and one female, approximately the same young age . . . maybe eighteen to twenty years old.

They must have been dead at least a few days, if not more. But I wasn't the coroner and the lighting wasn't very good, so I was just guessing. The putrid, horrid smell should have led me directly to the bodies, but the whole apartment building smelled like death warmed over.

When I checked the bodies a little closer, I noticed something very familiar. It seemed to me that I had come across a murder scene similar to this before. In fact, these two people had been killed in the same fashion as the victims in my last multiple murder investigation. But these murders were recent—just a few days old. And the killer from the case in question was locked up in prison, so I knew that someone else had to have killed these two people. Maybe a copycat killer? I thought to myself.

I had one of the uniformed officers contact the coroner's office and forensics team to investigate this murder scene. While he did that, I had other officers section off the room so nobody could corrupt the crime scene. As I was directing traffic, my captain came into the room. And just at that moment, I heard a loud commotion coming from another area of the apartment building, one floor below. I could hear one or two officers yell, "Halt! Police!" Then I heard what sounded like muffled gun shots. Maybe as many as ten or twelve shots total.

Many of us in the room were curious and ran out to see what all the commotion was about. We ran down the cluttered steps to the next floor below. When we entered the main hallway, I could see a crowd of policemen standing around at the end of the long hall approximately one hundred feet from us. We ran to get a closer look.

Captain Blake and I pushed through the crowd of uniformed police officers to the head of the class to see a raggedy-clothed man, who fit the description of our suspect, lying dead in a urine-soaked, foul-smelling hallway.

I quickly searched the man's body for his weapon, but I didn't find one. We searched the immediate area, but still no weapon. All we found was a small paper sack clutched in the man's left hand.

I checked the bag that the bum had been carrying; it contained only food. He had two pieces of moldy bread covered with a white substance that looked and smelled like mayonnaise, but no lunchmeat. The bag also contained a little shriveled plum. For crying out loud ... This guy was only carrying his lunch. For this, he had been gunned down by three different police officers.

"This guy doesn't have a gun," I shouted. "Why did you shoot him?"

"He jumped up and ran out of the room as we were searching for the robber. He was dressed in the same clothing that was described to us earlier. We were also told that he had a paper sack full of money. That's what I saw him carrying in his left hand. Then, when we yelled for him to stop, he quickly turned and reached into his waistband with his right hand," said the officer. He was still shaking from the ordeal. It was probably the first time he'd ever shot a man.

"But why did you have to shoot him?" I asked the young officer.

"I thought he was going for a gun," he replied, still shaking. "It's dark in here...and the darkness played tricks on our eyes. Why did he run if he wasn't guilty?" asked the frightened and confused uniformed officer.

"Well, you guys are going to have a lot of explaining to do, especially if he isn't the robber. I can't really tell if it's him, with all this blood all over his face and body. Let the forensics investigators take a powder burn test on his hands. We'll see if he has fired a gun in the last hour or so," I said, trying to soothe the officers' nerves.

But Captain Blake scolded the three officers. They were told to visit him in the morning for disciplinary action. He also ordered a few of the uniformed officers that weren't working on the double murder investigation on the floor above to search for a gun and a bag of money, while the rest of the officers continued their search for the suspect. They were certain he hadn't escaped our perimeter. I wasn't so sure. I believed the suspect might have escaped during the time we had been waiting for our backup units to arrive.

While the officers continued their search for the suspect, my two detective friends and I ran back upstairs to check on the double murder investigation. Captain Blake was already there barking out orders when we walked in.

"Detective Hero, what do you think about this double murder?" asked Captain Blake.

"Well, sir, I've seen these type of killings before," I said. "Like in the Weltman murders."

"That's the same thing I was thinking," he said.

"But the perpetrator from that case is locked away in prison. So I know *that* person couldn't have killed these people," I said.

"So what are you saying, Detective Hero?" asked Captain Blake.

"I believe we have a copycat murderer. It might be the guy we are looking for now. He might be our killer in this double homicide. But right now, it's still too early to say. Let the team of investigators do their work. Once we get the autopsy reports, they should give us some answers."

"I just can't get over it. They were mutilated just like your other victims," said Captain Blake.

"They sure are," I replied. "Their throats are slit from ear to ear, and the man's manhood is severed."

"What about the dead female victim?" he asked.

I looked over the body of the female victim once again, then said, "The female was butchered and bludgeoned with some type of large butcher knife, probably the same one that was used on the male victim. The breasts are caved in, just like the murdered women in my last multiple murder investigation. Also, the woman's hair was cut and shortened...and the cut hair was deliberately placed around her head as if it were a halo. Just as before. We must have a copycat."

"Detective Hero, do you have any ideas?" Captain Blake asked.

"No. But I think I'll drive up to the prison and have a talk with Elaine Weltman, the perpetrator from my last multiple murder investigation. She might have some idea about who might have killed these two people. It was definitely some maniac that committed these murders."

"Good. Detective Hero, I would like you to take over this investigation," said Captain Blake.

"But sir, I'm already working on the park murders along with my two out-of-state detectives."

"Yes, I know. But I can't afford to take anyone off of the serial killer squad. I need you to close this case. I know I can count on you."

"Yes, sir," I said, as I watched the investigators search for evidence.

While coroner, Doc Grady checked the victims, the photographer was busy snapping photos and making videos, all the while trying not to disturb any of the pertinent evidence.

"Detective Hero. Would you step over here for a minute?" Dr. Grady asked.

"What can I do for you, Doc?" I said, walking over to him.

"What do these remind you of?" he asked, handing me a clear plastic evidence bag to examine. It contained strands of golden blonde hair.

"You took these off of both bodies?" I asked.

"Yes sir. I took at least three or more off of each body. ... But something just doesn't fit."

"What do you mean? What doesn't fit?"

"These hairs were placed—neatly on the bodies—after they had been killed. I mean, I don't see any dried blood on them. They should be covered in blood if the suspect and victims came in contact with each other. But these are pristine."

"What if the suspect was standing or kneeling over them and somehow shook her hair over their dead bodies?" I asked.

"Yeah, but just by coincidence there should at least be one hair with blood on it. I feel the hairs were placed on the bodies. Don't ask me why, or when. But I don't think they got on them as they were being murdered. But I'll know more when I get them under a microscope. My opinion could change."

"Well, I don't know how or when the hairs got on the victims, but I want to know whose hair it is. I hate to say this, but these hairs look like the same hairs that were found on the five murder victims in the Weltman murders—and that case is closed. The perp was caught, tried, and convicted," I said.

"We'll do a DNA check on them, so we'll know for sure if they belong to the person you convicted or if they are from somebody else. You know, there are millions of blondes in this country," said Dr. Grady.

Just as I handed the evidence bag of blonde hairs to a forensic investigator, my captain turned and left the room. He went to coordinate the murder investigation on the floor below. We didn't know for certain whether the person that had just been shot and killed was really the perp or just an innocent victim. We hoped to review the café's videotape and hopefully get a good look at the perpetrator's face. That would be all the evidence we would need to prove that the shooting by the three rookie officers had been justified.

Our flashlights just weren't powerful enough to light the murder scenes, so we had to bring in quite a few portable lights. It would also help them stay out of harm's way, with all the maggot-infested garbage and human waste. This place was like working in an open sewage reservoir.

While watching the forensics investigators do their work, my thoughts turned to those few long, blonde hairs found on the two murder victims. I thought of Elaine Weltman, and how she claimed to be innocent. But the evidence against her had been overwhelming. The jurors convicted her in less than two hours. Still, I never believed she could have done all five murders, even if it had been her hair that we had found at the murder scenes.

But now, two more dead bodies had turned up with blonde hairs found on their bodies. Even though the hairs looked similar, we still had to have them tested for DNA. That would prove, positively, whether or not it was the hair of the convicted criminal, Elaine Weltman. But it couldn't possibly be her hair...because she was in prison when these murders occurred.

That, however, didn't mean she might not have an idea who did. So I decided to visit her within a day or so. Right now though, I decided to leave this crime scene and return to the cafe to retrieve the videotape from the video machine.

# MURDER IN THE CITY PARTS I-II

I walked to the floor below where the investigators were still collecting evidence from the crime scene. Detectives Stanton and Banner were there watching the investigation. A few minutes before, the coroner had just taken away the two dead bodies from the room above and was now taking away the other victim that had been shot by the three rookie police officers. It had been over four hours since we had begun the search for the robber.

The uniformed officers finally completed their search of the building, but they were left empty-handed. My gut instincts had been correct. The robber, if not the man who had been shot, had somehow gotten away.

When my captain and the photographer left the building an hour or so later, so did my two detective friends and I. We returned to the cafe, to check out *that* murder scene.

When we reached the cafe, the coroner's assistant, Dr. Bradly, was just leaving with the dead customer. And a small team of investigators were there collecting evidence and interviewing witnesses. They also retrieved the bullets—fired by the suspect's gun—which had been imbedded in an oak wall. The slugs had gone through a chromed, steel hinge and then shattered into many pieces. They were a small caliber, possibly a twenty-two. But we wouldn't know for certain until they were checked by ballistics under a microscope.

We surmised that these bullets were Dum Dum bullets. When they hit the intended target, they explode on impact, ripping out large chunks of flesh as they make their way through the body, destroying as much tissue and bone as possible. These types of bullets are used for one purpose: to kill their intended victim. The bullets were tagged and placed into an evidence bag to be tested later.

When I asked the waitress for the videotape from the camera, I was shocked to learn that there wasn't any. The camera was only a prop. It didn't work...and was there only to appease the insurance company and to scare away robbers. This time, however, it hadn't worked. Now, instead of the suspect's photo, we would have to make a composite drawing from eyewitness accounts, including myself.

I let the investigative team do their work while Stanton, Banner, and I went back to our table in the back...to sit, relax, and have a drink or two. I wanted to eat my meal. Hopefully, in peace.

"I'll stop by the station tomorrow morning and pick up the reports," I told Banner and Stanton. "We'll go over them at the breakfast table. If there isn't any trouble from the serial task force investigation, all the reports should be completed and waiting for me."

"You know, we saw some of the task force at today's murder scene. Did they think these victims were killed by their serial killer?" asked Stanton.

"Yeah. They check any murder scene that they think involves their serial killer," I said.

"You never told us anything about that task force. You said you were on it at one time. Did you guys have any suspects in mind? How long has the task force been in existence?" asked Banner.

"Well, the task force has been together for a little more than a year. But the murders of the serial killer have been investigated for more than three years."

"Were all the serial killer's victims found in your city?" asked Stanton.

"All the murders occurred within a fifty mile radius," I said.

"What about the five victims in your last multiple murder investigation?" asked Banner. "Did the task force think any of those murders were committed by their killer?"

"Yeah... some," I said, nodding my head. "But after the evidence pointed to a different suspect, they dropped those murder victims from their investigation."

"What about the murder victims that were found today? Does the task force think they were killed by their serial killer?"

"Yep ... That's the reason some of their investigators checked out the murder scenes today. But they have to wait for the evidence to be tested."

"So they think their serial killer had something to do with those two murders. Did they have a psychological profile done on their killer?" asked Banner.

"Yep," I replied, "there was a psychological profile done."

"Baxter, not to change the subject... but why did the forensic investigator ask you about those blonde hairs that were found on the bodies? Were they found at any other murder scene?"

I nodded. "Yes, I have seen those types of hairs before on some of my other murder victims. But many people have long, blonde hair. Anyway, the person whose hair is in question is in prison right at this very minute. So I know she can't be the killer."

"What does the psychological profile state about the task force serial killer?" asked Banner.

"It stated that the killer was a calculated, intelligent, and manipulative male, between thirty and sixty years of age. He works either as a janitor or handyman...or possibly a professional, like an engineer or lawyer."

"What other insights did the profile give?" Banner asked.

"The killer is very cunning and pragmatic. He knows every move he will make ahead of time. He has no sense of fear. He thinks he will never be caught. ... But, time is on our side. He's going to make a mistake one day."

"Why did the task force investigators think the dead couple from the apartment building might be the work of their killer?" asked Stanton.

"Because they were murdered in the same fashion as the others. Their throats were cut from ear to ear, and they were butchered, unmercifully. It was actually overkill. Many of his victims had their penises severed and placed near their mouths. We think he was leaving us a message leaving his victims like that."

"Baxter, didn't you have a killer like that?" asked Stanton.

"Yes. She murdered five people and killed them in a similar fashion," I replied.

"So what's the difference between murder scenes?" asked Banner.

"Not much," I replied, "except Elaine Weltman left much of her signature at the murder scenes. The task force serial killer doesn't. Many of his murder scenes have very little in the way of evidence. He slices and stabs the victims so they will bleed to death very quickly and does it without leaving any fingerprints, footprints, hair, semen, saliva, or anything else for that matter. That's why when the investigator found those blonde hairs on both bodies I thought about Elaine Weltman. But I know she can't kill anyone where she's at."

"Where is she now?" asked Banner. "In a maximum-security cell or on death row?"

"She's in maximum security *on* death row. She's locked up twenty-three hours a day, seven days a week. When she does get out of her cell, four guards escort her. So this could be the most evidence that we have found from our serial killer."

"I don't know how your investigators found any evidence in all of that maggot-infested garbage and human waste all over the floor of the murder scene. The smell was so bad, my eyes burned," Stanton said. "It reminded me of the time I visited Los Angeles during a smog alert. That day I could have used a gas mask, and I could have used one today in that apartment building."

"It was pretty bad," I said, nodding in agreement. "I'd hate to have to investigate homicides in places like that every time."

"So, Baxter. Who do you think killed those two young kids that were found today?" asked Banner.

"I don't know. But after finding those blonde hairs at the murder scene, I want to visit Elaine Weltman. Maybe she knows something. This could be a copycat murder. Who knows?"

"You don't think your convicted criminal could have killed them, do you?" asked Banner.

"How could she? I told you, she's locked up in prison. There is no way in hell that she was responsible for those two murder victims."

"Then what about the blonde hairs?" asked Stanton.

"They have to belong to someone else," I replied. "The DNA testing will tell us the answer. The only problem is that the testing can take months. That is, if the task force doesn't get in line first."

"You know, it's getting late," Stanton said. "We should be getting back to our hotel. I still have some packing to do."

Banner nodded in agreement.

"Why don't we meet here in the morning?" I said. "I'll bring the investigative reports with me and we can read through them after we eat."

The detectives agreed, and we all made plans to meet up the next morning.

# Chapter 16

I arrived at the station with a pounding headache, courtesy of my typical, late-night drinking. I really needed a cup of strong, black coffee, but I didn't want to keep my two out-of-state detectives waiting. They had planned to leave today.

When I reached my desk, I noticed a thick stack of papers sitting there. I quickly glanced through them—some of the investigative reports had finally come in on the park murders.

As I glanced through the stack, I saw that the reports I had been waiting for were among them—the fingerprint analysis reports, along with the complete autopsy and ballistic reports. These were the reports that Stanton and Banner needed to close their investigations. I just hoped they included the answers that they needed.

I quickly placed the reports under my arm and walked out of the building, heading for my car. I was anxious to meet with my two friends at the café.

The two detectives were standing outside the front door of the cafe waiting for me as I walked up to greet them.

"Good morning, fellows," I said, holding up the reports for them to see. We headed inside, walking around the yellow tape that cordoned off the murder scene to get to our favorite table all the way in the back.

"Boy, my hands are sweating," Banner said, as we took our seats. "I am so excited my heart is pumping a hundred miles an hour. I hope these reports have the answers that I need to close my investigation." He rifled through the stack, then handed half to Detective Stanton.

A few seconds later, the waitress brought each of us coffee and then took our orders. While we sipped our coffee and waited for breakfast to arrive, the two detectives sorted through the reports to get to the fingerprint analysis on three of the victims. They didn't find one on the old man. A moment later, both detectives were smiling. Two of the dead victims' fingerprints matched the killers that they had been searching for. They finally had the evidence they needed to close their investigations after years of hard work.

Two serial killers at one murder scene had to be a billion to one shot. The third victim was also a wanted fugitive. He was wanted in several states on many different crimes and was a suspect in many murders and armed robberies. But the old man remained unidentified.

When Bonnie brought our breakfast, the two detectives put the reports to the side. They had a big appetite and wanted to enjoy their food this morning. They finally had some good news to take back to their superiors.

Searching for one devious person for that length of time can wear a person out. The investigation begins to eat at your mind until it consumes your being. You dream about it and have nightmares about it. But today, you could tell that Detectives Banner and Stanton had finally received the answers to their prayers. All the stress and aggravation that had built up in their bodies and minds over the years had suddenly been lifted. It didn't matter that the suspects would never get their day in court. My two friends didn't seem to mind. They smiled and hummed songs while eating their breakfast. I must say, I was happy for them. They had worked long and hard for this moment.

We finished our meals and then sat back to digest them while we smoked our cigarettes and drank our coffee. My head was still pounding, but it was no longer as bad. Another few hours and I'd be as good as new.

We went back to reading. I examined the shooting diagram of the park murders. We still couldn't figure out what exactly had transpired. Was the shooter that got away robbing them? All four victims?

"Well, I have my suspect's identity," said Banner gleefully.

"Which one is it?" I kidded.

"The female ... I've been hunting her for so long. I really wanted to understand how a human being could do such cruel and inhumane things to another. She used evil and sadistic torture and murder to subdue her prey."

"Unfortunately Joseph, that's what makes this crazy world go round." I turned my attention to Stanton and asked, "Which suspect were you looking for, Eddy?"

"It turns out that the male lying underneath the female was my suspect. I just couldn't tell from my photo. But I know who he is now."

"Let's look over the shooting diagram. Do they know who shot the first bullet?" Banner asked, looking at me.

I was about to answer when I noticed a rather tall man standing alongside our table.

"Can I help you, sir?" I asked.

"Yes, you can. I am looking for a Detective Hero."

"I'm Detective Hero. What can I do for you?"

"I'm Detective Francis Wilmont, working for the homicide department out of Twin Falls, Minnesota. I stopped by your department to talk to you about a murder you are currently investigating. Captain Blake told me you could be found at this cafe. I believe you are investigating the park murders, are you not?" He had blond hair and sounded like he was from Sweden.

I nodded in agreement and then said, "Yes, I'm investigating the park murders. What can I do for you, Detective Wilmont?"

"The fax I received stated that you had my suspect in custody. I would like permission to interrogate him. You may take part in the interrogation if you want."

"Please, sit down. Take a load off of your feet," I said, pointing to the only empty chair at our table. "We were just going over the reports on that case at this very moment. . . . Oh! Let me introduce you to my two friends. They are—"

Banner cut me off in mid-sentence and introduced himself, as did Stanton.

"I am Detective Joseph Banner," he said, standing up to shake hands with Detective Wilmont.

"And I am Detective Eddy Stanton," he said. He reached across the table and shook Detective Wilmont's hand. "Please, Detective Wilmont, have a seat and join us."

"Thank you," he said.

The second he sat down, Bonnie brought him a cup of coffee.

"My two friends here are also working on this investigation," I interjected. "Let me rephrase that. They just finished working on this investigation."

"Oh, do you two detectives work in Detective Hero's department?" asked Wilmont, looking to Stanton and Banner for an answer. I answered for them.

"No. They are out-of-state homicide detectives hunting serial killers."

"That's what I'm doing. I'm also hunting a serial killer. ... Detective Hero, do you think my suspect is involved in the park murders? I've been hunting this killer for the last five years," said Wilmont, as he lit a cigarette.

"Detective Wilmont, maybe you're hunting the same suspect as Detectives Banner and Stanton," I said, smiling at my two friends.

"I don't know," he replied. "Can I look at some of the investigative reports on the park murders?"

"Sure," I replied. "We were just going over the shooting diagram now."

Banner looked at Wilmont and said, "While we're going over the reports, why don't you tell us about the suspect you've been hunting?"

"All right," replied Wilmont, eager to tell his story. "I have been hunting a monster for five years. This guy has killed over fourteen women at last count. Those are the ones we know about. ... We think he may have killed over thirty women!"

"Why do you think your suspect has killed thirty women?" I asked.

"We have sixteen women missing in the Twin Falls area alone, and counting those that were found murdered ... Well, that totals thirty," Wilmont said. "And our district attorney said he can prosecute my killer on at least twelve of the fourteen murdered females."

I pulled the autopsy and fingerprint analysis reports out of the stack and handed them to Wilmont. "These are the autopsy and fingerprint analysis reports," I said. "See if any names ring a bell."

As he took the reports, Wilmont looked at me, frowning. "Autopsy reports? Why would I want autopsy reports? I just want to talk to my suspect. ... Did he murder these victims in the park?" He sighed. "I just hope we aren't chasing the same suspect."

"I don't think you understand, Detective Wilmont," I said, shaking my head. "If your suspect was involved in the park murders, he's either one of the victims or he's the shooter. Do you have a name for your suspect?"

"Yes," replied Wilmont. "His name is Johnny Napolin. He's a hardcore gangster-type that likes to rape and torture women. He likes to strangle them as he sodomizes them."

"I also handed you the fingerprint analysis reports. See if Napolin's name is among the victims," I said.

"I thought you had him in custody?" Wilmont said, looking to me for an answer.

"He is," I replied. "They're keeping him at the morgue."

"Why? Are your jails full?"

"Detective Wilmont," I said, shaking my head in disbelief, "I can't believe you. Are you for real? ... He's dead. ... If your suspect is one of those people found at the park, he's as dead as a doornail!"

Wilmont wasn't listening to me; he was reading the investigative reports. Finally, he looked up. "Detective Hero, you're right," he said. "I just read Napolin's autopsy report. ... He's dead as a doornail." He cursed, setting the report back down. "We'll probably never know how many people he's killed. And we'll probably never find the missing women that we feel he's somehow responsible for."

"We have the same problem," said Banner, pointing to Stanton.

"Detective Banner, which suspects were you and Detective Stanton searching for? You weren't chasing my suspect, were you?" asked Wilmont.

"No. My suspect was the dead female," replied Banner.

"Mine was the dead male that was lying underneath the dead female," said Stanton. He showed Wilmont the shooting diagram. "If I remember correctly, Detective Wilmont, your suspect, Johnny Napolin, was the one lying about thirty feet from the dead couple. He was the male with his manhood severed. The autopsy states he died first."

"Oh my god, how gross," Wilmont said. "Why would someone do that? Why would someone cut off his manhood?"

"This particular person wanted it as a memento. A souvenir," said Banner.

"A souvenir? Nobody in their right mind would keep someone's manhood as a souvenir," Wilmont said, shaking his head in disbelief. "Any normal killer would have taken a ring or a piece of their victim's jewelry."

"Detective Wilmont, you're probably right. But this person made a necklace out of them. We found nine of them at the park murder scene—all stuffed—on a piece of string tied together to form a necklace," I said.

"You've got to be kidding," he said, shaking his head in disgust.

"No, I'm not kidding. It was found lying near your suspect...along with his own severed penis. It hadn't been attached to the necklace yet."

"We think," explained Banner, "that my suspect killed or thought she had killed her intended victim—which was your suspect, Johnny Napolin. But before she could finish the job...two other males happened upon the scene—the old man and Stanton's suspect. We believe my suspect came out from behind the bushes, half-dressed, and began flirting with them as she walked towards them."

"Where was my suspect at this time?" asked Wilmont.

"We believe," replied Banner, "when the female came out from behind the thick brush, Johnny Napolin was still lying in the deep brush, hidden from view, as his life slowly seeped from his wounded body. When she left him for dead and walked towards the two males, we believe Johnny Napolin somehow pulled his body into the open and began firing his weapon at her."

"Detective Wilmont, this is total conjecture on our parts, mind you," interjected Stanton. "In fact, we were talking about this very thing when you came in."

Then I put my two cents in. "Detective Wilmont, we believe your suspect, with his penis severed and his chest bleeding profusely from several stab wounds created by a large butcher knife, gathered enough strength to stumble a few steps out of the brush and squeeze off two or three rounds from his forty-five. Then he died from his wounds and fell back into the deep brush," I said.

"I wonder why he was in that park in the first place?" asked Wilmont.

Before Stanton or I could answer Wilmont's question, Banner spoke up. "We believe that Napolin went down into that park to rape and murder that woman to satisfy his sick need. But she turned the tables around on him. He wasn't aware that she had the same thing in mind—that she was going to torture and murder him for her own pleasure."

"All I can say is... it couldn't have happened to a better guy. He finally got what he deserved," Wilmont said. "This time, it seems, he got a little taste of his own medicine."

"But your suspect got the last laugh, Detective Wilmont. He was able to shoot the female in the back with one of his shots. ... But not the fatal one," Banner said.

Wilmont thought for a moment and then asked Banner, "So Napolin shot *your* suspect?"

"Yes, but he didn't kill her," Banner replied. "The autopsy report shows she died from a bullet wound to the head, fired from the gun of Stanton's suspect."

Then Stanton gave his opinion to what had occurred on that fateful day at the park. "We believe my suspect thought he was going to get laid by the female, but she surprised him, like she surprised Johnny Napolin...and used her butcher knife on him. She nearly severed his manhood...and stabbed him in the chest several times before he was able to shoot her with his weapon."

"But," I said, "he didn't die from her stab wounds. He died from someone firing a twenty-two-caliber weapon—at both him and the female."

"Who shot the twenty-two?" Wilmont asked.

I took a long drag on my cigarette, then said, "We believe a shooter standing behind the old man fired the fatal bullet into the chest of the male, and also shot one into the back of the female. We also believe Stanton's suspect fired one bullet under the chin of the female and then began firing his weapon at the shooter standing behind and in direct line of the old man. That's when the old man was hit by one of the .357 slugs."

"Where did it hit him?" asked Wilmont.

"It smashed through his frontal facial area," I said. "His teeth were completely shattered from the blast and couldn't be used for a dental record check because of the severe damage. And his fingerprints weren't in the FBI's criminal database, so we have absolutely no idea of his identity. Every time we run down a lead, we hit a dead-end."

"Talk about dead-ends," exclaimed Wilmont. "We hit a dead-end after every sadistic murder Johnny Napolin committed. We knew he would continue to kill as long as he was free to act upon his devious nature. This guy was such a brutal animal that he once ripped the head off of his victim's shoulders, literally by hand, and then sodomized the victim while it lay dead and bleeding. This guy was a sadistic, psychopathic, and demented killer. Thank god he won't kill anyone else."

"Did your department ever get a psychological profile on your suspect?" I asked Wilmont.

"Sure, after the thirteenth brutal murder that was committed. ... But then again, we found very little evidence. Napolin could change his identity like a chameleon changes its color. But then we got lucky one night and found the victim within a few days of her murder. And we also found a bloody fingerprint on the floor near the victim's body."

"When did you find that evidence? Was it during the first year of your investigation?" Banner asked.

"No. It was the fourth year of my investigation. ... It took over four years before we had a suspect with an identity. We were always investigating the boyfriend or ex-husband."

"Detective Wilmont, you never told us about the psychological profile that was done," I said.

"Oh, the profile. ... Well, the psychologist stated that our serial killer was a white male, approximately thirty to forty years of age, between 5' and 5'9" tall, weighing between one hundred and fifty to one hundred and seventy pounds. And he was very egotistical and selfish."

"That sounds like your typical serial killer," I said.

"You're absolutely right, Detective Hero," Wilmont said. "Napolin was only on earth to satisfy his own pleasures. He would do what he wanted, when he wanted, and with whom he wanted to do it, and not give a damn about the consequences. He had no conscience!"

"I guess not," said Stanton.

"When he was young," Wilmont added, "he was orphaned. He was underfed and never held in the arms of a loved one—or shown any love. He had what is known as Detached Deficit Disorder behavior. He also had Attention Deficit Syndrome since childhood."

"So what you're telling us is that he didn't like anyone," I said.

"That's right, Detective Hero," replied Wilmont. "He didn't have feelings for anyone other than himself. He couldn't identify with others. He couldn't feel love for another. ...Napolin's troubles at the orphanage began at age six, when one of the younger orphans wouldn't look at him or talk to him because he was too young and couldn't speak. When the baby didn't answer him, Napolin hit and beat it until it was a bloody pulp. He killed the baby because it refused to talk to him."

"Man, I hate the guy already," exclaimed Stanton. "Did he know that he'd killed the baby?"

"I don't think so," replied Wilmont. "He was still angry at it and beating it when one of the attendants came into the room and tried to save it. But it was too late. The baby was already dead."

"So what did the staff do? Did they call the police and have Napolin's ass hauled off to jail?" asked Stanton.

"What ... a six-year-old kid? ... No. They just kept him away from the other children. Napolin ate, slept, and played by himself."

"Did that help?" asked Stanton.

"No," Wilmont said, shaking his head. "It made things worse. To get attention he would bang his head against the wall until he was covered in blood. He felt no pain while he was in his fit of rage."

"So what happened when he did that?" Stanton asked.

"When the attendants showed up to clean his wounds he became angry with them," Wilmont said. "He didn't want his wounds cleaned. He wanted to play. And when they refused his request, he became even angrier. He only thought of his own gratification—even as a child. This was the type of person Johnny Napolin was. He was beyond reproach. He was beyond rehabilitation. He was beyond redemption. ... When he killed that little baby, the staff supervisor asked him if he felt sorry for his actions. Do you know what his reply was?"

"I can't wait to hear it," I said.

Wilmont took a long drag on his cigarette before answering. "He told them it was the baby's fault that he became angry…because the baby refused to talk to him. When the baby refused to give him the attention he needed, he tried getting it by beating him. It was always someone else's fault," Wilmont said. "Never his. … This was how Napolin grew up."

"When did he kill for a second time?" I asked.

"When he was ten, he killed his first foster parent—by choking the woman because she refused to let him go outside to play."

"How in the world could a ten-year-old kid kill an adult woman?" asked Stanton.

"When he became enraged, he had the strength of five men."

"Did he know that he had killed her?" Banner asked.

"I'm not positive," Wilmont said, "but I think he did."

"Did anyone call the police? Or did anyone know that a murder had even occurred?" asked Banner.

"Not until Napolin began throwing rocks at the streetlights…then the police were called to the neighborhood. When they escorted him to his foster parent's house to talk to the responsible party, they found the woman lying dead on the kitchen floor. … At first, the kid acted surprised and hurt. But as the police questioned him about his foster mother's death, his true feelings emerged."

"Did they ever get a confession out of him?" Banner asked.

"Yep. Within ten minutes, he had told the police that he had grabbed her by the neck and she passed out and fell to the floor. He had absolutely no remorse for his actions. When the police asked him if he knew his foster mother was dead, he told them he didn't care...that he just wanted to go outside to play and she wouldn't let him."

"So what did they do to him?" asked Stanton.

"He was sent to Juvenile Hall for that incident. But he didn't stay long there, either. He committed crimes that the system wasn't used to. They could control all the other juveniles, but they couldn't control him—no matter how much they punished him. If they beat him, he laughed at them. If they locked him up, he would find a way to get out of his room. And the minute he was out, he would injure another kid...or a guard."

"Why would he do that?" asked Stanton.

"His excuse was always the same," Wilmont said, taking a long drag on his cigarette.

"Which was?" I asked impatiently.

"They didn't pay enough attention to him. That was always his excuse. Me, me, me. That's all he cared about. He didn't care who he hurt. The more the merrier."

"What did the courts do?" asked Stanton.

"Well, Juvenile Hall refused to keep him because he was contaminating all the other juvenile delinquents. So they had him transferred to a maximum-security juvenile detention center."

"Did that do any good?" asked Stanton.

"They put him among the hard-core juveniles—many of whom had killed at least one person in their life. But the kid was only ten-years-old, and the judge thought that his transfer was a bit too harsh."

"So what did the judge do?" asked Stanton.

Wilmont sat back in his chair and shook his head in disgust. "They transferred him from maximum-security and had him placed into another foster home."

"What happened at that place?" I asked. "Did he kill another foster parent?"

"No," he replied. "This time it was only animals."

"What did he do, kill a pet dog?" Stanton asked.

"No...but something just as bad. He was feeding baby kittens to starved guard dogs."

"Whose bright idea was it to put him into another foster home?" Banner asked.

"Well, a judge signed the decree, but it was social services that moved him from foster home to foster home after each psychotic episode. They couldn't place him in any state or city facility."

"Why not?" I asked.

"They refused to accept him," he said.

"Why were they allowed to refuse him?" asked Stanton.

"Each facility had him at one time or another but couldn't control his outrageous actions. ... He always believed he hadn't done anything wrong."

"That kid must have been mentally incompetent," I said.

"That's a possibility. One side of his brain never developed properly, or so says the psychologist. The judge finally ordered the state to protect him from himself," said Wilmont.

"What did the judge do?" Stanton asked.

"He was forced to lock him away in a padded cell at a maximum-security mental institution that had been built back in the eighteen sixties."

"Couldn't they find a more modern facility?" asked Stanton.

"The state *must have* updated the building since the eighteen sixties?" interjected Banner.

"Nope. The place hasn't changed a bit since that time," Wilmont said, taking a sip of his coffee.

"Did Napolin hurt anyone at that facility?" Stanton asked.

"No. He wasn't able to kill anyone for a few years," Wilmont replied.

"Why is that?" asked Banner.

"He was kept locked up in a straight jacket—and they made him wear a helmet at all times so he couldn't damage his head."

"When did he leave that state facility? After his eighteenth birthday?" Banner asked.

"Long before that," Wilmont said. "Believe it or not, the ACLU came to his rescue. They petitioned the courts to hear his case."

Stanton and Banner looked on in disbelief.

"Why in the hell did they get involved?" I asked, disgustedly.

"They believed the state was violating the boy's civil rights and that his punishment was cruel and inhumane," Wilmont replied.

"It sounds to me as though your suspect was the cruel and inhumane one," said Banner matter-of-factly.

"So what happened in the courts?" I asked.

"The state fought the lawsuit by voicing the concerns and terror of the victims. However, the judge didn't allow the victims to tell their own stories. He said it would be prejudicial to the court."

"That sounds right. That's what a stupid judge would do," I said, mockingly.

"The judge ruled that the victims had no place in this case or in his courtroom. It was only about the plaintiff, the boy. ... The state was shoved to the side in every instance in that trial," said Wilmont.

"So what was the outcome of the trial?" asked Banner.

"The judge ordered the boy placed into a halfway house or another foster home. He ruled that there was absolutely no basis for Napolin's incarceration at the state mental institution."

"Then the judge should be held responsible for any of his criminal acts," said Banner, putting out his cigarette in the ashtray.

"The state was also ordered to pay a fine to the court and to set up a small trust fund for the boy, to use as he wished, when he turned twenty-one years of age."

"That money should have gone to his victims' families," Banner said, "or at least to pay for the attorney fees."

"Well I'll tell you one thing. That boy's attorneys looked very foolish after the trial," exclaimed Wilmont.

"Why is that?" asked Stanton.

"The first month the boy was placed in a halfway house, people began disappearing in the neighborhood. He learned to keep his dirty deeds quiet. When he hurt someone or killed someone, he would never admit it. He knew that if he told anyone, he would be in big trouble."

"So what happened?" asked Stanton.

"We wouldn't find the missing kid for days, if not weeks. By that time, all the pertinent evidence was gone or washed away. The state knew that Johnny had something to do with the missing kids, but could never prove it. Then, when the kids' dead and deteriorating bodies were found, it was too late. ... We could never pin it on him."

"So what did the authorities do to him?" asked Banner, seemingly very interested in the answer.

"The state had no other choice but to move him, over and over again. They never let him stay in one place more than a week or two. It seemed, once he got bored with the place he would look for other ways to keep himself occupied."

"Why, what would he do?" asked Banner.

Wilmont stared into his coffee cup as he answered Banner's question. "He would go out and find a little boy or girl to torture and kill. He would cover their mutilated bodies with leaves and other objects and dump them in places where they couldn't be seen, unless you walked right on top of them."

"Man, I thought my suspect had a rough childhood. This guy was born with evil genes. The biological parents were probably monsters, too," exclaimed Stanton.

"Yeah, they were. I know because I read their background reports. The father was a total psychopath. He was born with extra rage hormones—always fighting. The psychologists believe that the father, and the son were sodomized when they were no more than six months old," said Wilmont.

Banner nodded. "I think that would make anybody insane," he said.

"That type of behavior continued until Napolin's father was put into prison for attempted murder and was killed during his stay," Wilmont added. "When he wasn't in solitary confinement, he was always fighting with other inmates...and many of those fights ended by him stabbing the other prisoner with a homemade shiv. But he had one fight too many."

"I take it he lost that fight?" I asked.

Wilmont nodded. "Someone slit his throat from ear to ear, then pissed into his mouth. The only reason his son, Johnny, didn't end up in jail or prison was due to the fact that his lawyers were the best that money could buy. They did a tremendous job for their psychotic client. Napolin's lawyers were able to get his cases reduced or dismissed by bribing certain officials or by threatening them with fictitious newspaper reports accusing the court of prejudicial action and being unprofessional."

"They should have been banned from practicing law and then jailed," I said.

"They should have, but they weren't," replied Wilmont. "Their strategy worked. Johnny was given his trust fund from the state when he turned twenty-one. He was given an account worth more than two hundred and fifty thousand dollars."

"That's typical. The murderer is the victim. So us taxpayers are the real losers," Banner said, shaking his head in disgust.

"You're right, Detective Banner...because taxpayers did have to pay the bill for Napolin's trust fund. In fact, he had been living on the interest from it—from thirty-year, tax free bonds—since his release from the state's mental institution."

"This story is literally making me sick," said Banner.

"He was the only person I knew that had ACLU attorneys working for him twenty-four hours a day, seven days a week, for fifty-two weeks of the year. He didn't even have to pay their wages for work rendered," Wilmont said.

"Why didn't they charge him? He had money from his trust fund that he could have paid them with," said Banner.

"They thought he was a victim of the state," Wilmont replied. "They thought his incarceration made him what he is today. But I'm sorry ... He was born a monster. The state didn't make him like that. It was in his genes."

"I believe that, too," I said. "I believe that type of criminal behavior is hereditary."

Wilmont continued telling us about Napolin's parents— next came his mother.

"The guy's birth mother was a paranoid, drug-addicted schizophrenic. She never worked a day in her life, and neither did the father. They lived on welfare and sold dope and stolen property. When her baby would cry, she would shoot it up with her drugs."

"What kind of drugs?" I asked.

"Usually heroin. Her first two babies died from mysterious reasons. The coroner believed the mother filled their bodies with heroin or some other type of opiate."

"So why didn't the police arrest her for the babies' deaths?" asked Banner.

"Nothing to hold her on because of a lack of evidence," replied Wilmont. "In each instance, by the time the paramedics were called to the scene the baby had been dead for days. When asked why she had waited so long to call for help, she stated that she thought her baby was just sleeping. They never took the mother to jail for the deaths of her infants. Instead, they sent her to the state's only mental institution, where many years later, her son had lived for a time."

"I told you, it's hereditary," I said, matter-of-factly.

"Yeah ... I think you're right. And she was just as uncontrollable as her son—especially when she didn't take her medication. But when her medication was controlled and not abused, she could fool the doctors into thinking she was back to normal, hoping they would release her back into society."

"Did they?" asked Stanton.

"Yes they did, for a time. But the state found out that she had delivered another baby and took it away from her. And then the courts came to her defense and had the state return her baby to her."

"When are these judges going to learn...and stop believing these sob stories that criminals tell?" asked Banner.

"I don't know if that will ever happen," Wilmont said. "But she thought that she had beaten the system, once again."

"Did anything ever happen to that baby?" asked Banner.

"Yeah!" Wilmont said. "While the baby boy was in her possession, he was sodomized by the father every night for months until a social worker stopped by the house to check up on him to see how he was doing. She noticed immediately that something was terribly wrong because the baby wouldn't stop crying. She took him to the emergency room. That's when it was determined that the baby had been sexually abused. That baby was Johnny Napolin."

"It's a wonder that little Johnny survived," said Banner.

"Yes, he survived...but just barely. His insides needed immediate surgery to save him. The tissue in the rectum and stomach had been ground like hamburger. It was a miracle Napolin survived."

"What happened to the parents? Were they punished?" asked Banner.

"Yep. The father ended up in prison for that. The mother also served time in prison for the same charge and a neglect charge. She also died in prison. She was given rat poison in place of her usual drug. Thinking it was her favorite drug of choice, heroin, she injected it into her vein."

"Ah, such a fitting way to die for such an inhumane person," said Banner.

"You know," blurted Stanton, wanting to get into the conversation, "I finally finished reading the reports of my suspect's parents just last night. I talked about this a little bit a few days ago, but I didn't know as much as I know now."

Stanton began telling us the story behind his suspect's parents.

"The father of my suspect was also a very bad apple. He killed his first human being at the age of fourteen—a black man. His own father was a racist, as was his grandfather—both were members of the KKK. And one time they brought a black man to one of their KKK meetings to lynch him. But before they did that, they had a few of the members' sons beat the guy with ax handles and rifle butts. They beat him unmercifully while he pleaded for his life."

"I bet you they didn't like what he had to say," kidded Banner.

"I don't know about that," replied Stanton. "But what I do know is that the black guy explained to them that he had a family and that they counted on him to support them. He pleaded that he had a wife and six children—that they would be lost without him. They lynched him anyway—and for no apparent reason other than the color of his skin. This is the type of life that my suspect's father lived. And he instilled all of his hatred into his son."

"I wonder how the father treated his wife?" asked Banner.

"He beat her daily. He would literally keep her bruised and cut, so she wouldn't go out to see anyone else. He was a highly jealous man. He wanted her by his side at all times," said Stanton.

"I wonder why husbands that supposedly love their wives always beat them?" I asked.

"This husband figured that if he kept his wife beaten up and ugly, nobody else would want her. So my suspect had to endure seeing his mother get beat, unmercifully. But at the age of fourteen, he snapped. He grabbed an ax and swung it over his head, and in an instant, he had decapitated his father. He said later, it was like hitting a baseball with a baseball bat."

"Like I said ... Like father, like son," said Wilmont, nodding his head.

"By coincidence, his father had killed his own father at the age of fifteen," Stanton said.

"What a family," interjected Banner.

"When my suspect was taken to court for killing his own father," Stanton said, "the judge decided against any type of punishment. He was given a free ride for protecting his mother. The only trouble was, he killed her, too."

"You're kidding. When did he do that?" asked Banner.

"Just a few months after he killed his father."

"When was the father killed?" asked Banner.

"I just told you. About three months before the mother's death," replied Stanton. "And the kid confessed to the police that he had killed his mother while arguing over alcohol. She wanted it—he wouldn't allow her to have it. But he maintained it was an accident. He stated in the police report that she fought with him trying to get a bottle of vodka. When he shoved her away, she slipped and fell and hit her head on the floor. The coroner's report stated that she died instantly."

"Did they prosecute him for that crime?" I asked.

"Yep. The prosecutor stated that he had hit her with a blunt object, but the investigators couldn't find the murder weapon. That didn't matter. The judge believed the prosecutor's story and not the kid's, and placed him into the Juvenile Detention Center for two years, until his sixteenth birthday."

"He should have been charged as an adult, not a juvenile," said Banner.

"He should have. By his sixteenth birthday, he had already killed two people. But they had no choice but to free him. Before age fourteen, he had never killed anyone.

He maimed a few kids, but never killed anyone. At least, that we know of," said Stanton.

"I also read the background reports of my suspect's parents and grandparents," said Banner.

"Why would the investigators do a background check on the suspect's grandparents?" I asked.

"The department's psychologists asked for it," Banner replied.

"Why?" asked Stanton.

Banner thought for a minute and then said, "You have to start somewhere to understand why my suspect acted the way he did. I, too, wanted to know what made this type of evil human being tick—and to see if my suspect's relatives had any skeletons in their closets." Looking at Wilmont, he added, "I also talked a little bit about this before with Detective Hero and Detective Stanton. So you might as well hear it, too. Maybe it will help all of us better understand these monsters' evil deeds."

"I don't think we'll ever understand how an evil person's mind works," I said.

"I do. I also believe the answer is in the person's genes. That's why the psychologist went as far back as her great-grandfather, down to her father," said Banner.

"Great grandfather? I thought a report on the grandparents was a waste of time. Why read about the suspect's great-grandparents?" I asked.

"Believe me, it opened up my eyes. I understand why my suspect is the way he is," said Banner, matter-of-factly.

"Well, let's hear it," I said.

And Banner obliged us. "The great-grandfather was born in California, just after the Civil War. And a few months after he married, he went away on a Merchant Marine ship to see the world and to make his vast fortune, leaving a smart, young, pert, and caring wife behind. When he returned home, she was a shell of the person that he had married. She had lived through a very high fever, and it had cooked her brain."

"Was she left paralyzed?" asked Wilmont.

"No. She was all right, but she must have gotten amnesia because she lost all use of her mental faculties and didn't even recognize her own husband. She couldn't talk...and wasn't aware of her surroundings. She was in a vegetative state. But that didn't matter to her husband. She was still his wife...so he continued to use her for his own sexual gratification."

"That sick bastard," said Wilmont.

Banner nodded in agreement. "She lived, giving birth to twelve babies...but only one survived past three months of age. They all died from mysterious deaths, except a baby girl. The mother died when the girl turned thirteen."

"What happened to the child?" asked Wilmont.

Banner took a deep breath and then answered. "She was taken away from her father...when it was learned that he was having sexual relations with her."

"If I would have been the cop investigating that crime, I would have killed the guy myself," Wilmont said. "Detective Banner, what happened to the girl's father?"

"He was sent to prison and died there...from Hepatitis C."

"What happened to the daughter?" asked Wilmont.

"The daughter was a ward of the state. She was raped while staying in a state mental institution."

"Why didn't the state find her a foster home instead of the nut house?" Wilmont asked.

"She was slightly retarded and had never attended school, so I guess nobody wanted her. And at the age of fourteen, she had gotten pregnant while at the institution and had her first child, a girl. The attendant that made her pregnant had to marry her or go to jail for the rape. He accepted the former and the three of them moved away and lived as a family. He was my suspect's grandfather...and the woman, his grandmother," said Banner.

"Don't tell me. He began abusing his family," I said.

Banner nodded. "Yep. The abuse began immediately. He beat his wife, daily."

"What excuse did he use to abuse his wife?" asked Wilmont.

"A wife beater doesn't need an excuse. But if I were to take a guess...I would say that he was angry over the fact that he had been forced into marriage with a person he despised. And then one day he became so enraged at her that he killed her and buried her under the house."

"Didn't anyone become suspicious when his wife wasn't around anymore?" asked Wilmont.

"Not right away."

"Did he remarry?" asked Wilmont.

Banner took a long drag on his cigarette and then answered. "Not exactly," he said. "He replaced his wife with his daughter just like his dead wife's father had done."

"That's sick!" said Wilmont.

"The daughter was his surrogate wife in every sense of the word. She lost her virginity at the age of five, to her father," said Banner, between sips of coffee.

"Boy, when I hear stuff like that I want to lash out at the perpetrator and break his neck. How could someone do something like that to a little five-year-old girl?" asked Wilmont.

Banner looked at Wilmont and said in a low voice, "She became pregnant by him at the age of thirteen and had a baby boy—my suspect's father. He was an incest victim, as was my suspect's mother."

"That is really sick," Stanton said. "The mother of your suspect's father is also the sister of your suspect's father. How confusing."

"I'm getting a little ahead of myself," Banner said. "I'll try and keep things simple. But this story is anything but simple. ... Anyway, to get back to what I was saying. My suspect's grandfather was very mean...and beat his so-called new wife—or daughter—nearly every day, just as he had with his first wife. He didn't pay attention to his son until the boy was nearly five... and then he taught him a life of crime. But when the boy was about ten or eleven years of age, his father's world came tumbling down."

"What happened? I hope somebody killed him," said Wilmont.

"No, not at that time. ... His neighbor's python snake had gotten out of its cage and crawled under the house," said Banner.

Wilmont blurted out, "Don't tell me the snake ate him? What a way to go—being swallowed by a snake!"

"No ... I wish it had! ... Animal control was called in to retrieve the snake from under the house. But the officer got quite a surprise. Besides retrieving the snake, he also noticed a body buried there in the dirt. So the police were called," said Banner.

"What did the police do? Did they arrest him or let him go?" asked Wilmont.

"The father was taken to the precinct for questioning and held for seventy-two hours on suspicion of murder while the coroner was doing the autopsy. And the minute the police found out it was the guy's wife, they arrested him for murder and held him until his trial."

"Don't tell me. He was acquitted," said Wilmont.

"Not this time. He was convicted and thrown into prison for life. He ended up dying there," said Banner.

"How did that happen?" Wilmont asked. "I hope he felt a lot of pain before he died."

"One day, when he couldn't get his way...he lashed out at a prison guard."

"You don't do that," exclaimed Stanton. "That's a no-no in prison. What happened to him?"

"He not only tried to grab the guard's nightstick but also tried to stab him with a homemade shiv," Banner said.

"You don't do that either. What did the guards do to him?" I asked.

"What do you think they did?" replied Banner. "They stepped in and retaliated—and beat him to a bloody pulp. And when he begged for help and medical attention, they refused his request. Instead of taking him to the prison hospital, they threw him in his cell. He died later that night suffocating on his own vomit. … It couldn't have happened to a nicer guy."

"Detective Banner, you've told us about the incest between your suspect's grandfather and his daughter. Did anything happen sexually between mother and son, once your suspect's grandfather was out of the picture?" asked Wilmont.

"Yeah," he replied. "When my suspect's grandfather went to prison, his son became the surrogate father and began abusing his mother for his sexual pleasures and gratification, just as his father had. … That was learned behavior."

"Why didn't she call the police?" asked Wilmont.

Banner shrugged. "She didn't complain because she never spoke. She was like a deaf mute."

"I couldn't live like that. I think I would have ended my life," I said.

"It's funny you should say that," Banner said. "One fine day, just after one of her beatings, she placed a few big spoonfuls of arsenic in her cup of tea and drank it.
Shortly thereafter, the son moved from town to town until he found a vulnerable woman similar to his mother."

"Where did he find her?" asked Wilmont.

Banner sat back in his chair. "He found her in an alley, passed out, nude and beat up. Then he carried her to his room in a vacant, condemned building and cared for her until her injuries had healed. Over the next few days, they became good friends, and during their many discussions, he found out that she was only fourteen years old and that her stepfather had sexually abused her and her two sisters since they were young children. And that her stepfather would take them from town to town and plead with each town's local church members for food, clothes, money, and anything else that they thought the people would give them. ... When the townsfolk finally got tired of the stepfather's antics and laziness...they demanded the family leave their city. But the stepfather refused to leave empty-handed."

"What did he do, rape *their* women?" asked Wilmont.

"No. But before he left their city, the stepfather stole nearly all of the church's valuables. Then the family drove their old, dilapidated car to the next small town and began their scam all over again. There, the stepfather used his stepchildren to beg for money and a place to live. The family stayed until the church members caught onto his scam and called the police."

"What did the police do, arrest him?" asked Wilmont.

"Nope. The stepfather was always one step ahead of the law—and long gone before they arrived."

"Did the police chase after him?" asked Wilmont.

"No. The police figured as long as he owed the townsfolk money and had stolen their valuables, he would never return to their town."

"Why did he need to beg for money?" asked Wilmont.

"He would use the money to buy himself alcohol so he could stay in a drunken stupor all day long. He was always soused to the gills, but always handled it well."

"Hey, that sounds a little like me," I joked.

All three detectives gave me dirty looks.

"Like I was saying. My suspect's mother's family was just as loony as her father's family. They were snake charmers and snake worshipers. They drank arsenic and other poisons and handled many different types of deadly, poisonous snakes while they prayed to their god. They believed that god would save them from any evil that tried to take control of their bodies and minds."

"Yeah, I've heard about cults like that," Stanton said. "Those people are just plain crazy."

Banner nodded in agreement. "They also believed in having sex among the family members. My suspect's mother was told at an early age that she was on earth to please the men in her life. Her birth father, not her stepfather, showed her the way. He also taught her two sisters the joys of sex. They were never allowed to have boyfriends."

"What did they tell their friends?" asked Wilmont.

"They always had to lie about their family life—and steal if they wanted to eat. If they disobeyed their father's orders, they were beaten and put into a small, dark closet for days, if not weeks at a time, without food or water or having someplace to relieve one's bladder. They had to sit in their own urine and human waste."

"That's sick," exclaimed Wilmont. "There go my rage hormones again. ... How could a family member do that to another family member?"

Banner added, "Sometimes they were chained to the basement staircase where the rats and wild mice gnawed on their bodies—with no way to defend themselves. ... There was one particular time when one of the girls went into the basement to help free her sister. She was terrified that her father would return home any minute. He did."

"What did he do to them?" asked Stanton consumed by Banner's story.

"He bound them both to the staircase and left them without food and water for three long days. Then, one day at their church, the birth father, while handling two diamondback rattlers to prove his faith in the Lord, was bitten many times. Within a few minutes he had swelled up ten times his normal size and died."

"It couldn't have happened to a better guy," I said, smiling.

"A few months later, the wife remarried—to another church member. That's when the stepfather took over as the father figure. He began using the family for his own selfishness. Once he had tasted the forbidden fruits, he had no qualms against prostituting his women out to acquaintances he had met that day or week, just so he could buy his alcohol and sit at the nudie bar all day long."

"Why didn't the mother stop him from selling her daughters?" asked Wilmont.

"She tried. The stepfather and wife would argue for hours. He became so disgusted over his wife's constant bickering that she suddenly became deathly ill, just after a moving experience at their church."

"What happened?" Stanton asked. "Did she get bit by one of those poisonous snakes?"

"No. But she did drink from a bottle of poison. And the second she drank from it, she felt the devil's wrath. She was struck to her knees and doubled over writhing in agony while spitting up gobs of flesh and blood. She died on the church floor."

"Did they call the police?" asked Stanton.

"No, they didn't call the police or paramedics. But when the parish priest wanted the bottle of poison checked for tampering, the girls' stepfather reached out to grab it and it slipped from his hands. It smashed into little pieces on the cement floor, spilling its evil liquid."

"Did the police ever investigate the woman's death?" asked Stanton.

"I don't think so. The stepfather was never charged with any crime, even though he had just purchased a life insurance policy on her a few months before her death. However, it wasn't enough money to satisfy his spending habits."

"What spending habits?" I asked.

"He liked giving money to the working women at the different nudie bars he visited and would even bring along his stepdaughters on his drinking binges," Banner replied. "They made sure nobody stole his roll of bills from his pants pockets. He even gave away his stepdaughter's prostitution earnings in big tips to the nude dancers instead of using the money to feed and clothe the girls."

"If I had been one of those girls, I would have run away or called the police," said Stanton, leaning his chair against the wall.

Banner nodded in agreement. "The stepfather sent the girls to live with their uncle for a while, so he could recapture his sex life and remarry. Then he went on a honeymoon with a new wife—and new mother for his stepdaughters. When my suspect's mother heard that her stepfather was getting remarried, she wanted no part in their family...and she tried anything and everything to earn her freedom. That's when she became pregnant by her uncle, her dead mother's brother. One of the other sisters had also become pregnant by him."

"Did they bring their pregnancy to term or did they abort it?" I asked.

"Abort it? Why?" asked Banner.

"Come on. They were incest victims. The kids will grow two heads. That's just not something normal families do," I said.

Banner gave me an uneasy smile. "My suspect's mother had a baby girl—my suspect. And her complete family tree is full of psychopaths and evil rapists. Many of the offspring from both family trees were full of degenerates and incest victims, pedophiles and violent sexual abusers with very sick and evil, criminal minds."

"You can say that again," I retorted.

Banner nodded. "My suspect's body was full of criminal, diseased genes. That's what drove her to commit her sickening, brutal mutilations. Because she stayed within the family and didn't have any outside interaction with other friends, the two offspring born to the two sisters became boyfriend and girlfriend, even though they were incest victims with the same father, who was also their great uncle."

"Even so. That's still no reason to kill innocent people," said Stanton.

"But all that rage built up inside her from all the years of sexual abuse by people that supposedly loved her and were supposedly there to protect her, exploded. Her inbreeding caused many deformities on the inside of her body. You couldn't see them from the outside," Banner said.

"I never heard anything so crazy," Stanton exclaimed. "What was wrong with the inside of her body?"

Banner replied, "Many of her vital organs were deformed. She could never have children because of it."

"The father is supposed to protect his children, not abuse them," I said to Stanton.

"And when her incestuous father wasn't sexually abusing her...she was learning a trade from him," exclaimed Banner.

"Oh great. What trade would that be, prostitution?" asked Wilmont.

"Taxidermy," Banner replied.

"I thought maybe she went door to door selling Bibles. It was such a religious family," I said, jokingly.

"As a matter of fact, it was!" replied Banner. "Because the family continued with their Bible reading and Holy Roller-type activities—except my suspect's mother. When she wasn't living with her family...she was shacked up with another member from the church. That was just for her extracurricular activities. But she always returned home to repent after a few days of sinning. How could anyone have a normal life in a dysfunctional family like that?"

"Detective Banner, how many people was your suspect accused of murdering?" asked Wilmont.

"We know of at least nine...and possibly more in other states. We haven't added them all up yet. Once I make out my report to my superiors, we will probably close at least ten murders that we can actually pin on her, including Napolin's. When I return to my department, I'll send out a fax to every precinct in the country. We really don't know for sure, but that amount correlates with the amount of souvenirs on her homemade, phallic necklace, plus the one that was found lying on the ground at the park, which was Napolin's, I believe."

"God, that necklace. That's sick," said Stanton, shaking his head in disgust.

"The psychologist said she snapped just around the same time she went for a doctor's visit without her parent's knowledge or approval. She wanted a child very badly," said Banner.

"That's not a difficult problem to solve," Wilmont said.

"Except the doctor told her that due to deformed ovaries, she would never be able to have children. It was then that she began her vendetta against the male population. That could be the answer to her vicious behavior—and the eating of her victim's testicles," Banner said.

"But why would she eat their testicles?" I asked.

"She would eat her victim's testicles?" Wilmont asked, shaking his head in disbelief. "There was definitely something not working upstairs in her attic."

"She wasn't playing with a full deck of cards, that's for sure. But now, we'll never know what made her tick. The doctors and psychologists would have loved to study her abnormal and demented brain," Banner said.

Detective Wilmont nodded in agreement, then asked me an important question.

"Excuse me, Detective Hero. Stanton, Banner, and I have theorized about our three serial killers and how they died at that park. But what about the fourth victim—the old man that hasn't been identified yet? Do you think there was another shooter?"

"There has to be," I replied. "There were three types of bullets found in the deceased victims and only two guns found at the murder scene. You're a detective, Wilmont, you figure it out!"

"What were the three types of bullets that were found?" asked Wilmont.

After yawning, I answered his question. "There were two different bullets that were dug out of the female: A .357 slug fired by the male victim lying underneath her, who had a .22 slug inside his body, and a .45 slug that was fired from thirty feet away by the male victim with the severed penis"

"What about the old man? Was he shot or stabbed?" Wilmont asked.

"The old man had one or two .357 slugs inside his body. I believe the guy lying underneath the female fired the gun that killed him. One slug caught the old man directly in his face and literally exploded. It damn near tore his whole face off."

Looking at the shooting diagram, Wilmont questioned me about another shooter. "Detective Hero, I agree with you that Stanton's killer shot the old man. But look at this diagram." He pointed to the report. "It shows that the old man could have fired those shots from the .22 caliber weapon that hit Stanton and Banner's killers. If there was another shooter, he had to be standing a few feet behind the old man, possibly hiding and firing his weapon from behind one of the parked cars. And if that's the case, the old man would have been in direct line of fire. So why didn't he get shot in the back?"

I nodded and replied, "That's a good question. If there was another shooter, firing from behind a car in direct line of fire with the old man, maybe the old man knelt down and ducked to get out of the line of fire."

"That's possible," Wilmont said, nodding his head.

"Maybe he was already dead and lying in the mud before the shooter began firing," I added.

"That could also be true," Wilmont said, nodding in agreement.

"We won't know for sure until we catch the shooter or find a witness to the shootings. Either one could tell us what we want to know. ... I wish I had received the photos of the murder scene. That might have shown us a better picture of the four victims," I said.

"When do you think you'll get them, Baxter?" Banner asked.

"I'll bet you they'll be sitting there when I return to the station later today," I replied, glancing over the old man's autopsy report. "If you guys want to wait and stick around until tomorrow I'm sure I could have copies of the photos for you to take back with you."

"I don't think so," Stanton said, smiling. "You can fax them to us. I want to get back to my wife. ... I hope she remembers me."

Stanton changed the subject and asked me about the dead bodies found at the apartment building. "Who's investigating those murders?"

"My captain ordered me to investigate the matter," I said.

"What two dead bodies are you talking about, Detective Hero?" Wilmont asked, quizzically.

"I put on some entertainment for my two guests yesterday," I said jokingly, pointing to Banner and Stanton.

"What happened? That is, if you don't mind me asking?" asked Wilmont.

I nodded, then told him what had happened, adding, "I should be getting the reports on those three victims from the apartment building and the customer that was killed here at the café very soon."

"Well, I have enough information and all the evidence I need to close my serial killer investigation," Banner said.

Stanton nodded. "Me too. I never thought this day would come, but it has. When I return to work tomorrow, our whole department will be celebrating this occasion."

"Speaking of celebrations, I know it's a little early, but why don't we have a drink to celebrate our new friendships," I said.

"That sounds good to me," Banner said, smiling.

Stanton agreed. "What the hell. I don't mind. I think I can have one drink," he said.

When everything was said and done, we said goodbye and went our separate ways. When I finally drove away, I wondered whether I would ever see them again.

# Chapter 17

The next morning, I woke up with another pounding headache. My eyes hurt each time I opened them. I had celebrated a little too much the night before—so much so that I could barely remember the drive home from the café. I hadn't been that drunk in a very long time.

I sat up and slid to the edge of the bed, then reached over to the nightstand for my nearly empty pack of cigarettes. I pulled one from the pack, put it to my mouth, grabbed the lighter from the nightstand, and lit it. After taking a long drag and coughing up the phlegm that had accumulated in my throat during the night, I was ready to begin my day.

Because of my hangover, I stumbled around the house like a blind man in unfamiliar surroundings, bumping into everything that I passed trying to get to the bathroom to shower.

When I finished, I quickly dressed into a clean suit. I had worn the other for nearly a week straight. Now I felt like a new man...I felt as though I had had a complete overhaul, even though my piston was still knocking.

With all my chores complete, I still had enough time to drink a cup or two of my favorite Jamaican Brew. I made it strong and black. And after smoking another five or so cigarettes and finishing the pot of coffee, I was ready for work. I grabbed my suit jacket and walked out my front door into the crisp, cool morning air.

A few minutes later, I was in my car and heading eagerly for my precinct. I hoped to have the photos of the park murder scene sitting on my desk when I arrived. I wanted to compare the photos to the shooting diagram.

On the way, I passed the vacant, condemned apartment buildings. These massive structures had once been images of hope and prosperity. Now they were images of hopelessness and nightmares.

I slowed the vehicle, noticing the victims of this squalor discreetly slithering into its bosom. That's when I saw him—the man I thought to be the cafe robber. He was wearing the same clothes that the robber had been wearing the day of the robbery. I didn't know if he had noticed me or not. I quickly made a U-turn to get a closer look. I had to work fast. He was heading for one of the vacant buildings. I knew from experience that once he was sucked into that blackness, my chances of finding him were slim. I knew that if I didn't stop him before he entered that hellhole, I would lose him once again.

I quickly found a parking space without bringing attention to myself. Then I reached for my hand radio to call for backup, but hurriedly threw it down onto the floor of my vehicle when it refused to work. For the hell of it, I tried the car's police radio...and that also refused to work. I even tried using my cell phone but the tall buildings blocked my reception.

As I jumped out of the car and slammed the car door shut, I felt uneasy. I still had a hangover, with barely enough energy to begin my hunt. But I took a deep breath and gathered what little strength I had.

The suspect was approximately one hundred feet ahead of me. Instead of running after him, I walked very briskly so I wouldn't draw attention to myself and blow my cover. And I stayed close to the side of the buildings, walking in the shadows so I couldn't be seen. I was slowly catching up to him. And I believed I still had enough time to overtake him before he reached the door of the condemned apartment building.

A few minutes later, I was within twenty-five feet of him, but he was within ten feet of the apartment building's front door.

Just as I was about to catch him, someone from across the street yelled from an open, upper window—"Run...5-O." My cover had been blown. I ran out from the shadows after my suspect. Just as I yelled for him to stop, he quickly opened the door to the apartment building and slipped into the dark, foul-smelling den of derelicts.

I stopped at the door, deciding whether or not to chase after him. I decided against it. It was too dangerous in my current state. Instead, I holstered my weapon and turned to return to my car. A second later, I heard a gunshot and felt a rush of hot air whiz past my right ear. I had felt the wind from a bullet—a bullet that rushed past my head and into a wooden telephone pole just a few yards behind me.

I turned to give chase. Now, it was personal. He had come within a fraction of an inch of blowing my head off my shoulders. I wanted this guy. And now I was *sure* that he was the cafe bandit—which meant that the guy that had been shot by the three inexperienced uniformed officers was not...but boy they sure looked a lot alike.

When I shut the door behind me, I knew I should have turned around right then and walked back to my car. Instead, I slowly stumbled through that foul-smelling darkness. I heard many different sounds coming from many parts of the apartment building. I could hear shuffling of feet, just a few yards ahead of me. My only problem was...I couldn't see in the dark—and my flashlight was lying on the back seat of my car. But every ten feet or so, I would get a glimmer of light shining through a small crack of a boarded up window.

I knew I was taking a chance, but the guy had gotten my blood boiling when he decided to take a shot at me. I could be walking into a bullet right at this very moment—and my bulletproof vest was in the trunk of my car. My only protection was my gun and my brain—and my brain wasn't working at one hundred percent.

I crept down a long corridor until I came to a dead-end. I had to decide which way the shooter would go. Would he try the hallway to the left or the hallway to the right? I tried to stay as quiet as possible so I could hear a noise that would give me the answer. But my heart was racing like a quarter horse on speed. I was sure my suspect could hear the beat of my heart.

I waited for a second, leaning against the wall to catch my breath. Suddenly, I heard a noise come from the hallway to my left. I decided to look in that direction. But just as I was about to move, I heard another sound coming from the opposite direction. I had to make a decision. But the wrong one could be fatal.

I decided to try the hallway to the left. I made a quick jog around the corner hoping to surprise my suspect. But as I did, I heard another gunshot fired in my direction. Trying to get out of the way of a speeding bullet, I slipped on the maggot-infested garbage lying on the floor and fell, hitting my head on the sharp edge of the floor molding.

The next thing I knew, I was blinking my eyes, trying to clear it of the blood that was seeping out of a nice, half-inch long gash just above my left eyelid. I didn't know how long I'd been unconscious, but after checking my watch, I guessed around two hours.

I slowly raised myself and checked my pockets to make sure I had all my valuables and wallet. I also checked my body to make sure I didn't have any other injuries. I rested against the wall for a few minutes, gathering enough strength and energy to leave the premises. Then I walked back through that long, dark corridor and stumbled out the front door. My eyes burned as I walked into the bright sunlight. After nearly a week of constant rain and dark clouds, finally, the sun was out.

Dejectedly, I returned to my car. I took my wet and smelly jacket off and threw it into the back seat. Once inside, I had to sit there for a few minutes to gather my thoughts and strength...and while doing so, I looked around the area hoping to spot my suspect. I promised myself then and there that I would catch that guy, dead or alive.

Looking around, I noticed that many of the drug addicts and criminal minds were watching me as I sat in my car. They were obviously waiting for me to leave the area. None of them wanted a confrontation with the police. They scatter in every direction, like roaches, when they see or hear the law coming. That's fine. But nobody gets away with shooting at a police officer. Not if I can help it. The alleged café robber had been very lucky. But his day would come, I promised myself.

As I drove away, the streets began to fill once again with derelicts, degenerates, drug addicts, the homeless, and the mentally incompetent.

I was feeling angry and hurt as I headed to my precinct. I would be a few hours late. I just hoped my superiors would understand.

I looked in my rearview mirror at the gash over my eye. I figured it would take at least six or seven stitches to close the wound. I pinched the two ripped sides of the bleeding wound together to stop the bleeding. That helped a little bit, but my head was still pounding...like a sledgehammer hitting a steel anvil.

And my suit, which I had purchased just weeks earlier, was completely ruined. Not only was it covered in human waste but it was also stained with my blood. Sometimes, I thought, it's just not worth the effort to get out of bed in the morning.

I finally arrived at the precinct and parked my car. While stumbling to the front door, I dabbed at the bleeding gash over my eye trying to stop the dripping blood from blinding me. When I signed in at the front desk, all eyes were watching me. My brother detectives were too surprised to ask any questions...and I was too upset and hurt to stop and chat with them. I went to the restroom, took a damp cloth and wiped away any blood, fecal matter, garbage or dirt from my head, pants and shoes. I had left my jacket in the car. My shirt and tie were clean but a little bloody and I didn't smell as badly as I had. Happy with the outcome I returned to my desk.

I noticed that there was another stack of reports sitting there, along with the photos of the park murder scene and the vacant apartment murder scene.

Just as I sat down in my chair, Captain Blake stopped by to speak with me.

"Detective Hero ... You look terrible. What the hell happened to you? Were you in a bar fight?" he asked, standing in front of my desk.

"No sir. I really don't want to talk about it right at this moment," I said, holding my handkerchief over my bleeding eyebrow.

Blake gave me a dirty look, then said, "Detective Hero, stop by my office...I need to speak with you." He paused, then added, "Take your time, as long as it's not more than five minutes." Then he turned and walked away to his office.

I immediately rose from my chair, grabbed the reports from the top of my desk, and walked directly to my captain's office. The door was wide open, and I saw that Blake was alone, sitting at his desk. I entered the room and stood waiting.

When he looked up, I said, "Yes, sir, Captain Blake ... You wanted to speak with me?"

"Yes, Hero. Please...sit down."

I took my seat thinking I was going to get reamed out for being over two hours late and looking like a drunken bum that had been in a bar fight.

But instead, Blake surprised me. "I had a few telephone calls thanking our department for the help we gave their detectives," he said. "I've also had calls from other police departments wanting me to fax them any and all information concerning the park murders. I just wanted to express my thanks for your good work."

I was stunned by my captain's words, so it took me a few seconds to say, "Thank you, sir."

And then Blake got down to what was really on his mind. "Have you found the identity of the fourth park victim? We can't close our investigation until his identity is known. The three out-of-state detectives that visited us were able to close their investigations. Now, it's our turn... And please, keep me abreast of your new investigation."

"What investigation are you talking about, Captain?"

"The two bodies you found in that vacant apartment building. Have you forgotten, Detective Hero? I ordered you to investigate the matter."

"No, sir...I haven't forgotten. I was just hoping you would have given it to someone else. I thought maybe the task force would investigate it, before they pushed it aside." I continued to blot my cut to stop the bleeding.

Blake shook his head. "Hero, you know they're too busy to handle an outside investigation. Anyway, I believe you are the best man to handle the job. You found them ... It's your case. Now find the guilty party that's responsible for those two dead bodies."

I looked directly into his eyes and nodded.

I thought our conversation was over, so I started to rise from my chair, but then Blake said, "One other thing, Detective..."

"What's that, sir?" I asked, sitting back down.

"Make sure you see the nurse and get some medical attention for the wound over your eye," he said, pointing to my bleeding eyebrow. "How did that happen?"

"If you must know, Captain, I ran into our cafe robbery and murder suspect this morning."

"You mean you actually scuffled with the suspect? Did he use his fist or a knife to cause your wound?" Before I could answer, he said, "You should have waited for backup. I always tell you guys to wait for backup!"

"I know I shouldn't have gone after him all alone, Captain. But after he shot at me yesterday at the cafe, I wanted to catch him, and I wanted him badly."

"You still should have waited for backup to arrive," he snapped.

"Captain, I tried calling for backup on my car radio, but it doesn't work. None of my police radios work properly."

Blake gave me a quizzical look. "Don't tell me you have radio trouble, too. I have been hearing complaints all week about the radios not working. I'll tell you, like I've told the others. Why don't you take your car to the garage and have our technician repair the damn radio?"

"I had planned to do that this morning. But...when I saw my suspect, I followed him instead. I came very close to capturing that guy."

"It looks to me like you came close to getting yourself killed," he said, pointing to my open wound.

I gave Blake a dirty look. "He didn't cut my head open, if that's what you're thinking. This happened when I slipped and fell on some slimy garbage in one of those rat and maggot-infested apartment buildings. My head hit the wooden molding at the bottom of the wall. That's what caused this gash over my eye. That's why I was so late this morning. I passed out for nearly two hours. That's why my new suit of clothes needs to be burned. I laid on that dirty, slimy floor rolling in all of that garbage and human waste. I was lucky the rats didn't eat me."

Blake snickered. "It's a wonder your suspect didn't come back and shoot you."

"He tried," I said. "He fired one shot at me just before he entered the apartment building. I still have to dig the bullet out of a telephone pole and match it to the cafe robbery bullets that killed the innocent customer."

"Well, get it done. I won't keep you here any longer, but don't leave this building until you see the nurse. Is that understood?" Blake said, adding, "And go home and change into some clean clothes."

"Yes, sir. Thank you, Captain Blake. I'll get started on my new investigation as soon as I get my cut looked at and change clothes." I stood up and then walked out of his office, carrying the photos and reports in one hand and holding my handkerchief over my cut with the other as I headed to the nurse's office.

When I got there, the clinic was empty of patients, so I was able to get immediate attention. The nurse put in ten stitches to close the big gash over my eye. But she refused to numb the cut area before she stitched me up—and made sure I felt the pain as she sutured my wound. I could hear and feel my flesh rip as she stuck the sewing needle into each side of my skin.

## MURDER IN THE CITY PARTS I-II

The nurse had very little compassion for me. I believed she was getting revenge for all the jokes I had made about her sexual orientation. I had called her a bull dyke, but of course, I had only been kidding. But after this incident, I don't think she cared if I had been kidding or not, although she did hand me two pills to take later for my pain. But they were just aspirin, the same type of aspirin I had taken this morning for my hangover. I thanked her and continued on my way...and to my home.

After a shower and a change of clothes, I headed directly to the police garage to take care of my radio problems.

When I pulled into the garage, there was only one mechanic on duty—that's all our budget could spare. He was also the technician that fixed our police radios and scanners.

"Jeff, can I get my police car radio repaired today?" I asked.

"Yes, but you'll have to leave your car."

"Can I get a loner while it's being repaired?"

"Yeah, but we only have one car that we use for a loner, and it's sitting over there," he said, pointing to an old and abused automobile.

And then I remembered about the problem with my hand radio and said, "Hey, Jeff... Can I exchange my broken hand-held radio for a working model?"

"You could, if we had any to exchange, but we don't. You'll have to leave it to be repaired."

"How long will that take?" I asked, turning off my car's ignition.

"I don't know off hand. I have a few ahead of yours."

"One day? Two? How many?"

"A little longer than that," he said. "Probably two weeks. But don't hold me to it. That's just an estimate."

"Well, at least I'll have a radio in the loner," I said.

I jumped out of my parked vehicle, then walked over to the beat-up vehicle and sat behind the wheel. The key was already in the ignition, so I started the engine up without any difficulty.

However, when I tried the police radio...that was a different story.

"Jeff, this radio doesn't work either," I yelled.

"I know. It hasn't worked in over a year."

"Why didn't you tell me? I'd rather drive my own car and have a patrol unit loan me one of their hand-held radios until mine is fixed."

"Whatever you want. You're the one that counts. But I can't fix the police radio in your car if you're driving it."

"How long will it take you to fix it if I leave my car?"

"I could start on it...within two or three days."

"How long to fix it?" I asked.

"It would be ready for you within one week. That is, if I'm not ordered to work on something else," Jeff said.

"All right, I'll leave my car. I'll see if I can borrow a hand-held radio for now. I'll see you in one week, so please, don't let me down. I need my police radio. I've already lost two suspects because I couldn't call for backup!" I put the car into gear and drove away from the police garage, shaking my head in disgust.

I had to drive back to the precinct to hopefully borrow a hand-held police radio from one of the patrol units. Each officer had one. I was sure I could borrow one...at least for a few days.

When I reached the station's parking lot, I quickly pulled my car between two parked patrol cars as its occupants were just getting ready to go out on patrol.

"Hey guys, I'm in a bind," I said. "Can I use one of your hand-held radios for a few days, until I get mine back from the repair shop?"

After telling them my short comings with my radios, they reluctantly let me borrow one of theirs.

I thanked them and backed out of the lot and headed for the coroner's office, turning the borrowed radio on to see if it worked—it did.

However, I didn't know if I was going to make it to my destination. The loner was suddenly acting up. It began to spit and sputter, as though it had watered down gas. Then it stalled out once or twice while I was stopped for a red light. After a few minutes, I was able to restart the engine. And after what seemed like hours, I finally made it to my destination.

As usual, the coroner's office was up to its ears in work. Technicians were busy testing evidence from different investigations, and the medical examiner was working on the autopsies of the two apartment murders while his helpers and assistants were cutting up the innocent victim from the cafe robbery.

I walked over to speak with the coroner.

"Dr. Grady, what can you tell me about the two bodies I found at that condemned apartment building two days ago?" I asked.

He stopped his work, then turned and looked up at me. "Damn, Hero, what the hell happened to you? You look as though you're having a rough day." He held out his hand for me to shake. "What the hell happened to your eye? Did you get into a scuffle with someone?"

"I'm surprised you noticed, Doc," I said. "But don't worry about me. If you must know, I had a little run in with one of my suspects this morning. But...I'm not here to talk about myself. I want to know about the two dead bodies that were found at that apartment building."

"Well, these two young people were killed approximately five days ago. I've seen this killer's work before."

"What do you mean, Doc?" I asked.

"You worked on a case similar to these murders. The one that the girl was convicted of. She might be the killer of these two bodies also."

"It can't be," I said, shaking my head. "That person is locked up in jail. It's got to be a copycat killer."

Grady shook his head. "I don't have all the evidence tested, so my report isn't complete. But I say the person that killed these two bodies is the same person that killed those five bodies in your last multiple murder investigation."

"I don't believe it," I said, shaking my head in disbelief.

"I could be wrong. Like I said, all the evidence isn't in yet. But I have a right to my own opinion. Unless you can talk me out of it."

I looked Doc Grady directly in the eyes. "I told you, that person is in prison."

"How do you know?" he snapped. "Are you positive?"

"I'll telephone the warden's office right now, so we can put this question to rest," I said, grabbing the telephone hanging on the wall a few feet away. I dialed the number to the warden's office.

When the warden answered, I told him who I was and the name of the prisoner I was interested in. He looked at his prisoner list and confirmed that the person I had inquired about was still serving out a life sentence, while waiting for her appeals to go through the courts on her death penalty conviction. I thanked the warden, then hung up the telephone.

"Well, what did he say?" asked Dr. Grady.

"I told you, Doc. That person is sitting in prison at this very moment."

"Then you're right, Hero. You have one hell of a copycat murderer out there. I hope you catch him and get him off the street. But one thing I didn't mention."

"What's that, Doc?"

"The two people that you found at that condemned apartment building were sick. Very sick."

"What do you mean? Do you mean crazy or unhealthy?"

"I mean unhealthy. If they hadn't been murdered, they wouldn't have had more than a week to live without some medical attention."

"What was wrong with them?"

"They each had walking pneumonia. So did the victim that the three rookie police officers shot and killed. He also had walking pneumonia, which had already turned into pericarditis. He didn't have more than a day or two to live. We also know he wasn't the cafe robbery suspect."

"Why is that, Doc?"

"His prints didn't match the one that was picked up off the cafe counter...and there wasn't any evidence of any powder burns on the victim either. He was an innocent victim."

"Are you positive about that, Doc? If you are, I feel sorry for those three rookie cops."

"I know what you mean, Hero. I'm afraid those rookies are going to lose their jobs over this particular incident."

"I had a feeling something like this was going to happen. When we didn't find a gun lying around his body, I knew he wasn't the suspect we had been searching for," I said, shaking my head in disgust.

Just then, we were interrupted by a uniformed police officer. He handed me a note to read. The note stated that I should drive over to a certain address—there was another dead body that had just been found—and to also tell the coroner about this situation because his expertise was needed there, too. After I read the note, I handed it to Dr. Grady so he could read it.

Grady read it, mumbled something under his breath, and said, "When will this all end? We haven't had a break in over a year! We can't go on at this pace!"

"I know what you mean, Doc," I said.

"I guess I'll meet you over there," he said.

Luckily, the loner started without any trouble. However, within two miles from the coroner's office, the car stalled while stopped at a red light. After trying a number of times to restart this bucket of rusty bolts, without luck, I might add, I had to push the car to the side of the road.

I remembered my hand-held radio. I grabbed it and turned it on. But when I tried to call out, I couldn't get anyone. The damn radio wouldn't transmit. It would receive, but not transmit. This radio wasn't any good to me either. I threw it into the back seat of the car, where it hit the side of the door and broke into tiny pieces. I was really pissed off. Nothing was going right for me this morning. My cell phone's battery was dead and there wasn't a pay phone in sight.

As I walked along the side of the road trying to hitch a ride using my thumb, my head began pounding and the wound over my eye was aching.

Nearly twenty minutes had passed, and I still hadn't gotten a ride. But then I noticed the medical examiner's truck coming down the road. It was Doc Grady. Luckily, before he passed me, I was able to flag him down. He happily offered me a ride to the murder scene.

"What the heck happened to you?" he asked, as I shut the door. "Did your car run out of gas?" He put the truck into gear and headed for our destination.

"I have no idea, Doc. That piece of crap I got from the garage just died, and I couldn't get the damn thing restarted," I said angrily, shaking my head in disgust.

"You should have used your car radio to call for a tow truck."

"I tried that. But that damn thing didn't work, either. Please, Doc, I really don't want to talk about it right now. I just haven't had a good day."

"You really do look as though you were in a drunken brawl."

"I told you before, Doc," I snapped, "I wasn't in a bar fight."

"It sure looks like it."

"I told you...I had a little accident this morning," I said, as we finally reached the murder scene.

There were a few policemen already at the crime scene securing it——which was another rat-infested, condemned apartment building only a few blocks away from where we'd found the other two dead bodies.

So Grady and I hopped out of the truck and proceeded into the building. And I'm afraid this crime scene smelled as bad as the last one.

There was an officer standing guard in the hallway, just twenty-five feet from the front entrance.

"What's the story, officer?" I asked.

"My partner and I were searching the premises when we stumbled across this dead body," he said, pointing to the nude, male body lying on the dirty floor in one of the smelly rooms.

"What made you come into this Garden of Eden?" I asked.

"We believed we were chasing the cafe murder suspect. He looked like the man in the composite drawing that we were given. When we ordered him to stop, he turned, fired his weapon, and then ran into this apartment building. We stopped looking for him when we found the dead body."

"Why didn't you continue your search for the suspect?" I asked.

"We waited for backup and the dogs. It was just too dark in that apartment building to warrant a search of the rooms. I didn't want to risk anyone getting killed, especially my partner—or me," said the officer.

"You did the right thing, officer. Good work," I said, patting him on the back. "You look familiar to me. Do I know you?"

"Yes sir. I believe my partner loaned you his hand-held radio."

"That's right. Where is your partner? I would like to tell him that the radio he loaned me doesn't work."

"It worked. I heard it," said the officer.

"Oh, yeah. It worked. It would receive, it just wouldn't transmit," I said, giving the officer a dirty look.

"Oh, I never tried to call out with it. I always used my radio," he said, holding out his radio for me to see. "Most of the time, we use our car radio."

"Well, you can tell him for me that his radio doesn't work at all now."

"Why is that?" asked the officer.

"I threw it against the door panel of the car and it broke into about a hundred pieces."

The officer just shook his head in disbelief as he began setting up overhead lights around different parts of the room of the murder scene.

# MURDER IN THE CITY PARTS I-II

The young male, approximately twenty to thirty years of age, had been dead for at least five days, but not more than one week. His throat had been slit from ear to ear, and his penis had been severed and placed into his closed left hand, within a few inches of his open mouth.

Suddenly, I thought about the Palter murder investigation. This murder looked as though it had been committed exactly the same way. But how could that be, I thought to myself. That killer was behind bars at the state prison. And I had verified that concern with a telephone call to the warden this very morning while I had been visiting the coroner. So...this murder had to be committed by a copycat.

I decided that I would make it a point to visit Palter's murderer—Elaine Weltman—within the next day or so.

While I was concentrating my thoughts on other problems, the coroner was kneeling over the body collecting evidence.

"Detective Hero, look what I've found," Dr. Grady said, handing me a small evidence bag to examine. "Have you seen them anywhere before?"

I grabbed the bag and examined it. I couldn't believe my eyes. "I'll be damned. Not the same long, blonde hairs on this body, too. We got them off those two bodies found at the apartment building two days ago...and now from this body. And again, I don't see any bloodstains on them, Doc. Why?"

"I can't tell you that, Hero. I'll know more when I get them to the lab and view them under a microscope. We are still running the DNA tests on the others. We should have the preliminary reports within a few days. The others could take a month or more," he said, as I returned the evidence bag to him.

"We've got to have a copycat murderer on our hands, Doc. ... I wonder if our cafe robber has anything to do with them?"

"Why do you think he had something to do with this murder?" asked Dr. Grady.

"I tracked him down in the apartment building where we found the two nude bodies, and according to the officers, they tracked him to this place, where *this* dead and mutilated body was found. He's got to be involved somehow."

"I don't know about that, but this body has been dead approximately one day longer than the other two bodies that were found at the other condemned apartment building."

"What are you trying to tell me, Doc?"

"I would say all three victims were killed within a twenty-four hour period."

"Are you sure?"

"Pretty sure," he replied. Then he sat back on the dirty floor, trying to catch his breath.

"How can you work in all of this filth and foul-smelling garbage, Doc?" I asked.

He took a deep breath. "If I keep working in conditions such as these ... I'm going to die!" he said. "All of this rotting, garbage stinks. I can hardly breathe."

"I think we're all having a hard time breathing in this ungodly, putrid air, Doc."

He gave me a quizzical look, then added, "And I keep tripping over the rats as they fight to retain their territory. It looks as though the rats have used the victim's blood for a swimming hole and the victim's body as their very own restaurant. You can see that the rats were having a feast. They gnawed the heck out of this body. And those other two nude bodies found at the other condemned apartment building had also been chewed on by rats. If I stay here any longer, these rats might begin biting *my* body."

"I've never heard you complain so much about your work."

"I don't usually complain about where my work takes me, but in this place, a person could catch a number of different types of diseases—TB, or cholera. Even the plague could be picked up in places like this. This place is a breeding ground for deadly bacteria."

"Well, I guess I've done enough here," I said, feeling a sudden overwhelming urge to leave the building. "I'll let the photographer and the forensic investigators complete their jobs. I'm going to the cafe to have a late lunch." It was a wonder I even had an appetite.

"What's your hurry, Hero?" asked Grady.

"I want to get out of here before Captain Blake comes and orders me to take over this investigation."

Just as I exited the building, I remembered that I didn't have a ride. I was trapped. I stood for a minute thinking about hiring a cab to take me to my destination when my captain appeared on the scene and walked over to me.

"Don't go anywhere, Detective Hero," said Captain Blake. "I want to talk with you about this murder. I was told that this murder victim was killed just like the two bodies that you found a few days ago in that condemned apartment building a few blocks over. Was this body killed in the same fashion?"

"I guess there are a few similarities, Captain. But we won't know for a couple of days until more tests are conducted. I would say we have a copycat killer on our hands," I said.

"What makes you think it's a copycat? Why couldn't it be the same person that killed the five victims from your last big investigation?" he asked.

I shook my head. "It's not possible. That person is in prison. As a matter of fact, I called the warden at the state prison this morning asking that very question."

"I want you to put this murder on your docket, too, Hero. These three murders have to be connected with the others."

"Are you sure, Captain?"

"If not, we have one hell of a copycat on our hands, and we'd better stop him and quick. I'm counting on you, Hero."

"Yes, sir. I'll do my best."

Blake nodded and told me to drive out to that prison and confront the person in question.

"I want you to talk to that convicted murderer and see if you can learn anything about these recent murders," he said. "Your convicted murderer may have befriended a person on the outside to perpetrate these recent murders to throw us off the scent. I want you to find out whatever you can. Is that understood, Hero?"

I nodded. "Only one problem, Captain. I don't have a car."

"Why not? Where is it?"

"It's in the police garage getting the police radio repaired."

"Well, doesn't the garage give you a car to use while yours is in their garage?"

"Yeah, except the loner they gave me died on the highway. I need a ride back to the garage so I can pick up my car."

"Fine. I'm leaving now anyway. You can ride back with me," he said.

The Captain dropped me off at the lot where my car was being repaired. I told Jeff where he could find his worthless loner, then took possession of my own car.

When I climbed in, I saw a stack of papers sitting on the front seat and realized that I had forgotten to take my murder scene photos, investigative reports, and the composite drawings of the two vagabonds wanted for questioning.

I hadn't started reading the new reports yet. I would read them later while eating my lunch. At least the composite drawings were back in my possession. Before driving away, I left a stack of them on a table in the garage for any law enforcement officer that appeared there. I would hand the rest out myself.

As soon as I pulled out of the police garage, I decided to drive to the apartment building where I'd had my little scuffle earlier that morning. I wanted to find the bullet that had just barely missed my head and ended up in a telephone pole. I was sure it was there.

I arrived at my destination ten minutes later and parked my car. There wasn't a soul around. I was glad. I wanted to do my work without stirring up the bees.

I quickly found the telephone pole in question, but the bullet hole was two feet higher than I was. I looked around for something to stand on and found a discarded five-gallon, plastic bucket just a few feet from where I was standing. I flipped it over, placed it on the ground near the pole, and then climbed on top of it. Then, I reached into my pocket for my pocketknife and used it to dig the bullet out of the wooden pole. The bullet was imbedded about half an inch deep.

After a few short minutes of digging, I had my prize. I looked at the bullet up close. It was of a small caliber and also a Dum Dum bullet, similar to the one taken out of the cafe wall—except this one was still in one piece. Now, we could compare this one to the others. I believed these bullets came out of the same gun. I would know for certain in a day or so.

I placed the bullet into a small, plastic evidence bag and placed it into my jacket pocket.

Now I was ready for a nice, home cooked meal. My appetite was finally coming back, so I returned to my car and drove to the cafe. When I entered the place, I noticed that the yellow police tape wasn't there anymore. The investigation team must have concluded their work.

As I walked to my table all the way in the back, I received dirty, cold stares from the cafe's patrons. They probably thought I was a barfly because of my injured face, and my eye had become much blacker. However, the minute I sat down, Bonnie brought me a double scotch on the rocks. She looked at me as though I was a stranger, and didn't say a word about the cut, or my blackened eye.

When I finished my drink, I ordered another. While waiting for my meal, I remembered the investigative reports and photos in my car. I retrieved them and then returned to my table to look them over.

The autopsy reports stated that all three victims found at the condemned apartments had a respiratory disease. Somebody did them a favor putting them out of their misery. They were also drug addicts. There was methamphetamine, heroin, and cocaine in all of their systems. I suppose one would have to do some type of drug to live in that rat and maggot-infested squalor.

When my meal finally arrived, I set the investigative reports and photos aside and concentrated on my food. It was my first meal all day, and I ate it like a starving man.

Just minutes later, after finishing my meal, I sat back to digest it.

# MURDER IN THE CITY PARTS I-II

I lit a cigarette then looked at my watch. In less than twenty minutes, my work for the day would be finished. That thought brightened up my spirits.

Now I was ready to go home and lie down on my favorite couch to think about my new investigations and what I needed to do to go forward. I still had to read the witness reports. That is, if there were any. People from that part of town tend to hide from law enforcement. They are very shy when it comes to the police. So...it's not uncommon not to have any witnesses.

And I still had thirty or so autopsy, forensic, and investigative reports to read through on these new investigations.

As I stood up to leave, I heard a police radio. A uniformed policeman was heading in my direction.

"Detective Hero, Captain Blake wants you to investigate a murder scene," said the officer.

"I was just out there," I told the officer. "I'm heading for home in just a few minutes. You can see I'm not in the best shape today."

"But Detective Hero, Captain Blake told me I was to escort you if need be," he said.

"Okay, son, don't get in a huff."

"I'm not, sir. But we should get going."

"So tell me, son," I said, leaving a few crumbled bills on the table as a tip before gathering up my reports, "where is this murder scene? It's not the one at the condemned apartment building on the West Side, is it? The one where your buddies stumbled upon the body?"

"No sir. This is an armed robbery," he said.

"Have them call the robbery division," I said, confused. "I'm in homicide."

"Yes sir, I know. But this is an armed robbery that went bad. And there are two dead victims to prove it."

"You're kidding? Who are the victims?"

"I believe they are the store owners," said the officer.

I nodded. "I'll follow you to the murder scene."

As we walked out of the café to the parking lot, I asked him if he knew who the perp was.

He believed it to be the same person that had committed the cafe robbery and murder.

"That's what I've been told, anyway," he said. "That's why Captain Blake asked for you. He thought you might want to help in the investigation, seeing you had a personal interest in the suspect."

"Who told you that?"

"Captain Blake mentioned that you had a run in with the cafe robber this morning. You must have scuffled with someone. Your eye looks like someone popped you a good one."

As we got into our separate cars, I yelled out to the officer, "I'll follow you over there!"

He nodded in agreement and peeled out of the driveway. I followed.

We were near the area where I had chased the two vagabonds from the park murders, so I kept an eye open as we first drove past the park, then a dilapidated, condemned apartment complex. I slowed down to search for them as I drove by, and to my amazement, they came walking out of the same apartment building where I'd chased them before.

I reached for my car radio to call for backup, but then remembered that it didn't work. I thought about honking my horn to get the uniformed officer's attention, but he was too far ahead of me. I only had an instant to react. I knew that if I honked my horn, I would give myself away. And that would have given the two vagabonds enough time to flee.

I had to think fast. What should I do? If I went after them, I would lose sight of the officer's patrol car that I was following to another murder scene. And if I continued to follow the patrol car, I would lose my two subjects. I decided they were more important.

I quickly made a U-turn and headed towards the two subjects, pulling my car over to the curb about twenty feet behind them. Just as I went to open my car door, I heard a loud honk from a car close by. It was the uniformed police officer that I had been following just minutes earlier. He had seen me make the U-turn, so he did the same and followed me. But when he honked his horn to get my attention, he also got the attention of my two vagabonds. When they spotted me, they took off like a bat out of hell. They separated and ran into the apartment complex. The officer and I ran after them. This time, I had gotten a good look at one of them. But I thought I was hallucinating. The guy looked identical to the cafe killer. I knew then that they were one and the same. I was sure of it—or so I thought.

We tried following them as best we could, but we lost them. There must have been fifty drifters scattering in every direction to get out of harm's way—just like before. I wondered if these people had a secret signal.

With so much confusion, the officer and I stopped in our tracks. This time, we waited for backup. The uniformed officer called it in on his working radio, so we walked back to the street and waited for them to arrive. Within ten minutes, they were on the scene.

I explained our problem and handed them composite drawings of the subjects. Many of the uniformed officers had already received the drawings at the station. They began searching the area for the two vagabonds.

I left them to finish what the officer and I had started. Then the officer and I returned to our cars and continued on our way to the murder scene.

We finally arrived at our destination without any other distractions and parked our cars near the collection of patrol cars already there.

As I stepped out of my vehicle into the warm night air, I watched—looking through a big store window—as the forensic investigators, the coroner's team, and other law enforcement dissected the crime scene, all the while, Captain Blake bellowed out orders, throwing his weight around. I could also see one of the victim's lying in a big pool of blood on the dirty floor.

I had a funny suspicion that I was about to add another murder investigation to my already full docket.

# Chapter 18

I walked through the store's front door, dodging the investigators as they worked, and saw an old Korean or Chinese couple lying dead in a large pool of dark, red blood. They had been shot twice at close range and in the heart, possibly by a small caliber weapon, such as a .22 revolver. Ballistics would tell us for certain.

As I looked around, I saw that the cash register drawer was wide open and emptied of all its contents. There were also hundreds of lottery tickets missing.

A few questions popped into my mind. I wondered if the uniformed officers were interviewing witnesses—that is, if there were any. And I also wondered why I had been called to this location.

I stood and watched as the investigation progressed, hoping Captain Blake wouldn't notice me. But oh how wrong I was.

He finished barking out orders to his underlings and walked over to me.

"Detective Hero, I'm glad you're here. How are you feeling?" he asked.

"I'm a little tired, but aren't we all."

"Yes. ... What do you think of this murder scene?"

"What do you mean, Captain?"

"We believe it was done by your cafe killer. We've recovered the videotape and have replayed it. The murderer was in plain view. His face resembles the composite drawing that was completed from eyewitness accounts, including your own. But we haven't found any fingerprints. We believe he might have been wearing gloves. That's all right though; we got his prints off of the cafe counter, so we should have a match very soon. But something puzzles me about these murders. There was no reason for this to happen. The old Korean couple obeyed the killer's every command."

"How long had they been in this country?"

"They arrived in this country three years ago...and lived in the back room of their store to make ends meet. They were not a threat to anyone. ... There was no reason for this scumbag to murder them," Blake said, shaking his head.

"Captain, scumbags don't need a reason to kill."

"I want you to catch this guy, Hero," he snapped.

"Was there any eyewitnesses seen on the tape?"

Blake shook his head. "We watched the tape a few minutes before the robbery and a few minutes after. The only person that was in this store at the time of the robbery was the killer."

"Who telephoned the police?" I asked.

"The store owner's son. He got here five minutes after the killing, but he didn't see anything." He looked around again at the scene, then turned back to me. "Hero, I want you to view the videotape and tell me if you think this killer and the cafe killer are one and the same. That is, if you can still see out of your one good eye." He laughed.

"Where are they viewing it, in the back room?"

"Yes, but walk back there carefully. I don't want the forensic evidence contaminated from your dirty shoes."

I walked into the back room where ten uniformed officers were viewing the store's videotape, burning the impression of the killer's face into their minds. I watched the tape with utter disdain and contempt for the killer. And after staring intently at the face on the screen, I was certain that it was the same person that had killed the customer at the cafe and robbed the place of its money.

Hopefully, the bullets from the cafe killing and the bullets from these store murders would match and confirm my suspicions. Fingerprints would also help, but the videotape revealed that the killer had, indeed, been wearing gloves.

When I was finished watching the tape, I went in search of the captain. I found him barking orders to the young and inexperienced uniformed police officers. I interrupted him anyway.

"Excuse me, Captain," I said.

"Yes, Detective Hero, what is it? Can't you see I'm very busy right at this moment?"

"I don't mean to interrupt, but I wanted to give you my opinion on the perpetrator in the videotape."

"Well Hero, let's hear it," said Blake.

"Sir, I believe this murderer and the cafe killer are one and the same. And the bullets from the victims should confirm my opinion. I also believe that the small-caliber bullets that were used in the park murders were also used in these two murders...and the cafe murder."

"How did you come to that conclusion?" Blake asked.

"I just have a hunch. But I won't know for certain until the ballistic tests come back. And when that will be...I have no idea!"

"Why is that?" asked Blake.

"Because, sir...I have to wait for my reports while the task force gets first priority for everything, including testing evidence at the forensics lab."

But Blake didn't want to hear it. "I told you, Hero—the task force is very important to this department and to our governor. But we'll talk about that later. Right now I want you to go home and get some rest." Blake pointed towards the front door. "You look like hell!"

"But Captain ... What about this investigation?" I asked.

"You can catch up with the investigation tomorrow. Just keep me informed on your progress."

I drove to my home to relax and rest my aching head. Once there, I tried to rest, but my thirst got the better of me. I got up and retrieved my twenty-year-old bottle of scotch—pre-war vintage. I quit counting shots after ten. After that, I was too numb to think or feel anything. Regardless, something moved me to pick up the autopsy, fingerprint analysis, ballistics, and forensic evidence reports on the cafe and apartment murders.

I started with the ballistics report. It stated that the small-caliber bullets that had been taken out of the dead male and female from the park murders were too fragmented and in too many smashed pieces to be of any use to make a confirmable, comparative study to the bullet recovered from the cafe victim. That testing was inconclusive. However, the report did state that the bullets were of the same caliber and type: A .22 Dum Dum.

I would have to wait until the bullets were recovered from the two party store victims, and then tested, before I would know if we had a match to any of the other bullets in question—including the bullet that I had recovered from the telephone pole.

I believed that all of these murders were somehow tied together, including the dead bodies that had been found in the condemned apartment buildings. But I believed those victims had been killed by a different killer. Now I had to prove it.

The next morning, I quickly dressed and then headed to the station. After picking up any new reports, I planned to make the long drive out to the state prison in order to see Elaine Weltman.

As I arrived at my desk, I was surprised to see another small stack of evidence and analysis reports waiting, along with a stack of photographs taken at the latest murder scenes. I didn't have any time to waste, so I grabbed the reports and photos and turned to exit the building. Before I could get out of the front door, I was stopped by Captain Blake.

"Detective Hero, can I see you for a minute in my office?" he asked.

I followed him to his office and then closed the door.

"What can I do for you, Captain?" I asked.

"I see you picked up the evidence and autopsy reports. I talked with the medical examiner's office to expedite your ballistics tests, autopsy reports, and anything else you might need to clean up these new investigations. I want this animal caught. This crime wave has to stop. I'll do anything I can to help in your endeavor."

"Thank you, Captain," I said. "I can use all the help I can get. I'm sure once I get the ballistic reports, I should be able to tie all of these murders together."

"I hope so...and soon."

"This morning I'm going to the prison to talk to the inmate responsible for the Palter murders. She might be able to shed some light on the three murder victims found at those condemned apartment buildings. I believe she knows who killed them," I said, lighting a cigarette.

He smiled. "Well, find out. ... And Hero, if there's anything else I can do for you, don't hesitate to ask. That's what I'm here for."

I nodded. "There is one thing you could help me with, Captain."

"What do you need?"

"I need a workable police radio. I lost my suspect twice now because I had no radio to call for backup. I *really* need a radio. If I happen to run into my suspects again, they'll get away unless I can get backup to surround the area as quickly as possible."

"I'll see what I can do," he said. "Our budget for this year has already been spent, so we don't have the funds to purchase new ones, but I'll see if I can get the technician to help you out."

"But sir," I whined, "I've already tried that. It's going to take him two weeks or more before he will even look at it. I need one *now*!"

"I'll have him work overtime if that's what it takes."

"He's already working overtime!"

"Don't worry, Hero," he said. "I will do my best to find you a working police radio."

"Thank you, sir," I said, putting my cigarette butt out in his ashtray. I turned to walk out of his office.

But Blake had more to say. "One other thing, Detective Hero." I turned to face him. "Today, you look much better than yesterday. Yesterday you looked like a person that had been on a drunken binge for a month. I'm glad you cleaned yourself up."

"Yeah, I even put on a new suit...just for you, Captain."

Blake smiled and nodded. "That's all for now, Hero. You can go."

"Thank you, Captain," I said, then walked out of his office to the parking lot.

I jumped into my car and headed for the state prison. It was a good hour and a half drive, but if I could get the answers I was looking for, I figured it would be well worth my time.

The drive was definitely a long one. It gave me time to think. And the one thing I thought about was my new investigations. I kept turning the evidence over and over in my mind. The more I thought about it, the more I became convinced that the apartment murders and the robbery murders were all tied together. I was sure of it. That is, until I began questioning prison officials.

When I entered the prison walls and spoke with a guard, I asked to see Warden Parker first. I wanted to get his thoughts about Weltman's outlook on life behind bars...and maybe some insight on her thoughts about the murders of which she had been convicted.

I was quickly escorted to the warden's office. Warden Parker was alone and sitting behind his desk, smoking a big cigar.

I introduced myself. "Good afternoon," I said, holding out my hand. "I'm Homicide Detective Baxter Hero out of East St. Louis."

"I'm glad to meet you, Detective Hero," he said. "Please have a seat."

I obliged him and sat in a chair directly in front of his desk before lighting a cigarette.

"I spoke with you on the phone yesterday concerning one of your female prisoners," I said. "She was convicted of five murders and was sentenced to the death penalty, plus five life sentences without the chance for parole. I would like your approval to speak with her in one of your interview rooms."

"What does Elaine Weltman know that could possibly have any consequence to you or your department?"

"I'm hoping she might have some pertinent information concerning my most recent homicide investigations."

Warden Parker gave me a concerned look. "This convicted murderer that you want to interview has been a thorn in our shoes." He shook his head in frustration.

"Why do you say that? Has she given your staff a hard time?" I asked.

He nodded, then added, "She is a real alley cat—and doesn't know what the word 'cooperate' means. She has told anyone that would listen that she's not guilty of any crimes, much less the murders of five innocent people. ... She's a lost cause if you ask me."

"I know what you mean, Warden. She did the same thing at her trial. She yelled, shouted, and bellowed...and even stomped her feet."

Parker shook his head in disgust. "I wouldn't have put up with her antics if I had been the judge conducting the trial."

"He didn't. After the first or second outburst, he had the guard gag her."

"That's what I should have my guards do when she screams foul language and spits at them. I should have them gag her! She's pathetic. I don't feel sorry for her in the least," Parker said, blowing his smelly cigar smoke in my direction.

"Well, I'd still like to talk with her, Warden, if that's at all possible?" I asked, putting my cigarette butt out in his ashtray, then lighting another.

"Of course," replied Parker. "But she might not want to speak with you. I hope you haven't driven all this way for nothing."

"Me too."

Parker gave me a puzzled look. "What does she know that's so important that would make you take a two hour drive without knowing if she will even talk with you?"

I took a deep drag on my cigarette, then gave him my answer. "I told you. I'm hoping she can shine some light on another investigation. We came across three dead bodies recently that could have been done by the same killer."

"So ... What's that got to do with Elaine Weltman?"

"They all have her signature on them."

"You mean a copycat killer is out there?" asked Parker, rolling his cigar between his fingers.

"There has to be. I know your prisoner couldn't have committed those murders due to the fact that she's been in your prison...locked up in one of your comfortable cells. So I have to believe that someone she may know killed these particular victims."

"But why?" asked Parker.

"I think she's trying to win her freedom."

"How? She got the death penalty! She's never going to get out of here alive...unless she escapes somehow."

"Not by escaping...in court."

"In court! How?" asked Parker.

"I know her appeal is coming up for review, and if she can convince the Appellate Court that someone else killed the people in question...then she can say that they also killed the people that she was convicted of killing."

"That sounds logical."

"Furthermore," I told him, "I believe she talked someone into committing these murders to help her in that endeavor."

"When were these three murders committed?" asked Parker, puffing on his cigar.

"The medical examiner believes all of the murders were committed within a twenty-four hour period, not more than a week ago."

"A week you say?"

"Yes. All three murders were committed six or seven days ago. Why?"

Parker sat quietly for a moment, puffing away on his big cigar. "It just so happens," he said, "that Elaine Weltman was rushed to the prison hospital about ten days ago."

"Why? What happened to her?"

"I think she had appendicitis."

"Is that what the prison doctor told you?"

"Well, her abdomen swelled up so much the prison doctor had her flown to City hospital before her appendix exploded and poisoned her body."

"City hospital?" I leaned forward, wanting to hear his every word.

"Yeah," replied Parker. "She was rushed by helicopter with a ruptured appendix to the emergency room where she was operated on."

"So how long was she there?"

"She just returned from there a few days ago."

"Wait a minute, Warden Parker. Are you telling me she wasn't locked up in prison but was at City hospital one week ago?" I asked, staring into his eyes, not believing what I had just heard.

"That's right. But she had round the clock surveillance by uniformed police officers."

"How long was she there?" I asked him.

"I think she was at the hospital for a total of eight days. ... But there was no way she could have gotten out of there without being noticed."

"I'm sure you think so. But this means she could have committed those three murders."

"I don't agree with you," said Parker, puffing away on his cigar. "She had a ruptured appendix and was guarded twenty-four hours a day, for god's sake."

"If there's a will, there's a way, Warden," I said, exhaling a large cloud of cigarette smoke as I spoke. "I would like to interview the policemen that guarded her room during the time she was at that hospital, and I also want to speak with Weltman. She could be up to her eyeballs in these three murders."

"I don't know. I don't think so. But you can speak with her."

"I would have bet my life that she couldn't have committed those murders...that it was a copycat. But now I'm not so sure." I shook my head in disgust.

Parker nodded. "And while you're interviewing the prisoner, I'll contact the policemen and prison guards that were involved in her twenty-four hour security. I'll try and have them here before you leave today. Then you can ask them the questions that might be important to your investigations. I'll have to wake some of them out of bed, though."

"Thanks, Warden," I said, standing up and putting my cigarette out in the ashtray. "I would like to interview the prisoner now, if that's all right with you?"

"Sure thing. I'll have the guard escort you to the interview room. The prisoner should be waiting for you by the time you reach it," he said.

A few seconds later, a guard came and escorted me from the office to the interview room, four flights below in the prison's basement.

The warden was right. Before entering the room, I looked through the door's glass window and saw that the prisoner was already sitting in a chair, all locked in chains, and smoking a cigarette.

I slowly opened the door to the interview room. She seemed very surprised to see me, then that surprise turned to anger.

"What the hell are *you* doing here?" she yelled, tossing her lit cigarette at me. It hit me in the chest, leaving a small, black burnt mark on my brand new suit.

"And hello to you, too, Miss Weltman. I came all the way here to see how you liked your new surroundings," I remarked, rather snidely, as I wiped the ash from my suit coat.

"Oh, I didn't know you cared. Why the hell should I talk to you at all?" she asked, practically spitting at me.

"Come on now. Don't be like that. I came here to see if you needed anything. Maybe I can bring you cigarettes or candy. What do you need?"

"I need to get out of here. I didn't kill anyone. You pinned those five murders on me because you couldn't find the real killer," she growled.

I shook my head angrily. "I'm sorry you feel that way. And I'm sorry to hear that you were very ill. How are you feeling now?"

"Probably better than you. ... I see one of your suspects popped you in the eye. You finally got what you deserved." She laughed.

"We are not here to talk about me and my problems. We are here to talk about you and your problems. So tell me, what happened to you?"

"What do you mean, what happened to me? When?"

"The guard told me you were in the prison hospital for a while. Is that true?" I asked, trying to catch her in a lie.

"What is that, a trick question? You know damn well that I had a ruptured appendix," she snarled.

"Did they operate on you?"

"Who?"

"The prison doctor? Is he a good surgeon?"

"The prison doctor saved my life."

"Oh, he operated on you then?"

"If you'd stop talking and let me finish, I'll tell you."

"I'm sorry. Please continue."

She gave me a dirty look. "Warden Parker and the guards thought I ruptured my appendix on purpose. They thought I drank gallons of salt water to make my abdomen swell, so he wouldn't let the prison doctor transfer me to City hospital."

"So what happened?"

"After the prison doctor pleaded with Warden Parker concerning my health, the warden changed his mind and had me flown by helicopter to City hospital's emergency room, where they operated on me as soon as they wheeled me in."

"You were in that bad of shape, huh?" I asked, lighting a cigarette.

"The surgeons said if I had arrived just five minutes later, I would have been dead. So if it weren't for the prison doctor pleading my case, I'd *be* dead. But that's what the warden and everyone wants anyway," she said, as she lit a cigarette from the pack sitting on the table in front of her.

"Have you had any visitors lately?"

"A few. Why do you ask?"

"Did your parents come to visit yet?"

Weltman stared at the floor and took a long, deep drag on her cigarette. "Which ones," she asked sarcastically. "The birth parents or my adopted parents?"

I gave her a dirty look. "Well, your birth parents are dead. You saw to that. So I must have been talking about your adopted parents."

"Oh, them! They never even came to my trial. Why would they come to visit me?"

"But you had other visitors, didn't you, Elaine?"

"That's for me to know and for you to find out!"

I smiled. "I know you had visitors. I'm curious, what did you talk about? The weather ... Your case, what?"

"I don't think it's any of your business. Who I talk to and what I talk about is my business and nobody else's." She blew smoke in my face.

"It's my business if it involves murder," I said, looking her directly in the eyes.

"Oh, that's why you're here. You're trying to pin another murder on me, is that it? You need another scapegoat!"

"I don't pin anything on anyone! I just gather the evidence!"

"What's the matter? Is your boss giving you such a hard time that you have to come up with a suspect, and I'm it? You can't find the real murderer...so you pick me...Again. I guess I'm an easy mark, huh? Well, I've got news for you and your boss," she snarled.

"What's that?"

"I'm not guilty of *any* murder," she shouted.

"You don't have to shout, Miss Weltman... I can hear you just fine. You know, most all prisoners say they're innocent."

"I *am* innocent! I didn't kill the people I was convicted of killing...and I haven't killed anyone else. I don't care if you charge me with a hundred murders. I'm not guilty!" she said, as she thrashed about in her chair.

The guard stuck his head inside the room when he heard the commotion, but relaxed when he saw that everything was all right. He quickly shut the door, and I went back to questioning Weltman.

"Let's see. Where was I? Oh, yes. ... How long were you in the hospital?" I asked, trying to calm her down by changing the subject.

"I was in City hospital for a total of eight days. So including the two-day stay in the prison hospital, that's a total of ten days."

"When did the prison doctor decide you should go to City hospital?"

She paused, then said, "I was in the prison hospital for one day and my appendix swelled up to three times its normal size. The doctor had to argue and plead with the warden for nearly two days before the warden finally gave in to the doctor's wishes. That's when the prison doctor finally called in the helicopter."

"Did you have any visitors while you were in City hospital?"

"You know I did. But they didn't kill anyone either. You'll have to find another scapegoat for your investigations. I can't help you."

"In that case, Miss Weltman, I'm going to interview every guard and visitor that came to your hospital room. And I'm going to find out if you had enough time to leave the grounds, murder your victims, and then return to the hospital without being noticed," I said, looking directly into her eyes.

"I can't believe this!" she snorted. "Are you really serious?"

"Yes, very serious," I replied, as we stared at each other. "And if you had anything to do with these recent murders, I'll hang you and whoever helped you. Is that clear?"

She laughed. "You're wasting your time. And what more can they do? Kill me again after I'm dead? What makes you think I had anything to do with these murders? When I wasn't in my cell, I was being operated on at City hospital. The rest of the time, I was recuperating. I couldn't even walk until the eighth day. And a day later, I was back in this prison. ... You're way off base, just like you were when you arrested me for killing those five people."

"I wouldn't be such a smart ass, Weltman. I only gather the evidence. As far as your last five murders, the district attorney is the person that charged you with those crimes. And a jury convicted you, I didn't. But that's history. I'm here because we just found three more dead bodies. And if the evidence points to you, that's what I'll tell the district attorney. Nothing more, nothing less," I said, lighting another cigarette.

"But I didn't do it," she shouted, pounding her fists on the table. "How many times do I have to tell you that!"

"Well, if you didn't commit these recent murders, then you had one of your friends commit them for you."

"Why do you keep accusing me for something that I had nothing to do with?"

"I'll tell you why, Miss Weltman. They had your signature all over them. It had to be you or somebody you know that committed these recent murders...and you know it. Now give me the names of your visitors!"

"Why should I? You're a detective. Do what the taxpayers pay you to do. Investigate!" she snapped.

"I will! And I have an idea where it will lead me."

"And where is that?"

"I believe the evidence will lead straight to you and your friends," I said, staring into her eyes.

"Hell, even if you don't have the evidence against me, I'm sure you'll make some up."

"Why do you say that? I have nothing against you one way or the other."

She gave me a dirty look. "But that's how you work. Arrest anyone, as long as it quiets your superiors and the media. Well, I'll tell you once more. I'm innocent! I've never killed anyone!"

"Then why are you here?"

"I'm sitting here in prison because of your incompetence," she replied. "And now you come here and tell me I've committed murder again. I can't believe I'm hearing this. I just got out of the hospital after nearly dying...and now I'm being accused of murder all over again. Get out of here! Leave me alone! I don't want to see your ugly, beat-up face again."

"You can call me whatever you like, Miss Weltman, but that won't change my opinion of you...or hinder my investigation."

She shook her head in frustration and then shouted, "Guard! Guard! Let me out of here. I'm finished with this interview!"

As the guard entered the room, I stood up from my chair and left. I had asked enough questions. I had gotten the answers that I thought I would. And being away from the prison for eight days, Weltman might well be my murderer. Now I would have to interview everyone that had come into contact with her during that eight-day period.

A guard escorted me back to the warden's office. I was hoping Warden Parker would have the list of the names of the guards and police officers that had guarded Weltman's room during the time in question, so I could make arrangements to interview each and every one of them. But when I walked into his office, I noticed him and six other people sitting in chairs all around the room. Silence filled the air—that is, until the warden spoke to me.

"Detective Hero, you wanted to speak with the people that had guarded the prisoner, Elaine Weltman, at City hospital. These are the six that guarded her during that eight-day period. You can use my office to interview them separately, while the others wait in my outer office." Warden Parker stood up and left the office, leaving me in charge.

I walked behind Warden Parker's desk, sat in his chair, and introduced myself to the six guards. "Hello, I'm Detective Hero. I will interview you one at a time. The rest of you can wait outside the office until I call for you. I'll interview you first." I pointed to a bald and fat male guard that was sitting closest to me. The others walked to the outer office.

"I'm sorry. What is your name and how long have you worked here?" I asked him.

"I'm Red McCloud. I've been a guard at this prison for fourteen years."

"Mr. McCloud, when did you guard the female prisoner?"

"When? What do you mean?"

"When you guarded Elaine Weltman at City hospital, what were your hours?"

He thought for a moment, then answered, "I was on from eight in the morning till five in the evening."

"What days did you work during the prisoner's eight-day stay?" I asked.

"I worked those same hours every day of her hospital stay."

"What did you do during this time?"

He shrugged his shoulders. "Most of the time I sat outside the prisoner's room reading a newspaper."

Then I asked him a very important question. "Mr. McCloud, did you ever leave your post for any length of time during the prisoner's eight-day stay?"

He gave me a perplexing, almost scared look. "The only time I can recall leaving the area was to go to the bathroom."

I could tell from his body language that he was holding back, not telling me everything, so I pressed him. "You're sure that's the only time you left the prisoner alone?"

"Well, maybe if I was called away by a nurse," he replied rather meekly.

I pressed him further. "If you were to put it in minutes, how many minutes were you away from the prisoner's room?"

McCloud scratched his head, thinking, then replied, "I would say, not more than an hour or so. Maybe a little longer...give or take five or ten minutes. Why? What has Weltman done? What is she being accused of?"

"That doesn't concern you! What concerns you is the dereliction of duty. You're supposed to stay at your post at all times. She could have escaped in that length of time and killed innocent people. Did you ever think of that?"

"What? How could she? She had just been operated on. She was too ill to leave the hospital. ... Anyway, I would have noticed if she was gone."

I shook my head. "Not if you weren't at your post. She could have easily slipped out and slipped right back in without being noticed."

"I don't think so!"

I took a long drag on my cigarette, then asked, "Mr. McCloud, did you handcuff her to her bedpost when you left her immediate area?"

He shook his head. "No," he said, sounding defensive. "She had just been operated on. She couldn't even sit up because she was too weak."

"Are you sure?"

"She nearly died. At least, that's what the doctor had told me."

I wrote down a few of his answers in my little notepad and then excused him. "Thank you, Mr. McCloud, I think I've heard enough. When you leave here, have one of the other officer's come in—and don't say a word of this to anyone. I'll contact you and Warden Parker if I need to interview you again." He left the room holding his head to the ground, sulking and acting as though he had just been scolded.

The next person to come into the room to be interviewed was a female guard—a short, beautiful and slender woman with light-brown hair. She sat in the same chair McCloud had used.

I introduced myself. "Hello, I'm Detective Hero."

"And I'm Sally Rupa," she said.

"I'm glad to meet you, Miss Rupa. I just want to ask you a few questions about the female prisoner, Elaine Weltman. You had the privilege of guarding her at City hospital, didn't you? Is it Miss or Mrs.?"

"You were right the first time. And yes, I did guard Miss Weltman while she was staying at City hospital. Why?"

"What was your work schedule for guarding the prisoner?"

"I came on right after Red."

"Who is Red?" I asked.

"The guard that you just got through interviewing,"

"Oh, you mean Mr. McCloud."

"Yes. I came on directly after his shift. I started at five p.m. and the shift ended at midnight."

"You worked those same hours all eight days of Weltman's stay?"

"No. I worked those hours for seven straight days."

"Which seven straight days? Were you there from the prisoner's first day at City hospital?" I asked, snuffing out my cigarette in the ashtray, then lighting another.

"Yes. I didn't work the eighth day of her stay."

"Can you remember ever leaving the area for any long period of time?"

She thought for a minute, then replied, "I can only recall one time that I was gone for any length of time. You know, other than to use the bathroom."

"Miss Rupa, do you remember why you had to leave your post?"

"Yes, I do," she said, rubbing her palms together in a nervous gesture. "I had a little scuffle with one of the hospital's visitors."

"Was he visiting your prisoner?"

"No. I don't think so. He was visiting one of the patients a few rooms down from the prisoner."

"So what was the problem?"

"He had been giving one of the nurses a hard time. And when I intervened, the visitor got a little irate."

"Why was this visitor angry with you? ... Oh, was this visitor a male or female?"

"The visitor was a young male. I would say in his early twenties. ... And he was angry with me...for interfering in his argument."

"So what happened?"

"Well, after arguing with him for a few minutes, we got into a little scuffle and he refused to cooperate with me, so I put him in handcuffs and threatened to arrest him if he didn't behave."

"Then what did you do? Did you release him after he calmed down?"

She nodded. "Yes. I made him sit in the waiting room until he cooled down."

"So how long do you think you were away from Weltman's hospital room?"

"From what I remember of that incident, it couldn't have been more than an hour, maybe a little longer."

"Did you ever check to see if your prisoner was still in the room?"

"I had no reason to check in on her. The nurses did that. I just sat outside of the room and left when my time was up. I never had a problem with her the whole time I was guarding her."

Then I asked her the sixty-four thousand-dollar question: "Was she handcuffed to her bed?"

Rupa slumped in her seat, looked down at the floor, and said, "No."

"So you don't know if she was in her room or somewhere else during that time in question, do you, Miss Rupa?" I asked.

She looked up at me. "Well, if you put it like that, then you're right. I really don't know if she was in her room. But she was recuperating from major surgery. I had no reason to believe that she would or could leave the room."

But that wasn't a good enough answer, so I pressed her. "Why didn't you handcuff her to her bed?"

She shrugged her shoulders. "She never gave me any reason not to trust her. Anyway, she was a very ill person."

"How do you know if she was ill or not...if you never checked on her?"

"Well, that's what the doctor told me."

"Can you remember when he checked on her? ... And if you can remember the doctor's name or even what he looked like, it would really be a big help in my investigation."

She had to think for a minute, then said, "Now that I think back on it, the doctor did come to her room very late at night."

"Do you remember what time he visited the patient?" I asked, lighting a new cigarette.

"It had to be between nine or ten at night. Maybe even later than that."

"Did he visit just that one time?"

"No. He stopped by on three different occasions. Then I didn't see him after that."

"Do you remember what days the doctor showed up? Did you notice anything out of the ordinary or strange about him? ... Did you get his name?"

"He came by the day after she was operated on. Then he stopped by the next two nights in a row. But I never got his name, and we never talked to each other."

"Wait a minute. You see this doctor on three different nights and you don't ask for his name or why he was there?" I asked, shaking my head in disbelief.

She shrugged her shoulders. "I thought he was just checking on her like all doctors do. She had just been operated on. ... I didn't think anything about his presence."

"Miss Rupa, if you don't know the doctor's name, do you know if he was the surgeon or her family doctor?"

"I'm sure he was one or the other. But you're making a big deal out of nothing."

"I could be, but I'm an investigator. That's my job. I ask questions. It's up to me to sort out what is pertinent and what isn't. Is that all right with you?"

"I'm sorry," she said, in a soft voice.

"Forget it. ... Now let me ask you this: Did you ever see anyone visit your prisoner, besides her doctor or the hospital staff?"

She shook her head. "I don't remember any other visitors coming to her room. However, I remember one instance."

"What happened?

She leaned back in her chair, then told me what had occurred. "Well, I had just returned from the restroom when I noticed a young man backing out of her room. He was the same young man that I had scuffled with a few days before. When I confronted him about what he was doing, he explained to me that he had walked into the wrong room."

"And you believed him?"

She nodded. "I just figured it was an innocent, honest mistake," she said.

"How long were you away from the room?"

"Not more than fifteen or twenty minutes."

"Did you ever think that the visitor might have been lying to you?  He could have been in that room for ten or fifteen minutes and given her a weapon.  Did you ever search the prisoner's room after that little incident?"

"No I didn't.  Like I said before, I thought it was an honest mistake.  The visitor went into the wrong room.  That was it."

"Do you remember whether there was anyone *else* that visited Weltman during your shift for those seven days?"

She thought for a minute.  "No," she finally said. "That was it."  Then she added, "But I did see that same young man a few times on that floor during my shift.  However, I never saw him near the prisoner's room again."

"Miss Rupa, do you remember what that young man looked like?" I asked, pulling out a folded copy of the composite drawing of the cafe robber.  "Did he look anything like this?" I showed her the picture.

She took a good look, then shrugged her shoulders.  "I guess he might look similar, but I can't say for sure.  I never really got a good look at his face or hair."

"I don't believe this," I told her angrily.  "You see this young guy a few times and you can't remember what he looked like?  Is that what you're telling me, Miss Rupa? ... You're in law enforcement.  You're supposed to notice things like that. ... By the way, was this visitor also the same person that you had detained?"

"First of all, I had no reason to believe this guy was a threat to me.  And second of all, he always wore a funny-looking hat. ... I noticed his hat instead of his face."

"But does he look like the drawing?" I asked, holding it up to her again.

"Well, I guess it's a close resemblance.  Why?  What did this guy do?"

"He's wanted in a cafe robbery gone bad. He's wanted for armed robbery and murder. So take another look at the drawing. Is the person in this drawing the same person you saw near Weltman's hospital room?"

"I'm sorry," she said. "I just can't say for sure. They look similar. That's all I can say. Why don't you check with City hospital?"

"I plan on it."

"They may know the person's identity and that doctor's. I'm sorry I couldn't be more helpful. I don't want to lead you on a wild goose chase, hunting the wrong man."

I smiled, then told her, "Well Miss Rupa, at least you're honest about it."

But she wanted an explanation from me. "What is this all about?" she asked, giving me a confused look. "Why is this female prisoner and her visitors so important?"

"I'm trying to find out if your prisoner was involved in three recent murders. I'm investigating whether she had the time to leave the hospital and roam the city looking for victims to mutilate."

"If you want my opinion, she couldn't have gone anywhere," she said. "She was in poor shape for three or four days after surgery. I don't think she was in any shape to even walk."

"How would you know?" I asked, looking directly into her eyes. "You stated to me that you never checked the prisoner's room. You didn't even think to check when you saw a stranger coming out of the room."

"I had no reason to check her room. I've told you that."

"Yes you did, but you were away from the area for hours."

"Yes I was. But during that period of time, she was recuperating in her bed. I'm sure of it."

"Miss Rupa, how long do you think it would take for that prisoner to sneak out of the hospital and find a vulnerable victim to slice and dice? Did you ever think about that?"

"Not really," she replied sheepishly. "I just think you're way off base on this one."

"Well, I'm not going to argue with you about it, Miss Rupa. You have your opinion, and I have mine. I think I've heard enough. If I need you for another interview, I'll contact you through Warden Parker. "

"Very good. May I leave now?"

"Yes, but send in one of your buddies. Have the person that worked the shift after yours come in. I want to go in the order of your shift hours," I said, lighting another cigarette.

A minute later, another prison guard walked into Warden Parker's office.

"Have a seat. You are Jason Perry, correct?" I asked. "Miss Rupa gave me your name."

"Yes, that's right."

"I'm Detective Hero. I need to ask you a few questions concerning your time at City hospital guarding the female prisoner, Elaine Weltman."

"What would you like to know?" he asked.

"What were your shift hours for guarding that prisoner?"

"My shift started right after Rupa's ended," he said. "It began at midnight and ended at four in the morning."

"Mr. Perry, did you guard Weltman all eight days of her hospital visit?"

"No. I guarded her for only five days."

"What day did your duty begin ... And did you guard her for five straight days or was there a day or two in between?"

He thought for a moment, then replied, "My guard duty ran for five straight days and began three days after her surgery."

"So... your guard duty ended the same morning that Weltman left the hospital?"

"Yes. She was escorted back to prison a few hours after my shift ended."

I then asked Mr. Perry if he had seen anything out of the ordinary or suspicious while guarding her room.

"Not that I can remember," he replied, scratching his head. "Usually it was dead quiet. ... I saw one nurse visit her all the time I was guarding that room."

"Why did the nurse have to visit the prisoner so early in the morning? What was so important that she had to go in there at that particular time?"

Perry searched his mind for an answer, then after nearly thirty seconds of dead silence, he smiled and said, "She was there to check the equipment."

"Can you remember, Mr. Perry, what day that was?"

"I believe it was the day before my last day on duty. I had taken Officer Dellerd's shift."

"Which days did Officer Dellerd guard the prisoner?"

"Dellerd was there for the first three days of her eight-day incarceration."

"Do you remember seeing any doctors going in or out of that room?" I asked.

Perry nodded. "Yes. I remember one doctor in particular. At the time I didn't think too much about it though."

"What did this doctor look like, Mr. Perry. That is, if you can remember?"

"Sure I remember. He was short, fat, old, and bald...and he must have forgotten to wear his eyeglasses because he kept squinting, like he couldn't see what he was looking at," he said, fidgeting in his seat.

I asked him what day the doctor had stopped by the prisoner's room.

"I believe it was my first day of guard duty," he replied. "A few days after the prisoner's surgery."

"Did you ask him for his identity badge...or his name?"

"No, I didn't," he replied matter-of-factly. "I just figured he was the surgeon looking in on his patient."

I wanted to know more, so I asked him if he had gone into the prisoner's room with the doctor to see what he was doing to her.

"No. He was just in and out. He wasn't in there for more than two minutes, and then he walked away towards the elevators," Perry said, staring at the floor.

"Did he ever return to check on the prisoner again?" I asked.

He shook his head. "No, I didn't see him after that day."

"Mr. Perry, let me ask you the same question that I asked the others before you. And I hope you don't give me the same answer."

"What question is that, Detective?"

"Was your prisoner handcuffed to her bed?"

"No," he answered.

I was disgusted by his answer and let him know it.

"You know, there's one thing I don't understand."

"What's that?"

"You had a convicted murderer in that room and nobody bothered to handcuff her to the bed or to even check to see if she was even in the room. Why is that, Mr. Perry?"

He wiped his perspiring forehead with his handkerchief and replied in a rather meek voice, "She wasn't a threat to me. Hell, she had just been operated on a few days before. She couldn't lift her head, let alone leave her bed."

I shook my head in disgust. "Mr. Perry, as far as I'm concerned, everyone that I've interviewed today regarding that female prisoner was derelict in their duties, and I'm disgusted by the way she was guarded. She killed five people, for god's sake. You people acted as if she was just another patient for the hospital. You're lucky none of you were killed by her."

"I don't know what you're all upset about. She didn't escape," he said.

I gave him a dirty look. "How do you know she didn't escape or leave her room? You never checked on her!"

"I didn't need to check on her," he replied. "She didn't give me any trouble. And she was escorted back to the prison without any difficulties. I don't know what all the fuss is about."

"I'll tell you like I've told your friends out there," I said, pointing to the outer room. "I'm investigating three recent murders that were committed during the time that your prisoner was a guest at City hospital. And they all point to her."

"You think that *she* committed those murders? I don't know how!"

I looked Perry in the eye. "From the information that I've gathered so far, she had plenty of opportunity to leave the hospital, commit her crimes, and sneak back without anyone knowing about it."

"I still say you're way off base with your suspicions," he retorted.

"But if she did, she would have the perfect alibi, wouldn't she? Just like the ones you guards have given her."

"I don't know how you have come to that conclusion, but I don't believe it!"

"You don't have to believe it," I snarled. "What's important, Mr. Perry, is what *I* believe. And I believe you have answered enough questions for one day. If Officer Dellerd is in the outer office, ask him to come in. I want to interview him next."

Perry stood up to leave the office.

"Is that it then?" he asked.

"That's it. I pretty well have the big picture."

Perry walked out of the room, and a minute later, a uniformed police officer came through the door.

"Come in, please. Have a seat," I said, pointing to the chair in front of Warden Parker's desk. "Are you Officer Dellerd?"

"Yes, I'm John Dellerd," he answered, in a deep voice. "What is it that you want from me?"

I told him I just needed to ask him a few questions.

"Questions? About what?"

"Concerning a female prisoner. You do work for the City hospital police force, don't you, Mr. Dellerd?"

"Yes, but I'm on loan from the County Sheriff's office and for the last year have worked at City hospital."

"Mr. Dellerd, when you had to guard Elaine Weltman last week, what time did your shift start?" I asked, lighting a cigarette.

"Yes, I remember that prisoner. ... I had the same hours as Perry, but I only worked for three days."

"What days did you guard the room?"

He told me that he had been ordered to guard that prisoner the minute she came out of surgery.

"I guarded her from midnight to four in the morning," he added.

"Why did you only work for three days when her stay was for eight days?" I asked.

He shrugged his shoulders. "I really don't know. My captain transferred me to another area after three days."

"What ... To guard another prisoner?"

"No. I was chosen to lead a group of law enforcement officers after a prison escapee."

I was getting bored asking the same questions over and over. But I had a job to do so I continued.

"Officer Dellard, while you were guarding the prisoner, did you leave the area for any length of time?"

"No, never. I didn't even leave to go to the restroom."

Then I asked him that all-important question: "Do you know if the prisoner had any visitors while you were guarding her?"

"Just the nurse."

"Anyone else?"

He thought for a second, then said, "I saw her doctor visit her to check her vital signs."

"How do you know what he did, Mr. Dellerd ... Did you enter the room while the doctor was checking her?"

"No. I stayed out of that room for the most part. She wasn't going anywhere. Hell, she'd just had major surgery."

"That's just what the others keep reminding me," I said. "Do you think that taking out an appendix is major surgery?"

"Of course," he said.

"Well Officer Dellerd, you're wrong," I said, as I put my cigarette out in the nearly full ashtray. "It's minor surgery. She could have gotten up and walked the first day after surgery. But enough of that. ... You mentioned a doctor. Did you only see one doctor visit her room or more than one?"

"Only one. That was it. ... But hell, I was only there for three days."

"What did that doctor look like, if you can remember?" I asked, believing I already knew the answer.

And I was right.

He told me that the doctor was an old, chubby man with a bald head who wore thick eyeglasses.

"They were so thick it's a wonder he could see at all," he added.

"How do you know he was a doctor?" I asked. "Did you ask him for his name or hospital identification?"

Dellerd told me that he knew the guy was a doctor because he always carried a black doctor's bag.

Then he added, "But come to think of it, I never did see his City hospital identification badge."

"Did you ask him for it?"

He nodded, saying, "I remember asking him about it. He told me he left it in his suit jacket, back in his office."

"Did you order him to retrieve it?"

"Not exactly," he said, squirming in his seat. "I told him to wear it at all times for his own protection. But I didn't order him to do anything."

I gave him a dirty look. "Did you check his identity with the head nurse on that floor?"

He told me that he didn't bother. "There wasn't anything suspicious about him," he said.

I couldn't believe what I was hearing. "Wait a minute, Dellerd," I snapped. "He doesn't wear his identification badge checking on a prisoner and you don't think to check his identity with the front desk? Aren't you a police officer?"

"Yes I am," he answered. "And a good one."

"But Officer Dellerd, aren't you trained to notice things like that?" I asked, opening a fresh pack of cigarettes.

"Yes," he snapped, "but it was *his* hospital. ... What does it matter anyway? What the hell does this doctor have to do with anything?"

"Right at this moment, I'm not certain. Right now, I'm just gathering information. That's why I'm interviewing you. But I will tell you one thing—I'm closer to finding a killer to my victims than I was before I started these interviews."

I took out the composite drawing from my shirt pocket, unfolded it, and showed Officer Dellerd.

"What is that?" asked Dellerd, grabbing the drawing and stared intently at the picture. "You know, I've seen this guy before."

"Was he at the hospital during Weltman's stay? Did he visit her?"

"He didn't visit her during my shift. But I did see him on my first night guarding Weltman."

"What was he doing there?"

"He seemed to be waiting for something. I noticed him when I walked to the front desk to retrieve a newspaper."

"Was he acting suspicious or what?" I asked, lighting a cigarette.

"Not really," he answered. "He was sitting in a chair in the waiting room."

"Was that room near Weltman's room?"

"No, it's completely at the opposite end of the hallway, away from Weltman's room. But I know that the visitor I saw in that waiting room is also the same person in your composite drawing. ... Who is this guy?"

"That, my friend, is a suspect in three murders and two armed robberies," I said, taking the drawing away from him, then folding it up and placing it into my shirt pocket.

"Do you know his identity, Detective?"

"No, not yet. I hope to shortly. I think we have the guy's fingerprint, but all of the evidence and investigative reports haven't come in yet."

"Do you think he's connected to Weltman?"

I shrugged my shoulders and told him that I didn't know. "But I'm certain he's involved in my investigation somehow."

"Why? Do you have anything pointing in that direction?"

"No, not yet. I just have that gut feeling. I don't have any hard evidence to speak of, just conjecture, speculation, and twenty-five years of on the job experience."

"Well, if you believe it, that's all that counts, I guess."

"Officer Dellerd, I've taken up enough of your time," I said. "If I need to interview you at another time, I'll contact Warden Parker. I thank you for taking time out of your day and speaking with me. I really appreciate it." I put out my cigarette in the overflowing ashtray.

"I'm glad I could help," he said. "Do you want me to send in the next person?"

"Yes, please. I would like to speak with the person that worked the shift after Guard Perry."

Officer Dellerd left the room, and a female guard entered. She sat down in the chair in front of me. She was tall and slender—a very pretty woman who looked more like a model than a prison guard, with long, straight brown hair that fell a few inches below her breasts. She couldn't have weighed more than one hundred pounds. She was definitely a knockout.

I introduced myself. "Hello, I'm Detective Hero. I'm investigating several murders that you might be able to help me solve."

"Okay, if you say so," she said in a sweet southern voice.

"May I ask your name?"

"I'm Sergeant Judy Mullins."

"Sergeant, do you remember a female prisoner you guarded at City hospital, Elaine Weltman. Does that name ring a bell?"

She nodded. "Yes, I guarded the prisoner in question."

"Miss Mullins, how many days did you guard the prisoner during her eight-day stay?"

"I guarded her all eight days—from four to eight in the morning."

"Did you see anyone visit her room, even if it was a nurse or doctor?"

She thought for a moment, then told me that most of the time, it was very quiet.

"But," she added, "I do remember a nurse coming by to check on the prisoner."

"Do you remember the day on which that occurred?"

She nodded. "It was a few days after Weltman had surgery. I didn't see anyone else come near the room until the sixth or seventh day of my eight-day tour."

"Your eight-day tour? We aren't in the military, Sergeant Mullins," I said, chuckling. "So who else came to the room?"

"A Rehab therapist. He took the prisoner for a few hours of rehabilitation," she replied.

"What time did this take place?" I asked, surprised. "Usually, rehab is done after breakfast or in the afternoon, not in the middle of the night. Isn't that right?"

She shrugged her shoulders. "I don't know, I'm not a rehab therapist. Anyway, he didn't come in the middle of the night; it was early in the morning."

"So what time was that?"

"Around five a.m."

"And what time did they return?" I asked, lighting a cigarette.

"It had to be after my shift ended," Mullins said.

"So that means that Weltman was out of her room for at least a good three hours, if not longer. Did you mention this to the person taking over the next shift?"

She nodded. "I believe I mentioned something about it, but I could be mistaken. If you want to find out what time Weltman was returned to the room, you'll have to ask the head nurse or the therapist at the rehab department."

"Do you remember what this therapist looked like? Was he a little, old, bald-headed, fat man that wore glasses as thick as coke bottles?"

"No, it was a young guy, I think," she said, scratching her head. "I remember he was really cute. Or was he a visitor? ... Maybe it *was* an old fat man. I'm just not too sure now."

To say the least, I was getting a little perturbed by her answers. I tried to make it a little easier for her.

"Do you think you could remember what he looked like if I showed you a picture?"

"If it's the rehab guy's picture, yeah. 'Cause I helped him push the prisoner's bed a few yards past my area and got a decent look at him for a quick second or two. And I'd know him if I saw him again, that's for sure."

I handed her the composite drawing. When she saw it, I knew she had seen him before.

"What is it? Do you remember something?" I asked.

"Well," she said, squinting, "I'm looking at this picture, and I can't tell if it's the same person or not. I mean his hair was short, but this face is too plain. It does look very similar though. Maybe if I saw a photo and not this stiff drawing."

"Does the drawing look like the therapist or not?" I asked, shaking my head in frustration.

She studied the drawing for a few more seconds. "He does look close to your composite drawing, but then, so do a thousand other guys. Why don't you check with the rehab department at City hospital? They can tell you who that therapist was and then you can interview him."

"I will do that. Thank you for reminding me, Sergeant. ... Now then, do you remember if a doctor visited the room during your shift?" I asked.

She shook her head. "No, I don't remember seeing any doctor. I remember seeing a nurse though."

"Yes, you told me that earlier," I reminded her.

Then suddenly, a light bulb went off inside her head and she blurted out, "I did see an old guy dressed in a long white overcoat come off the elevator as I was getting on. He could have been a doctor or male nurse I suppose. But I wasn't really paying attention. I do remember saying to myself that he looked like the Pillsbury Dough Boy. Come to think of it, that guy also wore thick-lensed, wire-rim eyeglasses. I don't know if he was a doctor or janitor though. I wasn't paying that much attention."

"But he did get off the elevator on your floor?" I asked.

"Yes, he was on the same floor as the prisoner," she answered.

"Okay, that will do it for now, Miss Mullins. I don't think I'll need to see you again. If you would, please have the last person come in for their interview. And thank you for your cooperation."

She stood up and walked out of the room to the outer office, and I extinguished my cigarette.

Thirty seconds later, the last person to be interviewed walked into the warden's office. He was the oldest of the group. He must have been close to retirement, like me.

"Hello, I'm Detective Hero," I said, as we shook hands.

"My name is John Roberts," he replied, "and I've been a guard at this prison for nearly forty-five years."

"That's quite a feat, Mr. Roberts," I said, smiling.

"Thank you. Now what can I do for you?"

"Right now I just need a few minutes of your time. Please have a seat," I said. "I need to ask you a few questions about the female prisoner, Elaine Weltman, who you guarded recently at City hospital. I need to know the time your shift started and ended. I also need to know what days you guarded the prisoner."

"Well, I only worked one day, from five in the evening to midnight. I guarded her on the eighth and final day of her stay. She left that next morning for the prison."

"Why did you only work one day out of her eight-day stay?"

"I filled in that night for one of the other guards. He was ill and couldn't come to work, so I helped out."

"Did the prisoner have any visitors during your shift?"

"I don't think so."

"Think hard now, Mr. Roberts. Did anything out of the ordinary or anything suspicious happen anytime during your shift?" I asked, looking deep into his eyes.

"There was one disruption that I remember. An hour into my shift there was a fire in the hospital storage closet at the far end of the hallway," Roberts said.

"So what did you do?"

"I ran over to help put out the fire."

I sat back in my chair, looked him in the eyes, and asked, "How long were you away from your post?"

He thought for a moment, then said, "At least two or three hours, possibly longer. I moved patients away from that smoke-filled hallway to another area of the hospital. Then I waited for the fire department."

"Mr. Roberts, did you ever notice anyone entering or leaving the prisoner's room?"

"No, but there was a young man waiting near the area. In fact, he was sitting in my chair when I returned to my post to guard the prisoner."

"Did you say anything to him?"

"Yes. I confronted him about him being in my chair."

"And?" I asked impatiently.

"He explained to me that he was just relaxing and reading the newspaper. Then I asked him if he was related to the prisoner."

"What did he say to that?" I asked.

"He replied that he had been visiting another patient at the end of the hall, so I didn't think anymore about it until now."

"So what happened to the visitor?"

"I don't know. I chased him out of my chair, then he walked away towards the elevators."

"Mr. Roberts, did you get a good look at his face and profile?"

"Yes, I talked with him for a good five minutes," he said matter-of-factly. "I questioned him about signing in at the nurse's station before being allowed to visit the prisoner. That's when he told me he had just been reading the newspaper."

"Did you get a good look at him?" I asked, hoping he had.

He nodded. "Yeah, I got a good look at him. Why?"

"Does he look like the guy in this drawing?" I handed him the composite drawing of my suspect.

"Yep. If it's not him, it's his twin," he said, as he studied the picture.

"You're sure? The others weren't."

"Why? What did they say?" asked Roberts.

"They maintained that the young man they saw looked similar, but not exact. Are you saying that the young man you talked with was this guy?" I asked, pointing to the composite drawing.

"I'm sure of it. Why? What is he a suspect of?" he asked, placing the drawing on the desk.

"He's wanted for armed robbery and triple homicide—and he could also be involved with Weltman in other recently found corpses. If you ever happen to see that guy again, Mr. Roberts, arrest him. Or hold him until I can interrogate him."

"Do you think he knows Weltman? I've never seen him here, as a visitor or prisoner."

"I don't know. But I'm sure going to find out."

"Good luck," replied Roberts.

"Mr. Roberts, you have given me a reason to question Miss Weltman again. I'm wondering now if that guy is her boyfriend or related to her."

"If she did leave the hospital, like you theorize, Detective, why didn't she just run and make her escape?"

"I don't know about that, unless she's trying to commit the perfect murder. If she can make people believe that she was in the hospital having major surgery, then she couldn't possibly have committed these murders. But if this suspect in the composite drawing is her boyfriend, he better walk soft and carry a big stick."

"Why do you say that, Detective? She doesn't act like a hard ass."

I shook my head in disbelief. "She killed her last boyfriend when she found out that he—the person she was in love with and had been making love to—was her own father. ... She mutilated his body."

"Well, if I see this guy, what do I do, arrest him?"

I couldn't believe what he was asking me. "Hell yes ... arrest him! I told you, he's wanted in connection with a triple homicide and armed robbery. Hell, arrest him for jaywalking if you have to. We've got an APB out on this character. We nearly caught him a few different times, but he got away from us. He's definitely a sly one."

"He sounds like it, but time is his worst enemy," said Roberts.

"He's a wise, old master at deception and hiding. But sooner or later, I'll catch up with him," I said, leaning back in the chair.

"Hell, he couldn't be that old. He's got to be maybe in his early twenties or late teens."

"I was just being facetious, Mr. Roberts. But enough of that. You've really been a big help to my investigation."

"Good. I'm glad I could be of some use," he said, smiling.

"I think that will be all for now, Mr. Roberts. If I need you for another interview, I'll contact Warden Parker to set it up. But you've helped out immensely. I won't keep you any longer. You may go back to work," I said, as we shook hands.

"Thank you, Detective Hero. I'm glad I've been helpful. When a man gets my age, he feels all used up, not useful. It's nice to get a pat on the back once in a while."

Once Roberts left, I leaned back in the chair, excited by the news the old man had given me. Now I wanted to talk with that femme fatale again...before I left the prison for the return trip to the precinct. I wanted to look deep into her eyes and ask her some very important questions. I wanted to watch for a reaction.

I was just beginning to put two and two together.

I now believed that Weltman had the time to commit the three murders in the condemned apartment buildings, or she had someone else do it to throw the police off the track. Most likely, the young man in my drawing had helped her commit the murders—or he had committed them himself. I also believed he committed the cafe and store murders. I was sure he was up to his ears in those crimes. But, who was he? He wasn't in the FBI fingerprint database.

I also thought about that old man at the hospital masquerading as a doctor. I was sure he also had something to do with my investigation. I just couldn't put my finger on it. But there was something about that guy that kept running through my mind. Who was he? Was he really a doctor? Was he somehow related to this young man and that female prisoner? These were the pertinent questions that needed to be answered. I truly believed that Elaine Weltman had the correct answers. I just had to get them out of her somehow.

I waited for Warden Parker to return to his office. But after waiting nearly five long minutes, I became impatient and walked to the outer office to use the copying machine. I began making copies of my composite drawing to leave for the officers at the prison, just in case that young man ever came to visit. I had made about twenty copies when the warden finally showed up. I quickly turned the machine off and followed him into his office.

"Warden Parker, I would like to interview Elaine Weltman again before I leave the prison. Your guards have given me some excellent information. I want to confront the prisoner about what I have just learned to get her reaction," I said.

"You want to talk with Elaine Weltman—again?" he asked.

"Yes, sir, I do."

"All right, I'll call the guard's station and have one of them escort her to the interview room. You can meet them there," the warden said.

"How long will that take?" I asked, lighting a cigarette.

"They'll be waiting for you by the time you get there," he replied. He picked up the telephone to set up the interview.

I turned and walked out of the room, heading for the women's cells four flights below. I hoped—but wasn't certain—Miss Weltman would talk with me. She had left our last interview, just a few hours before, very upset.

By the time I reached the interview room, Weltman was already there. She was seated in the chair, her arms and legs wrapped in thick, heavy chains and locks. They weighed almost as much as she did. I slowly opened the door and walked in.

"Oh, it's you again. I told you, I don't want to talk with you," she snapped.

"Why is that?" I asked, dropping my cigarette butt to the floor.

"Why? You've ruined my life." She turned her head away.

"Please," I begged, "I just need to clear up a few things before I drive back to the city. I was hoping you could clear them up for me."

"Why in the hell should I help you?" she said. "I am kept under lock and key for murders I didn't commit. If I lose my appeals, I'll get the death penalty ... And you want me to help you. You're trying to hang me. You won't be happy unless you can put the noose around my neck."

"That's not true. I'm just doing my job," I told her sheepishly, trying not to upset her.

"Detective," she snapped, "if you had done your job correctly, I wouldn't be in this god forsaken place!"

I reminded Miss Weltman of another reason for her demise.

"You're here, Miss Weltman, because all the evidence pointed to you. But I don't want to talk about that. I have other things I need to clear up."

"Like what?" she asked, giving me a dirty look, then lighting a cigarette from the pack sitting on the table in front of her.

"Just a few questions. I would have asked them before, but I didn't know what I know now."

"Oh, really. I thought you wanted to talk to me about my innocence. But instead, you probably want to hang another crime on me—because you and your department can't do your jobs properly. What is it now? You arrested me before because I was an easy target. And you hung everything you could on me, didn't you, Detective *Hero*?"

"I didn't want to talk about this, but seeing how you brought it up, I will. First of all, the evidence against you was overwhelming. We had hair and fluid samples that matched your DNA. And secondly, we had your fingerprint on the murder weapon and the victim's blood on the blouse you wore the night of the murder."

"And I had a reasonable and logical explanation for each of those pieces of evidence that was brought up at my trial," she said, blowing her cigarette smoke in my eyes.

Then I let her have it with both barrels.

"There was much more evidence against you. I could go on and on, but it doesn't do anyone any good to hash over your case. A jury of your peers found you guilty. I just uncovered the evidence and presented it to the district attorney."

She shook her head, pounding her fists on the tabletop. "I told you *and* the jury that the blood that was found on my blouse was from a finger cut. Jim Palter cut himself with the butcher knife when we were cutting the rope to the lengths we needed to tie him to the bedposts. He didn't even know he'd cut his finger until I noticed the blood on my new blouse."

"There...you said it yourself," I told her matter-of-factly. "That proves that you were at Palter's apartment the night of his murder."

"I *told* you I was at his place at the trial," she snorted, throwing her cigarette to the floor, then lighting another. "I didn't deny that. But I didn't kill him. He was my biological father, my birth father. Why would I want to kill my own father?"

I gave her a dirty look. "At the time, Miss Weltman, he was your boyfriend. And when you found out his true identity—that you were really screwing your own father instead of your boyfriend—you flipped out. You killed him."

"You're right, Mr. Homicide Detective," she said sarcastically, "I did find out his true identity that night. It was right after finding a bagful of phony identification cards and badges in a commode drawer. And I wondered what the hell was going on. I was so upset about what I had just found that I ran out of Jim's apartment, crying and hyperventilating. I could hardly catch my breath."

I looked deep into her eyes and told her, "You ran so you wouldn't be caught. You were crying and hyperventilating out of fear of being caught."

"When I left his apartment he was still alive and tied to the bedposts. I swear it," she said, pounding her fists on the tabletop in frustration.

"I'm sorry, Miss Weltman. But you are in denial."

"Denial?" she replied angrily. "You're crazy. I'm telling you the truth, just like I did at my trial. I've said this since you first questioned me."

But I reminded her of what she had just told me. "You said it yourself, Miss Weltman—you were very upset with him when you found out his true identity. And you must have gone into shock and didn't know what you were doing. That's the defense you should have used at your trial. But instead, you plead not guilty," I said, shaking my head in disbelief.

"I said it because I'm *not* guilty. I never killed anyone," she snapped, throwing her cigarette butt to the floor, then lighting another.

I tried to soothe her hurt feelings. "Miss Weltman, this isn't easy for either one of us to talk about. Let me ask you the questions I came here to ask, and then I'll get out of here and leave you in peace."

She gave me a dirty look. "Go ahead and ask your questions. I can't stop you, but I can't promise that I'll answer them. But go ahead. Ask away."

"Did you have any visitors during your stay at City hospital?" I asked.

"Just the nurse when she gave me my medication."

"Is that it? That is the only visitor you had?"

"That's it. Either a nurse or a doctor would come into my room to check up on me," she replied, staring at the floor.

I pressed her further. "I want you to think hard, Miss Weltman. Didn't your boyfriend visit you during your hospital stay?"

She looked up, puzzled. "What are you talking about? I don't have a boyfriend."

"Look at this picture, Elaine," I said, as I unfolded the composite drawing and showed it to her. "Do you know anyone that looks like this guy?"

"No, not at all. I've never seen him before," she said, looking away from the drawing and my eyes.

But I pressed her, knowing she was lying. "I was told that this young man was seen leaving your room. Not once, but a few different times."

"Who told you that?" she said, giving me a cold look. Then she seemed to think better of her response. "Oh yeah. But now that I think about it, I do remember a young man that walked into my room. But by mistake. He turned right around and walked back out when he found out that he was in the wrong room."

"So you didn't know him and you didn't talk to him when he barged into your room? Is that what you want me to believe?" I asked, lighting a cigarette.

She stared into my eyes, not saying a word, then after a long pause, she blurted out, "Yes, I spoke with him, but just for a few seconds."

She seemed very nervous with this line of questioning, and I didn't want her to get flustered or upset with me, so I changed the subject. "Well, let's forget about that for a minute. Let me ask you about your doctor. What did he look like?"

She thought for a moment, then told me that he was a little pudgy, balding, nearly blind, old man.

"What did he want?"

She shrugged her shoulders. "I guess he just wanted to know how I was feeling."

"Was he the doctor that performed your surgery?"

"No, I don't think so," she said, shaking her head. "I met the surgeon just before I was wheeled into the operating room. I thought the pudgy doctor was one of the surgeon's partners or friends. I never asked him, and that doctor never talked that much anyway. But now that I think about it, he did act pretty strangely at times."

"What do you mean?" I asked.

"Well, he came to my room early one morning and wheeled me to the rehabilitation room, but the room was empty when we got there. Then, he stepped out of the room and left me all alone. And I didn't see him again. That's what I meant by strange."

"Where was your guard through all of this?"

"I have no idea," she replied half-heartedly. "I didn't see him guarding the door. He just wasn't around."

"Did the doctor ever return to the room for your rehab treatment?"

"No, he didn't," she said.

"So how did you get back to your hospital room?"

"Another therapist found me."

"Did *he* give you the rehab that you required?"

"No. Because he said I didn't have a prescription from the doctor for rehabilitation."

"So when did you finally return to your hospital room?" I asked.

"About four or five hours later, when my police guard came and got me."

I then asked her why she didn't ask someone for help during that four to five-hour waiting period.

"I didn't know what the hell was going on, that's why," she replied, angrily. "And it was so early in the morning that I was too tired to notice anything."

"Yes, that is strange. ... It just doesn't make sense. Why would a doctor take you to the rehab room when it's the job of the therapist or his assistant?"

"That's what I'd like to know," she replied.

"Oh well. That's not important right now. I'll have to return to City hospital to get that question answered. What *is* important is the identity of this young man in the drawing. I want to know his name, and I think you know what it is," I said, tapping my figure against the picture.

"I told you," she whined, "I don't know that guy. ... Do you think the young man at the hospital is the guy in this composite drawing?"

I nodded. "I believe so. Although I don't know for sure, but others have identified the two to be one and the same, and I believe you know him. Or you're related to him somehow." She remained quiet, staring at the floor. "If you won't tell me, Miss Weltman, I guarantee that I'll catch up to him very soon. I only hope that when I catch him, he'll still be alive."

"What do you mean? What is so important about his identity? Why should I know him?" she asked, rubbing her sweaty palms together.

"That's a good question, Elaine. But I feel you already know that answer."

"No I don't. Please tell me."

So I did. I told her my theory, reading her body language. "I believe your visitor helped you escape from City hospital, and helped you kill three more victims."

"Why would I do that?" she asked meekly.

"Why? I believe you and your boyfriend are sadistic, psychopathic killers," I said, leaning over the table, making face-to-face contact.

"Oh please, tell me more. Tell me what's on your mind," said Weltman, being sarcastic.

So I obliged her and further explained my theory. "I also believe your boyfriend is involved in armed robberies and murder." As I said this, I looked deep into her eyes to see her reaction to my words, but I only received a blank stare. Then, speaking to nobody in particular, I added, "I just have to figure out what that little bald, fat man has to do with all of this. I have a feeling he's also involved in this insanity."

"This is ridiculous! I can't believe I'm hearing this! I'm in the damn hospital, having major surgery, and you think I somehow snuck out to find people to murder!"

"That's right, I do," I said, looking into her eyes, trying to read her mind.

"You're nuts, Detective. You say you've been in the police business for thirty-five years...and that's the best you can come up with? Great! I bet all of your convicted suspects are innocent like me," she said, flicking her lit cigarette butt against the wall.

"Go ahead, get it off your chest. I can take it."

She gave me an evil, dirty look and said, "If that's the best you can do, Detective, I think this city is in big trouble. ... You come in here acting like a friend of mine, then set me up ... You not only accuse me of more murders but you also think I'm in this big conspiracy with some guy I don't even know, who you seem to think is my boyfriend or relative."

"Yes I do, and I guarantee I'll find out as soon as I catch him."

"Well, please leave me the hell alone. I'm already in prison for life and waiting for my execution. You can't hurt me any more than you already have. I'm living in hell now. So just stay out of my life!"

"Please, Miss Weltman, I don't want you to be angry with me."

"This interview is over," she snapped. "If you're going to charge me, do it. That's all I've got to say." She turned her eyes to the floor.

"Fine! I'm sure we'll be seeing each other again. Probably in a courtroom. ... You're not fooling anyone with your denials."

"Then show me your proof," said Weltman, lighting another cigarette.

"You're absolutely right, Miss Weltman. Right now, this is all speculation on my part. But soon, I'll have all the evidence I need to put you away once and for all, in a nice, little room on death row. And no appeal will save you."

"Great! Why wait? Why don't you just shoot me now and get it over with? Why wait to gather the evidence?

Why wait for a trial? Save the taxpayers money and just kill me once and for all. Detective Hero, you make me sick!" She threw her cigarette to the floor and yelled out, "Guard! Guard! This interview is over. Take me back to my cell!"

"I'm sure we'll meet again," I told her, then I stood up and walked out of the room.

# Chapter 19

Driving away from the prison, back to the city, my thoughts were on my investigation and the list of things that still needed to be done. First, I needed to visit City hospital, where Elaine Weltman had recently been a guest.

I wanted to call my superiors to tell them of my plans, but my cell phone refused to transmit and using my police radio was out of the question. I just hoped I didn't run into my suspects again...I had no way to call for back up.

But my thoughts concerning Elaine Weltman continued to cloud my mind. I was nearly certain now that she was involved in these recent condemned apartment building killings. But where did the young man come into the situation? And what did the old man have to do with all this madness—was he really a doctor?

I drove directly to City hospital to find the answers. After a thirty-minute drive, I arrived at the hospital parking lot. I quickly parked my car and walked to the floor where Elaine Weltman had stayed. I found the nurse's station and asked to see the floor supervisor.

While waiting, I noticed an officer sitting in a chair outside a room at the end of the long hallway. I wondered whether he was guarding the same room that had housed Weltman. A few minutes later, the head nurse showed up.

"Yes, I'm Nurse Brachit. I'm top dog on this floor. What can I do for you?"

"I'm Detective Hero," I said. "I need to ask you a few questions concerning a homicide investigation I'm conducting."

"Of course. Ask away!"

"You had a female prisoner here about ten days ago by the name of Elaine Weltman. Does that name ring a bell?"

She nodded. "Yes, she was a patient here. I believe it was for a ruptured appendix. What about it?"

"Do you remember if she had any visitors?"

She thought for a moment. "Not that I can remember," she said. "But they would have to sign in at this desk. Let me get the record book. I'll be back in a minute." Nurse Brachit then left the little cubicle, walked into a back room, and returned carrying a black book. She plopped it onto the desktop and opened it to the page in question. "This is the sign-in book for people visiting the prisoners, including Elaine Weltman." She quickly checked the list. "I'm sorry. She didn't have anyone visit her."

"Are you sure?"

"No one signed the book, anyway."

"Can I have a look?"

Nurse Brachit nodded and passed me the book, so I took a look. She was right. No one had signed in. "Not one visitor," I said. "I wonder, did you ever see anyone that looks like this." I unfolded the composite drawing of my suspect and showed it to her. "Does he look familiar?"

She nodded. "He does look familiar, I must say. Yes! That is the man that was here a few times during Elaine Weltman's stay. But I never asked whom he was visiting. You would have to talk to the police officers that guarded that room."

"I've already done that. That's why I'm here now. You can't remember if this guy was visiting another patient?"

"No, I don't ask visitors questions unless they come to me. I'm very busy helping all the patients."

I then asked her if she knew the name of the doctor who had performed Weltman's surgery.

"Let me get the chart." She reached behind the counter and grabbed a chart hanging from the wall. "Here it is," she said, turning to the correct page. "Her doctor was a Dr. Rhodes. He's a very old but fine surgeon."

"What do you know about him?" I asked.

Her reply didn't tell me much.

"Although I've never seen him or talked with him, he comes in for emergency surgeries. That's as much as I know about him."

"Do you know if he ever visited the prisoner's room to check on her condition?" I asked.

"I don't know. The surgeon or doctor usually visits the patient only in the pre-op room. I've never seen any doctor with a patient on this floor."

"Why is that?"

"The doctor only comes to do the surgery and that's it. The only doctor the prisoner might see is the prison doctor or the surgeon. Once surgery is completed, the prisoner's health is left in the hands of the nurses."

"Why doesn't the doctor come to see how his patient is responding to surgery?" I asked her.

"Prisoners aren't treated like the regular paying patients. The taxpayers are footing the bill, so there aren't any special privileges or extras for the prisoners. In fact, the prisoner you're inquiring about was kept a lot longer than normal."

"Yes, I know. I talked with the guards that were posted at her hospital door."

"She was here for more than a week," Brachit added. "Eight days to be exact. ... She was brought in by helicopter and taken directly to surgery."

"So what happens once the patient is brought in for surgery?"

"The doctor is called in...for the sole purpose of doing the surgery. And when he's finished with the surgery, his job is finished," she replied matter-of-factly.

"Where does the prisoner go from there? Does the patient go to ICU, or do they keep them in the surgery room until they awaken?"

She told me that once surgery is performed, the prisoner is taken to her room to recuperate, which is guarded by police officers twenty-four hours a day until the prisoner is returned to the prison hospital.

"Do you know if Elaine Weltman was taken to the rehab department?" I asked her.

"No, she wasn't. There wasn't any prescription from the surgeon or any doctor for rehabilitation. There was no need for it."

"Are you sure?"

She thought for a moment, then said, "Let me take that back. Someone had taken her out of her room without staff approval. When she was found, she was two floors below this one, in her hospital bed, asleep."

"Did she say who wheeled her out of her room?"

She nodded. "Weltman said that someone had taken her from her room and left her in the hallway. That was all she knew. When the officer that had been guarding her was questioned by his superiors, he said a doctor had taken her out of the room for rehab treatment."

"But Nurse Brachit, you said there wasn't any prescription for rehab."

"That's right. We knew nothing about it. Come to think of it, there were a few strange things that happened during that prisoner's stay."

"Like what?"

"Well, for one, we had a fire in a small closet that could only have been set by an arsonist."

"What did the fire marshal say about it?"

"Not much. And he never found the reason behind the fire. ... Then there was a little misunderstanding between that guy in your composite drawing and a guard. But it was straightened out."

"What happened?"

Brachit told me that the prisoner was taken out of her room without authorization. "We thought she had escaped until the officer explained the situation. We never did find out who came to take her away."

I then asked Nurse Brachit if she thought Weltman might have had the chance to leave or sneak out of the hospital without anyone's knowledge and then sneak back in.

She shook her head. "I doubt it very much. But she was left alone more than three hours on one day that I know of."

"Weltman told me that she was away from her room for nearly four hours," I said.

"That's possible. However, the room was guarded every minute of every day. If the police guarding her are away from the room for any length of time, then she could possibly sneak out. But if she did that, she would have stayed gone. She would never have come back."

"But you did say that it's possible she could have left her room without anyone noticing. Is that right, Nurse Brachit?"

"Yes, but highly unlikely. The prisoner's room is well guarded, so after five in the evening, the room isn't checked until the morning. Unless there's an emergency."

"Are you serious?"

"Yes. The prisoner is left unchecked by hospital staff for ten to twelve hours, unless for an emergency. If for some reason the guard had left his post, the prisoner could have easily had the chance to come and go as she pleased."

"From what I've been told, Nurse Brachit, by the people that guarded Weltman, she certainly had plenty of time to leave the hospital and return without anyone knowing."

"I'm sure the hospital would have a videotape of the main entrance at the security office that would show you if she ever left the building," she said.

I shook my head. "She would have used a back or side entrance. Any door but the main one. I don't think the videotape would help me."

"It was just a thought."

"Yes, and a good one. I'll keep it in mind. ... Let me ask you this: Did you ever see a little, fat, and bald man with thick glasses near Weltman's room, or maybe just visiting on this floor?"

She thought for a moment, then said, "No, but there is a lot of traffic on this floor during the day. Besides, I'm all over the hospital checking up on the nurses and patients."

"I wish I had a composite drawing or photo of the old man I'm referring to. I was told by a number of guards, who I questioned earlier today, about this man's identity. Many of them had seen this man on this floor."

"Is that right?"

"Yes. They also thought he was the one who took the prisoner out of the room and moved her two floors away."

"Didn't the guards tell you his name?"

"Unfortunately, no. I don't know who he is, but I'm going to find out. I believe he may be involved in my investigation. I don't know how at this moment, but I'm certain he is."

"You might want to speak with the nurses that were on duty at that time, during the prisoner's stay. They might have more answers than I have."

"Yes, I will do that. But at another time. I want to have a photo for them to look at before I question them." I paused. "Is that the room that the prisoners stay in?" I asked, pointing towards an officer sitting in a chair, guarding a room at the long end of the hallway.

"Yes," she replied, "that's the only room that we use. We can put as many as four different prisoners at one time in that room."

Just to see what kind of reaction I would get from Nurse Brachit, I asked her the sixty-four thousand-dollar question. "Why aren't the prisoners handcuffed to their beds?"

That question caught her by surprise, and after a few seconds of silence, she said, "Usually the patients need the use of their hands. With the guard posted just outside of the room, it's not really necessary. We've never had any trouble with a prisoner, yet. They are usually in no shape to move, let alone escape."

"What if that room were full of prisoners? Would you handcuff them then?"

She nodded. "I'm sure if we did have four different prisoners in that room, then we would probably insist on the prisoners being handcuffed. However, if they behaved themselves, then it wouldn't be needed."

"Don't you keep them doped up so they don't want to go anywhere?"

She shook her head. "Heck no. We use as little pain medication as possible. Our hospital director doesn't like to waste money on these types of patients. The best pain medication that's given after surgery is aspirin. Nothing more. It's very rare that they are given any type of narcotic pain medication. That's a no-no. They get better drugs in prison anyway!"

I nodded. "Well, Nurse Brachit, I guess I've asked you enough questions for now. I'll come back another time, when I have a picture of the old man. I want to find out who this guy is." And then I asked her one last question: "Nurse Brachit, do you know of any doctor or therapist that looks like the old guy I described to you earlier in our conversation?"

"Not that I know of. That description doesn't ring a bell. Why don't you go down to the rehab department two floors below us?"

"I might just do that before I leave," I said, reaching out to shake her hand. "Thank you."

"It's no bother, Detective Hero," said Nurse Brachit.

I turned and headed for the elevators to take me to the rehab department.

I found the rehab department without any trouble, and peeked into the weight room where all the exercise machines were kept. I saw three or four patients using the equipment and two therapists helping them...but neither therapist fit the description. I then walked into the room and spoke with one of them.

"Sir," I asked, "do you know of a therapist that works in this department that's near retirement age. The guy I'm looking for is short, fat, bald, and nearly blind. He wears very thick, wire-rimmed eyeglasses. I was told that he might be a therapist here, but I didn't get his name."

"I've been working here for five years, and I don't know of any therapist that fits that description. That sounds like one of the doctors that works in the emergency room. In fact, there are a few doctors that fit that description," he said.

"You don't have a name, do you?"

"No. You might want to speak with the emergency department." He turned away to work with his patient.

I thanked him and walked away. I was undecided about questioning the people in the emergency room. However, I was very near there. So I followed the signs on the walls and within a few minutes, I had found it. I stopped at the front counter and waited to talk with the receptionist.

"Yes, can I help you?" she asked.

"I would like to talk with the person in charge," I said.

"What is this pertaining to?"

"I'm Detective Hero. And I'm investigating a homicide."

"Just a minute. I'll let you speak with Dr. Door." She left the area for a few minutes and returned with another female.

"Yes, I'm Dr. Door," she said, introducing herself. "Can I help you, Detective?"

"I hope so. ... I'm interested in a particular patient that you people operated on. It was a female prisoner by the name of Elaine Weltman. She was here for a ruptured appendix about ten or twelve days ago. I'm not sure of the exact date."

"Let me check the computer. You said Elaine Weltman?" I nodded in agreement, as she searched the computer in front of her. "Yes, she was here for emergency surgery. Let's see, thirteen days ago, I believe."

"Yes, I think Warden Parks also stated she had her surgery thirteen days ago," I replied.

Reading from the computer, she said, "The records state that Miss Weltman was in very bad shape when she arrived. If she had arrived five minutes later, she'd have been dead."

"Dr. Door, do you know if you have any doctors that work in your unit that are short, fat, bald, and wear thick, wire-rimmed glasses?"

She thought for a minute, then said, "That sounds like two different doctors that work here part-time."

"Who was the attending physician that operated on Weltman?"

Door checked the computer records again, and within a few seconds, she had the answer. "That was Dr. Rhodes. He was called in to do the operation."

"What does this doctor look like?" I asked.

"He's short and pudgy...and wears very thick-lensed, wire-rimmed glasses. He reminds me of the Pillsbury Dough

Boy. But he's only one of the two doctors that fit your description."

"Do you have his office telephone number and address?"

She shook her head. "No, he works out of his home and is semi-retired. I can give you his home address if you'd like."

"I would rather have a phone number," I said.

Dr. Door looked through her hospital directory. A minute later, she found his number. "Here it is." She scribbled the telephone number on a scrap of paper and handed it to me.

"Do you have the other doctor's name and telephone number?"

"Yes, but that doctor didn't do the surgery on the prisoner. Do you still want it?"

"Yes, please."

"Dr. Venialo is female. Does that matter?"

I nodded. "Yes, actually, it does. The person I'm after is a male. At least, I think so. My eyewitness accounts never mentioned a female."

"Well, you didn't tell me that, Detective Hero. Do you have a picture of the person you're looking for?"

"No, I wish I did. I haven't had the chance to get a drawing made up. You wouldn't happen to have a picture of this Dr. Rhodes, would you, Dr. Door?"

She shook her head. "No. I'm sorry, I don't." Then she added, "You know, he hasn't been around lately, either."

"What do you mean?"

"Well, we tried contacting him a few days ago but he didn't answer his phone. And we left the message with his answering service, but he never returned our calls."

"How long has it been since you called him?"

"It's been well over a week," she said. "However, he might have had an out-of-town emergency."

"Why, has he done that before?"

She nodded. "Yes, he has. The last time we needed him for an emergency surgery, he disappeared for nearly two weeks."

"Didn't he give you any notice before he left?"

"No. That's why he only works here part-time. We don't worry about him too much. He usually shows up within a week or two."

"Dr. Door, maybe I can find him for you? I don't know exactly how important he is to my investigation, but I want to find out if he is involved or not. Do you know of any reason why Dr. Rhodes would take Weltman out of her hospital room and wheel her two floors below in her hospital bed?"

"Did he do that?"

"I'm not sure. I'm trying to verify my eyewitness accounts. But when the guards finally located Weltman, she was found just outside the rehab room. Would the emergency room doctor visit the prisoner after surgery?"

She shook her head no. "There isn't any reason for him to see the prisoner. Are you sure it was Dr. Rhodes and not someone else?"

"No, I'm not. I'm just going from eyewitness accounts. I'm trying to find all the pieces to the puzzle and then fit them into the correct spots. ... I guess I'll go and try to figure this out. I don't think I have anything else to ask you. If I've forgotten something, I'll come back for another interview, if that's all right with you."

"I can't stop you," she said, shrugging.

"Thank you for your time and trouble, Dr. Door," I said, then turned and walked away.

Before leaving the hospital, I decided to take a quick look at the hospital's security tapes. I figured they might show me a picture of Weltman or my robbery suspect...or maybe even the fat little doctor.

I headed toward the hospital's security department, two floors up.

I entered the room and introduced myself. I then told the senior security officer about my investigation and asked him to show me the tapes of the dates in question. There were nearly thirty of them to look at, and each was approximately eight hours long.

I wanted to watch them at home and pleaded with the officer to release them, promising to return them the minute I had finished viewing them.

There was some disagreement, but we settled our differences. I would be allowed to keep them for one week...and then I would have to return them, whether I was finished with them or not. Then, if need be, I could sign out the remaining tapes that I had not yet seen. I gave the senior security officer my approval and thanks as he placed all the tapes into a brown paper sack.

I jumped into my car and headed for the station, all the while thinking about my investigation. One question that kept running through my mind concerned the Pillsbury Dough Boy look-alike. I wondered why that old man would take the prisoner out of her room and leave her for someone else to find. Perhaps I was just being too paranoid, making something out of nothing. Maybe he was just doing his job and helping his patient. I couldn't be sure.

Instead of going back to the station, I went directly home. My workday was finished anyway, and I needed a drink, badly. I'd briefly thought about stopping by the forensics lab, the coroner's office, and the station to check my desk to pick up any new evidence and autopsy reports that may have been left there for me—I was especially interested to see if my ballistics report had come in—but I decided to save those chores for the morning. My need to quench my thirst was more important.

Once home, I walked directly to the kitchen cabinet and grabbed a glass and my bottle of scotch. I poured myself a shot. I downed that, and then another, and another, before I took the bottle and glass into the living room and plopped my butt onto my couch. Lately, I had been spending more time on my couch than I had in my own bed.

I stared at the ceiling as thoughts swirled in my mind. I decided to find Dr. Rhodes and ask him a few questions, even though I half-heartedly felt that he was an innocent victim in all of this. But now that I had his name, address, and telephone number, I would clear up this confusion, once and for all.

The next morning, I shook the cobwebs out of my head and began getting ready for work. I wanted to head straight for the station and pick up any new investigative reports...then visit the forensics lab for any additional information. Once I had accomplished that task, I would locate and speak with that fat little doctor.

When I reached my desk, my head was still pounding in spite of the aspirin I had taken. Even so, I was very happy to see another stack of reports sitting on top of it. I eased myself into my chair and began glancing through them, searching for the ballistics analysis report. I was anxious to find out if the cafe and store murders had been committed by the same gun that was used in the park murders. I had a feeling they were, but I needed the proof before I could act upon it.

Looking through the thick stack of reports, I couldn't find the one that I wanted. However, I did find the one concerning the bullets that had killed the cafe customer and the two storeowners who had been married for fifty-two years—they had been fired from the same gun, which meant that the shooter in both investigations shot and killed all three victims. This was also confirmed from the videotape retrieved from the party store, and from eyewitness accounts.

I had to stop reading. My head was throbbing again, and my vision was beginning to blur. I needed black coffee and donuts to fill my empty stomach.

I left my desk and walked to the snack room, which was adjacent to the dispatch center.

As I poured myself coffee, trying to come to terms with my pounding head, I heard a frantic call coming over the dispatcher's radio. It was another armed robbery in progress. I listened intently as a female police officer screamed into her radio from the scene of the crime. She said that she had stumbled upon an armed robber just as he was leaving the crime scene...and that shots were fired, with one hitting her in the neck and collarbone, and another striking an innocent store worker, killing him. Gasping for air, she screamed for backup and an ambulance.

Suddenly, the station came alive. Everyone was running either to their patrol cars or to the dispatch room. I had a strange and strong feeling that my suspect was indeed the culprit in this crime. My gut instinct was sure of it.

I strained my ears, listening to the wounded female officer's every word before her radio suddenly went silent. A few minutes later, the silence was broken. Her backup had arrived.

Just then, Captain Blake walked into the snack room and ordered me to follow him to the scene of the crime— another party store. I obeyed his order and followed him, in silence, as we quickly walked to our separate vehicles. Captain Blake drove like a mad man, racing to the murder scene, while I followed behind in my vehicle, doing seventy miles an hour just to keep up with him. I figured we would both be dead before we arrived at our destination.

Even though our sirens were blaring, the oncoming cars refused to stop. More than once, I had to swerve to keep from having a bad accident. Finally, after a harrowing ten minutes of driving hell, we arrived at the murder scene, where ten or more patrol cars and its occupants were already guarding the area and the entrance to the party store.

Captain Blake and I parked our cars and then ran to the wounded officer who was sitting up against the front door frame holding a white towel over her wound. The towel had turned a dark red, her blood dripping like water from a leaky pipe. If the ambulance didn't come soon she would surely bleed to death.

I wasn't yet cleared to check out the crime scene—there was still too much confusion in the air—so I lit a cigarette and looked around. I wasn't surprised to recognize my surroundings. This little run-down party store was in the same area as the abandoned and condemned apartment complex.

I was drawn from my thoughts by the sounds of the forensics and coroner's team arriving on the scene. Captain Blake and I stepped to the side as they entered through the party store's front door. By the time Blake and I entered, it was overrun with wandering patrol officers and investigators. Captain Blake didn't say a word. He was more or less in shock. But within a few minutes, he was his old self, barking out orders to everyone involved, including Doc Grady.

Seconds later, walking about, I saw the store attendant lying on the floor behind the counter in a pool of his own blood, dead. I thought that was the final tally: one dead, one wounded. But I was mistaken. One of the investigators searching the back room found two more innocent victims lying dead—each shot once in the back of the head, execution style, with their hands tied behind their backs and rags stuffed into their mouths.

I couldn't understand why someone with a brain would do that to another human being. But then, I looked at the open and empty cash register drawer and quickly found my answer: money. That's what it was all about. Simply greed and money.

The cowards kill so there aren't any witnesses to identify them. But in the end, they are all caught and convicted. Cold-blooded killers rarely get away with killings like these. Criminals always leave some damning evidence behind...and glancing over this crime scene, I began to think that this guy *wanted* to get caught.

I began looking for the store's security tape, hoping it would identify the killer. But the videotape in the machine behind the counter was gone. Thankfully, they had a backup tape, which had escaped the notice of the killer.

I rewound the tape and played it, while many of the investigators and uniformed officers stood near and watched the sickening scene explode on the screen. Even though the killings were hard to stomach, we did learn something—the killer's identity. He was the same suspect that was wanted in the cafe and other store murders. Now his victims totaled six dead and one wounded.

We had to catch this guy and catch him quick. That was the order given to the uniformed patrol officers from Captain Blake. By now, all of the officers had a composite drawing of the suspect. He didn't have a record, and we still didn't know his name. But we knew what he looked like and where he lived at times—the condemned apartment buildings. That's where we had to concentrate our efforts at finding him. A number of officers were sent to begin searching that area and those filthy, abandoned apartment buildings.

I stayed behind at the crime scene and waited for my orders from Captain Blake. I had a pretty good idea already of what he was going to say. But just as he began spewing his demands, we were interrupted by a rather large individual wearing a long, gray, wool coat, a gray fedora, and black, wingtip shoes. He reminded me of a very large and tall Frank Sinatra, and had "federal officer" written all over him. I stared at him as he stood in front of me. Just as I was about to open my mouth to ask him a question, he beat me to the punch.

"Excuse me, sir. I'm Detective Kendall working out of the homicide department from upstate, about one hundred and thirty miles from here." He produced his identification and badge and held it out for all to see. "I was directed to this place from your station commander. I'm here investigating a homicide that's similar to the ones a Detective Hero is investigating. I would like to talk with him, if I may?" His voice was as big as he was, with a Texas drawl.

"That's me. I'm the guy you're looking for," I blurted out. Captain Blake shot me a dirty look, so I stopped to introduce the two. "Excuse me, Detective Kendall, this is Captain Blake. He's in charge of this investigation."

Kendall acknowledged Blake with a nod and smile. He looked around the room, then said, "This is the same type of case I'm investigating: An armed robbery gone bad. Was this victim killed by a small caliber weapon?"

"We believe so," I replied. "We still have to have to run a ballistics test once the autopsy is conducted. ... Detective Kendall, you were talking about an armed robbery that happened in your neck of the woods. Is that why you're here now?"

"Yes. It happened about seven days ago. Maybe eight. I'm not sure. I've been working nonstop since I began my investigation. But I would like to go over the facts of my case with you," Kendall said, looking at me.

"If it's all right with Captain Blake, then it's all right with me. I'm still waiting for my orders," I said.

Blake smiled, patted my back a few times, and said, "Detective Hero, I want you to put this case on your already full agenda. We know it's connected to your others. We know that *your* suspect is the vicious killer behind all these robberies and murders. Have you determined yet whether he's also connected to your park murders?"

"No sir," I said, shaking my head. "I haven't received all of the ballistics reports yet. And I'm still waiting to hear from the forensics lab. Captain, I thought you were going to talk with them concerning my investigations?"

"I did speak with them," he said. "I made them aware of your concerns."

"Well, I don't think you've gotten through to them yet," I replied, aware that Kendall was listening in.

"Why do you say that, Hero?" Blake asked.

"Because," I replied, "the forensics technicians were supposed to work strictly on my evidence, but they're still way behind and still giving the serial killer task force first priority. Nothing has changed for me. Both the forensics lab and the coroner are still moving at a snail's pace when it comes to testing my evidence."

"You have to remember, Detective Hero," Blake explained, "that those departments have been working very long hours. They're short on manpower. If I squawk at them, they seem to work even slower. That's why I decided not to rock the boat. We'd get more done that way. In fact, why don't you head over there when you're finished with this investigation? See if the forensics lab has your ballistics analysis tests finished. You can have Detective Kendall tag along with you."

"That's a good idea. I'm through here anyway," I said. "If I stay, I'll just be in the way of the investigators."

Walking out, I was glad to see that the ambulance had finally arrived.

I watched as the paramedics lifted the wounded female officer onto a stretcher and finally carried her into the waiting ambulance. It was a wonder that she was still alive. She must have lost at least three pints of blood, if not more, while waiting for that damn ambulance to arrive. They were only ten minutes away, and it still took them nearly twice that to reach their intended destination.

Just as the ambulance sped away, so did the coroner's van with the three dead victims. Kendall and I left the scene soon after.

He and I were approximately the same age, so we had at least one thing in common: We were both near retirement. During our short drive to the forensics lab, he told me about his current investigation. The only evidence he had was the suspect's photo, which he showed me. It became clear that we were chasing the same suspect.

Within ten minutes, we had arrived at the lab. The coroner's van had just pulled into the lot a few minutes ahead of us. We watched as the coroner's team of investigators unloaded the three dead bodies taken from the crime scene. Kendall and I sat and stared in disbelief. I wanted this killer so bad I could taste it...and I was sure Detective Kendall felt the same way.

We sat in the car talking as the coroner's workers carried the dead bodies into the building.

"You know, Detective Kendall, when you first came onto the crime scene, I thought you were here for the park murders."

"When did the park murders occur?" he asked.

"Within the last two weeks. In fact, I'm still investigating that case."

"What happened? ... Is Park the family's last name?"

"No, it's not their name, that's where the murders occurred—at a park not too far from here. In fact, I just finished working with three out-of-town detectives concerning the park murders and their suspects."

"Did they catch their suspects?"

I smiled. "You could say that."

"How many people were killed?"

"There were four dead bodies in the park murders. Three of those bodies were the three detectives' suspects."

"Boy, that's very strange. Did the suspects know one another?"

I thought for a moment, then said, "We don't really know what actually occurred in the park on that day. We'll probably never know. What I *do* know is that I helped clear up three important serial killer investigations."

"The three suspects the three detectives were hunting for were all serial killers?" Kendall asked, surprised.

"That's right. And I'm sure that will never happen again. ... Their investigations are complete and closed, while mine is still continuing."

"Why is that?"

"Because I have one more victim to identify before I can close it. Speaking of that..." I motioned for us to go into the building.

First, I went to talk with Dr. Stork, the supervisor of the forensics lab and ballistics. Detective Kendall tagged along. I wanted to pick up any new completed evidence reports that his department had for me, especially the ballistics report on the small-caliber bullets found in the bodies of a few of the park victims. My gut feeling told me the same gun was used in both the park murders and the cafe and party store murders. I was sure of it—but I needed the evidence to verify my theory and was hoping Dr. Stork could help me with that problem.

As we entered the lab, I noticed a big difference from other days I had visited; it was quiet for a change.

But the autopsy room right next door was busier than ever. They were getting ready to start three more autopsies.

Just as Kendall and I began walking towards Stork's office, I noticed Dr. Stork standing in the far corner of the room peering into a microscope. Kendall and I walked over to him.

"Hello, Dr. Stork," I said. "I came in to see if there were any more analysis reports concerning my investigations. Do you have any for me?"

He didn't stir. Finally, after a few long minutes, he turned away from his microscope and looked at me. "Please Detective Hero," he said, "don't you notice how quiet it is in here today?"

"Yes, I'm surprised. I haven't seen it like this in quite a while."

"That's because I'm the only one working in here right at this moment."

"Where are all of your technicians?" I asked.

"They're currently working another armed robbery and murder investigation."

"I know. I just came from that murder scene."

Dr. Stork turned to look pointedly at Detective Kendall.

"Oh, excuse me, Doc. This is Detective Kendall from upstate. He's here working on a similar case. He believes his suspect and my suspect are one and the same."

"I'm glad to meet you, Detective Kendall," Dr. Stork said, as the two shook hands.

"I really need any reports you might have for me. I am especially interested in the ballistics reports. They are very important to me. They can tie my two murder investigations together," I said. "We already know that the person who committed the party store murders also committed the cafe murder. Now I want to know if he was also involved in the park murders."

"Well, I'm sorry. We finished half of them, but we still need to compare them to the other bullets. When my staff returns from their vacation, I'll have them get right on it. That is, if they aren't taken away for another emergency," said Stork, sarcastically.

"I really need those tests, Doc. Right now I can only go on speculation and conjecture."

"Detective Hero, did you ever find the third gun used in the park murders?" Stork asked, peering at me over the rim of his eyeglasses.

"Not yet," I said, shaking my head. "We're still looking for it."

"I think that old man was one of the shooters," Stork said.

"How can you say that, Doc? You didn't get any powder burns from his hands, did you?" I asked.

"We did get a positive paraffin test, but due to the fact that the victim's hand had been immersed in that thick, soft, red mud, and mixed with the water, the powder residue was very minute, which means he could have been wrestling with one of the other victims who had the gun."

"I think all of us will be surprised when we find out who ended up with that gun," I said. "But I believe there was another shooter. And the old man was just an innocent victim."

But Stork disagreed. "I still say that old man was one of the shooters. You seem to think there was another shooter standing directly behind the old man. That's very possible, but I don't think so."

"Why do you say that?" I asked. "All the evidence isn't in yet."

"If there had been another shooter standing directly behind the old man, he would have gotten a .22 bullet in the back. I said that before." He sounded adamant.

But I refused to give in. "I told you, Doc, your theory is conjecture just as mine is. That's why I want those ballistics tests done. That should give us our answer."

"If I were you, Hero, I would go back to that park and look for that small caliber gun," Stork said.

"I've done that. And so have nearly twenty other investigators. We went over that murder scene at the park with a fine-tooth comb."

"Yes, but it was muddy, wet, cold, and raining when our investigators looked over that area. Detective Hero, you even said that you had overlooked two of the guns during your examination of the victims."

"That's true," I said, "but I was also interrupted when I ran after my suspect. I guess I could go back to the park for a fast look—that is, if Detective Kendall doesn't mind riding along?" I looked at Kendall.

"Sure, I don't mind," he said. "I'll be glad to help. I would like to hear more about these park murders, though. It sounds like a very interesting case."

"Good. We can drive over to a small cafe not too far from the park and have a late lunch. What do you say, Detective?" I asked.

"That sounds good to me. I could use something to eat."

"Great. But first, I want to stop at the station for a minute to pick up the investigative and autopsy reports sitting on my desk. I want to read them while we're relaxing over drinks and dinner."

We thanked Dr. Stork for his time and then headed for the station. While Detective Kendall waited in the car, I ran in and picked up the reports. I was in and out within a few minutes.

When I returned to the car, Kendall and I decided to eat later and visit the park first. I didn't know what we would find...if anything. Although I had once believed there to be a third gun, which the investigators and I had somehow overlooked, now I wasn't so sure. There was a slight chance, however, that Dr. Stork was right. So I thought I would give it the old college try and search the area again.

When we arrived at the park, the sun was shining but the ground was still soft, damp, and muddy—which meant that the murder scene was still covered in thick, soft, red mud. But we pressed on anyway, splitting the crime scene in half. Detective Kendall searched the right half and I searched the left—the area where the old man had fallen.

I began running the scene through my mind. I remembered that the old man's dead body had been buried face down in four or five inches of red mud. So I began to dig into the muddy ground where the old man had fallen, thinking that the gun might have fallen there and sunk. I couldn't recall seeing anyone digging deep in that area during the crime scene investigation.

I never thought about looking in the mud at that time. I was sure that if the gun had been at the crime scene that night, the investigators would have found it. But the more I thought about it, the more I believed that they had overlooked it, as I had. So I continued to dig through the mud, as deep as I could, until I was up to my elbow in it.

Twenty minutes of digging produced absolutely nothing. But then, after digging nearly a foot deep, I finally struck gold. I pulled out a metal object encased in mud. I was so excited by my find that I set to work right away, cleaning it off using the bottom of my shirt. But once I had cleaned off the mud, I found that it was a just a pair of thick-lensed, wire-rimmed glasses.

Now I was really confused. Who did these glasses belong to? I didn't think they belonged to the old man. He didn't have any valuables or identification on him when his dead body was searched, but his autopsy report would have told me if he had worn glasses.

As far as the weapon was concerned, I thought that if there *had* been another gun, it was gone now.

I placed the pair of glasses into an evidence bag and put it into my jacket pocket. I found Kendall, and we drove over to the cafe for some good food and conversation.

Detective Kendall and I headed into the cafe to my favorite table in the back room, then ordered drinks before deciding on our meals.

"Detective Kendall, this is where many of my investigations are solved," I told him. "In fact, while dining with two of the three out-of-state homicide detectives, our suspect not only robbed this café but also killed one of the customers."

"You mean this happened while you guys were sitting here, like we are now?" he asked.

"It sure did. The two detectives were freshening up in the restroom while I was sitting at this very table relaxing and enjoying my time away from work. Then there was a commotion up near the front counter."

"What happened?"

"I walked up to see what all the fuss was about, and all hell broke loose. When one of the customers intervened and wrestled with the suspect, the suspect fired his weapon. That's when one of the rounds struck a customer standing in the crowd. I was nearly shot as well. We gave chase, but he got away."

"That's too bad."

I nodded. "You're absolutely right. But the two out-of-state detectives sure had an exciting time while they were here. Plus, they were able to solve and close their investigations. Maybe you'll be as lucky." I took a sip of my double scotch and toasted Detective Kendall's friendship.

"I don't know if I want to get that involved in one of your investigations," he said, smiling. "You know I forgot to mention this earlier, but I brought along a couple of bullets from my victims. I was hoping that your ballistics department would run a comparative test with them and the bullets that your coroner retrieved from the bodies of your party store victims."

"Why didn't you say something while we were at the forensics lab?"

"I was going to, but when I heard that supervisor give you hell for wanting your work done, I didn't want to upset him any more than he already was."

"You're right. That's a good reason. I wouldn't want someone I didn't know jumping all over me either. You did the right thing by keeping quiet."

"Do you want them, so you can have them tested?" he asked.

"Yeah, I'll have them tested when I visit the lab tomorrow. Then I'll remind them about *my* ballistics tests so they'll get'em done."

Detective Kendall handed me a small plastic bag containing the bullets, and I placed them into my jacket pocket.

A few minutes later, our meals were delivered to our tables. While eating, I began reading the investigative reports on the different murder investigations assigned to me. I was interested in the autopsy report of the old man found dead at the park and his personal property list. I wanted to see if there was an eyeglass case listed—or any evidence that showed the old man had worn glasses.

I went through nearly half of the reports before I found my answer. It was in the old man's autopsy report. It stated there were two slight indentations on each side of his upper nose. This, I thought, could have been the marks left from his wire-rimmed glasses. Now I was sure the glasses that I had found in the mud at the park was the property of the old man.

I quickly ordered another double scotch. One of the pieces of the puzzle had just fallen into place. But I needed more of them to fall into place. Hopefully, I'd have the answers I needed very shortly.

For some reason, I kept thinking about the old man I had found lying dead in the mud and the pudgy doctor involved with Weltman's surgery. I couldn't get the two of them out of my mind—especially the doctor, whom I would try to reach the following morning by telephone. If I didn't get a response, I would then drive to the address I had been given. I hoped he might have some information for me concerning the young man I thought to be my suspect—or seen something while visiting with Weltman.

I also thought about Detective Kendall's investigation. His police department wasn't too far away from City hospital where Elaine Weltman had had emergency surgery on her ruptured appendix.

I figured my suspect could have pulled an armed robbery in Kendall's city before or after he visited with Weltman. If he helped her sneak out of the hospital, they could have pulled the armed robberies together...and completed their run in a very short time. If so, she could have been driving the getaway car. Again, that was speculation on my part. But I hoped to have the answers very soon.

Then, I remembered the videotapes I had received from the hospital's security department—thirty, eight-hour tapes that I needed to view. They might have the answers I needed to wrap up my current investigation. And they might solve Kendall's investigation, too.

I continued reading reports as we ate our dinner and drank our alcoholic beverages. And by the time we had finished our meals I had all the reports read. But I didn't find any other important information that would help me close my park murder investigation any time soon.

With dinner out of the way, we relaxed, smoked our cigarettes, and drank our liquor. I decided to spend a little time getting to know my new partner.

"Detective Kendall, how long have you been in law enforcement?"

"Too long," he replied. "I applied to the police academy a few days before my twentieth birthday and graduated number one in my class."

"Did you ever have to walk a beat?"

He shook his head. "Not exactly. I drove a patrol car for five years during the day while going to night school to earn a college degree. When I graduated with honors, I was selected by my captain to take the test for detective and to earn my gold shield."

"I take it the test went well?"

He nodded. "I passed the test with flying colors the first time around."

"How old were you when you received your gold shield?"

"Twenty-five. I had the department record for being the youngest homicide detective. That is, up until a year ago. Now there's a new kid on the block."

"I wouldn't worry about it," I said. "He doesn't have your experience."

"This kid came right out of college. He'll probably be captain in another year. ... But seriously, I've been in the homicide department for thirty-six years."

"Thirty-six years? How old are you?" I asked.

"I'll be sixty-two years old in another three weeks."

"You could have retired with a nice pension by now."

"I know, but I don't have anything better to do. I'm a widower and live alone. If I didn't work for the police department, the other detectives wouldn't have anyone to laugh at." He shrugged.

"It sounds to me like our lives are very similar," I said, smiling. "I also live alone. My wife divorced me more than ten years ago."

"Don't tell me. She didn't like worrying about you, always thinking the worst," he surmised.

"That could have been one reason, but basically, she didn't like my obsessive drinking, among other things. ... And the detectives in my department act like yours. They always make jokes about me for one thing or another."

"Like what?"

"They make fun of the way I dress or the way I stumble into work in the mornings trying to hide my hangover. They're always quick to judge. But I don't care what they say. I pretty much stay to myself and do my job as best I can. That's all I can do."

"Are you sure your name isn't Detective Kendall? You're treated by your peers the same way I am."

"How do you put up with it? Do you talk back to them or do you just ignore them?"

"I just ignore them. I work alone, and I refuse to have a partner. I stay away from them and they do likewise," Kendall said.

"I wonder why we put up with it."

"I put up with it because I love my job. I'm helping society mend its fences. I thought I could make America a little safer. Maybe I thought I could benefit mankind. Hell, I don't know. Sometimes I question my value as a person. Except when a case comes together and the perpetrator is caught and convicted. That makes up for all those unbearable nuances that threaten my sanity and peace of mind. I could go on and on, but who would listen," he said.

"You sure said a mouthful." I chugged my fifth double scotch, then said, "I feel the same way. You know, we are very much alike, you and I." I lifted my glass. "You're even keeping up with my drinking."

"No, you're wrong. I'm one drink ahead of you. I've had six double scotch and sodas. ... And it's just starting to kick in."

"Do you have a hotel room for the night?"

"Yes, your station commander made all the arrangements for me."

"When we're finished here, I'll drive you to your car. Tomorrow morning I'll meet you here for breakfast...at eight-thirty. ... It looks like you'll have a partner for a while," I said, then raised my glass in a toast to him.

"What will we do after breakfast?" Kendall asked.

"I thought we would head over to the forensics lab. I want to get your bullets tested and compared to ours."

"How long do you think it will take?"

"I don't know, but I'll wait until we get those reports even if it means waiting there all day long."

"*Then* what's on your agenda?"

"I thought we would contact Dr. Rhodes about some information he may have concerning my investigations. I hope he does anyway."

"Does this Dr. Rhodes have any information pertinent to my investigation?" asked Kendall.

"I should hope so. I'm hoping he can tell us something that we don't already know about our suspect."

"Like what?"

"He might have seen something suspicious going on between a female prisoner by the name of Elaine Weltman and our suspect," I said. "But, it's getting late. We should be leaving pretty soon. We've both had a long day, and if I drink any more, I'll be an accident waiting to happen. So, what do you say, Detective? Let's call it a day."

"That's fine with me. I have to call my department anyway. I can only stay for another day, so I hope we can come up with some conclusive evidence."

"Such as?"

"Such as, I'm hoping my two bullets match up with the ones fired by your suspect. Then my investigation will pretty much be closed. That is, once the suspect is caught and convicted."

I nodded. "Let's get going then," I said.

We paid our bills and left the cafe in high spirits. We were both pretty well soused to the gills, but I was still capable of driving without causing an accident.

After dropping Kendall off at his car, I made it home without incident. I thought about drinking a few shots from my bottle of scotch but decided against it.

And then I remembered about the bagful of videotapes in the back seat of my car. I stumbled out the front door to the car and retrieved them, then stumbled back into the house.

I went directly to the living room and turned on my video machine. I grabbed one of the tapes from the paper bag and placed it into the machine. It would have taken me a year to watch all of these tapes had I played them on regular speed. Instead, I played them on fast forward. When I saw a person that looked like one of my suspects, I slowed the speed to normal. I looked at four of the tapes without seeing anything of importance before I passed out on the couch.

# Chapter 20

I awoke to the ringing of my alarm clock. It sounded as though the decibel level was a hundred times louder than normal. My head was pounding out the Morse code for help. But even this couldn't keep me down. I reached deep down and used some of the energy I had stored for days like this.

I had many important chores to do this morning. First, I had to meet Detective Kendall for breakfast. Then we would go to the forensics lab. But I had one stop to make before I went to the café—the station. I wanted to make a phone call to the mysterious Dr. Rhodes.

On the way to work, I had to pass by the condemned apartments near the park. Out of habit, my eyes searched the area. That's when I noticed two guys step out from between two of the condemned apartment buildings. And I was sure one of them was the killer and armed robber. But which one? Both subjects looked very much alike.

By instinct, I reached for my police radio to call for backup, but relented when I remembered that it didn't work.

When I looked up to check on the location of the suspects, they were gone.

I quickly pulled the car over to the side of the road and strained my neck looking for them, but they were nowhere to be seen. Shaking my head, I put my car into gear and proceeded to the station.

At the station, I was disappointed again to find that my desk was empty. No new reports. Instead of getting angry, I eased myself into my chair and reached for the phone, then pulled a scrap of paper out of my pants pocket containing Dr. Rhodes' telephone number. I unfolded it and quickly punched in the numbers.

I thought it was his home phone number, but I had reached Dr. Rhodes' answering service instead. I explained the situation to the lady on the other end of the phone and had her forward my call to Dr. Rhodes' home phone. Still no answer.

When I asked the service questions concerning their client, they mentioned that they hadn't heard from the doctor in over a week.

However, the answering service didn't seem too worried; they said he had disappeared before. They told me there were times when Dr. Rhodes wouldn't contact them for weeks. On one particular occasion, he had left the area for a short vacation and hadn't told the answering service anything about it until he returned nearly two weeks later.

I thanked the answering service for their time and told them that I'd try contacting the doctor another time. I also left a short message, asking Dr. Rhodes to come into the station for an interview.

I hung up the phone and decided to drive to the doctor's address later in the day. I also put in a telephone call to the AMA, asking them for a photo of Dr. Rhodes, but they refused to cooperate unless confronted with a subpoena from the courts. With that, I quickly gave up on the idea.

But then a bell went off in my head. I suddenly remembered hearing that name before—Dr. Rhodes. I was *sure* I had heard that name before? But when? Where? That's when an explosion went off in my head. He was the man who had been the family doctor of the Weinburg sisters—the sisters who had been mutilated and murdered in their apartment.

Were these two men one and the same? Unfortunately, I wouldn't have the answer to that question until I could meet with the man in question.

To say the least, I was very curious about this doctor...and I wanted to meet him now more than ever. But first, I had to meet Detective Kendall at the cafe. I also needed a cup of black coffee and something to fill my stomach. I was beginning to get the shakes.

Detective Kendall would be in town for only one more day, so I wanted to get a few things completed before he left our beautiful city. I didn't want him to return to his department empty-handed. And if I could help it, he wouldn't.

Driving from the station to the cafe, I once again passed the burned out apartment buildings where I had last seen my suspect. I kept a close eye on the area, but I didn't see him this time.

When I finally reached the cafe's parking lot, I saw Detective Kendall standing outside the front door smoking a cigarette.

I parked my car and then strode over to where he was standing.

"Good morning, Detective," I said, smiling. "I hope you weren't waiting very long. I had to stop by the station for a minute to make an important phone call. I got here as soon as I could."

"I just arrived a minute ago myself," Kendall said, stamping out his cigarette on the ground.

"Good. Shall we go in and fill our stomachs?"

"I'm game. Detective Hero, are you feeling as bad as I look?" Kendall asked, as we walked to the back of the cafe.

"I believe I do. I took four aspirin this morning to stop my pounding headache, but they haven't worked yet."

"I thought you'd be used to hangovers by now."

"After thirty years of hard drinking, I should be."

Kendall nodded. "I don't think my body ever gets used to hangovers like the one I have today."

"I hope you're up to taking a little ride in the car after breakfast," I said.

"Why ... What's on your agenda for today? ... I hope we can get those bullets analyzed."

"We'll drive to the forensics lab right after we eat our breakfast, but I want to make a little detour before we go there."

"Where do you want to go?"

"I want to stop by an address of a doctor. He may have some very important information concerning my investigations. Then again, he may not know anything of value. But I want to exclude him or include him, once I've interviewed him. ... I think I've seen and talked to this doctor before, but I'm not sure."

"Oh, yeah? You think you know the person that you want to interview?"

"I believe he was the family doctor of two of my victims in an investigation I closed a few months back."

"Can't you visit this guy another time?" Kendall asked. "I have to leave in the morning, and I really need to have my bullets analyzed and compared to the ones that your department has."

"It will only take fifteen minutes to drive there," I promised him. "Then we'll drive to the lab and stay there until they've analyzed all of the bullets that were collected from the many different crime scenes. I promise you that we will not leave until they have tested them all, including the two bullets that you gave me."

"That sounds good to me," he said. "Shall we order breakfast now?"

We each ordered the same meal. We did things so similarly we could have been brothers.

It was almost eleven o'clock before we finally left the cafe and headed for the doctor's address, which was on the other side of town in the richest part of the city. I had visited this part of town many times this past year, interviewing suspects in another investigation.

We finally arrived at Dr. Rhodes' address, and as I parked my car in the long driveway right next to a hundred thousand dollar blue Mercedes Benz, I noticed that one of the neighbors had become curious enough to come out of her home to watch what we were doing.

I stepped out of the car, walked up to the front door, and rang the bell. No one answered. I then looked through the picture window hoping to find life, but everything was quiet—and nothing seemed out of place. So I wrote a little message on the back of my business card and stuck it between the doorjamb and door.

While walking back to the car, the neighbor confronted me.

"The Doc hasn't been home for over a week," she said, stepping in front of me. She was a large woman who looked like the sort to snoop around on her neighbors. "I haven't seen him lately. He must have gone on an emergency."

"Ma'am, you don't know when he'll return, do you?" I asked.

She shook her head no, saying, "We don't talk to each other much. But I watch out for our neighborhood."

"Is that his car in the driveway?" I asked.

"Well, he has an older car that he uses when he makes his house calls," she said. "That way he doesn't have to worry about being carjacked or robbed when he goes into those impoverished areas. He's the only doctor that makes house calls."

"What kind of car does he drive?"

"I don't know the make, but it's a brown car. It was a little beat up and dented. He only drove his blue car for special occasions. He used to drive it all the time when his wife was still living with him. But when she left him, he retreated to his home."

"So I take it the doctor stays around the house a lot?"

"He usually stays around the house during the day and works at night. He's a very reclusive and eccentric type of person."

"Ma'am, you wouldn't happen to have a picture of the doctor, would you?"

"No, I'm sorry, I don't," she said. "I don't believe he liked his body enough to have his picture taken."

"Why is that?"

"He's always been a little fat all the years I've known him, and he's a very shy person. His glasses are so thick, I don't know how he can see at all. But they say he's an excellent doctor."

I reached into my jacket pocket and pulled out my business card, then handed it to her. "If you see Dr. Rhodes, would you contact the number on the card?" I said. "I really need to speak with him."

"Maybe he's in there lying dead on the floor?" she said, pointing towards the house. "But at least he should have a photo of himself in there. Why don't you just kick the front door down and see for yourself?"

"We can't do that, ma'am. We have to have a search warrant before we can go breaking down doors."

"I don't believe it. Cops can do anything they want and get away with it," she said.

"Our department doesn't act like that, ma'am. But I thank you for your time and information." With that said, I returned to the car.

"Well, did you learn anything?" asked Kendall, as I entered the vehicle and shut the door.

"No. Not much."

We left the doctor's residence and headed for the forensics lab.

My head began to pound, so I searched my jacket pocket for my aspirin. My hand touched on the wire-rimmed eyeglasses. I had forgotten to show them to the doctor's neighbor. She might have recognized them as the doctors and saved me a trip to the morgue. I decided that I could always return there to ask her if I didn't find the answer at the morgue.

When we reached the forensics lab, I saw that all hell had broken loose. Many of the technicians were gathering their tools of the trade and running out of the building to the parking lot. While Kendall waited in the lobby, I quickly searched out Dr. Stork near his office.

"Dr. Stork, what's going on? What's all the fuss about?" I asked.

"Haven't you heard? There's been another armed robbery and murder." He gave me a dirty look, as though it were my fault. "It just came over the police radio a few minutes ago. Didn't you hear it?" he asked, as he walked past me.

"No, my police scanner and radio are out of order. But that's not important. Where did the robbery and murder take place?" I asked, following him.

"Just two stores down from that last one, yesterday. We had just finished the investigative work at that scene not thirty minutes before this call came in. The police officers only took the yellow tape down twenty minutes ago, and now this. It's déjà vu all over again." He stopped in his tracks.

"Dr. Stork, how many people were killed?"

"I'm not quite sure, but someone has got to stop all this killing. This city can't handle it. It's too much for the city to bear."

"I'll follow you over there."

I remembered seeing my suspect in that area around the same time that this robbery had occurred.

I wondered if I could have stopped that killing if I had stopped to search the area this morning.

Detective Kendall and I returned to my car and followed the forensics team to the crime scene.

Dr. Stork was right. This murder scene was just two stores away from yesterday's crime scene. This killer had big balls to commit robberies and murders in the same area in this short of time. Why would he take the chance? Well, I didn't know the answer to that question, but I wanted to find out...and soon. Someone had to reel in this lunatic before his murders ended up in double figures. We already had one serial task force set up. We didn't need another one.

When Kendall and I reached the murder scene, the place was already full of investigators.

When I entered through the front door of the store, I saw Captain Blake barking orders to anyone that would listen. Detective Kendall quickly crouched behind me, trying to stay invisible. He didn't want to feel the wrath of Captain Blake. I didn't blame him a bit.

"It's good to see you here, Detective Hero," Blake said, smiling. "I believe you will have another case to add to your already full docket. If this proves to be your suspect, you have the case. If this person is not your suspect, I'll give it to another homicide detective. That is, if I have the manpower available. But for now, it's yours."

I acknowledged his words with a quick nod.

*Hell,* I thought to myself, *I just can't win.* I needed another case like I needed a hole in my head.

I stayed away from the investigative teams as Detective Kendall followed me slowly around the crime scene.

Looking around, I noticed the open and empty cash register drawer, just like yesterday's robbery. Also, the videotape had been ripped out of the machine and unfortunately, this store didn't have a backup.

But all the telltale signs pointed to my suspect—and the bullets in the two dead victims would most likely confirm my beliefs once they were compared to all the others.

Both victims were young, adult males in their early twenties and lying about four feet from each other. One had been shot in the heart and the other, in the side of the head. The one who had been shot in the head looked as though he was coming from the back room to help his friend. But I guess he just wasn't fast enough to get out of the way of the bullets.

These two victims shouldn't have died. We should have captured this killer by now.

I wanted to send surveillance crews out around the city, but I was denied. I was told there was no money in the budget to pay for the overtime.

Suddenly, a uniformed patrol officer came running into the store, to my table, and spoke the words I had longed to hear.

"Detective Hero, we think we have the suspect cornered in the condemned apartment buildings up the street. We're waiting for the dogs and backup to arrive. We have other officers surrounding the buildings as we speak."

"Officer, how big of area do they have cordoned off?" I asked.

"I believe we have nearly a two-square block area surrounded. We're going to get that bastard now." The officer then turned and ran towards the front door.

Detective Kendall and I followed the officer out of the store and down the street. I looked over to Kendall for assurance as we ran the few blocks to the area where the suspect was supposedly cornered. If I remembered correctly, we'd had him cornered a few days before, yet he'd somehow managed to escape.

I was completely out of breath and sweating up a storm by the time we reached the apartment complex. There must have been at least one hundred police officers surrounding the complex. The area they had cordoned off was more than a two-block square, just like the last time we'd had the guy cornered. But I thought this time might be different. My gut told me so.

Detective Kendall and I, with guns drawn, crowded in front of one of the apartment buildings waiting for orders to enter the premises. I thought I was the senior officer in charge, but then I heard Captain Blake's voice spewing orders once again. He was still barking orders as we entered the apartment building—forty uniformed police officers armed with their flashlights and guns drawn followed close behind. We would search one building—out of the four—at a time, while uniformed officers stood guard outside near every exit and entranceway. No one could go in or out without authorization. When we were satisfied that the building had been thoroughly searched, we would move on to the next condemned apartment building.

We were going to find the suspect this time.

However, after hours of searching, we weren't having much luck. The dogs couldn't pick up a decent scent with all the human waste and garbage lying in every room of each apartment unit, and they coughed and sneezed more and more as the search continued. I couldn't blame the dogs, though. The foul smelling odors were enough to knock out a professional trash collector. We should have used *them* to track down the killer instead of the dogs.

We had searched every nook and cranny in three out of the four buildings without any luck. In fact, the dogs had given up. Their handlers took them out; we weren't as lucky.

These buildings were completely empty of occupants. I, along with everyone else, was beginning to feel frustrated. The first cops on the scene remained certain that they had the killer cut off and surrounded. But now I wasn't so sure.

Captain Blake was still busy barking out orders and offering comfort to the uniformed patrol officers for their unselfish effort and inability to locate the suspect. As he spoke, we moved on to the last of the buildings yet to be searched. We had searched nearly sixteen hundred units in three of those foul-smelling buildings—and that proved to be too much for many of the younger officers, who were suddenly becoming ill and throwing up. These officers were taken to the hospital for checkups, while others left for a change of clothes. This left about twenty officers to check the last building. If we didn't find the suspect here, we were shit out of luck. He would have beaten us again.

Detective Kendall and I was the last to enter the apartment building. But as we did, I had a funny feeling come over me, like a premonition. I could sense that the suspect was definitely in this building, and I told my peers this. They didn't say a word, remaining focused on trying not to breathe in the foul-smelling air.

I could sense the young officers were feeling sick to their stomachs. The only thing *I* felt was my pounding head. Luckily, my hangover blocked my nasal passages, so my sniffer wasn't working all that well. But I could tell that Kendall was affected by the putrid smell. He kept taking quick, short breaths, trying not to fill his lungs with it. At least he would have something of interest to tell his buddies at his precinct, I thought.

Our group had searched the first four floors for the suspect but came up empty-handed. Some of the officers began leaving the building. Detective Kendall and I turned to follow them out. When we reached the second floor, a sudden, loud noise caught my attention, four floors above us. Then we heard about ten loud pops, as if guns had been fired. Kendall and I looked at each other in disbelief and ran up the stairs towards the sounds.

We finally reached the room where the noise had begun and echoed through to the lower floors. There were six police officers holding their beams of light at one wall of the building. Their other hands held their guns, smoke still spewing from the mouths of the barrels.

In the dim beams of our flashlights, I could barely make out the two fallen people lying on the filthy floor in their own pool of blood. I walked over to them to get a better look. One of the bleeding victims was a young adult male, maybe in his early twenties. The other was a young, adult female, also in her early twenties. The male was fatally wounded, but the female was still alive—barely. Her breathing was very shallow and blood was pumping from her chest onto the floor. You could hear and feel the pain and excitement in the young police officers' voices as they screamed into their radios for an ambulance.

I bent down to get a closer look at the young, male victim. He was definitely our suspect.

The officers were happy about this turn of events, but I wasn't. There was one thing that they had failed to notice: the suspect's gun was nowhere in sight.

"Where is the gun?" I yelled to the officers in the room. "If this is our suspect, where is his gun?" I looked into a few of the officers' eyes through the dim light and haze and saw confusion in them.

"Find the gun," shouted Captain Blake.

While shining my flashlight around the room, I noticed something very strange—the wall near where the victims lay seemed to be ajar. Upon closer inspection, the wall actually slid to and fro on rollers...and behind it, there was a small room approximately two feet wide by eight feet long, which could easily hide six averaged-sized people from intruders, like us.

After looking over the scene, it seemed to me that the victims had tried to hide, but they didn't make it to their hiding place in time. I would soon learn how wrong I was.

As two uniformed officers were giving the wounded female medical attention, I walked over to see how she was doing. She was barely breathing and was slipping in and out of consciousness.

Calls had gone out for an ambulance, forensics, and the coroner. They were still working the crime scene one block away. In the meantime, technicians were to bring in the overhead lights to help in the search of the suspect's weapon.

The officer who had shot the two victims was trying to explain his reasoning behind the shooting and made the excuse that when one of the officers slid back the phony wall, the suspect and female jumped out after them. He thought they were trying to attack him and that the guy was going to shoot him, so the officer shot first.

The only problem was that we couldn't find any weapons on either victim. Nor did we find any weapons in the immediate area. We needed that gun to tie the dead male to the armed robberies and murders. Even though he was the spitting image of the composite drawing, and I had identified him as the suspect, we still needed that weapon to make a case against him. Even if the fingerprint that was taken from the cafe counter matched the victim's, we still needed the gun. It would make my case that much stronger.

Within minutes, the room was overrun with uniformed officers. Soon after, forensics and the coroner arrived, along with the lighting technicians. And then, a few minutes later, the paramedics showed up to take the female victim to the emergency room at City hospital for immediate surgery.

Detective Kendall and I walked by the female victim's stretcher as the paramedics slowly carried her out of the room. I was about to ask one of them a question about her condition when the victim blurted out an inaudible sentence. She could barely speak, and her breathing was erratic and shallow.

The paramedics hurriedly carried her down the six flights of stairs to the waiting ambulance while I stayed right next to her stretcher and strained my neck to hear her words. A few minutes later, the paramedics, having reached the ambulance, set the stretcher on the ground and opened up the rear doors. Just as they lifted her stretcher, she spoke again. This time, I heard her clearly.

"I know who killed him," she whispered, then she coughed and spat up blood.

I tried to get her to repeat her words, but she wouldn't respond. She had passed out. The paramedics tried to revive her using electric shock, but she didn't respond. They began CPR as they raced away to the hospital.

I wanted to follow the ambulance to the hospital so I could speak with her as soon as she regained consciousness, but I decided against it. I would just be in the way. The minute she arrived at the hospital, I knew she would be taken into the emergency room for immediate surgery to remove the bullet from her chest. That is, if she was still alive by the time she reached the hospital.

I figured I could interview her in a day or so, if and when she had recovered from her wound. I was sure she wasn't going anywhere anytime soon.

Anyway, I had my guest, Detective Kendall, to entertain...and I still had a few chores left to do yet to help him close his investigation—like having his bullets compared to the ones from our murder scenes.

I also wanted to visit the morgue to look at the old man's body from the park murders—to see if the indentations on his nose fit the pattern from the wire-rimmed eyeglasses. If I could prove that they belonged to the old man, I could eventually find out his identity.

If I could find the manufacturer of the eyeglasses, and the optometrist that had filled the prescription, then I could find the owner's identity. If I had the forensics people do it, they would take two weeks or longer before they completed their testing. I didn't want to wait that long. And I didn't want to press my luck. I still had to have them do comparative tests on Kendall's suspect's bullets, and their reaction to my request, I was certain, would be one of anger.

At that moment, I decided to head for the medical examiner's building. I wanted to escape this disgusting place before my captain ordered me to investigate *this* shooting, too.

When Detective Kendall and I arrived at the medical examiner's building, the forensics lab was empty of technicians. There was nobody around. I presumed because they were still investigating the murder scene Kendall and I had just left. So we walked directly to the morgue, two floors below.

Once there, the first thing I noticed was the dead silence. This place was also absent of its workers. Only one attendant was on duty, and we followed him to the refrigerated room where the bodies were kept. He pulled out the drawer that was holding the body of the old man from the park murders. I had forgotten just how disgustingly grotesque the victim's face had looked—kind of like Frankenstein. A large portion of flesh from both cheeks, nose and mouth had been ripped apart by one of the gunman's bullets and sewn back together with large stitches by the coroner.

However, the part of the face that was important to my investigation was now intact. The indentations on the bridge of the upper nose were still very noticeable.

I pulled the wire-rimmed eyeglasses from my jacket pocket and placed them on the bridge of the victim's nose. They seemed to fit perfectly. I was sure these glasses had belonged to this victim and that the forensics lab could verify my findings concerning them.

Within minutes, I had completed my analysis and thanked the attendant. Detective Kendall and I returned to the lab, but it was still completely empty of working bodies. However, right next door, the medical examiner was bringing in the body from the apartment shooting. To kill time, we walked over to the autopsy room to speak with Dr. Grady.

As we entered, I noticed two other bodies still needing an autopsy. They were the two male bodies from this morning's party store robbery. On the other side of the room were bodies from yesterday's robbery, which also needed their autopsies completed. They looked to be about seventy-five percent complete.

This department had been busier than ever during the last week. I was sure if I had asked the wrong question, I would have gotten an angry response in return. I didn't want to step on anyone's feet.

Detective Kendall and I stayed to one side of the room, completely away from the work area, while two assistants got the murder suspect's body ready for the autopsy.

This wasn't the best place to wait for the forensics team to return, but I wanted to get the bullets from the two male bodies and have them analyzed.

We watched as Dr. Grady and his assistants began their work. But not on the murder victims from yesterday's or today's party store robberies; instead, Grady began cutting open the body of my suspect. Why? I thought to myself. Just as I was about to ask Doc Grady that very question, Detective Kendall became a bit squeamish and left the autopsy room. I followed to help him.

We decided to wait in the hallway while Dr. Grady did his work. During this time, I thought about the reasoning behind this particular autopsy at this particular time and assumed that Dr. Grady wanted to complete the suspect's autopsy first so we could close the case that much faster.

I suggested to Detective Kendall that we go eat dinner and have a few cocktails. But he didn't want to leave without some kind of confirmation on his suspect's bullets. He wasn't going to leave this city empty-handed.

Detective Kendall decided to wait in the hallway while I peeked into the autopsy room to see what was going on. Just then, the supervisor noticed me. He grabbed something from his table and headed towards me.

"I have something of importance for you, Detective Hero," Dr. Grady said, handing me three evidence bags—two small ones and a large one. The large one contained a print card of my suspect's fingerprints, the second contained two small-caliber bullets taken from the bodies of today's murder victims, and the third held a large-caliber bullet taken from the suspect's body.

"Thank you, Dr. Grady. I've been waiting for these for some time now," I said, as I checked out the two small-caliber bullets. "These look like the same type of bullet as the others. And they are both Dum Dum bullets."

"I'm glad to help you. I'm sorry that it took so long for the autopsies, but you know the state of our department."

"Yes, I'm well aware," I said.

"Now, if you can get the forensics lab to complete the ballistics and fingerprints that should be the final detail to help close your investigations."

"I hope so, but my friend outside in the hallway has to leave tomorrow morning, and he needs our lab to compare his suspect's bullets to ours. So I'm hoping they'll do it as soon as they return from the murder scene."

"Good luck, Detective Hero," said Dr. Grady.

I left the autopsy room to meet with Kendall, who was sitting in a chair in the hallway.

I sat next to him and told him the good news.

"Well, Detective Kendall, I have all the evidence I need to get your answers and my answers. When the forensics team arrives, I'll confront the supervisor and see if we can speed up the testing."

We waited and waited and waited. Finally, after waiting two long hours, the forensics team slowly stumbled into the lab. Detective Kendall and I watched as the investigators and technicians crept to their individual workstations. They were sluggish, as though they were very tired. I sensed they wanted to be at home and not at the lab—especially not to work overtime testing my evidence.

I rehearsed the words I wanted to say to Dr. Stork, hoping he wouldn't be too angry with me for asking his team of workers to finish not only the testing of my evidence, including this new evidence that had just been handed to me by the coroner, but also Kendall's.

I took a deep breath and walked into the lab to speak with Dr. Stork; Detective Kendall stayed outside in the hallway, not wanting to get involved in case an argument transpired.

I saw Stork standing alone near a microscope in a far corner of the room. As I approached him, he looked up.

"Dr. Stork," I said, "I see you're back from that filthy rat hole. Can I get you to analyze the bullets from today's victims?"

"What's the rush?" he asked.

"I really need to know if the bullets came from one gun or more than one gun. Then I can decide the next step in my investigation."

"Why ... Are you investigating those murders, too? ... Doesn't your department have any other investigators?"

"I guess not. They are all involved on the task force."

"So what? Let Captain Blake use one of those investigators for this recent murder spree."

"I wish you would tell Captain Blake that, Doc. But I still need the comparative test done."

"Yes, I heard you," he snapped.

"If you don't test all of the bullets, at least compare the ones from the park victims to the ones from the party store victims. I need to know if these two cases are tied together."

"We'll get to them as soon as we can."

"I also need to have two bullets tested and analyzed that Detective Kendall brought from his murder victim. We think his killer and our killer are one and the same. If you could do that for me, I'd really be indebted to you."

"Can't you see that we're up to our ears in work?" he said.

"Yes, I know that, but this is very important. I really need the tests done today."

"When we get to it! When I'm finished, I'll send the report right over to your department. We are so far behind on testing evidence it's ridiculous. ... Now you want me to stop what I'm doing and test your evidence. But not just *your* evidence, you want us to test *another jurisdiction's evidence*. Why not let us do all the country's criminal lab work? Gee, we like working twenty-hour days. ... Come on, Hero, what do you want from me?" Stork crossed his arms in front of him and eyed me, obviously unhappy.

"Dr. Stork, you know I wouldn't ask this of you if it wasn't of the utmost importance."

"Detective Hero, my people are tired. We've worked forty-six days straight."

"I know how overworked your department is. My department is busy also. I'm working on two different investigations at the same time, plus I was ordered by Captain Blake to help Detective Kendall with his investigation. I don't like it any more than you," I told him, trying my best to be sympathetic.

He sighed. "I'll see what can be done," he said, holding out his hand for my bags of evidence.

"I also have the suspect's fingerprints to be matched with the ones we found at the cafe murder scene—and if you could get your Latent technicians to check them, it would be deeply appreciated." Dr. Stork shot me another dirty look, so I added, "But the fingerprints don't have to be analyzed right this minute. Although, I do need the bullets analyzed ASAP. They are the most important evidence to my investigations."

"Leave all of your evidence with me, and I'll give you the results as soon as we are finished with the testing."

"Dr. Stork," I said, handing him all three bags of evidence, "if it's all right with you, I'd rather wait for the results."

"That's up to you. But I'll tell you now...you might be here for a while. It might take three or four hours to analyze all of the bullets."

"That's all right. You're doing me a favor. If you have to stay here and work on my evidence, the least I can do is stay here with you and give you moral support and encouragement."

"Please, don't do us any favors," he said. "Why don't you wait out in the hallway? You'll just be in the way here."

I agreed and walked out to the hallway, resuming my seat next to Detective Kendall.

"It looks like we'll be here for quite some time," I told Kendall. "Do you want to sit around here, or do you want to drive to the cafe and have a late dinner and a couple of drinks?"

"Why? How long do you think it will take before they finish their testing?" he asked.

"They are going to be at least two or three hours. Maybe longer."

"If it's going to take that long … Yeah, I could use another drink. In fact, I could use two or three."

"You talked me into it."

Four hours—and a number of drinks later—we returned to the lab.

I stopped by a drinking fountain near the testing room and threw some cold water on my face, trying to shake myself from my drunken stupor. Detective Kendall sat in the hallway, too drunk to move. It was a wonder he was able to stumble into the building at all.

I took a deep breath and walked into the lab. Dr. Stork acted as though he had been waiting for me. He arose from his desk, grabbed a manila folder from it, and walked towards me.

"I have something for you, Detective Hero," he said, handing me the folder containing my test results. "I hope you're satisfied with the results. My guys stopped everything they were working on to finish your project. They should get your thanks."

"Thank you, sir. I've been waiting for these results for quite a long time. I hope they give me the answers I need." I stumbled out of the lab and into the hallway to sit down.

"Did you get the test results?" asked Kendall, as I sat down in the chair next to him.

"I have them right here in my hand," I replied, showing him the manila folder. "Let's see what they have to say." I took one report, of three, from the folder and began reading it, but my eyes refused to focus. All the words ran together. I had to have Kendall read it to me.

"Well, the report states that the bullets that were found in the party store robberies, and my victim, were all shot from the same gun," Kendall said.

"Great!" I replied, happily.

"That means your two cases and mine are tied together."

"I think so. Damn, I forgot to ask Dr. Stork if they found the suspect's gun."

"Why don't you go back in there now and ask him?"

"I don't know if I can."

"What do you mean?"

"I mean...I'm too drunk to move."

Kendall shot me a disgruntled look, which got the better of me. I decided to seek out Stork.

"Well, I made it once without falling flat on my face," I said. "I guess I can chance it."

"Good luck," said Kendall.

I arose from my chair, staggered into the forensics lab, and sought out Dr. Stork once again. I found him sitting behind his desk.

"I'm sorry, Dr. Stork, but I forgot to ask you one question," I said.

"What's that?"

"Did your investigators find the suspect's gun?"

Stork gave me a somber look, shook his head. "No, we didn't find it. And we tore that place apart looking for it."

Hearing that knocked the wind out of my sails. I felt as though Mike Tyson had just punched me in the stomach.

"Damn, Dr. Stork. I need that gun to close the investigation and to verify that the young male that was killed this morning was my suspect. All I know right at this moment is that the bullets were fired from the same gun. What I need to know is—who fired the gun?"

"Did you read the fingerprint analysis report yet?"

"No, I haven't. Why?"

"Read it and find out."

"The suspect's fingerprints matched the ones taken from the cafe counter, didn't they?" I asked.

"I guess you *haven't* read the report," he said, sarcastically. After a few long seconds of silence, he obliged me. "No. The fingerprints don't match the one found at the cafe. One was very similar, but not exactly the same. It was missing a minute scar. Everything else matched."

I shook my head in disbelief. "I don't believe this! It has to be the same guy, Doc. I saw him with my own two eyes. If this guy isn't our suspect, then who is he?"

"I have no idea. He had no identification on him, and his fingerprints weren't in the FBI database files. Gun powder residue tests done on his hands and clothes proved negative," said Stork.

My shoulders slumped. "Then another innocent person was killed this morning," I said. "I don't believe this. On one hand, the same gun was used at three different murder scenes, but the person that matched the eyewitness accounts and the composite drawing isn't the killer. Yet, I saw the guy myself as he shot and killed a cafe customer. The guy that was killed this morning has to be my suspect." Then it dawned on me. "Or his twin brother."

I was so stunned by this turn of events that I didn't say another word to Dr. Stork; I simply turned and staggered out of the lab. It seemed all my strength and energy had just been drained from my body. But Detective Kendall had a right to know what I had just learned.

I sat down next to him. "Well, Kendall," I said, "I've got some good news and some bad news. Which would you like first?"

"Whatever. Just tell me," he said, and let out a big, stinking belch.

"The good news is...your bullets matched the others from my victims."

"I *know* that. What's the bad news?"

"The bad news is—"

"The fingerprints don't match the fingerprints that were found at the cafe murder scene," said Kendall, finishing my sentence.

"How did you know?"

"I was reading the reports while you were in the forensics lab. It's all there."

"Yeah, but what you don't know is, they didn't find the gun. It wasn't at the crime scene."

Kendall looked puzzled. "If that's not the suspect, then who did that officer kill?"

Before answering him, I lit a cigarette and took a long drag. "I believe he killed an innocent person. That's two innocent people killed and one wounded by the same people that are supposed to protect them."

"What are you talking about?"

"I'm saying that those innocent people were killed by their own police force," I snapped.

"Well, at least I'm not going home empty-handed," Kendall said. "I just won't be able to close my case—something I thought we were both going to be able to do."

"You can say that again. I thought I was gonna close two cases at once. Now, I only have half of my answers. We still have a murder suspect running rampant out there."

Kendall yawned. "You know, it's late. I should be getting back to my hotel room. I have to get up early for my flight home. I'll make a copy of the analysis report so I have something to show my captain. But I'll leave the investigation open, just in case the suspect comes back into my territory. I still have the composite drawing on our suspect. His face is burned into my mind."

"That guy must have a twin brother," I said. "I just can't believe these fingerprint results. But I guess I shouldn't dwell on it. ... It *is* getting rather late. Come on, I'll give you a lift to your hotel room."

"I left my car at the cafe parking lot. I have to drive the car back to the airport in the morning and return it to the rental company. So take me to the cafe."

"Your wish is my command," I said, as we staggered out the door to the parking lot.

When we arrived at the cafe parking lot, we said our goodbyes and then went our separate ways. His case was solved—to a point—but mine wasn't. I still had many questions to answer.

I still couldn't identify the old man from the park murders—nor my suspect in the armed robberies, who was also involved in the shooting deaths of two of the park victims—because the bullets taken out of those victims had been fired from the same gun that had killed the party store victims. Whether his bullets killed the park victims or not wasn't as important as his identity was. He was still a big threat to this city. And I was sure that he would kill and rob again—and soon.

Once home, I decided to watch some of the videotapes from the hospital hoping to spot Dr. Rhodes, my male suspect, or possibly the female prisoner, Elaine Weltman.

Over the next hour or so, I placed tape after tape into the machine and watched on fast forward until one frame on tape #14 caught my eye. It showed my male suspect entering the hospital through the main entrance. The one thing I noticed right away was that he was wearing gloves. This was great evidence—for what, I wasn't sure. But just to be on the safe side, I wanted the forensics lab to use this videotape to photograph and blow up the suspect's face; it might help identify him. I still needed a name to go with the face. At least now I had proof that he was at the hospital when Weltman was recuperating from her surgery.

Exhaustion finally caught up to me, so I shut off the video machine and lay down on the couch, all the while thinking about my investigation. I wondered what my suspect had to do with Weltman. Was he a boyfriend? A brother? And then I remembered that Weltman had been adopted. Was he her adopted brother? My thoughts were becoming too confusing. I shut my eyes to think, but instead fell fast asleep. I didn't wake up until early the next morning, just in time for work.

# Chapter 21

While getting ready for work, I thought about a dream I'd had during the night about the cafe robbery and murder. I remembered that the killer was wearing gloves at the time, but only one, which was on his gun hand.

When the forensics team checked the cafe counter for fingerprints, they only found one print that couldn't be matched with anyone from the café. Nor could it be identified through the FBI's computer files.

I also remembered in my dream that one of the cars found at the park was brown in color—the same color of car that the doctor's neighbor had mentioned, and Dr. Rhodes had owned.

For a second, I thought that maybe Dr. Rhodes could be the old man found dead at the park. But then, I decided against the idea. I didn't think the doctor would have gotten himself into such a predicament. He was probably out of town at a convention when the park killings were being committed. I was hoping to get the answer to that question and others very soon.

Suddenly, my belly began bellowing, telling me that it was time to eat.

So twenty minutes after awakening, I was out the door and heading for the café with reports in hand.

While walking towards my favorite back room table, I spied another person sitting there—their back to me. I was about to tell the person that the table had been reserved, but then I saw who it was.

"Detective Kendall, what the heck are you doing here this morning? I thought you had to fly back today?" I said.

"You're right. But I couldn't get out of bed this morning."

"Why, what happened?"

"Well, after the answering service called and woke me up, I fell back asleep."

"You shouldn't have done that," I said, shaking my head. "You should have gotten out of bed as soon as you heard your phone ring."

"My headache kept me in bed. I called my captain and explained to him that I needed one more day to complete my investigation."

"I'll bet he appreciated that. What excuse did you use?"

"I told him that we didn't get the lab results yet. So he allowed me to stay one extra day. But I gotta be back by tomorrow morning."

"Well, do you want to ride along with me today and help me with my investigation?"

"Sure... Why not!"

"Good. I have a few important chores to take care of this morning."

"Like what?" asked Kendall.

"Well, the first thing I want to do is drive back to the station and make a quick phone call to that doctor's answering service. If he hasn't gotten in touch with them yet, then I want to visit his neighbor again."

"Why do you need to speak with her again?"

"I want to show her the wire-rimmed eyeglasses that we found at the park. Maybe she can identify them."

"If you think those glasses belong to that doctor, then you think he's the victim from the park that hasn't been identified yet," said Kendall.

"Possibly. But like I said...it's just a hunch. That's why I want to see if Dr. Rhodes has checked in with his answering service. And then I want to ride out to the hospital and interview the injured female."

"What do you think she can tell you?"

"She may have some very important information for me. ... I wonder what she meant when she said, 'I know who killed them?'"

"Are you sure that's what she said?"

"Yeah, why?" I said.

"She was definitely in shock at the time," said Kendall.

"I'm sure she was. If you had gotten shot in the chest with a bullet from a .38 police special, you'd be in shock, too. But I'm certain she said those words. She said it, twice. I know I heard her!"

"You know... you had at least three drinks before we searched that apartment complex."

"So what are you saying? Do you think I was too drunk to hear the girl correctly?" I snarled.

"Not exactly. Now, don't take this the wrong way, Hero...I don't want to step on any toes. But you did have quite a bit to drink yesterday."

"Yeah ... So!"

Kendall hesitated before answering. "I'm just saying you may not have heard her correctly. She may not even remember yesterday."

"Well, I can't find out if I don't visit her. Right?"

"That's true," replied Kendall.

"I want to hear what she has to say, if anything. I also want to get that fingerprint analysis report Stork gave me rechecked and verified."

"How come?"

"I can't believe they don't match the fingerprint taken from the cafe. I have videotape of the suspect's face taken at City hospital the same day he was seen with a female prison inmate who had surgery there. That guy has to be my suspect."

"Who is the prison inmate you're talking about?"

"Elaine Weltman. She was the killer convicted a while back of five brutal murders—all of which, I might add, were badly mutilated. And now, we have more of the same type of mutilated dead bodies popping up all over the city."

"But you said she was locked up in prison during the time the murders were committed. Isn't that right?"

I nodded yes.

"Then why suspect her of the killings?" asked Kendall.

"Because they have her signature all over them," I said. "I believe Weltman committed these murders during the time that she was at City Hospital supposedly recuperating from surgery for a ruptured appendix. And I also believe that my suspect, who has committed all of these armed robberies, helped her in the killings."

"That's some theory. Why do you think that?"

"Because she wanted to show the public that someone else did the murders that she was accused and convicted of."

"What proof do you have that she did it?"

"So far, I've proved that she had the time to sneak out of the hospital, with or without help, most likely the former, and commit the murders. Then, sneak back into the hospital within a matter of an hour or so, without anyone seeing her or being the wiser."

"You're forgetting one thing, *Detective* Hero..."

"What's that?"

"If she was convicted of those murders, that means she's in prison, right?"

"Yeah, that's right. So!"

"So, the prisoners are guarded at the hospital. Are they not?" asked Kendall.

"They're supposed to be. But I've interviewed a number of the guards who had the job of guarding her room, and for one reason or another, left their post. And not just for a minute or two, either."

"Why? How long were they away?"

"Some were gone an hour, some longer. One guard was away from the room for more than three hours."

"That's incredible," replied Kendall.

"Yeah," I said, nodding, "and the head nurse told me that Weltman was treated only during daytime hours. For twelve hours of the day, she wasn't attended by anyone."

"Incredible," repeated Kendall.

"Not only that...but none of the guards bothered to handcuff her to the bed. What do you think of that?"

"You're kidding? I can't believe that. If that had happened in my city, someone would be losing their jobs over it, I'll tell you that," said Kendall.

"I hear ya."

"But you really think she's involved in more murders? How long was Weltman at the hospital?"

"For a total of eight days. I figure her surgery took three days to heal, at least well enough for her to walk and move around...and during those three days the guards were away from their posts for long periods of time—like three hours or more."

"Why would they stay away from their posts for so long without checking on their prisoner?"

"They thought she was too ill to worry about. She wasn't a threat to them, so they didn't pay much attention to her. ... And the other five days she was there, the guards were away from their posts, too."

"I can't believe the guards would do that," said Kendall, shaking his head in disbelief.

"They didn't expect any trouble from her," I told him. "But they didn't know her like I know her."

"What is she like?"

I took a long drag on my cigarette before putting it out in the ashtray. "She is a cold-blooded, calculated, sly, and very, very clever woman," I told him. "Highly intelligent and criminally motivated."

"When did you become aware of this person? When did she become a suspect?"

"I first heard about her from her adopted mother. She was frantic and worried that her daughter was coming out here to kill her birth mother."

"Did she kill her?"

"Yep ... And four others, including her biological father, whom she thought was her boyfriend and lover."

"Was she sleeping with this guy?" asked Kendall in disbelief.

I told him she was and detailed the case to him.

"She must have been mighty surprised and angry when she learned the truth about her birth father?"

"Instead of killing her mother right away, Weltman thought she would hurt her like she had been hurt by taking her birth mother's boyfriend away from her—a guy by the name of Jim Palter. But Weltman knew him by a different name."

"Are you telling me the guy Weltman thought was her lover used an alias?"

"Yep. Lots of 'em. It seemed he used a different name for each woman he dated."

"So this girl only wanted to hurt her birth mother at that time?"

I nodded. "Yeah. Weltman wanted to make her birth mother feel the betrayal and hatred that she had felt when she learned that she had been given away at birth."

"So why did she kill Palter?"

"I believe she became enraged and killed him when she figured out that she was screwing not her lover but her father."

"And now you think she might also be involved in some recent murders?"

"I do."

"When did these murders take place?" Kendall asked.

"Less than two weeks ago. We found the dead bodies badly decomposed about four or five days ago. But they had already been dead for four or five days before we stumbled over them."

"What do you mean, you stumbled over them?"

"I told you about the two other detectives that had visited me, just recently, didn't I?"

"Yes, vaguely."

"They were here during the cafe robbery and participated in the search and near capture of the suspect. After robbing the café and killing one of its patrons, the bandit fled the premises with me and the two out-of-state detectives chasing after him. And even though he had a big head start on us, we were able to follow him to an apartment complex not too far from the ones we searched yesterday." I stopped speaking to light another cigarette.

"So what happened?" asked Kendall.

"While we were searching the buildings, we stumbled over the dead bodies. We moved a mattress away from the wall and saw a dead male and female."

"How long had they been dead?"

"I told you! Approximately four days."

"How do you know Weltman committed *those* murders?"

"For one thing, they were both mutilated—overkill. But there were a few different things that got my attention."

"Like what?"

"The male's penis had been severed and placed into his left fist, near his mouth. The males that she was convicted of murdering also had their manhood severed and placed in a closed fist."

"Which fist? His left or right?"

"Same as all the other victims. It was in his left hand. And they had been stabbed more than thirty times. But the *kicker* was the long, blonde hairs that were found on the bodies of each victim."

"Did they belong to Weltman?"

"We don't know just yet. Looking at them through a microscope, they looked identical."

"What did the DNA tests state?" asked Kendall.

"I haven't gotten the report back from the lab yet. Sometimes they take weeks before they complete the tests."

"I know. We have the same trouble with the lab that we use. One lab even refused our evidence for testing. We had to contract with another lab outside the state."

It was getting late, and I had lots of work ahead of me, so I told Kendall, "Let's have one last cup of coffee before we leave. Then I have to run by the station real quick and make a few phone calls. You can wait in the car if you want."

"That's fine. My head hasn't settled down yet anyway."

We finished our coffee, paid the bill, and headed to my car.

While driving towards the station, we passed the apartment complex that we had searched the day before. While Kendall was resting his eyes, I was busy looking for my suspect. I wasn't sure if I was looking for a ghost, or if there really was another person out there that looked exactly like the dead young man—his twin.

Kendall stayed in the car—asleep—while I ran into the station and signed in at the front desk. Once at my desk, I phoned Dr. Rhodes's answering service and asked to speak with a supervisor.

A moment later, someone picked up the line.

"Yes, this is Mrs. Joyce. I'm the company supervisor."

"Hello, this is Detective Hero. Have you heard from Dr. Rhodes lately?"

"We have not heard from the doctor in nearly two weeks."

"Has he done this before?"

"He has, but this has been the longest time he has been away without contacting us. We will wait another three days. If he doesn't contact us within that time, we will contact the police."

I thanked her for her time and the helpful information then hung up the phone. On a hunch, I picked up the phone again and dialed the doctor's office number. But the phone rang and rang and rang. Nobody answered. Evidently, nobody was at home.

My next move was to drive to Dr. Rhodes's neighborhood and speak with his neighbor about the eyeglasses that I had found in the mud at the park. Would she recognize them as the doctor's?

Once that chore was accomplished, Kendall and I would then visit the hospital to speak with the wounded female that had been shot at the apartment building by the rookie policeman.

When I returned to the car, Kendall was snoring up a storm. I guess he was getting his much-needed rest. I started the car and headed for the doctor's place. Ten minutes later, I was parked in the doctor's driveway.

I waited in the car for a few minutes hoping the neighbor with whom I had talked the day before would venture outside of her home to see who I was, but nobody came near us.

Deciding what to do next, I looked over to Kendall for his opinion, but he was still sleeping like a newborn baby—no help to me.

But I wasn't going to leave until I had tried my best. I stepped out of my car, walked up the front steps to the neighbor's home, and rang the doorbell. No one answered. I rang the doorbell again and also knocked on the front door, but to no avail. There was no answer.

Just as I turned and walked down the steps, a car drove up into the next-door neighbor's driveway. The passenger door opened and out stepped the woman I had been looking for. She had a hard time getting her four hundred-pound, five-foot five-inch body out of the vehicle, but somehow managed...and walked slowly towards me.

When she was within earshot, I said, "Hello, remember me? I'm Detective Hero. I spoke with you yesterday about Dr. Rhodes."

"Yes, I remember you. What do you want now?" she asked, striding past me toward her front door.

"I'm sorry, I've forgotten your name."

"It's Doris."

"Doris, I would like you to look at something. Would you do that for me?" I pulled the wire-rimmed eyeglasses from my jacket pocket.

"What do you have there, Detective?"

"I would like you to look at this pair of eyeglasses and tell me if you've ever seen them before." I handed them to her.

"They do look familiar," she said, looking them over. "I didn't lose them, did I?"

"I don't think so. Doris, did you ever see Dr. Rhodes wear eyeglasses like these?"

She nodded. "He might have. The lenses are thick, similar to the thickness of the doctor's glasses. But I've seen him wear at least three different pairs at different times."

"But did he own a pair of wire-rimmed glasses?"

"Yes, but I couldn't swear that this pair is his."

"What do you think, though? Could they be his?" I asked, anxious.

"I'm sorry, but I couldn't say one hundred percent that these eyeglasses belong to Dr. Rhodes." Doris returned the eyeglasses to me.

I placed them back into my jacket pocket. "Well, I thank you for your time, and I thank you for your help."

I walked back to my car and headed for the hospital.

Detective Kendall remained asleep during the twenty-minute ride to the hospital; however, when I parked the car in the hospital parking lot, he finally woke.

"I'm glad to see you awake," I said. "Did you have a nice nap?"

"I sure did," he replied, smiling.

I then asked him what he wanted to do. "Do you want to interview this witness with me or just sit in the car?"

"I'll go in with you. I'm curious to hear what the girl has to say," he said.

"Yeah, but I'll do all the questioning. Is that understood?"

Kendall nodded.

I had planned to phone the hospital from the station, but I had forgotten about it. So now, I had to find out what floor the female victim was on. The receptionist told me that and more.

I was surprised to learn that the victim—a Miss Sue Adams—had been arrested and was being held on "suspicion," of what, I didn't know. A guard was posted just outside her room, and I had to show him my identification and gold shield, as did Detective Kendall before entering.

As I slowly opened the door, I saw the girl, who looked to be all of sixteen years old—with large bandages and heavy gauze covering her chest and midsection—sitting up in the hospital bed eating her lunch. She must have been feeling all right to be eating this soon after surgery, I thought.

She had color in her face and seemed to have a good appetite, eating nearly everything on her plate. And when I heard her burp, I figured that was the right time to ask her some questions.

As Kendall and I stood near the end of the bed, I introduced us. "Hello, I'm Detective Hero and he's Detective Kendall. Don't be frightened of us. I am here to ask you a few simple questions."

"What is Detective Kendall here for?" she asked.

I looked at Kendall. "He's just going to listen, for the time being," I said. "Your name is Sue Adams, correct?"

"Yes, I'm Sue Adams. What kind of questions?" she asked, as she reclined the bed with her remote control.

"I just want to know, Sue, if you remember what you said to me yesterday as the paramedics were carrying you down the stairs of that condemned apartment building?"

"Yes, I remember."

"What did you say?" I asked, stepping closer to her bed. "Who were you talking about yesterday? Your boyfriend, who was killed by the police officer?"

"He wasn't my boyfriend," she said.

"Then why were you with him?"

She hesitated for a few seconds before answering, then said, "I was already in that room when he came running into it and asked me to hide him. He didn't say from what, but I figured it was somebody he was frightened of."

"Are you saying that you didn't know that young man? Is that what you want me to believe?"

Again, she hesitated before speaking. After a long pause, she said, "Well, you could say I knew *of* him, but I didn't *know* him." She patted her hair. It seemed like a nervous gesture.

"How did you know *of* him?" I asked.

"He would come around once or twice a week usually looking for a place to sleep."

"Did he come alone?"

"Sometimes he came with another guy that looked just like him. I guess they were twins."

"Sue, did you know the names of these two young men?"

"No. Usually, they were around when the doctor visited us," she whispered. She seemed to be growing tired.

"What doctor is this? Who are you talking about?"

"Many of the kids living in that squalor and filth were coming down with some kind of disease or bug," she said. "Each vacant building had a couple of people that came down with it. So to get help, we pooled our money to pay for a doctor to treat the sick ones."

"Where did you guys get your money?"

"We panhandled and didn't eat. That's how we saved the money. None of us had any insurance, or transportation to the hospital, so we called the only doctor that made house calls and was reasonable."

"Where did you find this doctor's phone number?"

"I'm not sure. We either found it in the phone book or one of the other kids had his business card. He was the only doctor that would come to the ghetto."

"Why would this doctor risk his life in that area for so little money?"

"You know... I asked him that very question."

"What did he say?"

"He said he wanted to help the needy people of the city. And to give something back to the city that had given him so much. He gave the sick ones a shot and also a prescription for medicine. And if we didn't have the money to pay for the prescription, he said he would give it to us."

"If you don't remember his name, I know you can give me a description of him. Was he a fat, little bald old man that wore thick eyeglasses?"

"How did you know?" asked Adams, surprised. "He was just like you described: a pudgy, little, bald man that wore very thick glasses. He reminded me of the Pillsbury Dough Boy, and he drove an old, beat-up, dirty brown car."

"Do you know what kind of car it was?"

"I don't know the make or model, only the color. I'm not good with cars."

"Did he wear glasses that looked anything like these?" I pulled out the pair of wire-rimmed glasses from my jacket pocket and showed them to Adams.

"Gee, those condemned buildings are so dark that I didn't really notice. But I believe I did see him with the same type of eyeglasses. I remember he also wore some thick, black-rimmed glasses. Those were the ones I remembered. He looked spooky in them."

"Spooky? Why do you say that?"

"His eyes were magnified ten times their normal size. Sometimes, I had to stop myself from laughing out loud. They looked so weird on him. But now that I think about it, something about him seemed strange...because even though he acted very nice and cordial, sometimes he seemed to change right in mid-sentence."

"What do you mean? How did he change?"

"He seemed to become disoriented. Like he was in a fog and forgot where he was."

"Do you remember this doctor's name? Please try and remember."

"Let me see." She thought for a moment. "It's been a few weeks since I saw him last. I did see his car at another condemned building a few blocks from the one where I was shot. I can't remember what name he used. Although I do know I telephoned a Dr. Bennet's office to make the house call. And then when the doctor arrived, I asked him if he was Dr. Bennet, but he said he was filling in for Dr. Bennet. I do remember that. I just can't remember his name. I just can't. I'm sorry," Adams said, dropping her head.

"That's all right. Don't worry about it. Do you remember Dr. Bennet's telephone number?"

She shook her head no. "Now that I think about it, I believe I got the number from another person."

"Do you remember who gave it to you?" I asked.

"Yes, but she's dead. She was found about a week ago."

"Who found her?"

"I guess the police found her by accident."

"Our police department?"

"Yes. She was found in one of the condemned apartment buildings. She was killed with her boyfriend."

"Sue, do you know who killed them?"

"No, but I have my suspicions."

"What are your suspicions?"

"Every time my friends ended up dead, that doctor had visited them just a few hours before. I can't say for sure, but a group of us that live at the apartment building talked about their deaths a few different times." Adams raised her bed with her remote control unit so that she could talk more easily.

"So who do you think killed your friends?"

She thought for a moment. "Either the doctor had something to do with their deaths or someone else came into the apartment building when there was nobody else around."

"So you think that doctor had something to do with those two deaths. Is that what you're telling me?"

"Hell, I don't know... I'm not a detective! That's your job, isn't it?"

I nodded. "You're absolutely correct. But that's how investigators find their suspects."

"How's that?"

"By asking the public to help us. Just like you're helping us now. But let's forget about that doctor for a minute. Let's talk about that young man that was killed yesterday. You say you didn't know him. Is that right?"

"What would you like to know?"

"How did you know this young man, if he wasn't your boyfriend?"

"I told you before. He came to one of the apartments where I was staying. He would sit and talk with all of us. But he scared me at times," Adams said.

"Why is that?"

"He had this shiny little gun that he said he had found...and he would take it out of his waistband and point it at us like he was going to shoot us. That's why he frightened me."

"Did he ever use it on anybody that you know of?"

"I don't know, but one of the people staying at the apartment asked him if he'd ever shot anyone with it."

"What did he say?"

"He just gave us this eerie smile and said, 'What do you think?' He kept spinning it around his fingers, like a cowboy. That guy was crazy!"

"Where did his gun disappear to? We didn't find it at the apartment building yesterday."

"I don't know. I didn't see it yesterday. In fact, I hadn't seen him for a couple of days until he came running into the room and asked for help. That's when we tried hiding behind the sliding wall."

"Sue, yesterday when I walked alongside your stretcher, as the paramedics carried you to the ambulance, you said something about knowing who killed them. What did you mean by that?"

"Just what I said. I know who killed them."

"Killed who?"

"The two bodies that are hidden behind the sliding wall, one floor above the room where we were shot."

Her answer floored me. I gave Kendall a surprised look and then continued my questioning. "How do you know that there are two bodies in that apartment building? We didn't find anyone else there yesterday," I said, looking deep into her eyes.

"I know, because we carried them up to that room. The smell was becoming unbearable, and we wanted them out of sight."

I just couldn't digest her answer. "Are you telling me that there are two more dead bodies up in that apartment building?"

She nodded. "That's right. They're still there, if you didn't find them yesterday." Detective Kendall and I looked at each other in amazement.

"Who are they?" I asked.

"Just two nameless, unlucky people that found peace and happiness in death. Life was too unbearable for them, anyway. And I believe that crazy guy with the gun killed them. Or maybe that doctor."

"Boy, this one is for the books," I said. Then I asked Sue something I'd been wondering ever since my first run-in with those buildings. "Sue, that place you stayed at is so filthy and smelly that the dogs couldn't even pick up the scent of death. That's how bad that air is in that place. How can you stand to live in all that filth and garbage?"

She gave me a sad answer. "That's the only place I can afford," she said. Then she added, "At least I have a roof over my head when it rains and gets cold at night. It might not be the Ritz, but it was home to me."

"Sue, let me ask you one last question."

"Go ahead."

"You did say that the young man that was with you yesterday owned a small gun. Is that right?"

"Yes, I know he *had* one. But it could have been his friend's gun."

"Who was that? Do you know his friend's name?" I asked.

"No, I don't. But his friend looked exactly like him. And when I asked if they were twins, they just laughed and said 'no.' So, I figured they weren't siblings but were related, and I left it at that."

Just then, the nurse came into the room to give Adams a pain shot.

"Detective Kendall, I think this would be a good time to leave," I said, and he nodded in agreement. I thanked Sue for her help and added, "If there's anything else you can think of that would help me with my investigation, just call the number on my business card. I'll leave it on your nightstand." I placed the card on the nightstand, and then Kendall and I left.

My next destination was the condemned apartment buildings. I wanted to verify Sue's claim that there were two more dead bodies on the floor above.

On the way, I thought once again about the doctor. Adams mentioned a Dr. Bennet, but I was sure she had described the same doctor I was looking for—Dr. Rhodes.

Instinct told me they were one and the same. The more I thought about the doctor, the more I wanted to head straight for a judge to get a warrant to search his house. I figured that the eyewitness accounts and wire-rimmed eyeglasses would be reason enough. I hoped so, anyway.

I wanted and needed that search warrant. The pieces of my jigsaw puzzle were beginning to fall into place. I had connected and finished the outside edge—now I had to start filling in the middle. I could feel I was getting closer and closer to ending my investigations.

Sue Adams didn't have the information that I had. Depending on the time of death, it was likely that my perpetrator, Elaine Weltman, was the guilty party in these and other killings. I believed she'd killed them during her eight-day visit at City hospital, using her surgery as her alibi. I was sure of that.

And although I didn't believe that the doctor had anything to do with the apartment murders, I *did* believe that he might be involved in my other case concerning the park murders. But that was a long shot.

For the warrant, I decided to go to a personal friend of mine…a drinking friend, who happened to be an elected official, a judge—Judge Walker. I hoped he would grant my wish.

But the judge had other ideas. I had what he called "flimsy evidence," especially when no one had notified the police of any foul play or wrongdoing. So he denied my plea for the search warrant…and told me to come back with more evidence.

I was in a tough spot. Because the old man's face had been partially blown off and disfigured, it was useless to have someone that might know him come to the morgue to identify him.

So, for the time being, all I had was the wire-rimmed glasses and eyewitness accounts. Beyond that, nothing.

I decided to wait until the answering service had notified the police that the doctor was missing. Then I would return to the judge's office and request the warrant. I was sure to get it at that time.

Back on track, I decided to drive over to the condemned apartments that Kendall and I had searched the day before. I wasn't looking forward to it, and neither was Kendall. But we had no choice. Let me take that back. *I* had no choice. And Kendall was nice enough to tag along. Anyway, our curiosity had gotten the best of us.

We finally arrived at yesterday's crime scene. As we stepped out of the car, the many derelicts and homeless people must have smelled "cops" because they went running for cover, not wanting to be seen. However, no one running away fit the description of my suspect.

When we reached the entrance to the apartment building, I wondered whether I should call for backup or for the forensics investigators, but I decided against it. Not because I would have to use a pay phone to make the call but because we hadn't yet discovered the bodies. I wanted to substantiate her claim—*then* I'd put the call into the station.

With guns drawn and flashlights on, Kendall and I entered the dark, foul-smelling dwelling, trying not to step in anything. I had forgotten just how bad the air was in this place. I tried holding my breath, but that didn't work. I damn near passed out from lack of breathable air. Somehow though, Kendall and I put up with it.

We quickly walked up the stairs to the seventh floor. This was where Miss Adams had told us she had hidden the bodies. We found the particular room she had described and began searching the area. She mentioned she had hidden them behind a phony wall with a sliding door.

We walked to one side of the room and tried sliding the wall, but it wouldn't budge. We went to the adjacent side and tried sliding that wall. But it stayed stationary also. The next wall we tried won the prize. The wall slid maybe two feet, just enough room to squeeze into the hidden room. And sure enough, there were two dead bodies lying on the floor there.

The stench was unbearable. We had to cover our mouths and leave the room to gather our senses. It was much worse than the normal smell of human waste and moldy, maggot-infested garbage. After gagging and coughing, we stood silent for a minute or two, trying to build up our strength and courage.

"Go out to the street and phone the station for backup," I told Kendall. "And make sure you send for the investigators and medical examiner. I'll stay put and make sure nobody comes into the room and disturbs these rotting bodies."

"It'll be my pleasure," he said. "I can't stand to be in this place for another minute."

I watched as Kendall started down the steps.

But just as he began walking down the first flight of stairs, we saw someone else on the floor below. Kendall and I shined our flashlights on the subject's face and asked him what he was doing. Our eyes met.

It was our man. We were sure of it.

"It's him, it's our suspect," I yelled, reaching for my weapon.

But the suspect also had a gun, and he fired it at us before we could react. All we could do was dive for cover and watch as the suspect ran down the stairs and out of the building. We followed, weapons drawn and ready. But he had a good head start on us and was much faster and younger. When Kendall and I finally reached the street, the suspect was a good sixty yards ahead.

"Detective Kendall!" I yelled. "Find a phone and call for backup and the dogs. I don't want this guy to get away again. He's our killer. I'll chase after him on foot. You can use the car to catch up to me." I then threw him the keys to my car and continued running after the suspect.

"Will do," shouted Kendall, as he ran off to telephone for help.

By now, the suspect was more than a hundred yards ahead of me. He ran through the industrial area and into a subdivision. He was very evasive and hard to follow...and I was out of breath. I had to stop ten minutes after I started. My body was sopping wet from the perspiration flooding out of my pores. I began hacking and coughing, and knelt on the ground to catch my breath. I was too damn old for this type of athletic competition.

A few minutes later, Kendall drove up in my car and parked it.

"Where did he go? Did he get away?" he asked, walking over to me and patting me on the back.

"He's in this subdivision somewhere. Did you call for backup?" I asked, still trying to catch my breath.

"Yeah, they should be here any minute."

Just as he said those words, we heard the sirens of the patrol cars coming towards us. First one, then two, then others began lining up and filling the streets to hunt for our suspect. I slowly got to my feet and began barking orders. I had some officers and patrol units cordon off ten square city blocks. We wanted to catch this guy—and make sure he wasn't going to get away this time.

I still had my doubts. With such a big head start, the suspect had more than enough time to slip through our dragnet. But we still had to try. This guy was just too important to us not to. We wanted to get this guy off the street. He was a sadistic, psychotic killer ... And a monster in our eyes.

Just as I began giving out orders to the uniformed officers, Captain Blake showed up at the scene. He took over. I didn't mind at all. I was worn out from my little jog, chasing the suspect. When Blake finished barking out his orders, he turned his attentions towards me.

"Detective Hero, are you sure that this was our suspect?" he asked.

"Definitely! He even took a few pot shots at us with that .22. The spent bullets should be in the walls of the seventh floor in one of the condemned apartment buildings back there."

"Do you remember which apartment building?" Blake asked.

"Yeah. The same one we were at yesterday where the officer shot the unarmed suspect."

"All right, that's enough of that. It wasn't the officer's fault that those two kids got shot. That's the nature of this job. Deal with it," Blake said.

"I am," I snapped.

Then Blake scolded me for returning to yesterday's crime scene. "What were you doing at that apartment building, anyway? The crime scene has already been investigated by your peers."

"Excuse me, Captain. You said the investigators had already investigated yesterday's crime scene. But they forgot to take the dead bodies with them."

"What the hell are you talking about, Hero? There was only one dead body, and he's lying in the autopsy room at the medical examiner's building. The other person was only wounded and taken to the hospital...and she's doing fine."

"I'm not talking about those bodies, Captain. I'm talking about the ones we just discovered today, on the seventh floor of that condemned building."

"You mean two more dead bodies? How long have they been dead?"

"I don't know; I'm not the medical examiner. But I would say at least seven days or more. They've been dead awhile."

"You say the bodies are one floor above yesterday's crime scene?" asked Blake, confused.

"That's right," I replied, nodding my head. "The girl that was shot yesterday told us about them. She and her friends placed them into a hidden room one floor above the room where they lived."

"Why did they move the bodies? Didn't they know they were breaking the law?" asked Blake.

I shrugged my shoulders. "I guess the bodies stunk worse than what they were used to. So they moved them to another floor. I don't think they thought about the cops one way or another."

"How were they killed, and who killed them? Do you know?" asked Blake.

"I believe the female convicted of the murders in my last multiple murder investigation committed the ones we located today. They have her signature all over them."

"How could she do that? She's in prison."

"I'm sorry, Captain. But during the time in question, she was at City hospital having surgery. I believe she had the time to kill them and the others that were uncovered recently. All of these dead bodies were killed in similar ways."

"How do you know?"

"Overkill! They were mutilated. And the males had their genitals severed, just like the other male victims."

Blake shook his head. "I don't know how a woman that just had surgery could pull that off. It just doesn't sound logical."

"You might be right, Captain, except for one thing."

"What's that?"

"I have already interviewed the people in question that were guarding the prisoner during her hospital stay for surgery."

"What kind of surgery?"

"Abdominal surgery. She was there for a ruptured appendix. She stayed for a total of eight days. And during that time, many of the officers guarding her room were away from their post for a period of time that would allow her to escape, commit the crimes, and return without anyone the wiser."

"How could she escape out of her handcuffs?" asked Blake, scratching his head.

"That's a good question, Captain. That is, if she was handcuffed at all."

"Wasn't she handcuffed to her bed?"

"That's just it. Not one officer guarding her room handcuffed her ... At any time."

"That's unbelievable. Why didn't they handcuff her?" asked Blake.

"They didn't think she was a threat. Not only that, but they were away from their posts for hours at a time. Quite enough time for her to do her dastardly deeds."

Kendall interrupted our conversation. "But the wounded girl at the hospital thought a doctor might be involved."

"Just what do you have to do with this investigation, Detective, ah, ah... I'm sorry, I can't remember your name," Blake said.

"That's all right—I'm Detective Kendall from upstate. I was with Detective Hero during his interview with the female subject. I overheard the conversation."

"So what did she have to say?" Blake asked.

Kendall then described what he had heard.

"Is that true, Detective Hero?"

"Not exactly, Captain. Adams also stated that someone else might have killed her two friends after the doctor had left the building. She wasn't sure because she went out to get a prescription filled for her sick friends, and when she returned they were gone, including the doctor." Then, giving Kendall a cold look for interrupting my conversation, I added, "She also stated that she didn't know who killed her friends."

"Then you think our killer to these recent murders is the female convict?" Blake asked.

"Yes, sir, I do. Until I've got the evidence to the contrary, I'll stick to my theory and gut instinct."

"Thank you, Detective Hero. I'll let you take me to the victims now. Oh, by the way, Warden Parker from State prison called you. It seems he has some pertinent information for you," Blake said.

"Did he say what it was about, Captain?"

"No. He just said to contact him when you get some free time. He thought you might want to hear what he has to say."

"Thanks for passing along the message, Captain. I'll telephone him when I get the chance, which doesn't look like anytime soon."

"Well then, let's go see the bodies," said Blake, leading the way.

As half of the uniformed officers searched for my suspect, the other half, along with Blake, Kendall and myself, walked the two blocks to the building where the bodies lay.

I hesitated to walk up those seven flights of stairs again. Before we entered this den of darkness, Captain Blake barked orders to a few of the uniformed officers to get the portable overhead lighting system. In the meantime, we would have to make do with our flashlights.

We hadn't yet reached the fourth floor, and already many of the uniformed police officers were retreating for the outdoors. They couldn't stomach the foul-smelling odors. You could hear them squealing in pain.

We continued our tormenting climb until finally reaching the correct floor. And then we followed the strong odor of death to the bodies behind the phony wall. Our eyes watered.

The uniformed officers cordoned and taped off the crime scene while the rest of us did the investigating. Although the deceased bodies had been moved from one floor to another, it remained obvious that the two bodies, a young adult male and a young adult female, had been killed in a manner similar to the other victims that Elaine Weltman had been convicted of killing.

This particular male victim had been stabbed in the chest repeatedly, and his member had been completely severed—then shoved into his left fist. And the woman's fatal wounds were just as bad; her head was nearly decapitated, hanging on only by a few thick strands of decaying flesh, and her hair had been roughly chopped off. Her chest was caved in due to numerous knife wounds. Her murder was purely overkill.

However, there weren't any bloodstains around the bodies...because the murders occurred at the original murder scene, one floor below. So we would have to check there for any forensic evidence.

## MURDER IN THE CITY PARTS I-II

Any forensic or blood evidence was most likely mixed in amongst all the human waste and garbage. But we still had to investigate. Not only that, but there was also a possibility that the movers of the bodies might have already cleaned up the murder scene. We didn't know, but we still had to check it out.

As we were dissecting the crime scene, the technicians arrived with the overhead lighting and began setting them up, using a small portable generator as the energy source. Minutes later, the forensic team arrived, along with the medical examiner.

The room was now swarming with investigators and technicians, which meant that Detective Kendall and I were just in the way. We decided to leave and head to the café—and I wanted to get out of there before Captain Blake added this investigation to my already full agenda.

Just as we were heading for the door, one of the uniformed officers yelled for everyone to keep quiet. Suddenly, the room grew silent, which made it possible to hear the loud screaming coming from the officer's radio. A patrol unit had pulled over the armed robbery and murder suspect, three miles away.

I listened intently for confirmation on the subject, which I received when I heard the voice on the other end of the radio scream that they had captured the suspect. The second I heard where they had captured him, I motioned to Kendall to head out the door.

As we started to leave, Captain Blake stopped me. "Detective Hero, before you leave, put this case on your list. And I also want you to take the suspect that was just captured and interrogate him. Charge him with murder. I'll be at the station as soon as I'm finished here."

"Thank you, Captain. I'll see you at the station."

Kendall and I ran down the seven flights of stairs to the street in record time. We raced to the scene.

I saw the flashing lights of the police cruiser, and as I pulled alongside of it, I noticed that the suspect was already sitting handcuffed in the back seat. I also noticed a big canvas bag sitting on top of the front hood of the patrol car, with a number of different objects setting next to it. I stopped the car. Now I would see my suspect face to face.

Kendall and I jumped out of the car and walked over to the uniformed officer standing near the canvas bag.

"Good work, officer," I said, flashing him my badge. "I'm Detective Hero. You will probably receive a commendation for catching this killer and getting him off the street. … When did you know you had our suspect?"

"Well, originally, we pulled him over for a busted taillight. But when I asked him for his driver's license, he didn't have one. He told me his name, though—David Wells. And when I called it into dispatch, the license came back expired."

"So what did you do?"

"At first, I was only gonna write him a citation. But that was before I searched his car and found the canvas bag." He motioned to the bag on the hood of the car. "I found that it contained a gun."

"What kind of gun?" I asked.

"It looks like a .22 caliber with a full clip of Dum Dum bullets. When I found that, I placed the subject under arrest, handcuffed him, and put him in the back seat of the patrol car." The officer smiled.

"Did you read him his rights?" I asked.

"Yes, as soon as I arrested him."

I looked through the effects of the suspect's personal property. After checking the gun, I was sure it was the one that had been used in all of the recent armed robberies and murders.

I then walked to the side window of the patrol car and looked at the face of the captured suspect. I was sure he was the cafe robber. He did, however, look identical to the person that had been shot and killed at the condemned apartment building the day before. Now I would find out if that guy and my suspect were related. They sure looked like twins. But at least now we had his identity and would know very shortly if his fingerprint and the one taken from the cafe robbery were a match. We were home free if they were—which meant that we had finally captured our perp. If convicted, it would put him on death row.

I told the officer to drive the suspect and his personal property to the station, and I would follow him. I also told him to book the suspect, fingerprint him, and lock him in a holding cell. Then, he'd be mine. I would interrogate him and hopefully get his confession.

Five minutes later, Kendall and I were driving towards the station, excited by recent events. Kendall knew, with this arrest, that he now had the evidence to close his case for good.

"Well, Kendall, it looks like you'll go back a happy man," I said.

Kendall smiled. "If the bullets match the gun, we have him. ... Not to change the subject, but Sue Adams thought a doctor had killed those people at the apartment building."

"Yeah... what about it?"

"Well, I remember a murder case that I had not too long ago where an eyewitness told me about a doctor that had given the victim medical attention at a condemned building. The doctor sent the eyewitness to get medical supplies and a prescription filled for the victim. When she returned, both her friend and the doctor were gone. The victim was found a few days later, dead," said Kendall.

"Was the doctor a suspect?"

"There were many...because I didn't believe the young girl's story."

"Why?"

"Because of her drug habit. But that wasn't the only reason. There were so many people living throughout that building near where the victim was found that it was impossible to determine a viable suspect. Any one of them could have committed that murder. So we closed the case after a few weeks."

"Why?"

"Due to a lack of leads. They dried up."

"So why bring up that case now?"

"I just wanted to mention it. Whether or not it means anything, I don't know. If I remember correctly, the victim was mutilated, just like the victims we found today."

"Well, I appreciate your thoughts, Kendall, but I believe Elaine Weltman, along with an accomplice, killed those people. In fact, the guy that was just captured may be her accomplice," I said.

"Do you really believe that?" asked Kendall.

"I don't know, but I guarantee I'll find out if he was involved."

"What about the doctor? Do you think he's somehow involved in all of this?"

"If there is a doctor that plays a role in my investigation, he might be the unidentified victim from the park."

We finally arrived at our destination just a few minutes behind the patrol car. Once I parked the car, Kendall and I then walked happily into the station.

We were now beginning to get a good appetite for some food and drink but agreed to wait a little while longer before we went out to celebrate. And Kendall finally stopped complaining about his hangover. The smell from the condemned building had probably chased it away.

Kendall and I each had coffee and donuts while waiting for the officer to photograph and book my suspect—which took nearly an hour. And then it was my turn.

We escorted the suspect to the interrogating room, where I immediately read him his rights. And then we all took our seats around a small, wooden table.

"What am I being arrested for?" asked the suspect. He seemed confused.

"Didn't the officer explain that to you?"

"No, he didn't. So why was I arrested?"

"Why do you think?"

"I don't know! Why *was* I arrested?" he asked again.

Looking deep into his eyes, I said, "For armed robbery and murder."

"What? I didn't kill anyone ... Or rob anyone," he shouted.

"What's your name?" I asked.

"Dennis Wells," he answered, rather meekly.

But when I heard that name, a bell went off in my head. Something about his name just didn't sit well with me. I couldn't put my finger on it, so I let it rest...and concentrated on more urgent matters.

"I'm Detective Hero, and my friend is Detective Kendall," I said. "He's going to listen while I ask the questions. Okay?"

He nodded.

"All right then, let's talk about the stuff that was found in your car, Dennis."

"That stuff isn't mine," he said in a high, squeaky voice.

"You know, if it hadn't been for the stuff that was found in your car, you would have been home by now."

"Is that right?" asked Wells.

"That's right. The officer was just gonna give you a summons. But when he found that canvas bag in your car filled with objects that could be used for criminal activity, especially that gun, he had no other choice but to arrest you."

"I told you, that stuff isn't mine. It doesn't belong to me. In fact, I don't know anything about it or where it came from. This was the first time I used that car in two weeks."

"It is your car, isn't it?"

"No, it's not my car. It doesn't belong to me."

Suddenly it dawned on me. He had told the arresting officer his name was David. Not Dennis. "Wait a minute," I told him. "You told the arresting officer that your name was David. The same name that's on the car registration. Isn't that right?"

"Yes, but that's my brother's name, not mine."

"How are we to believe you? You didn't have any identification on you. Did you throw it away?"

"No. I never carry any. But you just have to believe me. I'm telling you the truth. My name is Dennis Wells, not David Wells."

"So you lied to the officer when you gave him your name?" I asked, looking into his eyes.

"Yes. I lied."

"Why did you have to lie to the officer?"

"Because I didn't have a driver's license," he said, his voice shaking. "I gave him my brother's name. I thought he had a valid driver's license...and I didn't want to spend the night in jail."

"So, now you say your name is what?"

He stared at the floor and answered, "Dennis Wells."

"So, let me get this straight, *Dennis*. Let me see if I understand you correctly. The car isn't yours; it's your brother's, right?" I asked sarcastically.

"That's right."

"The gun that was found in the car you were driving isn't yours, either. Is that what you're saying, *Dennis*?"

"That's right. The gun doesn't belong to me."

"Now you say the name you gave the officer isn't yours, either. Come on, give me a break." I got right up into his face. "I wasn't born yesterday. We recovered a fingerprint from the cafe you robbed...and where you killed that customer. If we get a match on that, we've got you cold," I said, giving him a mean and unholy look.

Wells wasn't fooling anyone. I knew he was lying...Kendall did, too. It would just be a matter of time before I got the truth out of him and shoved his lies down his throat.

"You better come clean, kid," Kendall said. "We are your only hope—the only thing keeping you off of death row. Tell us what we want to know, and we'll put in a word with the district attorney that you cooperated."

"Please, Detective Kendall," I said, holding my hand up. "Let me continue."

The room remained silent for a few minutes as the suspect thought about his future. I gave him a cigarette and lit it for him. He finished nearly half of it before finally getting up the nerve to speak.

"My brother found that gun," he said. "He was the person that robbed those places and killed those people. I didn't have anything to do with it. My brother is the guilty party." Wells hid his face in his hands.

"Where is your brother now?" I asked. "How can we get in touch with him to question him?"

"You can't—he's dead."

"Oh, that's a good one. When did he die?"

"He was killed yesterday. You should know . . . your policemen shot and killed him."

"Oh, how convenient. Blame it on your brother. *Bullshit*! His fingerprints didn't match the one that was found at the café. But I have a good suspicion that it will match yours," I said.

Then Kendall jumped into the conversation again. "You say the kid that was shot and killed yesterday at that condemned apartment building was your brother?"

"Yes. I heard about his death last night. I hadn't seen him in nearly two weeks. Since all of this crap started," he said, in a high-pitched voice, while flicking his cigarette butt to the floor. "May I have another cigarette?"

"Yeah, you can have another cigarette," I said, handing him one and lighting it for him. "Now…tell me exactly what you and your brother were up to. And start from the beginning. And I'll know if you're lying or not. But first… let me tell you that we're running your fingerprints through state and federal data banks, and we've sent the gun to ballistics for testing. We'll get that report within an hour or so. If you lie, we can't help you. You must tell us the truth the first time."

This was enough. Wells spilled his guts. He told me a story that blew my mind.

He remained silent for nearly a minute while squirming in his seat, then began speaking. "Well, it all started one day in the park. We were sitting down on a picnic table talking and smoking cigarettes when a car entered the park and stopped about fifty yards from us."

"Didn't the occupants in the car see you watching them?" asked Kendall.

Wells shook his head no. "The thick brush and foliage camouflaged us. We couldn't really see who was in that car until they got out of it. We saw two men. One was little, fat, and very old. The other was much, much younger."

"Was it raining or was the sun out?" I asked.

"It was raining, but not that hard. There was a slight drizzle."

"Hold on a minute, Wells," I told him. Then, giving Kendall a dirty look, I added, "And Detective Kendall … Please let me ask the questions."

"Don't worry, I won't say another word," he replied.

"Thank you. Now Dennis, continue."

"While we were watching this old man and this younger guy walking away from their car, we were walking closer to the scene to get a better view. Then the younger guy put his arm around the old man's waist, as if they were lovers. But then, they began to argue."

"Could you hear what they were arguing about?"

He shook his head. "No, I couldn't hear them that well. But about two minutes into their argument, I see this half naked lady appear out of nowhere."

"What was she doing?"

"At that particular time, I didn't know what the hell she was doing. She just came walking out of the bushes all of a sudden, about twenty feet from the two men. Her hair was askew, her blouse was hanging around her waist, and her naked boobs were bouncing in the drizzle."

"What time of day was this?"

"Around dusk. Darkness was just settling over the park."

My excitement grew as I began to realize that he was talking about the day of the park murders. "Okay, so what happened next?" I asked, anxious.

"Then the young man started flirting with the female that had just walked out of the bushes, while the old man walked away towards his car yelling at the young man the whole time."

"Now that you were closer to them, could you hear what the old man was yelling about?"

"No... I wasn't really listening. I was watching the naked girl. But then another guy appeared on the scene."

"Where did he come from?"

"He came stumbling out of the bushes naked with blood all over his chest. There was blood everywhere, spraying all over the ground. That man had death written all over his face."

"Was he with that female?"

"I don't know. But he came out of the bushes near the same place that she did. She came out walking naked from the waist up. He came out staggering and stumbling...with his pants shoved around his ankles. Then I saw something shiny in his hands...a gun I think. I watched as he aimed it towards the woman...as she stood next to the other guy, undressing him—that is, until he let out a loud scream." Wells nervously bit at his fingernails.

"What happened then?" I asked.

"The woman pulled out a butcher knife from under her blouse and started stabbing the guy that she was undressing—and then *he* pulled out a gun and shot her."

"Where did the guy get his gun?"

"He must have had it hidden behind his back. At the same time that he blew the woman's head off, the naked guy that had just wandered out of the bushes, and the old man, were shooting at the woman, too. It was happening so fast that it was hard to keep up with the action."

"So how do you know everything went down as you said if everything was happening so fast?"

"After everything happened, my brother and I talked it over later. I explained to him what I had seen, and he explained to me what he had seen."

"So what happened after everyone started shooting?"

"Well, first of all, my brother snuck over and knelt down behind one of the cars that was parked nearby so he could have a ringside seat. That's when the old man turned to look at him, and got a bullet right in the face. I saw his flesh fly all over the ground. Then I saw him fall forward into the mud, along with his gun."

"So what did you do? Did you retrieve the gun?"

"When we saw everyone lying on the ground bleeding, we ran over to see if we could help. But there wasn't much we could do. They were either dead or dying."

Wells shook his head in disbelief. "Then what did you do?"

"My brother got the brainy idea to take all of their valuables."

"Did you?"

"We took nearly everything they had. My brother ransacked the cars while I checked the victims."

"What did you take?"

"Not too much. The only person that had anything of value was the old man. I took his wallet and money. He didn't wear any jewelry."

"Why didn't you take the other two guns?"

"I couldn't find them. Anyway, I didn't have much time to look. We were afraid that someone would see us, so we took what we had and ran...up the hill."

"Did anyone see you in the park that night?"

"I don't think so. But we did see a car coming towards us...just as we exited the park. So we got away from there as quick as we could."

"You actually want me to believe that story?"

"Yes, it's the truth," he whined in his high-pitched, squeaky voice.

"Well, the way I see it, you're the one that's in possession of the gun that was used to kill lots of people. If the bullets from the gun match the bullets from the victims, it's all over for you, *Dennis*."

"Why? Just because you found a gun in the car I was driving?"

"Yeah! That, along with a positive ballistics test. With those two pieces of evidence, I have to believe you were involved... not only in the park murders but also the party store murders."

"But I wasn't," he whined.

"I don't believe you. The old man wasn't doing the shooting ... You were, as you hid behind one of the vehicles. Isn't that the way it happened?" I asked him, leaning forward again, crowding his space.

"No," he said, "I didn't have anything to do with those deaths ... Or any others. I told you the truth. My brother and I left as soon as we gathered up all the valuables. You have to believe me!"

"Then what did you do with all the valuables that you took from the murder scene? Do you still have them ... Or did you trade them for drugs?"

"I don't know where my brother hid the stuff. I told you, he's dead."

"So you want me to believe that you had nothing to do with the armed robberies and murders, and that your brother did it all by himself."

"Yeah, that's right."

"How convenient that your brother was shot and killed yesterday and isn't here to defend himself. That's pretty convenient for you, isn't it? Just blame the whole thing on your brother."

Just as I was getting ready to dissect his story and alibi, Captain Blake burst into the room and handed me the report on the gun. I quickly looked it over and found that the gun in question had been sold to a Doctor Bennet fifty years before. He'd recently had his name legally changed to Rhodes. It seems the doctor did abortions on the side. He had reason to hide his identity.

My investigation was beginning to get interesting. I decided to interrupt my interrogation and run by Judge Walker's office for a search warrant. The same warrant I had asked for before. I knew Judge Walker couldn't turn me down now.

Before leaving, I placed Wells back into the holding cell. I had to wait for the test results on Wells's evidence, anyway.

With that done, Kendall and I hurried to my car and drove away. During the drive, I explained to Kendall what I had learned about the gun found in Wells' canvas bag.

"What are we going to do now?" Kendall asked.

"Well, I want to get a search warrant to search Doctor Rhodes's home. Now we have something to go on."

A few minutes later, I pulled into the courthouse parking lot and parked the car. "Why don't you wait here in the car?" I told Kendall. "I'll only be a few minutes."

He nodded. "No problem. Take your time."

I arrived at the judge's office, walked past his secretary, and went straight into his inner room. "How are you doing, Judge?" I asked, smiling big.

"Hero, don't you knock before you barge into a room?" Walker asked, looking up from his desk. "You're lucky you're a friend of mine. If a lawyer had done that, I'd have thrown him in jail for contempt."

"I'm sorry, Judge. But I need your help."

"With what?"

"I need that search warrant for Dr. Rhodes's residence."

"I thought we went over this before? What's up?"

"Take a look at this forensics report and the gun owner's permit." I handed him both, then gave him a quick synopsis as he looked through them. "The serial number on that gun was used in a number of armed robberies and murders, and it was traced to a Dr. Bennet—who, it just so happens, has recently changed his name to Rhodes."

"So why do you need a warrant? Go pick him up and interview him," Walker said, puffing away on his cigar.

"That's just it," I said, shaking my head. "Dr. Rhodes hasn't been seen for nearly two weeks. I believe now that he may be the last unidentified victim from the park murders. And he might be more involved than that."

"What do you mean?"

"I'm not sure. I'm still investigating. That's why I need this search warrant."

"You'd better be sure, Hero. I don't want to get my butt caught in a sling over this. I've got enough trouble with the republicans. I don't need any more aggravation in my life."

"Don't worry about me. Hopefully, I'll find the information I need to wrap up my investigation."

I watched through a heavy haze of cigar smoke as Judge Walker signed the search warrant.

He then picked up the document from his desk and held it out to me. "Here," he said, "take this. And get out of my chambers."

I grabbed the important paper from his hand and left his office. I was eager to get to where I was going. I knew I was about to fit some of the bigger pieces into my puzzle.

We reached the doctor's residence in record time. And this time Kendall tagged along instead of staying in the car.

We walked up to the house and rang the front doorbell. Nobody answered. I rang the bell again and pounded on the door. Just then, I noticed Doris, the doctor's next door neighbor, eyeing my every move. I waved to her, then pounded on the door again. Still no answer.

I quickly walked back to my car and retrieved a few small and delicate tools from my car's glove box. I walked back to the front door and inserted a few of them into the door lock. Within ten seconds, the door sprang open.

As Kendall and I entered the house, I yelled out the doctor's name. It was dark and quiet inside. The house smelled of mildew and vinegar, but at least it had breathable air.

The first room we entered was a large living room. Sitting on a mantle over the fireplace was a picture of the doctor. He really did look like the Pillsbury Dough Boy. In this picture, he was wearing a pair of wire-rimmed eyeglasses, just like the ones I had found in the mud at the park. But that still wasn't enough information or evidence to verify the old man's identity. I would have to find his fingerprints from the house and match them to the body at the morgue. Then there would be no question of the park victim's identity. We would know for certain if the fingerprints matched.

I placed the photo in my dirty jacket pocket and continued to search the house for anything of importance.

I walked into an adjacent room, which was a library and den, and began to look at the doctor's massive and excellent book collection. While searching the titles, I ran across some thirty or forty personal journals or diaries. I picked out a few, just randomly, and began glancing through them. I couldn't believe what I was reading. I was stunned...to say the least. But I would have to read more in order to ascertain whether these diaries were fact or fiction.

I decided to investigate these books more closely at another time and began placing them into large paper bags, which I had found lying next to a small trashcan near the desk. I continued my quest for the truth and answers to my questions—especially the identity of the last unidentified park victim.

However, I didn't find anything else important to my investigation except for a single fingerprint, which I was able to pick up from a desktop. I wasn't sure whose print it was, but I would have it analyzed and compared to the victim's. I only needed one print for this purpose. And if it didn't match, I would have the forensics investigators dust the whole house for prints using a quick and simple method: a laser light.

We grabbed the doctor's property and placed it into the back seat of my car. Then Kendall and I headed for the forensic lab to have the fingerprint compared to the victim's.

My jigsaw puzzle was nearly complete. I needed just a few more important pieces. I didn't know which investigation I would close first—the park murders or the party store murders. It was just a matter of time now.

And I still had one other killer on the loose. One that killed his victims at condemned buildings. Wells was a suspect in those murders, too. I was suddenly anxious to get back to the station and interrogate him.

When we arrived at the medical examiner's parking lot, Kendall volunteered to remain in the car while I ran into the lab to retrieve my analysis reports. I really didn't believe that they had finished them yet, but I wanted to remain optimistic. I was too excited by recent events to have any negative thoughts. And I didn't want to cause any problems with that department. I didn't want to push it until all my other evidence had been tested and analyzed.

# MURDER IN THE CITY PARTS I-II

So when I met with Dr. Stork, I was very surprised by his willingness to cooperate with me. A sudden change had come over this lab. They had never reacted so quickly to my demands. Captain Blake must have come in loud and clear for me.

Before I could hand Dr. Stork my new evidence, he handed me the ballistics and fingerprint reports from the cafe and party store murders. I quickly glanced through them and found some of the answers that I had waited for, for so long. The fingerprint lifted from the cafe counter matched the fingerprint of my suspect, *Dennis* Wells. To say the least, I was ecstatic. That report was the kicker. And when I read the ballistics report, I was even happier. The bullets from the party store murders also matched the gun. We now had our armed robber and murderer. Now I wanted to see if he had been involved in the condemned apartment mutilations.

I still needed to identify the old man from the park murders. But until I had received confirmation from the fingerprint analysis report, I could only guess. I needed to know for certain. But I would know soon enough.

I handed Dr. Stork the new evidence I had taken from the doctor's house and thanked him for the good news.

"That's why we're here," he said.

"Doc, you have made my day. And if you can analyze the fingerprint that I gave you by the end of the day, I'd be very happy and indebted to you. I need to know if it matches the print taken from the last unidentified victim from the park murders. If it does, I'm home free. And I can wrap up three out of my four murder investigations. Thank your workers for me, Doc."

"I will."

After shaking his hand, I left the lab and ran back to the car to tell Kendall the good news.

"Well, the bullets matched the gun," I said, entering the car.

"You're kidding?" Kendall said, slapping his leg in joy.

"It's true. And the kicker is, the fingerprint found at the cafe matches Wells' fingerprint. He's definitely the armed robber and killer. It looks like you can go back home and close your investigation. You finally received the confirmation that you needed. Your extra day here was well spent."

"That sounds great. We'll have to stop and have a drink to celebrate."

"We will, but later. I want to get back to the station and finish my interrogation of Wells. I have to know about his relationship with Elaine Weltman. I'm sure he helped her mutilate those bodies that were found at the condemned buildings. Or at least he drove her from the hospital to the murder scene."

"Why would they do that?"

"Same reason I've said all along."

"And what's that?"

"She wanted to win her court appeal."

"How would she do that?"

"By saying someone else had killed those people. Her defense would be that she couldn't have done it because she was in the hospital having surgery."

"That's true. What are you going to do with the books from that doctor's house?"

"I'll have to make some time and read a few of them to make sense out of them. It's probably nothing, but some of the things I read...they sure made the hairs on the back of my neck stand on end."

"They're probably just his medical journals," Kendall said, glancing through the analysis reports.

"I'm sure you're right. But what's important now is my interrogation with Wells."

We made it back to the station in record time. Once inside, I walked directly to the holding cell and directed Dennis Wells to the interrogation room. Kendall stayed in the viewing room this time. I wanted no interruptions.

"Now, where were we, Mr. Wells," I said, leaning back in my chair. "I believe you were telling us your story. I'll let you continue in a minute. But I have a few simple questions I need answered first."

"I'll do my best," he said. "But first, could I have a cigarette?"

He had such a high-pitched and squeaky voice it was hard not to laugh.

"Sure, why not." I pulled a pack of cigarettes out of my jacket pocket and handed him one, then lit it for him.

"Thank you," said Wells. He took a long drag and then waited, expectantly.

"First, I must tell you that I've received the results from the testing of the evidence. Your fingerprint matched the one we lifted from the cafe counter. And the bullets that we pulled out of the murder victims from the cafe and party stores matched the gun that was found in your possession."

"But that gun isn't mine!"

"Not only did we find the gun in the canvas bag, but we also found a ski mask, a pair of black leather gloves, tape, and other objects that were used in quite a few armed robberies and cold-blooded murders. What do you have to say to that, *Dennis*?" I stared deep into his cold and calculating eyes.

There was no reaction. He remained silent for a good two minutes, quietly smoking his cigarette. You could see that he was deep in thought. Then suddenly, he came back to reality and said, "Okay, I'll admit. I was at that café."

"I know that... Now tell me something I don't know."

"But I only had breakfast there. I didn't rob, or kill anyone at that place."

"You actually expect me to believe that?" I said, laughing. "We've got you on videotape showing the whole crime from beginning to end." This was a lie, but he didn't know that.

"It's not me. It's my brother!"

"Oh, no. It's you, all right," I said, looking him directly in the eyes.

"Please believe me. I don't like guns. I never use guns."

But his whining didn't help him. And I told him so. "I believe you were one of the shooters at the park that day. You were ... weren't you?"

"No, I wasn't. I told you. That fat man was shooting at the couple. I only found the gun after it fell from his hand and sank into the mud."

"See, you admit that you had the gun."

"I admit I dug the gun out of the mud, but I never fired it that day—or any other. When my brother saw the gun, he took it away from me."

"There you go again, blaming it on your poor, dead brother who isn't here to defend himself. Isn't that convenient!"

"I don't know what else to say."

"Tell me the truth," I replied.

"I've been telling you the truth," Wells whined. He bowed his head in shame.

"Well, let's change the subject for a minute, Mr. Wells. Do you know Elaine Weltman?"

"No, I don't think so," he said, half-heartedly, looking up and in my direction. "Who is she?"

"You actually want me to believe that? If you lie to me about her, how can I believe anything you've said? I told you. You have to tell me the truth and the whole truth or I won't be able to help you. Let me make this perfectly clear. You are looking at the death house. Unless you're one hundred percent truthful with me, nobody will be able to save you. Do you understand?"

"Yes, I understand," Wells said, staring at the floor again.

"Now, let me ask you again, Mr. Wells. Do you know Elaine Weltman?"

He raised his head and whispered, "Yes, I know her."

"What? I can't hear you."

"Yes," he said, a little louder. "I know her."

"Who is she to you? Your girlfriend ... your wife?"

His answer floored me. "No. She's my sister."

"Your sister! Weltman was adopted."

"That's right, and so were we."

"Who's we?"

"My brother David and I. We lived with Elaine until the age of twelve, then we moved to our aunt's house."

"Did you and Elaine get along?"

"I've been close to her all of my life. We were adopted one month apart. But I'll tell you this."

"Yeah, what's that?"

"You sent an innocent girl to prison. Now you're about to send an innocent man there, too."

"Oh, is that right?" I answered sarcastically.

"That's right! I didn't kill anyone, and neither did my sister!"

"Did you ever visit her during the time she had abdominal surgery?" I asked.

"Yes, my brother and I both did."

"Did you help Weltman sneak out of the hospital?"

"No, of course not! She had surgery for a ruptured appendix. She couldn't go anywhere."

But I was sure he was lying. And to get at the truth, I lied again. "But I saw her with you or your brother at the entrance of the hospital. I know she left the hospital with you. So now all I want to know is, how long were you two away from the hospital before she returned?"

"*I* didn't take her out of the hospital."

"Then maybe it was your brother?" I said sarcastically.

"He didn't take her out either."

"Then where were you two going? You were very near the entranceway doors."

"She walked us to the main entrance and returned to her room. That was it!"

"Well, then how did she get out of her room if she was guarded twenty-four hours a day?"

He turned away and wouldn't look at me. "It was you who started that fire, wasn't it, Dennis?" I watched his body language as I asked the question...and reminded him again to tell the truth.

He sat silently for a minute, and after much thought, he said, "Maybe I should get myself a lawyer. I don't think I should say another word until I can get an attorney."

"He won't be able to help you," I said, leaning back in my seat. "We have all the evidence we need to see you on death row. So it's up to you. It's life or death. It's your choice."

You could see the innocence and the spirit of youth in his eyes. He was just a nervous, egotistical young punk. His life must have been challenging, being adopted and not knowing who his real parents were. I felt sorry for him a little bit. If I'd had a son, he might be just about the same age. But he had to take responsibility for his actions.

"So it's up to you, kid. What do you want to do? Do you want to tell me the truth or let some crummy lawyer send you to death row? What's it going to be?"

"I'm trying to be cooperative, but you don't believe me. I told you. I didn't kill anyone, and I didn't rob anyone."

"Then tell me how that bagful of property got into your car? Did it just suddenly appear?"

"No, my brother must have put it in there when he used the car."

"Well, tell me this, Mr. Wells. If your brother was killed yesterday, and someone who looked just like you shot at me this morning, and it wasn't you ... Who was it?"

He shrugged his shoulders. "I don't know. There must be someone that looks just like me."

"Okay, that's enough of that crap! If it wasn't you that shot at me, you're saying your dead brother did it? Give me a break! I wasn't born yesterday. Do I look like an idiot?"

"No, you don't look like an idiot," he said. "But I'm telling you, I didn't kill anyone or shoot at anyone. Maybe you should let me finish telling you my story."

"So go ahead and speak. Nobody's stopping you." I lit a cigarette and waited to hear his story.

"I already told you, didn't I? That the old man was shooting that gun...and we just found it in the mud."

"Yes, you told me that already. You didn't shoot anybody. It must have been the dead old man that shot all those people at the party stores, right?"

"No, of course not. But the one you want for those robberies and murders is my brother, David."

"I know, you told me that, too. But that's just too convenient. We didn't find his fingerprint at the cafe. We only found yours. Why is that, Dennis?"

"My brother wore gloves in the crimes that he committed. You found them in the canvas bag. It should show that in the videotape from the cafe. It should also show me, too. You'll see from the tape."

"That would be nice if the cafe had a video machine that had worked."

"They must have a machine, they have a camera. I saw it. It was hanging from the ceiling, right above the counter," Wells said, chewing on his fingernails.

"Yes, they have one, but it doesn't work. They just have it for show, to keep their insurance company off their backs. Now tell me something I don't know."

But before he did, he took a final drag on his cigarette, dropped it to the floor, and then stomped it out with his shoe. "All of this craziness started a while ago, when we heard that my sister was going to find and kill her birth mother," he said.

"How did you know that?"

"My adopted mother told us. That's why we came after my sister, to stop her before she did something stupid that would get her into trouble."

"Evidently, you didn't make it in time."

"I know. My brother and I followed her to this city, but she had a seven-day head start on us. We searched and searched for her, but we didn't have the information that she had."

"What kind of information are you talking about?"

"My sister had found some letters hidden away in our adopted mother's closet that mentioned her birth mother. Somehow, she learned of her whereabouts and went to find her."

"When did you finally find your sister? She *is* your sister, isn't she?"

"Yes, I've already told you that."

"Then why does she have a different last name than yours? Her last name is Weltman and yours is Wells. What gives?"

"Well, when we moved to our aunt's house, we used her husband's last name. I guess for insurance purposes. And we've kept them ever since."

"So when did you finally find your sister?"

"Like you said, we didn't find her soon enough. We found her one day after we had heard her birth father had been killed."

"Did you ask her if she killed him?"

"Well, we did talk to her about that situation. But all she told us was that she wanted to take her birth mother's boyfriend away from her."

"Why did she want to do that?"

"I guess so her birth mother would feel the hurt that she had felt, wondering why her real mother had given her away."

"Yep. She made her hurt all right. I guess she did that and then some."

"Well, when she found out that the person she had taken away from her birth mother and made passionate love to was really her birth father...that's when she snapped."

"She snapped all right. She mutilated the guy."

"No, that's when she snapped and ran out of the apartment in tears," Wells exclaimed.

"Is that what she told you?"

"She stated to me and my brother that they'd had intercourse and that he was still tied to the bedposts when she ran out the front door. That's when she saw this fat little balding man with very thick eyeglasses in the hallway. She believed he had something to do with the death of her birth father."

"Had she ever seen this man before? Did she know who he was?"

"She thought he was a doctor because he was carrying a black leather bag, similar to a medical bag. She had seen him coming out of an apartment a few doors down from the one she had just run out of. So we got involved to see what we could turn up. And the first thing we did was visit that same floor of the Admore apartment building to wait for that man to show up."

"Did he?"

"He did, a day or so later."

"What did you do then?"

"We followed him from the day we spotted him. And every time we followed him to one of those condemned buildings, someone always ended up dead. That's why we were in that park on that particular day."

"So you lied to me. You weren't sitting at the picnic table when the old man showed up. You had followed him from one of those condemned buildings. Isn't that right?"

"Yes, that's true. We saw him leave and then watched as he drove away in his dirty brown car. We thought we'd lost him until we ran to the end of the street and saw that he had stopped to pick up a hitchhiker. A few minutes later, we watched as they headed towards the park, so we took a shortcut through the wooded forest and beat him there. Then we sat on a picnic table and watched to see what the old man was up to."

"Couldn't he see you?"

He shook his head no. "We were hidden by the trees and bushes."

"What did you do then?"

"I told you before. We sat there as the scene unfolded. The doctor parked his car in front of one that was already there and the two men got out. That's when everything went crazy."

"Is that the story you want to stick with?" I asked.

"It's not a story. It's the truth. We followed this guy for months. And every time he visited one of those condemned buildings, dead bodies were found days or weeks later."

I laughed, then said, "That's a good one. But now... let me tell *you* what happened! When you started that fire in the closet at the hospital, you and Weltman snuck out when the police officer guarding her room left his post to investigate—and you made sure the fire was started at the far end of the long hallway."

"That's not true," Wells whined, shaking his head.

"Oh... but it is! And then you two drove into the city and murdered innocent, vulnerable people. Most of them living in those terrible abandoned apartment buildings. Then you drove her back to the hospital, snuck her up the back stairs, and back into her unguarded room. Does that pretty well cover it?"

He looked away from my eyes and remained silent. I waited patiently for his answer, but he remained mute.

I tried coaxing him back into the conversation. "What's wrong, did I knock the wind out of your sails?"

He still remained silent.

"Well, if you don't want to speak, let me speak for you." I continued telling him how I saw it. "When you and Weltman left the hospital, you traveled in your car looking for the poor and less fortunate. You didn't think anyone would care about those people you killed and mutilated. But you're wrong! *I* care about those people. They have a right to live just like you and me."

He gave me a confused look. "Why would we kill them?"

Getting up in his face, I said, "You killed them so Weltman would have an alibi for those earlier killings and win her appeal for a new trial. If you hadn't gotten caught, your plan might have worked. But let me ask you this: Why rob and kill the people at those party stores? Why did you do that?" As I asked this question, I kept my face near his, hoping he would hit or slap me, so I could knock him for a loop.

But he didn't take the bait.

"You're wrong," he said. "I'll say it one more time. *I didn't kill anyone!* It was my brother. And I didn't kill anyone from those buildings, either. I stayed and slept in some of those places."

"Yeah, and that's how you picked out your subjects. But enough of that. I think I've heard enough bullshit for one day. I think when reality sinks in, you'll come around and tell me the truth. It's amazing what one or two days in a cell all alone will do to one's mind." I stood him up and walked him back to his holding cell. "Have fun," I said, as I shut and locked the cell door behind him.

When I returned to the viewing room, only Kendall was there. My peers were nowhere to be found. Evidently, they were ignoring me. But I didn't care. I was about to close one case and would have another solved very shortly. I was in a mood to celebrate.

"I'm hungry and thirsty," I told Kendall. "What do you say we go to my favorite café and celebrate our new turn of events?"

He nodded. "But don't you want to see if forensics has finished your fingerprint analysis? If they match the old man's print with the one you lifted from the doctor's house, then you'll *really* have something to celebrate."

"Nah, we don't need to check on them," I said. "They don't need our help. We would just be in the way. They'll get that report to me later today or sometime tomorrow. I'm sure of it."

"Do you really believe that?" asked Kendall.

"If the lab technicians work on my evidence instead of setting it to the side and forgetting about it, I should have my answers very soon. But right now, let's forget about work and go celebrate." With that said, we walked out of the station, jumped into my car and headed to the cafe. It was a great day for a celebration.

Later that night, as I stepped out of my car, I remembered the thirty or so journals I had sitting in paper bags in the back seat. I wanted to read them in my spare time, so I grabbed them and stumbled my way to the front door.

Once I had entered my abode, I placed the two bags of journals on the living room floor and then turned my attention to my bottle of scotch. I grabbed it and a dirty glass from the kitchen counter, then headed to the living room to exercise my right arm.

As I relaxed on my couch, I took off my dirty jacket, my tie, and unbuttoned my shirt. Then I filled my glass with scotch, reached into one of the paper bags, and pulled out one of the doctor's journals.

Just as I opened the book, something else occurred to me—another journal. The old woman's diaries.

I got up, grabbed the two diaries off the end table, and began sifting through page after page, trying to find the right one. I didn't find it in the first diary, but I found it in the second. She talked about her husband—a doctor—who had been frightening her. She thought he was losing his mind. She mentioned that he had two or three distinct personalities. One of them would complain about a birthmark on his left hip, calling it the "mark of the devil." He wanted it cleansed from his body.

She described the birthmark as a one-inch round circle with two small bumps, resembling horns, on the top of it, and one bump on the bottom. He thought it looked like the face of the devil and wanted it burned or cut out, which he would have done himself, but he first had to numb the area by injection and was frightened of needles. I'd never heard of a doctor that didn't like shots.

Suddenly, a light bulb went off in my head. I remembered a similar mark on the old man from the park and wondered if it matched the description in the diary. If it did, that would be one more piece to add to the puzzle.

I decided to go to the morgue first thing in the morning and check the old man's body again. I would make the call to Warden Parker for an interview with Elaine Weltman afterwards.

I was getting tired, so I placed the diary on the table and picked up the doctor's journal. But before I could finish reading the first page, I passed out, sleeping soundly through the night.

The next morning, I drove directly to the morgue, anxious to check out the park victim.

Once there, I had the attendant show me the body. I looked on the victim's left hip and was surprised to see a small, round birthmark, exactly like the woman's diary had described—the face of a devil. I was elated. But I still lacked an identity. All I knew for certain was that the man mentioned in the diary was a doctor, and Pat Dawner's ex-husband. I just hoped the fingerprint lifted from Dr. Rhodes's house matched my park victim's print.

I thanked the attendant for his time and left. My mood had brightened even more thanks to my foresight.

Even so, I didn't stop at the forensics lab. I didn't want to act as though I was pushing them. I decided I would return there on my way back from State prison.

I wanted to interview Elaine Weltman today—to see her reaction when I told her what had transpired over the last couple of days concerning her brothers: namely, that one of them was a guest of the city and the other, a guest of the city's cemetery.

Just as I was leaving the building, I ran into Dr. Stork. He had completed the analysis on the fingerprints and handed me the report before departing. I looked it over, and there was the answer I had hoped for. The print from my victim and the print taken from Dr. Rhodes's house matched.

I walked out of the medical examiner's building floating on air. I now had the identity of my last park victim. I could close that case for good.

I folded up the report and placed it into my jacket pocket before stepping into my vehicle and heading for the station to make a call to Warden Parker.

I arrived and entered the station with a big smile on my face. But I signed in at the front desk amid dirty looks and scolding glares from my brother detectives. By their reaction, I could tell they were jealous of my good fortune. And as usual, I ignored their childish behavior.

But just to rub it in, all the way from the front desk to my desk, I sang childishly for all to hear. "I just closed my case. I just closed my case and another soon to follow."

My peers stared at me in disbelief, but I didn't care. I was in a happy-go-lucky kind of mood. I refused to let my hangover or anything else interfere with that.

When I reached my desk, I picked up my desk phone and called Warden Parker. Unfortunately, he was away from his desk, so I left a message with his secretary that I would be there within a few hours. She stated that he would be in his office all day and would be expecting me.

Just as I hung up the telephone, I noticed a thick stack of reports sitting in front of me. I ignored them. I already had many of the answers I needed to complete my puzzle.

My next move was to drive to the prison and interview the cold-blooded killer, Elaine Weltman.

During my drive to the prison, my only thoughts were on the questions that I was going to ask my convicted killer. I wondered if she would break down and spill her guts. But I was sure that once she heard the news about her adopted brothers, she would.

The drive seemed to go by faster than usual, and I was at the prison before I knew it. I parked the car, then strolled into the guard's station. The guard then phoned Warden Parker and afterwards escorted me to Parker's office. He was alone and sitting behind his big desk, smoking a stogie.

"What brings *you* here, Detective Hero?" asked Warden Parker, jumping up from his seat to meet me in the middle of the room. We shook hands.

"Well, Captain Blake told me you called the other day and that you had an important message for me. But I had to come here, anyway. I need to interview Elaine Weltman again. I have some very important information to tell her. I think I can get her to open up once I reveal my information."

"I hate to say it, but I think you've wasted your time coming here today."

"Hell, I'm in such a good mood I don't think anything I do today is a waste of my time. But I'm positive Weltman will definitely want to hear what I have to say. It concerns her brothers."

"I'm sorry to have to tell you this, Mr. Hero, but Elaine Weltman is no longer at this facility."

"She's not?"

"No, she's not."

"Then where is she? I drove a long ways to see her. Please Warden Parker, I'd like to speak with her today, if at all possible."

"I'm sorry, but she committed suicide the other day. That's what I wanted to tell you when I phoned. But you weren't there, so I left that message with your captain."

"Why would she want to commit suicide?"

"I don't know. She left a suicide note. It was addressed to you, so I saved it. I thought you might want to read it. I'll make a copy for you if you want one."

I nodded, too shocked to speak.

Parker walked to his copier and quickly made a copy. "Here it is," he said, handing it to me.

"Why would she leave a note for me? I had nothing to do with her suicide."

"I have no idea."

"If you don't mind, Warden Parker, I'll read it when I'm alone." I folded the paper and placed it into my jacket pocket. "I can't believe Weltman would commit suicide." And then I changed my tune. "Well, at least she saved the taxpayers money. I was about to charge her with a number of recent murders anyway, for which I'm sure she would have received the death penalty ... again. But I don't know why she would choose me as her scapegoat."

"She always maintained her innocence."

"Warden, every criminal in prison says they're innocent. Why don't people take responsibility for their actions anymore?"

"I don't know. I wonder about that myself at times."

"Well Warden, I guess I won't waste any more of your time. I thought I would be doing an interview, but I guess not. I thank you for your time and thank you for the note. I'm sure I'll get a kick out of it."

"Take care," said Warden Parker, as we shook hands.

I left his office and headed for the parking lot.

I couldn't understand why Weltman would leave me a suicide note. It wasn't my fault that she was in prison.

Twelve of her peers placed her there. I just gathered the evidence. These thoughts and others raced through my mind. I wondered if her brother knew that she was dead and had committed suicide. I would have to break the news to him anyway. I was sure he would want to know what had happened to her.

Throughout the drive home, I couldn't get Weltman out of my mind. She might have won a new trial on her appeal. But now, we'd never know.

Boy, I thought, this day was turning out great. Now I had every case sewed up. I knew the identity of the last park victim. I had the perpetrator locked up for committing the recent armed robberies and party store murders. And the murders at the condemned apartments would finally be closed. I now had all the pieces of my puzzle fit snugly into place. I was, to say the least, elated.

About twenty minutes after I'd left the prison, I began reading the suicide note, which Weltman had addressed to me.

*Dear Detective Hero, I know you were just doing your job, but you were completely wrong arresting me for my birth father's murder and four others, including my birth mother. But believe me when I tell you. I'm innocent! I didn't and couldn't kill anyone. I might have wanted to, but many people say it and never do it. I just couldn't get over the fact that I had been arrested, convicted, and condemned to death for those evil crimes. I nearly gave up on life, but then my two brothers decided to help me get out of this horrible place and started tracking down the real murderer, who we believed to be a little, fat doctor. If and when you see and talk to them, they will explain the situation to you. They know the whole story. In fact, they found that man...that sham of a doctor. And the last time I spoke with them, they were hot on his trail.*

*That was the very first time that I believed I had a chance to get my life back, to get out of this hideous, filthy place society calls prison.*

*I started smiling again. I believed in justice again. But that was short-lived when you came to visit me and accused me of more hideous murders. Then you threatened that you were gonna keep me on death row. I couldn't believe what I was hearing from your mouth. The hope I had built up suddenly evaporated into thin air. I was saddened by the thought of being accused and then tried again for murders I had nothing to do with. Then to make matters worse, you accused me of leaving the hospital just so I could go out and kill more people—just to have an alibi for my appeal.*

*Of course I wanted a new trial. I was railroaded into this prison. But you put a stop to that. I couldn't go through another horrible murder trial again. I hurt too much. And my body was becoming numb to my surroundings.*

*I won't give you and your department the satisfaction of putting me on trial again for something I didn't do. I'm sorry, I just can't. I just hope you think about me the next time you send someone to prison for life on circumstantial evidence.*

*I never denied I wasn't at the crime scene. But I was there before the murder took place. So I leave you to ponder your fate. You won't have to ponder mine anymore. Peace on earth.*

It was signed, Elaine Weltman.

That was the end of the note. I didn't know quite what to think of it. I folded it up and placed it into my jacket pocket to read again later. I felt bad for her but I wasn't going to let this note ruin my day. I was definitely saddened by it, but prisoners committed suicide all the time. There were over two hundred prison suicides last year alone. One more was only a statistic for the justice system. Then I remembered that, at one time, I did have a feeling in my gut that she was innocent. But that feeling went away when the evidence pointed to her.

Before I knew it, I found myself back in my city and at the station. It was well past lunchtime, and I still hadn't eaten. I had been filled up with happiness. Three investigations closed within two weeks. I wondered if that was a new record in my department.

I parked the car and then strode into the station. As I reached my desk, I noticed two bags sitting on top of it. One was a black medical bag; the other was a small, backpack type bag. Sitting nearby was a note addressed to me. It stated that these bags had been found an hour ago by the forensic investigators at a condemned building. They had recovered a doctor's black bag and a few of the park victims' wallets containing their identification. Great! Now they find it. But two weeks too late. Oh, well. Such is life!

I opened each bag and glanced into them. The investigators had every piece of evidence already bagged and tagged. Then I looked at my watch and noticed that it was later than I had thought.

I decided to head home and take the two bags with me so I could look through the evidence in the presence of my home. I was also anxious to read some of the doctor's journals. And while doing this, I could have a drink or two without feeling guilty.

The minute I got home, I placed the two bags on the living room table and then grabbed my bottle of scotch and a shot glass. I had a couple of drinks to soothe my old and aching body.

Then I began looking at the evidence. I opened the small backpack first. It was full of jewelry and wallets. I pulled out the wallets and looked at the identification in each one. But only one had a driver's license, and that belonged to Dr. Rhodes. That would have been my best piece of evidence to identify his body, especially if it had been found in his jacket pocket.

I placed the wallets back into the backpack and then inspected the few pieces of jewelry. There wasn't anything of value, except one item—a Rolex watch: A *platinum* Rolex watch. It wasn't the best, but it could have been sold for some good money. Most likely, it belonged to the doctor.

Once I had inspected all the items in the backpack, I then turned my attention to the black medical bag. I didn't know for certain whether it was Dr. Rhodes's bag or some other doctor's. Forensics would tell me later if the fingerprints from the bag matched his. But it was a medical bag. So, I speculated that it *was* his. I looked into the bag and saw some weird stuff. There were a couple of scalpels, cloth slippers, rubber and leather gloves, a butcher's apron, and a large butcher knife. But the last item really caught my attention. It was a powder blue, knitted sweater, with long, blonde hairs all over it. I wondered why a doctor would be carrying a woman's sweater in his medical bag.

If this was Dr. Rhodes's bag, then the hair on the sweater certainly wasn't his. He was bald. The forensics lab would have to send the hairs out for DNA testing, if they haven't done that already. I would take the evidence there in the morning just in case.

As I lifted the sweater out of the bag, I saw the owner's name—Dr. Bennet—stamped on the bottom in dull gold letters. And right next to that name was another stamp— also in gold letters. It said, Dr. Rhodes. This was indeed, Dr. Rhodes's bag.

I placed the evidence back into their respective bags and set them aside to read Dr. Rhodes's journals.

Each journal was written over a one-year period with approximately one hundred hand-written pages in each. I could read one within ten or fifteen minutes. They were in corresponding and numerical order, starting from one through forty, so I started from the beginning.

After reading the first paragraph, I knew I had some fanatical writings. I couldn't tell if this was his true story or just fiction. The more I read, the sicker the writing became.

He began his fun right out of medical school. He called mutilating bodies, "fun." I could not believe what I was reading. Was he writing a story line for a book he hoped to get published? This person he described in the journals killed like Rambo—by the hundreds.

These journals were incredibly morbid. He tells of falling in love and marrying his "true diamond," his wife...and how one part of him loved her, but his other side hated her. This was very confusing to me, but I continued to read page after page. I drank more and more as I read.

I was already a third of the way through the stack of books. Every journal talked about his wife and how suspicious and frightened she was of him. He talked about killing her, but then decided against it. I noticed that this handwriting was different at times, as though two or three different people had written it. Page after page talked about killings, mutilations, and planting different pieces of evidence—either to throw off the investigators or to pin the murders on innocent people.

But even after reading twenty journals, I still didn't know if these stories were true or just science fiction. Some parts were very difficult to read and made my stomach queasy. A few times, I wanted to quit reading completely. But I struggled on, reading this maniacal writing.

Dr. Rhodes talked about how he would medically treat people, which he called low-life scum, and then kill them by mutilating their bodies and severing the male's manhood. Some of these murders seemed like some I had investigated before. It brought back memories from years or decades past. But at the time, I thought this was just coincidental. He couldn't have been talking about the murders I had investigated, I was sure of that.

However, as I got to the end of the thick stack of journals, I became a little skeptical. Now I was in familiar territory. These murders and mutilations he was writing about sounded all too familiar.

When the doctor's wife finally left him, that's when he decided to change his name and start a new life. He also used the excuse that he was getting death threats from pro-life fanatics over the abortions he had been performing. So he decided to change his name from Bennet to Rhodes.

He talked about starting his murders immediately after his internship, killing at least one person every week or two...and continued right into his own practice. Most of his murders had been patients of his at one time or another. But other times he used his profession and his medical bag to get into the homes of unsuspecting victims, announcing that he was from the health department and the occupants had to be checked for a number of different diseases and viruses due to contaminated city tap water. He used this ruse for years. And stated it never failed him.

The doctor continued to kill and mutilate bodies even when he went out of town for conventions and special vacations. He liked the thought that he was a homicidal maniac. He nearly stopped when his wife threatened to leave him and expose him for what he really was. But he couldn't stop himself.

Then, when their only child died, he became even more frightening. His wife knew then that she had to leave him or he would kill her, too. She finally escaped and moved away, then changed her name to Dawney.

And around that time, the evil doctor began killing multiple subjects at the different places he visited. He stated in one of the last journals that he liked killing two or more people at once and would inject them with a special concoction that he had developed. It put the victim in a deep trance, so they wouldn't put up a fight. Then he would put on his apron, slippers, and rubber gloves—just as if he were in an operating room—and then mutilate their bodies or slit their throats while they were still alive and breathing.

One of his stories hit home … Hard. He talked about killing two old and dear, adorable sisters that had been his patients for nearly fifty years. He stated how he'd put them out of their misery…and did them a favor by ending their lives. Just then, it hit me. These were two murders that Elaine Weltman had been convicted of doing. *This can't be true,* I thought. What had I done? I had to have another drink, and fast.

After consuming two quick shots, I continued to read—about how he had killed some bastard who used vulnerable women for their money and then discarded them, like used toilet paper, after he had depleted their life savings. This man also made him outrageously angry, especially when he saw him with two very young girls—young enough to be the man's daughters.

Then one night, while visiting his patients, Dr. Rhodes saw one of the young girls run out of the man's apartment in tears, leaving the front door wide open. Seeing her upset like that made his blood boil. He decided to confront the man and tell him off. So he walked into the open apartment. And as he did, he heard a man shouting from a room at the far end of the hallway. When he went to investigate, he was surprised to see the man he hated tied to the four bedposts of the bed.

Seeing him like that gave Rhodes the upper hand and the urge to reap his revenge. So he opened up his medical bag, took out the needed items—gloves, slippers and apron—and put them on before injecting the victim with his special solution. He then proceeded to stab and mutilate his victim. Not with his scalpel but with a large butcher knife that he had picked up off the floor near the foot of the bed. Then he dragged the man into the kitchen, cut his throat, severed his penis, and placed the penis in the man's fist near his mouth, as though he were sucking it.

Rhodes stated that he wanted to show the public what this guy was: a cocksucker. And also to teach that young girl, whom he called a slut, a lesson.

After mutilating the body, the doctor found a blue sweater in the bedroom full of long, blonde hairs that belonged to the young girl who had just stormed out of the apartment. So he planted a few of the hairs on the victim's body...and then, days later, on a few others he had killed. He stated that he wanted *her* to pay for *his* killings...because in his eyes, the young girl was just low-life scum. But I knew her as Elaine Weltman. And the man he was talking about was Jim Palter.

I had to stop reading for a few minutes and catch my breath. I needed this time to reflect upon this new information. I set the journal to the side and pulled the medical bag close to me. I slowly looked into it...at the powder blue sweater and the long, blonde hairs. I wondered if these hairs really were Elaine Weltman's. Then I thought, boy, if they are, I really pulled a boner. I helped get an innocent girl convicted and condemned to death. Now I thought, maybe it *was* my fault that she had taken her own life.

But I couldn't think like that. I had done my job to the best of my ability. I was only *part* of the Justice system. I tried to put those thoughts completely out of my mind, but for some unknown reason, I couldn't. I couldn't get over what I had just read. I was overwhelmed by the hideous nature of the journals. It was as though a thunderbolt had just struck me in the side of the head.

I would have to tell my superiors about what I had learned. The truth had to be told. Now it would be up to them to decide the outcome of this new evidence. But I didn't think that would change anything. They believed that their justice system didn't make mistakes, nor did it execute innocent people. Or put innocent people into prison.

But I still had to ask myself, am I putting *another* innocent person in jail? I didn't know, and only time would tell if Dennis Wells was guilty or innocent.

After nearly a one month trial, Dennis Wells was convicted by twelve of his peers on three counts of armed robbery and five counts of first degree murder for the killing of the stores' shop workers and owners. He was sentenced to death. And, to put salt in his wounds, he was also convicted on three felony counts for using a gun while committing a felony.

Now, he and I would both have to live with the decision. However, during the court trial, Wells had threatened my life. He shouted that if he ever got out on parole or escaped from prison, he would kill me. But he only threatened me after he learned about his sister's suicide. He knew she hadn't committed the crimes that the state had convicted her of. Just as he ranted that he was innocent of the crimes that the state had convicted him of.

I, too, questioned the outcome of the trial. At one time, I had been very certain of Wells' guilt. Now I wasn't so sure.

The End...Or is it